INFORMATION TECHNOLOGY FOR PARTICIPATORY DEVELOPMENT

Prof. R. Raman Nair an Information Technology expert, has designed the Multimedia Library Automation System (McLAS 1993) in India and the KAU Library and Information System with building LANs, Digital Library and IT Training Facilities considered to be the best in the country. He has 14 books including *Peoples Library Movement, Computer Application to Library and Information Services,* and *Internet for Library and Information Services*, as well as 120 research papers and articles and many national and international conference presentations to his credit. He has organised various national level seminars including the *National Seminar on Right to Information* and national level IT courses and training programmes under various organizations which include *Managing Digital Libraries in Agriculture* (ICAR). *Modern Information Access Facilities* (NISSAT) and *Worldwide Web for Managing Agricultural Information* (CAGI)

Prof. Nair has associated with many expert committees on IT formed by professional organizations, universities and government. He is a research fellow of American Biographical Institute and is the founder member of Centre for South Indian Studies, life member of Rural Development Forestry Network (ODI, London), Asian Watershed Management Network (Katmandu, Nepal), ILA, IASLIC and AGLIS. In recognition of his outstanding contributions in library and information services he has been presented him the IASLIC S.M.Ganguly National Award for the year 1998.

INFORMATION TECHNOLOGY FOR PARTICIPATORY DEVELOPMENT

Prof. R. Raman Nair
Former Librarian
Kerala Agricultural University

Published for

CENTRE FOR INFORMATICS RESEARCH AND DEVELOPMENT

by

CONCEPT PUBLISHING COMPANY, NEW DELHI - 110059

ISBN 81-8069-025-3

First Published 2003

Published and Printed by
Ashok Kumar Mittal
Concept Publishing Company
A/15-16, Commercial Block, Mohan Garden
New Delhi-110059 (India)

Phones: 25351460, 25351794
Fax: 091–(11)–25357103
E-mail: publishing@conceptpub.com

PREFACE

Information is becoming the most important resource. Alvin Toffler remarks that Force and Wealth continue to be the property of the strong and rich. But knowledge or information has a revolutionary characteristic. It can be grasped by the wealthy and the poor as well. If one shares some wealth he has to loose a part of his wealth. But knowledge can be shared without any loss. Both become equal without loss to any and both get equal power to acquire other resources. Hence information is the most democratic source of power. This makes it a continuous threat to the powerful even as they use information to ensure detaining of the power in their hands. Hence every power holder, the government, the head of an organization, or the family controls the quantity, quality and distribution of knowledge within their domain. Many traditional rules and regulations prevented the poor from acquiring knowledge and information. Hence movement for access to education, knowledge and information forms the most important struggles that helped us to march towards an equalitarian society. Information kindled revolutions that achieved freedom and established and maintained democratic set-ups. Libraries have played an unique role in disseminating information to the common people all over the world. Now Information Technology (IT) enables provision of equal access to knowledge, information to everyone. So the libraries, the traditional information service providers have to absorb new technologies offered by IT and play the same role more effectively in the coming networked society.

True democracy cannot flourish unless all citizens have the right to participate in their governing, in the preparation of the plans and programmes for their development, and in their implementation, evaluation and monitoring. This accordingly asserts the citizen's right to inform and be informed. The concept of people's right to know was accepted by the country long back when it acceded to the UN

Human Rights Charter (1948) and ratified the subsequent U.N. Convention on Civil and Political Rights. The mechanism was incorporated into the domestic law in Information Technology Act, 2000. Now major share of Plan funds goes to lower levels of administration and huge sums of money are being dedicated to poverty alleviation through various programmes. But the proper planning, implementation, monitoring, evaluation and accountability are not possible without transparency and an effective mechanism to ensure people's right to know. The established media and government's information systems will not fully protect the people's right to know as well as extend information services to the poor and the disadvantaged. A vigorous, rural small town library and information service network like the one that existed in Kerala should come into dominance and harness IT to ensue people's access to information. This truth is now dawning upon ordinary people of the country.

In the development scenario, the terms accountability, decentralization, democracy, diversity, ownership, participation and transparency are becoming very popular. Participation is now the very important concept in planning and development. All these are dependent on information. Participation to be real and meaningful should be informed participation. So dissemination of information, access to information by the beneficiaries and ensuring people's right to information are very important for participatory development. Ensuring participation in development programmes, as well as participatory monitoring and evaluation of these programmes solely rest on the efficient information support systems that involve in developmental activities. But even though theoretical studies and publicity materials and statements widely acclaim these concepts and lists what and what measures have been adopted to ensure their implementation; in practice what is the extreme opposite happens. Even though outwardly many programmes seem to be participatory and decentralized, in reality it is not so. The clever keep the participants ignorant of the facts about the matters in which they have to involve, give distorted versions of things, or cleverly keep away the informed and knowledgeable, one who may differ or concerned experts who can understand; away from participation. So participation in planning, implementation, further monitoring, and evaluation can be ensured only if efficient information systems for the people exist to disseminate information and protect people's right to information.

Until recently it was impossible to extend information services of quality and relevance to remote areas where also it is essential when we think in terms of decentralized governance and development. But now information technology has opened before us the possibility for putting at the finger tip of any villager any data from anywhere in the world that he requires at the time when he requires it. Maintaining such an information access system is a hundred times less costlier than maintaining our rural libraries or the government's publicity divisions; but will give a thousand times more result than those traditional systems if information infrastructures are well planned. Hence our rural libraries requires to be uplifted by incorporating these provisions also. This will bring those libraries into live spheres of social activity and make the decentralized planning and development real by making participants informed. Those libraries have played a similar important role in our national movement. Kerala and West Bengal are some good examples for that. The inroad of IT in information management and the inertia of professionals and educational systems to absorb current developments are presently keeping libraries away. Even in Kerala decentralized development programmes have established a parallel information system for providing information support to development when a good network of 5000 and odd libraries that came up through people's initiative existed and they extended information services to remote corners of the state. This is a mistake in policy. The only difference of new information system is that it is fully IT based. But those who have successfully handled information for the rural people manually will handle it with the present tool more effectively than any one else. Instead of developing new institutions and systems for information support at local level government could have developed rural libraries as service outlets of state information infrastructures which would have pooled together; the more than a century old expertise in providing information to the rural people, the ocean of information of local relevance already stored in rural libraries which are not going to get digitized in the near future, as well as the currently generated digitized information.

This book brings together papers, presentations and invited lectures made in special sessions on information and decentralized administration on the occasion of the national seminar on right to information conducted at Thrissur in Kerala during December 1998 while the Information Technology Act was under consideration of the parliament. A classified arrangement of papers is followed here instead of the actual sequence of presentation. Along with the papers and other invited talks we have appended to this volume the IT policy statements of the Centre and selected States, as well as the IT Act that followed. The participants of the seminar included IT experts, librarians, NGO representatives, government officials, academicians and researchers. The papers and presentations stress or mention the aspects which form the most important factor of the participatory development programmes that failed to get due attention; the information systems for development as well as the failure to identify the right institutions that should provide information services as well as protect people's right to information.

Information resource is going to play a key role in social, cultural and political progress as well as in productive and sustainable economic development. The ease and speed with which new knowledge is produced, organized, packed, retrieved and disseminated through IT based systems and applied together with old knowledge our traditional libraries stored, will be the strategic determinant in whether the country, states, a region, an institution or individual prosper or lag behind in the new services based economy. This book should be of interest to development professionals who are government officials, academics, or those from civil society, information professionals, librarians and managers of community information centres and all readers interested in participatory development.

R. Raman Nair

Acknowledgements

National Seminar on 'Right to Information'

and this publication which forms the results of its special sessions
on

Information Technology for Local Administration
was supported at various stages

by

Centre for Agricultural Informatics
Varanasi and Cochin

Committee for Science, Technology and Environment
Government of Kerala

Indian Association of Special Libraries and Information Centres
Calcutta and its Study Circle at Thrissur

Kerala Agricultural University
Thrissur

Kerala Institute of Local Administration
Thrissur

Raja Rammohanroy Library Foundation
Calcutta

Informatics (India) Limited
Bangalore

CONTENTS

Appendices

CONTRIBUTORS

Sri Alha, Head, Library and Information Services Division, Central Institute of Agricultural Engineering, Nabi Bagh, Berasia Road, Bhopal-462 038

Sri Chandradath, Costford, Trichur

Sri Chandrakumaran Nair, Library and Information Services Division, Regional Cancer Centre, Thiruvananthapuram-695011

Prof. A.B. George, Retired Head of the Information System, Centre for Water Resource Development and Management, Calicut

Dr. V.K. Gopi, Associate Professor, Kerala Institute of Local Administration, Trichur-680561

Sri P. Govinda Pillai, Chairman, Kerala State Film Development Corporation, Trivandrum

Sri Haridas P. Nair, System Manager, Kerala State Remote Sensing and Environment Centre, Trivandrum

Dr. Jaya Soorya, Member, Executive Committee, KAU, Trichur

Sri Jayadevan, Member, Kerala Legislative Assembly

Sri Krishnan Kaniyamparambil, Former Minister for Agriculture, Kerala

Sri Naresh Reddy, CMC Limited, Chennai

Ms. Padma V. Upadhya, Librarian, Manipal Institute of Technology, Manipal-576 119.

Sri Parameswaran, Reader and Head, Department of Library and Information Science, University of Calicut, Calicut

Sri P.P. Pillai, Costford, Trichur

Dr. Prithvish Nag, Director, National Atlas and Thematic Mapping Organization, Calcutta

Dr. Prodhani, Library and Information Officer, ICAR Research Complex for NEH Region, Umroi Road, Umiam-793103, Meghalaya

Prof. C. Pythal, Department of Parasitology, College of Veterinary and Animal Sciences, Mannuthy, Trichur

Dr. Radhakrishnan Nair, Director, Kerala State Remote Sensing and Environment Centre and Land Use Commissioner, Trivandrum

Sri V.R. Raghunandanan, IRTC, Palakkad

Sri K. Rajasekharan, Librarian, Kerala Institute of Local Administration, Trichur-680561

Sri K.P. Rajendran, Member, Kerala Legislative Assembly

Sri T.K. Rama Krishnan, Former Minister, Cultural Affairs Fisheries and Rural Development, Kerala

Prof. R. Raman Nair, Librarian, Kerala Agricultural University, Trichur-680654

Dr. I.K. Ravichandrarao, Professor and Head, DRTC, ISI Campus, 8th Mile Mysore Road, Bangalore

Dr. N. Saifudeen, Land Resource Research Unit, Radio Tracer Laboratory, KAU, Trichur-680654

Sri Sajal Kanti Goswami, National Atlas and Thematic Mapping Organization, Calcutta

Sri Sreenivasulu, Librarian, National Institute of Agricultural Marketing, Jaipur-303 906

Dr. H.B. Nandwana, Assistant Professor, Department of Library and Information Science, Kota Open University, Kota-324 007

Dr. K.N. Syamasundaran Nair, Former Vice Chancellor, Kerala Agricultural University, Trichur-680654

Sri Teeka Ram Meena, IAS, Former Director, Kerala Institute of Local Administration, Trichur-680561

Sri A. Varadarajan, Department of Parasitology, College of Veterinary and Animal Sciences, Mannuthy, Trichur

Sri K. Veeranjaneyulu, Assistant Librarian, Acharya N.G. Ranga Agricultural University, Rajendra Nagar, Hyderabad-30

Sri S. Venugopal, Deputy Librarian, Bharathi Dasan University, Thiruchirappalli-620 024

Sri S.M. Vijayanand, IAS, Secretary and Commissioner, Local Administration, Government of Kerala

1

Introduction

Information and Participatory Planning and Development

Effective planning will not be possible without people's true participation in it. While people's involvement is necessary at all levels of planning, implementation and supervision, it is very important at the local levels. The three-tier district planning set-up has much room for the beneficiaries to cooperate with and participate in the process of planning and development. But to achieve this, decentralisation of planning in its full sense is essential. Economic planning is an endeavour in which human beings are intimately involved. As such, people's involvement is supposed to be the key to effective implementation of development programmes. The failure of planning in delivering desired results may be attributed to the absence of people's involvement.

People's involvement aims at securing people's commitment to the plan and programmes so that they are implemented effectively and in a desired way. The concept of people's involvement is not so obvious and it is usually interchangeably used, with people's participation and people's cooperation. In practice the term 'participation' has one of three possible connotations. In its most committed sense, participation means cooperating, taking part in something. The mere presence, even silence of an individual or organization at a meeting thus constitutes participation. Participation also means to having a share in something for which one assumes a certain responsibility. The third meaning of participation is being a partner in something and it calls for the collective pursuit of identical aims. We mean this form of participation when we talk of involvement, the term 'people' connotes individuals and social groups at large. These people are prospective beneficiaries of the plan. People's involvement in planning thus tries to ensure prospective beneficiaries' 'say' in formulation, execution and implementation of economic and social planning at all levels, particularly at the level of implementation.

People's involvement enriches the plan process in a number of ways. It helps to check the reliability of data, ensures commitment of the people to the projects formulated, restricts the vagaries of the technical and bureaucratic agencies making them to rationalize their proposals, reduces the scope for unreasonable pressures through informal channels and make the proposals to be based on the experience, knowledge and judgement of people at large. With the involvement of the people, a planner is not only better informed about the part played by economic progress in the process of growth, the cost and efficiency of group activities but he is also able to define the parameters of the behavioural equations that express people's reactions and economic process. It makes it possible to discover new ways of decision making in matters of economic and social policy in fulfilment of plan objectives. It would also make all classes feel themselves, part of the national community, strengthening the thread of national integration. People's participation in planning further helps to minimise the social cost of development and reduces conflict by making clear the area in which unbalances are tolerable.

Development should not only aim at increasing production but it should also reflect the values adopted by the society. These values can only be clarified and given expression if people at large are involved in planning. Participation by the people involves a fundamental choice whereby a new direction is given to the process of development and the existing social structure undergoes far reaching change. This in itself leads us to the concept of social democracy which emphasises that the people have to cooperate among themselves and with the various agencies responsible for the formulation and execution of the plan.

There are three phases of planning. Drawing up a plan is a technical one. Until recently when the experiments were done in this regard in Kerala and a few states it was considered that there is little scope for people's participation. Involvement of the people at this stage can help in defining objectives and priorities. Then people's participation can play much greater role in putting the plan into effect. People's involvement goes to arouse popular enthusiasm for the common venture. The next phase involves supervising the implementation of the plan. Supervision may be either a technical question or a political question. So far as it is a political question, there is scope for involving the people. People's involvement at this phase would bring about objectivity in supervision.

Participation is thus more needed at the local levels. Participation at the national level may go to decide the probable future of the nation. However the active cooperation of the population concerned is a condition for lasting success in regional development. The local population must be made to feel not only that they have an interest in the development of the region, but are responsible for its growth and success. At the local levels contact between official activities and the general public most commonly occurs and the project identified by the planners is either supported or rejected by the populace. Usually plans are made against difficulties due to ignorance; of the attitude and behaviour of the people in the face of changes imposed upon them by the central planning authority. Earlier the projects were executed either without the participation of the population or against the opposition and so they are doomed to failure.

In order that people's aspirations are translated into reality and people are actively involved in the process of planning, plan must be decentralised at local levels. Decentralisation of planning enables formulation and implementation of planning in conformity with the specified needs, deficiencies, resource potentials, ambitions and aspirations of the various areas of economy and thereby is able to secure the effective involvement of local people. Considering local involvement as the key to effective implementation of development programmes; now various steps are taken for decentralisation of planning and for involving people in plan implementation.

Decentralisation of planning in terms of local plans has been mentioned since the beginning of the era of planning in India. But till recently there was no concreate action. The pious statements made on decentralized planning were also too vague to be translated into action. Encirclement of a district may not satisfy the geographical and economic criterion for a spatial unit of planning. But the district will continue to be a unit of planning for long because of its convenience in terms of data base, administrative infrastructure and similar aspects. Almost all state governments have established some kind of district level planning set-up and it differs from state to state owing partly to the varying interest shown by the state leadership and partly due to the economic compulsions. The district level planning machinery in different states consists of two agencies—one mainly advisory and the other technical in nature. The first is known as District Development Committee; District Planning Board etc. and is a high powered body involving top officials and representatives of the people. The second tier of the district planning set-up usually called as the District Planning Unit formulates the district plan. This body though varies in composition from state to state, consists of mostly official and technical members.

The Working Group on District Planning, set up by the Planning Commission in September 1982, recommended a participatory approach to the district planning process, the participation extending through the stages of pre-planning, plan formulation, post-planning and implementation stages. It also outlined the methodology for district planning and stressed a massive training programme. The Planning Commission will continue to play a promotional and guiding role, in order to impart momentum to the decentralised planning process, in areas of providing data and information base, strengthening the district planning machinery, training to district level personnel and technical guidance through pilot projects.

In the light of the inventory of resources, infrastructure facilities, the felt needs and aspirations of the local people, the local planning unit formulates a perspective plan, five-year operational plans and annual action plan. It is believed that district and panchayat planning would help secure people's participation. The involvement of the people in the planning process in India has so far been restricted to the political executive, particularly to the Prime Minister and State Ministers. As early as during the first five year plan, Community Development Programme was launched to secure participation of the people in decision making and implementation of the development schemes. In accordance with the recommendation of the Mehta Committee (1957), Panchayati Raj institutions were established with an inter-linked three-tier structure of local self-governing bodies—Panchayat at village level, Samitis at the block level and Zilla Parishad at the district level. It was expected that the scheme would provide the necessary basic framework for implementing developmental activities in rural areas. Till recently these institutions due to excessive dependance, on the Government, failed to secure the desired popular support and participation.

1. Participation Leads to Equality

Securing full participation of the people and making the plan effective depends on various factors. There is need for separate inter-linked planning machineries right from the Planning Commission level to the village level. It would help pay exclusive attention to the development programmes. The block level administrative set-up is too burdened to carry the responsibility of executing development programmes effectively. The block level machinery needs to be suitably strengthened and restructured. It should have a different cadre for development planning including economists, statisticians, cartographers, geographers, agronomists, engineers, and other technical experts. It would be responsible for identifying growth centres and collecting information on implementing development programmes. It would also broaden the view of socio-political leadership at block level.

The non-officials, because of wider information basis, will also have a say in the selection of projects. The selection of projects will be in the light of broad principles agreed to and based on the discussion with local elected representatives, heads of department at the district level, voluntary agencies and people's committees; the Gram Sabhas. This saves the plan from being a pure academic exercise and bring about rationalising effect on the process of decision making. This helps securing a greater amount of people's participation because beneficiaries are involved in project selection. It is possible at the village level.

The task of implementing development programmes is entrusted to the block level planning unit. This unit is made responsible for seeking active involvement of the people at large and institutions. The outlook at the block level requires to be changed in favour of poor. This is possible by seeking the active involvement of local people from all classes as well as by more than proportionate representation to the poor in the task of implementing beneficiary oriented plans. The schemes are to be executed at the village level on community basis with the help of Gram Sabha in order to check distortion and misappropriation. Gram Sabha will have representation of all classes of society as a whole with a bias for the poor. If development programmes are implemented with the involvement of local people and beneficiaries, the problems of tackling socio-economic tension and achieving socio-economic equality can be solved to a great extent. The role of voluntary organisation to this end is important in the sense that they are able to provide sufficient dedication and involvement in implementing the development programmes and they are able to secure active involvement of the local people and beneficiaries.

Mobilization of the community resources to supplement the efforts of the government to achieve the goals of development is most important for self-reliant development of villages. It is however necessary that participatory planning is pursued at all levels. For any successful village development programme, participatory planning should be pursued both as an end and as a means. As an end, it is an inevitable extension of the national effort and commitment to bring the masses into mainstream of development process for establishing an egalitarian socio-economic order. Participatory planning, as a means, should subserve the object of self-reliance which is the base of an all-round development of a village. Self-reliant development of villages is of particular relevance to the Third World countries, to mobilise community resources to supplement the efforts of the government to achieve the goals of development. It is, however, necessary that participatory planning is pursued at all levels because it would create conditions wherein the services provided by the Government would be more effectively utilised for they would have a direct relevance to their felt needs. A crucial precondition to participatory planning is to understand the local situation, it is necessary to know the perception of development by the villagers. Unless the common man would not come forward to participate in the planning and development of their village, the plans would not be realistic. It is only when the development plan of a village is prepared according to their perception, they would identify themselves with such a plan. It would also ultimately lead to the mobilisation of the community resources.

People should participate in day to day decision making in all aspects of economic and social activities. This participation can be fruitfully organised through their own organisation which we may call as a "receiving mechanism". It can utilise their initiative and creativity and channelize their energies in management of their own welfare. Thus, the major responsibility of development management is shared by the community itself. The role of government agencies or the delivery systems become very nominal in this situation and it is required only to supplement the efforts of the community. For an effective participatory planning the community has to be involved in the following major tasks:

- Plan Formulation and Decision Making
- Implementation of Planned Activities
- Distribution of Benefits of Development
- Monitoring and Evaluation.

The implications of involvement of the community in these major tasks are more or less obvious. The first task of plan formulation and decision making is the most important for the successful functioning of the community in a collective manner and its formal organisation for its survival. Presently, in most of the states there is no participation of rural poor in decision making at the local level. Normally, the policies and programmes are handed over from above directly or indirectly and local people are required to fit in this framework. Even if there is some participation in decision making it is through their representatives and it cannot be relied upon. Keeping in view the socio-economic and political structures, prevailing in most developing countries, the participation by the people in the process of development can be meaningful and effective only if it is direct. In the initial phase the rich are likely to influence the decisions and setting the priorities in their favour. But, gradually, as the whole community gets involved in decision making process, it is unlikely that decisions would be grossly unfavourable to the interests of the poor. In course of time the poor will begin to participate more and more effectively and will be in a position to influence decisions in favour of the needs and interests of the majority.

The normal practice of people's participation in implementation of development programmes, particularly in community projects has been in the form of contribution of free labour, voluntary or otherwise. It is the poor who possesses only labour as their sole asset, who are asked to contribute it without any compensation. The rich on the other hand are not required to make proportionate sacrifices and it is they who benefit most from the community projects. This system should be changed and every section should share equal burden and responsibility of implementation. It can be done if we have defined the roles and responsibilities of each group and individual in project implementation.

Monitoring and evaluation are essential to provide feedback to the project management to improve the efficiency of the delivery of services and inputs. On this basis, corrective action or adjustment in the policies are made during implementation of the project. These aspects are very closely related to project, identification, formulation and overall decision making by the community. This is obvious from the fact that under integrated rural development programme the project ideas are not generated by the community or by the beneficiaries themselves. Consequently realistic projects are not formulated and there is dearth of innovative projects. If the participation in decision making is not there, there is also little participation in monitoring and evaluation of the projects. People's participation is necessary to provide information related to the progress of the project in order to identify problems, and constraints in implementation. Their involvement in monitoring and evaluation is also essential to identify not only 'how many' but also 'who' benefits from a particular project. People's direct participation in monitoring and evaluation is also likely to reduce mismanagement of resources in a project. The receiving mechanism should also be brought in to evaluate the performance of government personnel in projects and programmes being executed in its area to make the government personnel accountable to the people.

The participation in benefit sharing was left out in conventional growth oriented strategies by assuming that the benefits of development would percolate to the majority. As a result, the issue of equity in distribution was neglected. Since people's participation in the planning necessarily implies equitable sharing of benefits of development, it may be looked upon as the heart of the development strategy aiming at the amelioration of the poor. It is also the *sine qua non* of people's participation in development for 'people participate most freely and fully in what is theirs'.

The growth and complexity of development programmes for rural areas also increasingly call for close coordination at levels below the state. At these points, popular supervision over the official machinery has the potential to become an effective instrument of coordination. It is essential that horizontal pressures are exerted by people's representatives over what otherwise would remain just a line hierarchy of administration. Further, many of the multi-pronged developmental efforts need people's participation. But the initiative of the people can be uncoiled only through their involvement in the process of growth and change. While socio-economic development would limit without democracy, it is equally true that democracy will be just a shell without development. The two are, in fact, mutually reinforcing.

There has come about a sharper delineation of the concept and content of development. It now means more than economic growth. It centres round development of man; the surge towards satisfaction of basic human needs like food and shelter, education and health as well as his deeper psychic needs; the urge to feel significant. To have a say in shaping one's life and community's future has become an inalienable part of development. There is not only restlessness against deprivation and destitution but there is also the growing awareness that poverty can be overcome through purposeful action. The political, material and psychological needs clamour for satisfaction. The people want power to embark upon purposeful action to seek satisfaction at all these levels.

2. Decentralized Administration

Autonomy at the local level implies proper decentralisation of decision making powers at lower levels. It may, however, be added that decentralisation has generally been confused with deconcentrating of administrative powers from the centre to states, regions, districts, blocks, panchyats and there is hardly any effort to involve the people in the process. The experiments in democratic decentralisation have not been very successful in most states in India and the people's representative bodies have remained superseded for most part of their life in most of the states. Granting autonomy is not an easy task as it requires a strong political will to part away with powers. Not only delegation of powers to local level institutions will do but they should be backed by sufficient financial autonomy or availability of adequate resources at the local level. The higher level leadership, should promote the local level institutions. This can be achieved only when the top policy makers believe and sincerely strive for development of local level institutions and hand them over the job of the plan formulation, implementation, monitoring and evaluation at the local levels. This was successfully experimented only in Kerala and there a good awareness was created about it among the people. The delivery system would also need to be restructured in such a fashion that they clearly spell out the role of receiving mechanism in a well defined manner. It would be made clear as to at what level and at what stage the receiving mechanism should intervene and assist in the delivery of services and inputs. For this a process of planning from below has to be initiated in the real sense of the word. The Panchayats will have to be given control and management of schools and health subcentres or other village level institutions. All the funds coming for development from different agencies will also have to be channelized through the village body.

It is also important that Panchayats have a sound financial base. The realisation of taxes of the Panchayat should be made by the government's revenue department because these bodies having face to face relationship cannot realise their taxes rigorously. Some additional sources of income should also be created so that the Panchayats may have some additional resources at their command. For this purpose, Panchayats should be provided some assistance to take up industrial project based on local needs and resources. It would also provide employment opportunities to the local people. The idea is to make the local bodies self-sustaining so that they can provide the facilities and amenities to the people without depending on the government.

Panchayats should be encouraged and trained to handle planning and implementation functions by themselves. It may be difficult in the beginning for the people to design programmes by themselves. Therefore, the line agencies should provide technological backup to these institutions in such time as they are able to develop their own capabilities. It has to be recognized that the process of building up institutional capabilities in a heterogenous society where majority is illiterate or semiliterate is very difficult and time consuming. Therefore, those who are made responsible for this job should have patience and commitment towards this cause. The concerned officials would also have to be well equipped in the art of institution building.

Local leadership can play a vital role in organising the community members and mobilising social action for development and the Chinese and Japanese examples are worth emulating. In China 20 million local cadres carry communication both up and down, to and from top leadership and horizontally in the village neighbourhood and the commune. They are supervised from the top for understanding the 'big-picture' but are looked from below by the community organisation and by actually working with the peasants and workers in the farm or in the workshop. As in most developing countries there is no vertically linked specialist who comes from the centre or the region to help the farmers, a family planning worker who comes to persuade the families, health expert who comes to teach people to dig wells or boil water. The technical specialist comes and works with the local peasants and workers to build up local capability. But it is the local leadership which manages the central task of building up a local agricultural, industrial and cultural economy where everybody has a responsibility for it and takes part in it. Similarly, bureaucrats and technicians from higher organs of government are sent down to the commune to work and live with the peasants, thereby relating their development assignments to local perceptions. In every commune there is a community information centre which looks after all the information requirement of the commune and services similar to all that library and information services presently our state planning boards are having at State headquarters are accessible at the villages through these centres. Development and information support for that is not for planners or bureaucrats or leaders only, it is for everybody.

The crucial role played by leadership at all levels in modernisation of Japan is widely acclaimed. The functional elite were instrumental in reinterpreting traditional values of collectivity and cohesiveness and combining them with modern Western values. They remained an integral part of the community and worked with the local people. The development of their own village community was first and foremost for them of which they had a clear vision. This role of functional leaders is largely conspicuous by its absence in most developing countries. Because of general apathy towards supposedly non-manoeuvrable sociological factors and fear of conflict of interests, there is least inclination to go into the depth of problems associated with social change and participatory development including organisation of poor in rural societies.

For involving more and more people in the process of development, it will be necessary to organise functional groups as a part of receiving mechanism. Such groups can take care of the vulnerable sections of the society such as women and children and also the small and marginal farmers and landless labourers. Similarly, it would be useful to create community cadres in the village to handle some specified jobs of village development and general welfare. This would give a much desired broad base to the programmes and ensure their successful implementation through people's active support. There are a number of successful experiments in India and in other developing countries which are worth replicating. These cadres have worked wonderfully well and have helped in improving the delivery of services. The community cadres are given comprehensive training to understand and appreciate the technical contents of the programme and to disseminate knowledge horizontally by communicating with the people. They also maintain a vertical link with the line agencies of the government departments.

3. Effective Participation

One of the major impediments to implementation of effective participatory planning is the lack of local level library and information systems and the absence of a well defined methodology through which people can plan and manage their own development programmes. There should be a very efficient library and information system which forms part of state information infrastructure at every Panchayat which can fulfil the information needs of the people of the region. Methodology for planning and management should be simple enough so that the common people even if they are illiterate or semi-literate can find it convenient to participate in this process. The important steps involved in this methodology are described below.

The requirement would naturally be the collection, analysis and interpretation of data because it is the basic facts and figures that enable people to comprehend the existing situation and most pressing problems of the area in order to think of suitable projects and schemes. This should be done under the initiative of the local library and information system. There are some guiding principles which should be kept into focus while collecting data :

- data collected by the community itself is most reliable for participatory planning;
- minimum data collection should be the principle;
- any data which has no immediate use by the community should not be collected;
- data collected should have direct relevance to the planned activities;
- data collection instruments, formats, survey forms should be as simple as possible for comprehension by the people as well as easy to be tabulated by them; and
- data collection process should be done through community

volunteers which is the first step towards materialising participatory planning (mobilisation, training, planning and management) as well as mobilisation of local resources for the proposed projects and schemes.

Next step to follow is the identification of problems and felt needs of the community from the analysis of the collected information. This would lead to setting of priorities for area development. In this process, both the community leaders and field level functionaries of delivery systems should be involved. The following considerations should guide the prioritisation of schemes :

- needs of the community and priority given to these needs by the majority;
- community's interest in solving problems and willingness to provide resources;
- severity of the problem, its intensity and magnitude and immediate solutions; and
- linkages with other problems that is the cause or effect of another problem.

Then comes the framing of objectives of development of the area. The objectives would naturally be related to the problems identified above. The following rules should be observed in setting of objectives :

- objectives should emerge from the knowledge of the problems of the area;
- inter-relationship between different kinds of objectives should be taken into account;
- the proposed objectives should be acceptable to all the sections of the community, particularly the vulnerable sections and their leaders as also the government functionaries;
- feasibility of achieving objectives should be examined in the background of availability of inputs, i.e. manpower, material and finances from government as well as non-government sources;
- time-frame for achieving the objectives should be clearly specified;
- objectives should be quantifiable and measurable;

- location must be specified; and
- target beneficiaries should be defined.

Afterwards likely impediments and obstacles are to be analysed to effective implementation of programmes proposed for the area. For this purpose a clearcut strategy will have to be worked out so that the identified obstacles may be taken care of. The proposed strategy is to be formulated again keeping in mind the social inclinations, economic and geographic conditions and available resources.

Obviously, the focus should be on maximisation of benefits from the existing resources and infrastructure. Sometimes the set of objectives may need revision after this analysis has been completed. Some important components of the strategy are narrated below :

- to fix responsibility for specific tasks and to find out the type of manpower needed and if such manpower is not available then what type of training should be given to them;
- review of technical needs;
- the package of services required with each input;
- establishment of organisational structure and its linkages with government departments to implement individual activities;
- detailed action planning with time scheduling of each activity;
- budgeting, indicating the requirement of funds and the sources of funding including community resources; and
- designing a proper participatory monitoring system.

The last step would be to work out in details the institutional framework which would be needed to implement the programmes in an integrated manner. In this the existing people's institutions should be utilised because they are already functioning in the area and they have the proper backing. As already explained, a number of functional groups and sub-committees may be constituted so that almost every household is involved in the process of social development in one way or the other. By following the above mentioned steps the community can be finally guided to formulate a plan of action which would be a microcosm of the integrated social development plan. But before finally arriving at the plan of action, project proposals which have been discussed by the villagers number of times through the functional groups and allied bodies such as cooperatives can creatively be involved and the community can further reinforce its solidarity and cohesiveness. The distribution of benefits also becomes more egalitarian.

The above methodology can be successfully transacted into action if there is a simple manual in local language for planning by the community. It should also depict the step and planning activities through appropriate symbols and pictures so that even the illiterates can participate in this process. Some attempts have already been made in this direction in Kerala and manuals for participatory monitoring have been developed. Drawing from such experiments a detailed methodology and a manual, can be developed and should be tried in a few villages and then extended over a larger area. Obviously, the manual for village planning should include the physical, social and economic aspects of development.

Information Technology, which includes aspects from computer and communication technology, library science, electronics and various related fields, is the most dominant technology emerging in today's development scenario globally. Kofi Annan has remarked that recent developments in the field of communication and information technology are indeed revolutionary in nature. Information and knowledge are expanding in quantity and accessibility. In such fields as agriculture, health, education, human resources and environmental management or transport and business development, the consequences really could be revolutionary. Communication and Information technology have enormous potential especially for developing countries and in furthering sustainable development. The society which combines productively the knowledge embedded in IT based systems with the creative potential and knowledge embodied in people, will achieve sustainable development. The explosive developments in information technology field has aroused much interest among policy makers, the business sector, the media and the academic world in industrialized countries. But developing countries are facing numerous problems in harnessing information technology. Although the cost of using information and communication technologies to build national information infrastructures are high, the costs of not doing so are likely to be much higher. Developing countries are lagging behind in building innovative and distinctive knowledge societies and in harnessing IT for their development projects. Not investing in IT implies forgoing the possibilities for economic development. At the same time excessive emphasis on IT means the danger of diverting resources away from the basic economy, which is the very foundation, for the IT take off.

4. IT for Governance

The advent of Information Technology as a highly leveraged enabling tool for delivery of products and services has now redefined the fundamentals and changed the institutions and mechanisms of delivery for ever. This Information Age paradigm shift is characterized by Citizen and Business focus integration driven as it were by the choice of service providers and means of access. In this context the concept of public Governance has not gone unaffected. It too has seen a fundamental shift in the concept, manner and method by which the State has to deliver its services. This new practice of administration of the Public has developed into the concept of Electronic Governance. Hence the Electronic Governance (EG) has a wider meaning than mere computerization of stand alone back office operations. It means to fundamentally change as to how the Government operates and this implies a new set of responsibilities for the executive, legislature and the citizenry.

Electronic Governance is the application of Information Technology to the processes of Government functioning to bring about simple, moral, accountable, responsive and transparent governance. The Department of Electronics has taken upon itself the charge of translating this definition into definitive reality by harnessing advances in IT and the opportunities so presented to restructure Government, Citizen and Business interfaces with the objective of better governance; establishing institutional mechanisms to facilitate initiatives towards synergic utilization of IT as an enabling tool for efficiency and effectiveness in public administration; targeting to achieve at least one-fourth of the government dealings and services to be delivered electronically through computers, telecommunication etc.

For Electronic Governance Government should have an Intranet for ensuring smoother flow of data, communications and access to information by different departments. It should be made mandatory for all departments to put as much information as possible on to the Intranet in an easily searchable way. Transactions between various departments of the government is to be networked to enable transfer of files and paper through networks. All departments have to operate web sites which provide up-to-date information, forms, leaflets etc. E-mail has to become the normal contact method and arrangement for rapid response to e-mail queries is to be ensured. There should be a single web based front-end for all government services to the public. The access of information must be permitted in the language most comfortable to the public user, generally the local language. The most important aspect of e-governance is bringing a change in the mind set of the government servants who have been accustomed to work only in the manual mode. It is necessary to train all employees in basic computer usage. There should be workshops and seminars for all levels. Creation of the infrastructure for Information Technology in the entire country by building up national, state and local level information infrastructures. Communication of data to public, i.e accessibility and retrieval of data by public through Citizen Information System interface (Information Kiosks) in public places, such as shopping centres, post offices, railway stations, libraries, PCOs, selected STD/ISD booths at prominent places, is very important. While we identify and develop new application areas, it is necessary to connect to the old systems and databases to develop comprehensive information systems. These databases should integrate into a data warehouse for analytical data mining to support decision-making. Given the fact that different applications may work with different languages, a coherent data integration policy need to be developed. Government departments which have maximum interaction with the public like Electricity, Water, Telephone, Sanitation, Public Transport, Police, Land Records, Pension, Ration Cards, Birth Certificate, Death Certificate, Caste/Tribe Certificate etc. must be identified for the use of IT. A number of organizations both in the Centre and the States have taken commendable initiatives to develop hardware and software platforms to address the challenge of EG.

The EG initiative would have to address issues, like, identifying functional areas in every Government organization which need to be taken up for EG, identifying the appropriate hardware platforms and software application packages for cost effective delivery of public services, making this knowledge repository widely available through appropriate demonstration mechanisms and offering a basket of these models to the States.

Management of Change is the other most fundamental challenge to be addressed by the practice of EG. This would involve: delivery of public services like utilities, rural and urban development schemes through IT based technologies which would necessitate procedural and legal changes in the decision and delivery, in the decision making levels and delegation of authority, in legal provisions to give effect to the technology objectives.

These would lead to mandatory organizational and institutional changes effecting both people and methods at all interfaces of the delivery chain. For this, acceptance of this changed process would have to be properly understood, internalized, adopted and improved to enable full advantages of the technology. De-layering of the decision making levels leading to re-engineering and appropriate sizing of the decision making machinery will be another issue.

During the last few years there has been major initiatives among different Governments towards ushering in Information Technology and its tools in the functioning of government. The emphasis has been on providing better services to citizens and in improving the internal productivity. IT implementation in government is the most difficult process and hence requires careful planning and formulation of strategies for effective implementation.

One important point to be noted is the need to use local languages in the IT implementation process. It is heartening to note that, particularly because of the pioneering work done by C-DAC, the technology is now very much available. This by itself could give a major boost to IT implementation efforts. However, in the national context it is essential to have access to local level databases maintained in regional languages as well as to use appropriate interfaces to aggregate such data. Here, a focused effort would have to be made in improving the technologies for transliteration. Similarly, an effort would have to be undertaken for perfecting the OCR technology for local languages. This is critical as an effective OCR technology is required to convert the data that is scanned and stored in local languages into meaningful and workable databases. This could also help in substantially simplifying the efforts at content generation and data warehousing.

The emphasis of IT application in government currently is on conducting system studies to understand the workflows involved in each of the activities and attempt computerization of such workflows. This results in certain levels of simplification and rationalization and even an improvement in productivity. However, here also the basic issues involved in delay and red tapism within Government are not adequately addressed. Even in computerization of workflows, there will be a need to update the data periodically. In the event of each individual completing the work assigned to him, even in the present system delays would not have occurred. It will be extremely naive to assume that the updating of data would be regularly and periodically done just because the system is computerized. In fact, in the workflow computerization model there is a very real danger of substantive investments being made in hardware application, software and even in training and still the issue of prompt and regular updating of data not being effectively addressed. In the above context, it is clear that substantive administrative reforms would have to precede attempts at e-governance. In other words, the emphasis will have to be on simplifying procedures, rationalizing processes, restructuring Government and then use IT to institutionalize such changes. However, this is easier said than done. It is in these circumstances that attempts at e-governance based on creative and effective uses of relational databases needs to be attempted. In this approach, the data requirement for decision making are identified and emphasis is on structuring the relevant databases. IT implementation would have to be planned in such a manner that each transaction would automatically be derived from the database and in turn would update the database. For this, apart from the creation of databases there is also a need to network individual service delivery point or workflow processing points. A minimized structure of such a database would have to be first decided and a relevant network first created. Subsequently, additional modules to databases and add on networks would have to be created and integrated. What should be attempted is, mapping of physical resources as well as the voluminous data available across various government departments into a relational data structure and manipulating the same as suited to different levels of government machinery for their functions related to service rendering and planning.

At the national level a uniform citizen code is to be adopted. Once this is done each State may be asked to arrange its databases with one field earmarked for this code. This would facilitate easy retrieval of data and integration of databases at any point of time. Then it is to be ensured that the databases that are going to get generated as part of the census operations may also be digitized and made available for building up citizen databases. This would need amendments to the census act and a thorough study will be necessary to identify the uses of such data in building up comprehensive databases immediately.

Attention is to be given to dissemination of information gathered through IT based systems. A case in point is the information collected by remote sensing which could be of immense use in estimating the availability of resources and qualitatively alter the planning process. An effort to identify similar repositories of data and information relevant for providing better services to citizens through e-governance and a strategy for the desegregation of such data and its dissemination needs to be urgently formulated.

5. Information Required for Participation

Information is a critical input into the preparation of the local level plan. The local level information systems have to collect, organise and supply data required to assess the resource base of a district and the development problems of each of the commodity producing sectors, the infrastructure, social and special sectors. This has to provide the macro perspective for the sustainable development of the region.

If we examine the methods, processes and nature of the Panchayat and district level plans to be prepared we can understand the importance of information support systems in making them effective. The Constitution also lays down in Article 243 that the Panchayats be given powers and responsibilities with respect to preparation of plans for economic development and social justice and their implementation as may be entrusted to them including those in relation to matters listed in the Eleventh Schedule. The primary responsibility of the preparation of the plans is with the different tiers of Local Self-Government Institutions.The District Planning Committee is visualised only as a co-ordinating agency whose responsibility is to integrate the local plans prepared by the Local Self-Government Institutions.

Despite the wide acclaim about the value of information support in effective participation in planning and development the districts and panchayats are not having library and information support for planning which exist only at the state capital attached to Planning Boards.

The suggestive format for local level plan given in the 1969 Guidelines shows that without information support that is relevant and of high quality the plans prepared will not be foolproof. As per the guidelines the section 1 of the proposed plan document was to present a critical appraisal of the existing level of development in the district, based on available statistical and administrative data, the advice of knowledgeable farmers and entrepreneurs, experience of local officials, and systematic appraisal of ongoing programmes. The Plan has to consist of the following chapters as per the guidelines given:

- Introduction
- Infrastructure and social services
- Natural resources
- Administrative and institutional structure
- Economic activities
- Problems of employment
- Problems of backward communities
- Critical appraisal of the ongoing development schemes
- Local mobilisation of resources
- Programmes for backward communities

Preparation of this document requires the use of efficient library and information systems. On the basis of the above situational analysis a long term perspective for development and priorities of programmes were to be drawn up along with documents on programmes for development resources for the plan issues for the state government.

It is not sure that if any District or Panchayat is having a library and information system that can provide information support to people in preparing the district, panchayat level plan. At state level State Planning Board is having a big library and information support system that can be used by the top brass of planning who have access to other information systems containing information on the same aspect in the State capital. Even though we argue for the need to decentralise planning and development; extending this facility, providing quality library and information systems that can support people's planning to panchayats have not been thought off seriously till now.

The following were the sequence of steps suggested by experts and guidelines for the preparation of the local level plan:

- Formulation of the major objectives of the local level plan;
- Compilation of data for local planning;
- Bringing out the profile of the region in relation to the basic objectives;
- Formulating the main strategy and thrust of region's planning;
- Analysis of the existing programmes and projects with reference to the strategy outlined above and the proposals regarding modification of the ongoing programmes and projects, proposals for removal of inter-block disparities, assessment of unemployment/ underemployment and proposals for manpower planning and budgeting, inclusion of new projects and plans, inter-linkages between various projects and programmes, organisation and management to ensure that no implementation gap exists;
- Assessment of resources for allocation to various programmes and projects;
- A statement of physical and financial components of the region's plans;
- Statement of spatial dimensions of the district plan; and
- Relationships and links between the panchyat, district plan and regional and state development plans.

The people's planning process in Kerala is a bold experiment that attempts to take the planning process to the grassroot level and empower the local bodies, so that they function as institutions of self-government. The unique feature of the Kerala experiment is the high level of autonomy granted to the local bodies to determine their own priorities. Each tier of local government is given the freedom to independently determine its priorities and draw up its plans within certain broad guidelines issued by the State government. Planning is conceived as a genuine bottom up process starting from grassroots with maximum involvement of masses. Ordinary people are encouraged to actively participate not only in identifying problems but also in finding solutions and even in formulating the projects. The broad stages of the people's planning process are the following.

First stage of the people's planning process involves formulation of a strategic perspective for development for every grama panchayat and municipality. The main activities at this stage are the following:

- identifying the felt needs of the people;
- data collection and objective assessment of local resources and problems; and
- preparation of panchayat (municipal) development report (PDR).

The grama sabhas were organised in 1996 to identify the local problems, priorities and development perspectives of the people. It is estimated that nearly 2.5 million people participated in these meetings. The following participatory studies were undertaken in every grama panchayat and municipality:

- collection of secondary data,
- study of local geography and natural resources,
- review of ongoing schemes,
- documentation of local history,
- consolidation of grama sabha reports, and
- primary surveys and resource mapping.

The outcome of the above exercises will be a development report for each panchayat (municipality). The structure of the reports was more or less uniform with the first chapter reviewing the administrative and local history, highlighting the role of social movements in the village/town. Second chapter was devoted to the analysis of natural and human resources of the locality. Twelve chapters followed it, each covering a development sector. The current status of each sector is to be discussed, its ongoing schemes reviewed and problems identified along with a list of suggested recommendations. The report will embody the local perspective for development and was discussed and adopted at a panchayat (municipal) level seminar. It is estimated that more than 3 lakh persons participated in these seminars.

Second stage in the people's planning process is the formulation of the annual plan by the grama panchayats and municipalities. The report will propose a large number of suggestions for every development sector that might take many years for implementation. Taking into account the resource constraints, the grama panchayats and municipalities prioritised and selected proposals that could be taken up in the annual plan. Task forces, 12 in number of 10 to 12 members, were constituted in every grama panchayat and municipality to formulate projects based on the approved proposals. A uniform format was also laid down for preparation of project proposals.

Preparation of the annual plans of the higher tiers constituted the Stage III of the people's planning process. The preparation of the district plan may be considered as Stage IV of the people's planning process. The planning process that was far outlined above involves only feedback from below. But a basic weakness has been the absence of a systematic feedback from above, from a macro district development perspective. This has been responsible for the inadequate integration between the programmes of different tiers of local bodies and also insufficient attention being given to the spatial dimension of the planning process. The district plan should not be conceived merely as a consolidated list of projects and plans of different tiers of Local Self-Government Institutions. It is also a document providing a comprehensive perspective for development of the district. This perspective should guide the preparation of future local plans within the district. With the preparation of the district plan, it may be claimed that the cycle of decentralised planning is complete. The local plans at every level would be prepared henceforward with simultaneous feedback from both—above and below. The objectives of the district plan will be the following as per points discussed above:

- to make an objective assessment of the district and an assessment of the problems of resources use and provide a macro perspective for sustainable development of the district.
- to analyse the consolidated plan of the local self-governments in the district so as to identify contradictions, duplications and gaps and also link the local plans with the macro perspective.
- to formulate guidelines for the preparation of future local plans, so that the weaknesses identified can be avoided in future and the local plans are better integrated with the state level planning.

Accordingly a district plan would have three parts. First part will be perspective for district development, constitutes the bulk of the plan document. After an assessment of the resource base of the district, the development problems of each of the goods producing sectors, services producing sectors and infrastructure sectors is to be made. Separate analysis is envisaged for the problems faced by women and weaker sections. The sectoral analysis draws heavily from the methodology proposed by the earlier official guidelines. However, there is also an important departure. While utilising the district level database, secondary studies and expertise, the proposed methodology emphasises importance of integrating local level perceptions of the development problems at the district level.

The spatial plan is given wide consideration and besides, the discussions on the sectoral problems are done with clear reference to the spatial dimensions. Second part will consolidate plans of the local self-governments. The relevant information with respect to the pattern of plan finance, sectoral investment, Special Component Plan (SCP) and Tribal Sub Plan (TSP) and Women Component Plan (WCP) by different tiers alone needs to be presented. Analysis of sectoral investment pattern in terms of broad natural regions may also be undertaken. Finally, the consolidated plan of the local bodies have also got to be juxtaposed with the State and Central plan schemes implemented in the district. Last part will be guidelines: To what the local plans correspond to the district macro development perspective outlined in Part I? What are the reasons for the divergence and how can they be rectified? To what extent do the local plan proposals correspond to the local problems identified? To what extent are the local plans integrated and consistent with each other? On the basis of questions such as these, the guidelines for preparation of future local plans are to be formulated.

6. Content to be Organised in Local Libraries

Aspects on which information is to be collected, organised and disseminated by local libraries at Panchayat and district levels are the following.

Development Perspective for the District

- Resource base and development
- General Information on the region
- Development history of the region
- Bio-physical resources of the region
- Population and labour

Commodity Producing Sectors and Infrastructure in the Region

- Agriculture
- Animal husbandry
- Fisheries
- Industry
- Co-operation
- Urban development
- Energy
- Transport and communications
- Finance

Social and Special Sectors

- Health
- Drinking water and sanitation
- Education
- Social welfare
- Culture
- Scheduled Caste and Scheduled Tribe development
- Gender analysis

Consolidated Plan of the Local Self-governments

- Financing pattern .
- Sectoral investment
- Special Component Plan and Tribal Sub Plan
- Women component plan
- State and Central sector schemes and projects
- Critical review of the planning process

Guidelines

- Mandatory guidelines
- Suggestions

General information to be kept at the local library should include documents on the historical, cultural and political history of the region, documents revealing the decentralised planning campaign in the district etc. Information on the members' participation in grama sabhas and development seminars conducted should be available. Documents on the administrative structure of the district, the list of taluks, blocks, grama panchayats and municipalities and their area and population may be available in the district and local libraries. Administrative maps of the district and panchayat also should be kept prominently in the library.

The district central library and the local library should have documents and information on the geography of the district and the panchayat which will enable the assessment of its bio-physical resources of the region concerned while preparing the plan. Documents on the following aspects must be organised and appropriate maps on each aspect must be collected and preserved.

Geography	general topography of the district — hills, slopes, valleys, coastal plains, marshy lands etc.
Climate	seasons, rainfall, atmospheric temperature, directions of wind etc.
Water resources	rivers, canals, tanks, ground water potential, water-logging etc.
Land and minor mineral resources	clay, river sand, glass sand and rocks
Soil types	composition, fertility, drainage, etc.
Land utilisation	existing pattern
Bio wealth	details of natural vegetation, flora and fauna, and wild life.

Detailed information on the major environmental problems of the location should be collected and periodical exhibitions and discussions should be organised by the library on that aspect to educate the people so that they will take appropriate measures to prevent further environmental degradation while formulating plans.

Documents and information materials on population, migration and other factors that influence population growth of the region should be acquired and organised. These documents should enable to provide a view of the social and religious characteristics of the population and their skill and educational development.

Sufficient documents on the history of resource use should be available for use of the people. They should enable the study of the development problems in a historical perspective. The collection of the local library should have documents/ information on the following aspects :

- the influence of the independence movement and major events that occurred in the locality in connection with it;
- the struggles against caste oppression and for social reforms, and the consequences in social life that result from those struggles; and
- foundation of trade unions, peasant associations and other mass organisations and major events in the growth of these mass movements.

The information or documents collected should cover development of the economic sector, with sufficient coverage to the agrarian transformation of the region during the century, expansion of agriculture and changes in land use, commercialisation of agriculture and changes in the cropping pattern, land reforms and changes in agrarian relations, evolution of technology and productivity. The industrial evolution of the region, modern industries existing there, transport and communication network available and details of electrification must be available for reference at the local library. Details or documents on development of education and health care facilities must be available.

All the available documents and information on development and development problems of all sectors are to be collected and made available at the local library. They should cover the structural features of the development sector and the level of development like, for example, in agriculture the cropping pattern and the productivity of the crops. The documents on service sectors should be able to give a view of the quality of services. The documents should include regional level secondary data and status report, studies and other secondary literature available.

The library can take initiative in organising discussions on what are the causes for inadequate growth, low productivity, poor quality of services or the inadequate coverage of services? The discussions can be recorded in audio-video tapes. This can form a collection of the information and knowledge of the local level experts and officials as well as the local wisdom.

7. IT Policy Initiatives in the States

After the launching of the National Task Force on IT, initiatives were taken by various state governments for IT applications which could benefit the majority of the people. Karnataka was the first state to adopt an IT policy in 1997. Maharashtra, Tamil Nadu, Kerala and Andhra Pradesh followed it. In May 1998, the Central Government adopted the recommendations of the National Task Force on Information Technology and Software Development that each state government should formulate an IT policy. Now most of the state governments have set up IT departments and budget allocations are being set apart for IT promotion. In states, task forces have been set up and action plans have been prepared. The major weakness of most of the policy documents is the total lack of rural focus. Kerala and MP claims to have taken sufficient care of this aspect where the local body computerisation and networking got priority. Kerala's policy clearly declares its commitment to implement local body computerisation, to extend citizen services through the local bodies computerization programme and to use IT for empowerment of the people and for fulfilling the right to information of the community at large. The policy also has a distinct focus on developing resource based information system for the state, which could evolve as the knowledge base for the decentralised planning programme and other developmental initiatives in the state. This in turn could be the centre around which an integral decision support tool for planning and management could emerge.

Kerala's Information Technology Policy document has benefited from earlier initiatives of the Kerala State Planning Board in formulating a development-centred and bottom-up IT outlook; the report of the task force on electronic media; and the Pilot project proposal for a State level informatics system for strengthening the people's planning process and decentralised plan implementation.

The development experience of Kerala which is unique has attracted wide interest. Kerala having one of the world's lowest per capita incomes, has achieved high levels of literacy and life expectancy and low infant mortality and birth rates comparable to developed countries. Kerala initiated the People's Plan Campaign for the Ninth Plan, a statewide movement for community development as a strategy to make a breakthrough in the development stalemate that the economy has got into. The State Government has transferred, 35% of the state development budget as grant to the local bodies on local projects decided by the people from below. All the local bodies are producing study reports on the Panchayat, municipalities with participation of the local communities. A number of participatory and innovative models of micro development have been emerging throughout the state in sanitation, housing, safe drinking water, education, agriculture and micro enterprises building. A series of software applications for participatory e-governance, participatory services based on a citizen's database, Geographic Information system based resource management tools and community portals for development, and transparency in public administration are developed.

The Panchayat Resource Mapping Programme jointly undertaken by India Rural Technology Centre (IRTC), the Centre for Earth Science Studies (CESS) and the Kerala State Land Use Board (KSLUB) was an innovative effort to address some of the major impediments of local level planning. The programme involved generation of a fairly comprehensive database on land and water resources, peoples and the pattern of their utilization in map format. The maps used were the cadastral maps (used by revenue authorities for entering the plot numbers), which can be easily comprehended by the villagers. Subsequently, IRTC took the initiative of moving from resource maps and the reports of quick appraisal to drawing up an integrated plan for the panchayat and implementing it with active involvement of the local people.

Implementation of the plans prepared at the local level calls for a wide range of technical inputs, which shall include among others spatial data; information on the resource base in the locality, socio-economic status as well as detailed micro level information on specific sectors where development programmes shall be initiated on priority basis. Availability of such data at the panchayat and municipality level would inevitably strengthen the presence of block level and district level local bodies, which can look into issues related to area planning and prioritization based on the area plan. A reliable information base is essential for successful management of a local body and strategic decision-making. Lack of information contributes to problems such as ineffective development programmes and activities; uneconomical and badly planned investment projects, poor functioning of tax and utility systems and disregard of environmental impact of development on the population.

8. IT Application in Kerala

SLIDE project of Kerala is a best example of the use of IT for welfare measures. The task force on electronic media, constituted by the Kerala State Planning Board had recommended two pioneering efforts for application of information and communication technologies for the development of the State; an initiative for a total communication strategy for Kerala and a proposal to develop a comprehensive resource based information system for the State of Kerala. The project on total communication strategy for Kerala proposed to set up a state-wide video and computer network. The video channel shall be for educational television and for developmental communication. The computer network shall be for establishing an integrated database that can facilitate better decentralized planning by the local bodies, implementing computerized citizen services to make local body administration more responsive and efficient and providing Internet and Intranet services at the local body level with the specific purpose of empowering masses and ensuring transparency.

The programme for developing a comprehensive resource based information system for Kerala was aimed at setting up an integrated resource based database of various spatial variables relating to land, water and biomass, and non-spatial determinants like socio-economic variables.

Centre for Development of Imaging Technology (CDIT) prepared a pilot project for a State Level Informatics system for strengthening people's planning process and decentralized planning (SLIDE). The project aimed at creating a state-level developmental information system nucleating from an integrated database at the local body level.

It was envisaged that a major initiative for computerizing the administration of local bodies shall also be taken up as a part of the SLIDE project. Further, a geographic information system based rural and urban information system, focusing on the natural resource endowment of each local body, shall be created, integrated at the state-level, and updated on a regular basis as a continuation of the computerization programme. Project aims at building a mechanism for bridging the data gaps in local area planning the objectives of which are listed as the following in concerned documents :

- to demonstrate that it is possible to undertake participatory integrated resource based planning at the panchayat level, participative urban environment planning and management at the municipality and corporation level and participative, sustainable and environment based area planning at the block level.
- to demonstrate that it is possible to use sophisticated information systems for developmental action.
- to demonstrate that our panchayats, municipalities and blocks are capable of using computers to increase the quantum and efficiency of their work.
- to use the capabilities of computers, remote sensing and geographical information systems for planning and management at the panchayat, municipality and block level.
- to evolve a mechanism at the panchayat and block level for continuously updating the resource information system to use it for integrated and sustainable resource based planning at the farm, watershed, panchayat and block levels.
- to evolve a mechanism at the municipality level for continuously updating the urban information system to use it for environmental planning and management at the aforementioned level.
- to demystify geo-informatics and computer based information systems and to make assure at least a section of people on the potential of using them as tools for developmental action.
- to develop a mechanism to cross check and authenticate data collected by the departments at the Panchayat/ Municipality / Block level and integrate this data with the resource information system and urban information system on a regular basis.
- to inculcate a new culture of collecting data, updating it, ensuring the truthfulness and correctness of the data and utilising the data meaningfully for developmental work.
- to evolve a system of responsive and efficient administration at the local body level and to inculcate a culture of total transparency in all walks of administration.

Expected results output of SLIDE Project include a full-fledged information management mechanism in the hands of local personnel in corporations, municipalities and block panchayats ; a comprehensive database covering environmental, geographic, economic, social and cultural aspects of the Panchayat/ Municipality/ Block and a mechanism for its updating; a comprehensive manual on the development and use of the Rural Information System for facilities planning, farm and watershed management and economic planning at the panchayat and block level; a comprehensive manual on the development and use of an Urban Information System for facilitating planning, infrastructure management, urban environment management and economic planning at the municipality level; a mechanism for bringing together data on all developmental projects in the local body and regularly updating it; a time bound complaint/query redressal system linking the local body and various line departments; a comprehensive manual on computerisation of administration, accounting and other operations at the panchayat, municipality and block levels and new systems for responsive and efficient administration; a cadre of trained computer personnel at the various departments and the local body level capable of undertaking office automation and database operations and a cadre of trained developmental activists at the local body level familiar with data processing, cartography etc., and capable of utilising such data for developmental work.

The Information Kerala Mission (IKM) has been set up by the Kerala Government for computerizing local bodies. This project include linking up one thousand two hundred and fourteen local bodies with the District Planning Offices and the State Planning Board; developing applications for deployment at the local body level; establishing training centres in engineering colleges, polytechnics and other institutions and training around one and a half lakh people in various aspects of software and hardware; establishing district level help desks at selected engineering colleges and polytechnics; positioning selected professionals well-versed in network management, system administration, and database administration for providing all-round support in setting up and maintaining the wide area network; and deploying the applications at one thousand two hundred and fourteen local bodies, fourteen district planning offices and the State Planning Board. In terms of both, coverage and scope, IKM has emerged as one of the biggest Information and Communication Technology (ICT) deployment programme taken up in the country.

The IKM has been initiated as a sequel to the people's plan

campaign, which has already brought about sweeping changes in the functioning of the local bodies. The IKM has tried to imbibe the spirit of the people's plan campaign and has come up with an innovative, holistic and participatory information communication technology deployment programme. The state claims that the mission, if successfully implemented, can by itself create history in participative electronic system governance (e-governance) as well as in human centred social informatics system building. IKM is aimed at creating information systems capable of strengthening the grassroot level people's plan organization covering grama sabhas and ward sabhas, making the local body institutions more responsive and efficient, and developing mechanisms for improving transparency and ensuring the right to information of the community at large.

The Natural Resources Development and Management Systems Division (NRDMS) of Department of Science and Technology had been taking the lead in creating spatial databases for planning. However such initiatives were confined largely at district levels. Creation of micro level databases was attempted in Kerala as a part of the Panchayat Resource Mapping programme by the Integrated Rural Technology Centre. However scientists from the Department of Science and Technology were not too sure on the replicability of the programme throughout the state on the one hand and further they were concerned about the capabilities of the local community in putting to use such sophisticated databases on a regular basis for grassroot level planning.

Planning Commission approved the project. Kerala Information Network for local bodies submitted by Kerala State Planning Board for computerization of local bodies. The Government of Kerala decided to set up a mission group for the time bound implementation of the local body computerization programme.

The objectives of the mission are : to provide connectivity with the State Planning Board, the District Planning Office and 1214 local bodies within the State (Networking); to develop a mechanism for regular monitoring of the plan targets achieved by the local bodies, over the network (Plan Monitoring); to establish a mechanism for automating the various operations at the local body level like accounting, finance, project management, public services, statutory functions and general administration using appropriately developed information systems at the local body level thereby making a quantum leap in accountability, transparency and efficiency in public services

(Service Automation); to develop an integrated micro-level resource based developmental information system which could facilitate meaningful decentralized planning at the local body level (Database development); to provide trained man power for operationalising the hardware and software (Training); to provide continued technical support to ensure that the network applications are up and running.

For many people as well as institutions, computerization means procurement of hardware. In majority of cases they do not go beyond using standard application software for simple applications. Time and resources are seldom spent to develop application packages for specific purposes, which are essential for any meaningful computerization programme. The reason for this state of affairs is not a lack of capability or slackness but absence of understanding on application of Information Technology. In order to cover up the inability to implement projects within a time frame producing tangible results, institutions attempt to monopolise within their area of operations. Not only do these institutions lack the perspective to promote local entrepreneurship; the latter is perceived as potential threat to the former's existence.

Training is not given its due place in government level computerisation projects. As a result the employees continue to be alienated from the technology; even after the computerisation programme is over. There are two reasons for this. The main reason is the absence of the training component in the project plan itself. The second reason is the lack of linkages between the government level computerisation projects and the institutions imparting training.

Information Kerala Mission claims that it is committed to opening up new vistas in electronic governance. Information Kerala Mission uses the participative software development model that was tested. The User Requirement Document shall be prepared based on the system study report with active involvement of the end users. The Software Requirement Specification shall be developed based on the User Requirement Document. The software module developed based on these shall be subjected to extensive field tests. Conscious effort will be taken to consider the opinions of end users and other beneficiaries. Then identifying a set of local entrepreneurs, sharing the software requirement specifications with them, and using their capabilities and skills for developing various modules of the software will be part of the methodology adopted for Information Kerala

Mission. This is for strengthening local entrepreneurship in software developments. The detailed document of the project shall be the output of the discussion with local software[1] developers. The project also envisages to give a new direction to the existing computer training centres and to prepare them for a people oriented training programme.

A similar approach will be developed in making technical support available at the local level. There are numerous individuals and institutions working in the field of Information Technology across the State. It is considered important to utilize their technical skills in supporting the mechanisms developed as part of the IKM. For this IKM project to attempt the following :

- setting up a dial up modem based WAN to be upgraded to a dedicated line based WAN with WLL/VSAT if required.
- developing application software actively involving the users comprising panchayat staff, people's planning organisation and elected local body members with the involvement of identified local partners in industry.
- tapping local synergies in establishing proactive ICT support network comprising institutional structures, voluntary mechanisms and entrepreneur groups.
- training and orienting a critical mass of human ware at the local level to operationalise the software and hardware, to generate an environment conducive to e-governance based on people's involvement and to trigger micro ICT ventures at the local level through out the State banking upon the social activism component of the people's planning programme.
- to promote creation of spatial and non-spatial development knowledge-base through horizontal and vertical integration of various development initiatives in the State, at the micro level and to initiate action research programmes centred around this knowledge base.

9. Effective Strategies

It has been widely accepted that IT implementation in Government is the most difficult process and hence requires careful planning and formulation of strategies for effective implementation. Computerisation in Government has generally focused on computerisation of individual activities *per se*. This leads to mere automation of the existing manual work. The emphasis currently is on conducting system studies to understand the work flows involved in each of the activities and attempt computerisation of such work-flows. This results in certain levels of simplification and rationalisation and even an improvement in productivity. However, here also the basic issues involved in delay and red tapism within government are not adequately addressed. Even in computerisation of workflows, it is required to update the data periodically. In the event of each individual completing the work assigned to him, even in the present system, delays would not have occurred. It will be foolish to assume that the updating of data would be regularly and periodically done just because the system is computerised. In fact, in the workflow computerisation model there is a very real danger of substantive investments being made in hardware, application software and even in training and still the issue of prompt and regular updating of data not being effectively addressed.

So it is clear that substantive administrative reforms would be essential. In other words, the emphasis will have to be on simplifying procedures, rationalising processes, restructuring government and then use ICT to institutionalise such changes. In the above circumstances attempts at e-governance based on creative and effective uses of relational databases needs to be attempted. In this approach, the data requirement for decision making are identified and emphasis is on activities structuring the relevant databases. IT implementation would have to be planned in such a manner that each transaction would automatically be derived from an activities integrated database and in turn would update the database. For this, apart from creation of databases there is also a need to network individual service delivery or workflow processing points. A minimised structure of such a database would have to be first decided and an appropriate network first created. Subsequently, additional modules to databases and add-on networks would have to be created and integrated. What should be attempted is, mapping of physical resources as well as the voluminous data available across various government departments into relational database structure and manipulating the same as required at different levels of Government machinery for their functions related to service rendering and planning. The IT implementation programmes should define appropriate databases at the panchayat level integration linking the various local body level operations, processes and workflows. Subsequently various data available with the individual government departments and offices shall be mapped on appropriate databases and linked with the above efforts. The overall perspective would appropriately define various databases and link up the services and workflows being generated based on such databases. Since, almost all informal services at the local level are individual specific, the key to this approach would be the formulation of unique citizen ID codes. In Kerala, it is proposed to link the creation of citizen code with the building tax assessment process. The IKM has completed two software applications; an application software for monitoring of peoples and the plan targets, and an application for IT enabled services covering issue of certificates, handling of pensions and social welfare schemes and establishing an integrated citizens database for faster delivery systems. Three applications under development are an application for establishment operations in the local body, a community portal for web enabled value added services and an application for a watershed based decision support system using a Geographic Information System Technology. Three data products, an encyclopaedic repository on the Kerala Panchayat Raj Act and Rules, Allied Act and Rules, Government Orders and Notifications, people's directory of small IT enterprises in the state and a compendium on the Panchayat Nagar Palika elections 2000 are also developed by the mission.

One successful example of IT implementation in governance is the project initiated in AP for the "Computer-aided Administration of Registration Department" . It is a good example of use of IT in improving the quality of delivery mechanisms; project management and administration; training and motivation. The project has already become a role model for several other departments in the State of Andhra Pradesh, and other States in the country. Government of Andhra Pradesh has taken up the implementation of e-governance to utilize the benefits of the latest information technologies for the public benefit, convenience and welfare by automating and speeding up the people-government interface and bringing about total transparency in administration and functioning.

The main objectives of the project are : demystify the registration process; introducing a transparent system of valuation of properties easily accessible to the citizens; replacing the manual system of indexing; accessing and reporting; delivering the registration services across the counter within an hour; issuing the encumbrance certificate within minutes across the counter. This has been used in 212 Sub-Registrar offices spread over the State. The application of IT in land registration transformed the nature of relationship between the Government and public. IT automated the repetitive work, improved the operational efficiency; prepared the organization to face the future and made fundamental changes in delivery of services to the citizens.

2

Information: The Basic Resource for Development

PRITHVISH NAG

I feel myself extremely honoured for having this opportunity to speak to you all. It is undoubtedly a proud privilege to deliver this address on the occasion of this National Seminar. The topic of the seminar Right to Information is undoubtedly a thrilling one for me as well. The prestige of this gathering has been enhanced with the presence of the Honourable Chief Guest. I am delighted to be in the territory of libraries. Kerala's high literacy rate, reading habits of its people and large number of public libraries are envied by all. As per my own calculations, if all the 4,200 + libraries were evenly distributed over this state, there would be an average 'inter public library distance' of only 3.28 km. This implies that on an average a person has to travel a maximum of 1.64 km to get such library facilities. Obviously, such an infrastructure cannot be developed overnight. The formation of the All-Travancore Grandhasala Sangham in 1945 and its extension to Cochin area after independence and to Malabar area after the formation of Kerala state in 1956 were a few steps in right direction. In addition, the Malabar area was benefited by the Madras Public Libraries Act of 1948 which empowered the local bodies to collect library cess. Further, a library in Kerala has several other connotations as well. It becomes a centre for varieties of social, cultural and even political activities. As a geographer, I would like to call it a central place or a central point. Hence, under the patronage of libraries we may find activities like cultural entertainment, literacy programmes, functional literacy classes, nursery classes, sports and games. Being an author and associated with the publication of several books, I am thrilled to know the existence of the Kerala Author's Cooperative Society which started as early as 1945. This Society has also contributed to the library movement in Kerala. I strongly feel that this movement in Kerala is not confined to libraries and government administration, but it is a people's movement. It encompasses not only librarians but also the whole society. This facet of libraries in Kerala gives me some strength to stand in front of you all and give an address though not having any professional librarian background. The role of a librarian here has to be different from other parts of the country. I am sure that the librarians of Kerala will lead the country by their innovations, inspirations and ideas.

1. Experience of Kerala

So, we have come to this territory of libraries to learn from your experiences — not to inflict our views. I am sure that the Indian Association of Special Libraries and Information Centres and its members will be benefited by this National Seminar. IASLIC feels privileged to organize its annual seminar in Thrissur this year. Its excellent library and modern facilities are additional impetus for us.

As a thematic cartographer, we have been handling information on different aspects. Our natural association with the Geographical Information System (GIS) is well known. IT Task Force and the IT Industry have further aggravated the importance of information. Last year IASLIC organized a national seminar on Information Superhighway in the neighbouring city of Coimbatore. Earlier also this body, as it is evident from its name, has given due importance to information in the overall library activities. I am sure that the facets chosen on this topic, i.e. Right to Information, and the deliberations to be made in the seminar would open new and newer dimensions of the topic to the participants who have taken trouble to come here from different parts of the country. Obviously, I would say a few words on the role of information and the need for its availability and accessibility for bringing a fast approaching productive society. Perhaps the experience of libraries in Kerala would break new grounds and new ideas would emerge from this combination. The term information is not new nor is its significance unknown to anybody here. My modest approach to speak on the issues of information is only to bring forth a recapitulation on its significance for societal productivity, progress and development while deliberating on the various aspects of Right to Information, the topic of the seminar.

2. Information and Change

The socio-economic fabrics have been undergoing fast changes. In order to combat the fast accelerating heterogeneous problems emerging from these changes, the social systems have been warranting a considerable quantity of information for its probable solution. Information is accordingly an ingredient and a problem-solving tool. Its generation, mobilization and its appropriate use are important tasks. The administrators, planners, decision-makers, scientists, technologists, academicians, researchers, corporate managers and others who are intimately entrusted with the responsibilities for bringing changes to the society are, in fact, adequately constrained to do so without the use of information. Admittedly, it is the key factor for transformation of the society. In other words, information is the catalyst to bring a sea change in the economy as well.

3. Knowledge and Industry

Technology and innovations in all spheres of societal activities are the key factors for societal transformation. Evidently, in the history of industrial revolution, technology and innovations played a key role. The industrial revolution occurred in fact primarily as a sequel to technological progress, innovations, education and increasing capital stock in those days. The example of this industrial revolution is cited here as it is one of the most significant events to bring a sea change in the whole world therefor. Needless to say, innovations of technology in those days went a long way to make the revolution purposeful. The technological and mechanical innovations are the contributions of the scientists, technologists and researches. Their search for new ideas, new concepts and new knowledge to attain wisdom was possible by using information.

4. Science and Technology

The second world war too, thereafter, also brought about radical changes almost in all societies in the world, not to speak of this country alone. The move for the reconstruction of the social systems and the economy after the second war is expressly evident. The developmental processes started coming in this country immediately after the war and especially after the independence. To keep pace with this development, science and technology has been given adequate importance as the key instrument for development. The setting up of the National Committee for Science and Technology (NCST), establishment of the Department of Science and Technology and also the NISSAT thereafter are the best instances for the approaches made towards the development. Information is the reason to emerge knowledge which ultimately brings forth wisdom for its use in all spheres of societal activities, especially the science and technological researches.

5. Dimensions of Development

The term development is construed as an embodiment of multidimensional improvements of the society. These multidimensional improvements such as scientific, technological, economical and so on should contribute to social development. However, whatever may be the nature, type and characteristics of development, undeniably any of such developments are adequately incumbent on the use of information. But unfortunately, the importance of information to this effect was not felt with same degree of importance as today. Gone are the days when the classical economists as well as the new-classical schools of economics characterized the land, labour, capital and organization as the factors of production. They overlooked, the role of information as the instrument to process these factors of production. Gradually, however, and at rapid paces subsequently the truth that information acts as the instrument for change in all sectors of the economy and precisely as a virtual factor of production, started gaining recognition. Perhaps Kerala is the right place to investigate or experiment how the accessibility to information can possibly change the course of development.

6. Information and Productivity

Admittedly, "productivity is the application of information to an economic process or activity" as Paul Shay says. According to him "technological innovation is the main source of productivity growth, and the productivity growth is the main source of improvement of living standard". Again, the inputs for production are the natural resources. These natural resources are expanded, monitored and used by undertaking R & D activities. Needless to say, the R & D activities are involved in generating new information which creates new knowledge to help attain wisdom. The use of more wisdom in all spheres of human activities results in increasing production and in creating all-round productivity in the society. The information is thus the basic resource for production and productivity.

7. Invisible Resources

While there is no universally accepted definition of information. It is widely accepted as a valuable resource. It is a valuable resource for the rapidly changing factors for the societal progress and performances on the one hand, and the fast appearance of the changing situation of the technology almost in all fields on the other. Accordingly, it seems prudent to say that information is the invisible resource and, energy which do away with the imbecility of the individuals, organizations and unplanned and retarded growth of the society. In other words, it is that force which visualizes all human activities bringing about the structural changes in all sectors of the economy.

8. Right to Information

To ensure availability, accessibility and easy flow of information, horizontally and vertically, in all spheres of the societal activities is of current relevance. The exponential growth of information is explicit. Its obsolescence is also rapid. Constraints in identifying, locating, collecting, processing, storing and analyzing information for its right use at right time and by the right person are also adequately explicit and frequent. The ardent attempts at all levels to this regard are there, but the fruitful and aimed at results are yet to come out. In this juncture the topic chosen for the seminar Right to Information is timely and adequately relevant to the present situation. I hope and am confident that by delving deeply into various facets of the topic, during the elaborate deliberations in the seminar the ways and means would be unearthed for easy availability, accessibility and use of information in all sectors of the economy. With these few words, I wish the seminar a success.

Finally, I am grateful to the Vice Chancellor of the Kerala Agricultural University for kindly accepting our request to host this Conference. The Organizing Committee, its members and of course its Secretary have done an excellent job in making this gathering successful.

(Extracts from the Presidential Address at the Inagural Session of IASLIC 98 Conference).

3

Local Governments and Right to Information

TEEKA RAM MEENA AND V.K. GOPI

Democracy is the best form of governance at any level whether it be central, state or local. Openness and accessibility of people to information is a vital component of democracy. Democratic Government presupposes people's involvement and it is hardly possible unless people have information about the way the government business is transacted. Right to information or transparency measures would certainly create confidence in the minds of the public and make them true participants in a democracy. People often complain about misutilisation of funds, unnecessary delay and poor quality in various developmental or welfare schemes. Transparency is one of the effective ways to ensure fair and equitable delivery of goods and services to the people. Choice of government is, very important in a democracy depends upon availability of adequate, accurate, timely and reliable information. Transparency is also the most potent weapon against corruption and ensures a responsive administration reflecting the true will and aspirations of the people.

1. Transparency and Participation

People's involvement would be more real and purposeful if the Government is closer to the people. The seventy-third and seventy-fourth Amendments[1] made a new era in the federal democratic set-up of our country by making the Government nearer to the people. Public participation and intervention are easily possible in local governments, since they are very close to the people. In Kerala, the grama panchayats are endowed with more powers, functions and resources and to ensure public participation grama sabha's various committees and social audit are envisaged in tune with the spirit underlying 73rd and 74th amendments to the Constitution. But what prevails in the Local Administration System is minimum openness and maximum secrecy in day to day functions, whereas what the need of the hour is to bring about maximum transparency and openness and keep minimum secrecy. Right to information or Transparency is a pre-requisite for achieving public participation in government affairs at any level. In this paper an attempt is being made to assess government measures in this regard and to identify bottlenecks in transparent administration of local governments in the context of Kerala.

2. Objectives

More specifically the objectives of this study are the following :

- to examine government measures to ensure transparency;
- to identify bottle necks in transparent administration of local bodies;
- to suggest measures for making the system more open and accessible to the people; and
- to bring about "Right to information" as a fundamental right.

3. Methodology

Panchayat Raj and Municipal Acts, Rules, Government Orders, clarifications and guidelines were examined in detail to assess the government measures in this regard. State Finance Commission report and Sen Committee report were also made use of for the purpose. Discussions were also held with administrators, politicians and local government functionaries. Panchayat documents and registers were also consulted to classify them into secret and open documents.

4. Local Government System in Kerala

The three-tier Panchayati Raj system with the District Panchayat at the apex level, Block Panchayat at the intermediate level and Grama Panchayats at the grassroot level came into existence on 2nd October, 1995, the 125th birth anniversary of Mahatma Gandhi, the pioneer of Grama Swaraj. Urban Local Bodies (ULB's) governed by the Kerala Municipalities Act, 1994 also came into force on the same day. The local government system working in Kerala based on the Conformity Acts had the following characteristics :

- Grama Sabha/Ward committees at ward level.
- Three levels of Panchayats at Village, Block and District levels.
- Directly elected members.
- Presidents elected from among members (indirectly).
- One-third of seats at all levels reserved for women on rotation basis.
- Seats are reserved for SC/ST in proportionate to their population allotted by rotation.
- Reservation of chairpersons for SC's/ST's on population basis — 1/3 reservation for women.
- Election in every 5 years.
- State Election Commission for holding election.
- Finance Commission to look into financial matters and five yearly review of financial position.
- Continuous Audit of accounts.
- District Planning Committee (DPC) at district level.
- Metropolitan Planning Committee at corporation level.

Local governments in Kerala are in a privileged position with regard to powers, functions and resources. The Government has given functional autonomy to the 3 levels of panchayats. Their powers, duties and functions are laid down in schedules III, IV and V to the Act[2]. Earlier they were performing some conventional civic functions like sanitation, water supply, street lighting, drainage etc. However under the new Panchayati Raj / Municipal Acts, developmental functions were also entrusted to them as envisaged in the 73rd and 74th constitutional amendments.

In Kerala, local bodies enjoy much fiscal autonomy. During 1993-94 own revenue of the grama panchayats were around 44 per cent. For India the ratio was around 10 per cent for rural local bodies. ULB's enjoy much higher fiscal autonomy. The share of the own revenues in the total receipts of ULB's were around 68 per cent in 1993-94[3]. Under the peoples campaign for IXth plan in addition to their self-raised income 35-40 per cent of state plan funds are earmarked for the projects prepared by the LB's. During 1997-98 it was Rs. 1025.37 crore[4].

Administratively also local bodies enjoy much autonomy. They have administrative control over the staff transferred to it. They are authorised to sanction leave, take disciplinary action against officials and to impose minor punishment as part of the people empowerment process.

Kerala's Grama Panchayats are relatively larger in size when compared to those in other states. An average grama Panchayat is 37.83 sq.kms in area and has a population of 25199 (1991 census).

4. Government Measures to Ensure Transparency

4.1 Grama Sabha/Ward Committees

The Kerala Panchayat Raj Act, 1994 provides for constitution of Grama Sabha consisting of all voters in the village[5] and convening of its meeting twice in an year to discuss development issues pertaining to the village. Ward Committees are to be formed and convened once in 3 months as per Kerala Municipalities Act, 1994[6]. The Grama Sabha/ Ward committee can discuss any issues concerning the responsibilities transferred to it and can pass the resolution on the basis of majority. Beneficiaries are selected through Grama Sabhas. The right of Grama Sabha for beneficiary selection was upheld by the Hon'ble High Court of Kerala in a verdict and it states, " the selection should be made only through Grama Sabha and the Panchayat is only an approving authority and not a selecting authority".[7] The Grama Sabha acts as an important means to ensure transparency in the local government functioning.

4.2 Collective Decisions Through Committees

Kerala Panchayat Raj/Municipal Acts contain provisions for constituting various committees for discussions and decision-making. Standing committees are to be constituted—(1) for Grama Panchayats,(2) for Block Panchayats and (3) for District Panchayats[8] to look after various development sectors. Municipal Act provides for (4) Standing Committees for municipal councils and (5) for municipal corporations[9]. As per Section 163 of the Panchayat Raj Act the local bodies can create functional committees for various subjects like agriculture, public health, education, etc. Clause 164 provides for creation of sub-committees and ward committees. All these committees in a way bring many subjects to the knowledge of more people than otherwise and hence can be treated as a provision for more transparent functioning.

4.3 Public Works and Transparency

Public works constitute an important development activity of the local governments in Kerala. The Public Works Rules provide that the estimate of public works should include a note in local language about the materials used in public works, its quantity, estimated cost, labour charge, manpower required etc. to be exhibited in the work place and that is a provision to ensure right to information by public. The bills and accounts of the public works done by the Panchayats itself should be kept separately and made available for examination by any citizen on demand[10]. The execution of public works can be done by any Panchayat member, the social audit committee appointed by the Panchayats, the sub-committee appointed by the grama sabha, the committee of beneficiaries or the officers appointed by the Government for the purpose. The abstract of public works should be placed in the grama sabha and it should be exhibited in the work place. The details of the work should be displayed on the notice board of the Panchayat office. The selected list of beneficiaries should be placed in the next grama sabha with adequate justification. All these are measures in the Public Works Rules to execute public works in a more open and transparent manner.

4.4 Transparency Through Performance Audit

Local government system incorporates a new concept of performance auditing to ascertain the actual performance with regard to the functions of the local government institutions. It acts as a corrective mechanism and give suggestions to the local body to work in conformity with the rules and regulations of the Government. The performance audit report prepared by performance audit team and the decision of the local body on the report as well as the replies made by the president of the panchayat to the officer authorized by the audit authority shall be published on the notice board of the panchayat office[11] and this is a case of ensuring transparency in the functioning of the local bodies. Copies of these documents are available to the public on a nominal cost.

4.5 Transparency in Beneficiary Selection

Transparency has been incorporated in the selection of beneficiaries under the Panchayat Raj/Municipal administrative system. To ensure transparency the selection of beneficiary is determined by grama sabha based on predetermined criteria and with wide publicity, including the display of selected beneficiary list on the notice board[12]. All documents relating to beneficiary selection like application forms verification reports, enquiry reports and decision minutes are determined as public documents and the public have not only access to them but can have a copy of it on payment of nominal fees.

4.6 Press Galleries

The Government have already announced its policy decision to have press galleries in the Panchayat Councils in order to ensure that the Council meetings are transparent and accessible to the public through mass media. The provision for obtaining Xerox copies of any document by paying a nominal fee[13] could be seen as an excellent means to ensure transparent functioning of Local Governments.

The foregoing analysis leads to the conclusion that sufficient provisions are already there in the Acts and Rules to make the system more open and transparent. In addition with the acceptance of Sen Committee recommendations on transparency and right to information the system will be more open and accessible to the public.

5. Transparency — A Tool for Financial Control

Finance is the lifeblood of any organisation and in a Government it is financed by the public. So public should have a right to see how efficiently funds are raised and expended for their well-being. This can be done by making the financial management system transparent and open to the public. Transparency can be introduced in the areas of resource mobilisation, budgeting, accounting and audit. Local bodies in Kerala raise funds mainly through taxes and matters relating to tax assessment, collection, exemptions given, arrears of taxes, appeals on tax assessed and decisions taken may be made public through various means like grama sabhas, circulating through newsletters etc. Resource crunch is very common and it can be brought to the notice of the public through grama sabha. Budget proposals can be discussed at the grama sabha level to have a broader consensus. Annual accounts, annual financial statement, D.C.B. and administrative report also requires thorough scrutiny and inspection by public. Thus, audit function can be entrusted to the public by constituting social audit committees, women watchdog committees etc. at the Grama Panchayat level.

Since the citizen's right to information and the level of his access to it would constitute the best indication of democratisation of a society, more standardised measures are needed to open the financial system to the public.

6. Major Constraints to Transparency

6.1 Political Will

A major constraint in bringing openness and transparency in local government functioning is the lack of political will on the part of the political executives. Every political executive desires that the power of governance to be devolved down to him but not below that. If decision-making power is devolved down to the people, the political executive feels embarrassed as he does not have much say on any issue. Generally, political executive at any level is unwilling to make any effort to put any element of transparency into the government system including local governance unless he is pressurized to do so. In the name of the Official Secret Act, the political executive indulges in many misdeeds. Thus the corruption breeds. Panchayat Raj Act and People's planning process have made a breakthrough to do away with this.

6.2 Bureaucratic Attitude

The veil of secrecy that surrounds any government system is a shield for the inept bureaucracy, ill kept records and ill motivated activities. So bureaucracy always prefers to make the system not transparent to the extent possible under the guise of inability to bureaucratic provision that may or may not endow him to key the information out of toner by the public. The interpretation about the laws regarding official secrecy are of extreme nature, some views that the laws of official secrecy is pertaining to national security, defence and international relations and those laws have no applicability in the areas of development. On a safer side, many prefer to keep the official information away from public. In practice, the Official Secrets Act has been grossly misused. The unholy nexus between corrupt politicians and criminal and corrupt bureaucrats is the product of this archaic and draconian Act enacted in 1923 by the Britishers.

6.3 Legal Provisions

Indian Constitution and the laws governing public administration do not explicitly provide for ensuring the right to information by public. The need for a right to information act was being discussed at various levels for long. But nothing has materialized even now. The absence of any clear provision for providing information and the existence of certain provisions in the Official Secrets Act and Code of Conduct Rules create a condition not conducive for exercise of right to information by the public.

6.4 Lack of Awareness Among Public

Another drawback that works against emergence of a conducive environment for exercising even the slightest extend of the right to information is the lack of awareness among public regarding this basic right. Majority of people are under a mistaken notion that the politics and public affairs are not their area of activity and hence they keep away from it. This certainly reduces the chances of exercising the right to information by the public. This on the other hand enable the protagonist of the school of secrecy in public administration to keep everything away from public gaze.

7. Measures to Achieve Transparency in LA

7.1 Lobbying for Developing a Political Will

As identified earlier the lack of political will is one constraint that needs to be checked in making the right to information a reality, there is urgent need for lobbying for enacting the state legislation for making the right to information a public right. The only organised group who may probably lobby for a right to information act in the state should be the non-governmental organisations. As well interested individuals and intellectuals can create some pressure on the government to develop political will to enact the legislation and to ensure effective means for transparency in all spheres of public administration.

7.2 Intensive Training to Officials

One way to ensure transparency is to provide continuous training for the officials at various levels. Enactment of some provisions through the legislative or formulation of certain rules and procedures do not suffice. Unless the officials are exposed to the new culture of transparent functioning, the efforts cannot materialize. So the administrative and other training centres in the state should device new training schemes to inculcate new attitudes among the officials on the need to have more transparency.

7.3 NGO Intervention

NGOs are the only organized groups who can do a lot for the creation of a more transparent public administration system. An NGO, namely centre for transparency in administration had prepared a mode/right to information bill for the state and circulated the contents for public opinion. Similarly, NGOs can act as a strong force in awareness generation and can function as a pressure group.

7.4 Local Government Functioning to Public

More number of practicable committees and their transparent functioning can be a good measure for bringing the local government functionary in public gaze. Providing publicity to the various local government functioning can be a measure for awareness generation among the public and can act as a best ground for transparency in governmental affairs. Modern information technologies like networks and closed circuit television could be used for making people aware of local government activities and information. Monthly news bulletins, video films etc. can be of use for disseminating information to the common man.

7.5 Role of Mass Media

Mass media can play a very dominant role in bringing many informations concerned with local governance to the notice of the local public. The fear of reporting may ensure a lot of changes in the local government functioning in the right way.

7.6 Social Audit

Committees of interested citizens, women watchdog committees, beneficiary committees etc. can be created to have social audit of local government functioning.

7.7 Demystifying the Language Barrier

The language of local administration should be demystified so that the communication should be people friendly. The language does act as a serious barrier in keeping the local government functioning away from majority of the rural population. So all statutes, rules, regulations and orders should be in local language.

7.8 Strengthening Grama Sabha

Even though the importance of grama sabha has been well understood and necessary recommendations have been made for legislation, the transparency through grama sabha could be a reality only if the public keep proper vigil over its functioning. The role of grama sabha as a transparent mechanism could become meaningful if it meet more frequently with more number of members and properly discuss all the issues coming into the purview of it. Necessary legislation, political will and public enthusiasm are required to make the grama sabha more vital and meaningful.

8. The Best Form of Audit

Right to information is the best indicator of the extent of democratisation of any society. This right has been in someway in built in our legislative and judicial process but not very visible in the functioning of the executive. The denial of right to information by executive is done under the pretext of safeguarding public interest but in reality the private and vested interests are safeguarded. In a government system, nothing other than matters concerning with political and economic sovereignty of a country need to be kept away from the public scrutiny. The convenient interpretation of the Official Secrets Act suppresses the truth to come out. The honest elements in the Government at times become victim of it. In the case of development programmes nothing needs to be kept secret particularly when it is done with consensus opinion of the people.

9. Collective Will

Local governments are the institutions of the people to be governed based on their collective will. But many of the systems that existed in the recent past are not people friendly and are not transparent. Badly kept registers, delayed decision making and a variety of reasons make the officers of the local government unsystematic and hence unworthy of being open up to the public.

Therefore, there is need to open up the local government system and to bring the administration mere acceptable, accountable and closer to the people by eliminating all hindrances standing against it. Transparency in local administration could certainly reduce chances of corruption in a state like Kerala. Transparency could serve as a best form of audit. Participation of people in the local government affairs could only be possible if there is transparency in local administration. The efforts being made by the Local Administration Department in Kerala in this regard are commendable. It will go a long way to bring about transparency in the system. Transparency, if not the ultimate panacea for preventing corruption, the cancer in so far the developmental activities are concerned, will certainly work as an effective check on it.

REFERENCES

1. Constitution (Seventy-Third and Seventy-Fourth) Amendment Act, 1992.
2. Kerala, (Government of). Kerala Panchayat Raj Act, 1994.

3. Kerala, (Government of). State Planning Board.
4. Kerala, (Government of). Kerala State Planning Board. People's compaign for planning, p.112.
5. Kerala, (Government of). Kerala Panchayat Raj Act,1994.
6. Kerala, (Government of). Kerala Municipalities Raj Act, 1994.
7. Kerala, (Government of). High Court. O.P. No.18175/1996L. dated Friday, 4th April 1997.
8. Kerala, (Government of). Kerala Panchayat Raj Act, 1994.
9. Kerala, (Government of). Municipalities Act, 1994.
10. Kerala, (Government of). Kerala Panchayats Raj Public Works Rules, 1997. Kerala Gazette Vol. XLII, 24 September 1997.
11. Kerala, (Government of). Panchayats Raj (Inspection and Audit System) Rules, 1997.
12. Kerala, (Government of). Guidelines for beneficiary selection. G.O.(P) No.220/97/LAD dated 2nd October, 1997.
13. Kerala, (Government of). Kerala Panchayats Raj (Keeping of Records) Rules, 1998, Kerala Gazette, Vol. XLIII, dated 28th May, 1998.

4

Responsible Local Government: Need for Transparency

S. M. VIJAYANAND

I will be making a brief presentation on Kerala's experience with decentralization being implemented in a campaign approach with focus on transparency and right to information. As you are aware ever since the Constitution is amended in 1992 to give decentralized local government a mandate ; a clear function in the developmental domain of the country, various experiments have been going on in different parts particularly in states like Karnataka, Madhya Pradesh, West Bengal and to some extent in Maharashtra. Kerala started rather late but now it has to its credit a lot of innovative achievements in decentralizing power to the people in realizing the spirit of the constitutional amendment. In this context Kerala did it in a campaign approach and earmarked nearly forty per cent of the Plan funds to local bodies.

This is the second year of the decentralized planning. Out of the plan funds of three thousand and one hundred crore rupees the local bodies will be dealing with Rs.1178 crore. Out of this amount Rs.950 crore is given untie which is unique to Kerala. The plans are prepared from below. Government gives only general guidelines saying that use only forty per cent in the productive sector and not more than thirty per cent in the infrastructures. This is the only sealing. The rest is left to the local bodies to plan and implement. And again among the local bodies the Grama Panchayats are given most of the powers and most of the funds. Out of Rs.950 crore eighty-five per cent is given to rural local bodies — Panchayats. We have to remember that our rural population is eighty-five per cent. Out of the amount given to the Panchayats seventy per cent is given to Grama Panchayats. So ultimately the vision of power to the lowest is achieved.

1. Public Action for Societal Good

We have very strong Jilla Panchayats in Karnataka, Maharashtra and even West Bengal. Kerala is the first and only state to go in for strong Grama Panchayats. One reason for materializing this vision is the awareness created on such things by the public library movement in Kerala. Public action for societal good which in a way defines the success of the Kerala Model.

In this context a campaign was launched; because a slow movement, an evolutionary movement may not be successful. Power cannot be given in droplets or intricles. Because after sometimes you realize that the power has gone and you cannot bring it back easily. So here it is giving power at one blow. But there are a lot of problems associated with this big bang. All the structures have to be created on course. We never plan for it in advance.

We are trying to correct during the implementation process. Even today some papers carry news about some failures in some part of the State. We are admitting the mistakes and we are trying to correct them. In this context we are depending fully on transparency and right to information to see us through as a kind of a new check instead of Government sitting and policing from Trivandrum. We expect the people to access information; to see what is happening by the transparency provided and correct the mistakes at the beginning and consolidate the achievements of the initial phases. That is what we are hoping. Transparency is very closely linked to the ethos of decentralization. After all what the Panchayat needs. It needs you people sitting and discussing your issues. No; nothing is written down. Everything is in the knowledge domain of the participants.

2. Decentralization and Transparency

So decentralization and transparency go together. In our development process initiated now it is their right from the beginning. And then, in a sense the statement I am making is a bit cynical. It is very difficult to bring right to information in Delhi. You must have read about the experiments there. It is very difficult to bring it in a bureaucratic set-up at the state level. But it is easier at the Panchayat level when you are creating a whole new system, a whole new structure. So we found it very easy to introduce it. And it is very easy to provide information when it is dispersed all over. It is very easy to get information or a list from a Panchayat, but not from a Block or from a District. So the ease of operation and all these factors help in Panchayat Raj and Nagrapalika institutions. And some of us hope if it is a change from below; transparency will not stop at the Panchayat level once if it is there; once people realize that it has its dividends there will be demand for trānsparency at higher and higher levels and which ultimately have to be conceded and it will be realized.

3. Participatory Structure

When we started decentralization, though I said it in a big bang we have a very clear vision, a very coherent vision of that. I will not dwell upon its details here but will try to explain some of its features. One is that we really believe that power should go to the people. They have a say. They can participate. It was to create a participatory structure. It will not stop at the level of the Grama Panhayat. It will flow through the Grama Panchayat to the people as much as possible. There are limitations in our constitutional set-up. A mob cannot decide what it wants. There are certain restrictions in our constitutional behaviour, functioning and conduct. But within that we believe that most of the powers are to be given to the people which means the Grama Sabha. It is the general body that is elected. They decide the beneficiaries; they suggest what is to be done; the works to be undertaken. They have a right to know the accounts, why a decision is taken. Still these are in an experimental state, but we are trying to institutionalize these mechanisms of Grama Sabha.

A new development culture, that is what we are aiming at. Let us not fight. We can fight and we can have debates at higher levels. At the grassroot level we know the harsh reality and the people know what could be done to mitigate that. So let them come together. Let us see things sharply, polarized politically. So let us not fight at the Grama Panchayat level on what should be done. Many of our laws, regulations and the government orders point to this mission. Let us have norms and do the selection based on norms and not considering who belongs to which party or group. Our mission also believes in releasing from below, control from below, control by the people who will be more vigilant about their matters than those at some higher levels.

4. Specific Information

Here transparency is seen as empowerment. Transparency is conducive to participation. Participation does not mean mere giving of information. Participation actually means that the actors have a say in deciding; that is in taking a decision on utilization of the resources which are at their command. It is this mission of participation that is to be promoted through transparency. It certainly enhances the responsiveness; it brings about accountability and also a lot of power structures which are there now, the clicks which have been formed and pacified over the past half century. They will be resisting when transparency is taken to its logical conclusion. We are taming problems and some of them are quite serious like how to take this transparency to its final conclusion. Now coming to the process we found that at the Grama Panchayat level or at the municipality level people do not want very general kind of information. They want very accurate information. How much money for which team? What is the cost you pay for this item? So that is the information needs at the Grama Panchayat level.

Then there is a possibility of thorough scanning at the Grama Panchayat level. At the state level the Ministry of Urban Development throws open its files. How much of it will be scanned by the people. At the local level there will be more thorough scanning and more elaborate scrutiny. Then as I said they want specific information; accurate and specific. At the national level it is enough for us to say there is fifty per cent people below poverty line. We are fifty per cent illiterate. But at the local level people want to know who is poor, who is not poor, why he gets the house first etc. which are very specific questions and answers should be very clear, accurate and in a form that can be understood by the common man. This is a problem which we are tackling now. It is a very difficult problem also.

5. Repacking Information

We have thrown open everything. But a person comes and reads an engineer's estimate. I don't know whether anyone here is an engineer. Even I cannot make head and tail out of it. It is all in cubic quantities and very specialist language. We do not communicate to an estimate. What use is it to even an enlightened villager to go through an estimate because it does not tell him anything. Our budget document; why speak of an estimate; take a State budget or union budget, and try to make sense out of it. Of course you know for salary how much is provided for or whether your institute's allocation is provided for. That is very clear. But beyond all that the budgets are revealing the health of the finance of a nation or a state. It is very difficult to decide on that aspect. Budget documents are too voluminous to make sense out of it. Like this much of the data in Panchayat is also difficult for the common man to assimilate. The Panchayat Budget with all its annexures is also too voluminous. When in a schematic pattern how do you give more and more information to this kind of society; this kind of system that is a decentralized system.

What I am telling is not based on rigorous study but impressions gathered from discussions and experience. In the first level people are interested in knowing about schemes, about procedures; how do I get a licence, a house number, a ration card. At next level they will need information on laws and rules. What are the rules governing certain things in which they want to engage. Next will be coming information on fund flows. I am using here the word fund flow deliberately. Funds provided by government. How do they flow, to whom, what can they be used for. People want to know about that at the next stage. At a later stage decisions and their rationale. They want information on that. Why do a Panchayat take a resolution? Why this road and not that road? That is the next level of demand. These we are seeing now. We want this process to graduate into developmental game. Yes we know this is our village. This is the situation of the village as indicated by various indicators of developmental data on the basis of which a decision is to be taken. Finally, the most dangerous kind of information. What are your rights and what are your duties? When you have information on these two then people like us do not have anything to do. Things may have developed their own memento. I do not know whether it will ever happen. But it is our dream.

6. Audit by the People

Then the key features of the Kerala transparency system are the Grama Sabha where all of you can come, all the villagers can verify the accounts. People do not believe that Grama Sabhas will work in

Kerala because we do not have nucleus kind of villages. So one problem continues; how can people come and discuss. Did people have come; have they questioned.

Then how are beneficiaries selected. Again in keeping with the vision outlined earlier; you develop norms, let the Panchayat develop norms, publish the norms, let the norms be in an applicable form that is in an easily understandable form. Give weightage to the norms. Weightage is a very complex exercise. But we said give it out of hundred. So that people understand what one get out of 100 or that I have thirty. And with this norm we have to evaluate each applicant. Go to the Grama Sabha and justify your evaluation. Let them stop with that. After you are selected let any villager come and see anybody's application form. But I am not claiming that this perfection exists in the field. This perfection presently exists only in the law books. But that itself is an advancement. Now the entitlement is there. It is for the people to access and develop in the way they want.

Public works is the domain of corruption in our country. We were not able to root out corruption in this sphere. I am not even sure that we will be able to reduce it after decentralization. But we have been able to bring about the law which has not been done anywhere. In Rajasthan there is a movement going on called MKSS. It is a voluntary agency run by an ex IAS Officer. They go into the villages, get all the data, and with that discusses with the villagers to find out their velocity. That kind of things has not yet happened in our place. But it is now there in the law books and in some places initiatives have been taken in this regard. All the vouchers, all your estimates, the bills, all the payments, account books; they are all public documents. You can ask for a copy of any of them and get that. But as far we know only ten or fifteen people have asked for it. But if you ask you will get it. You can draw your own conclusion. But why this exercise is not done; we will discuss later. Even the accounts are public now. These legal provisions has been brought with the various Panchayat Acts and rules.

7. Facilitating Transparency

Now we want to go to the next step. Taxation will be transparent. Anybody can have a self-assessment. Tamil Nadu tried it and gave it up. Bangalore and Ahmedabad are trying it. But we have not given it up. But once the assessment comes we will know the field problems. Licences, permits, all these can be seen by anybody except things relating to privacy. These are some of the provisions for protecting people's right to information which we are building into Panchayat Raj.

What is the supporting action from the government's side for creating this environment? Of course the orders issued by Government; they are the most important; than the rules. It enables anyone to go to the court. So the structures for that we have decided. If the people ask and the Panchayat doesn't give information, should the Secretary or Director sit on judgement and direct about it. The government has decided to create an ombudsman kind of system which is prevalent in the west. Who can act as an ombire. We can ensure that the laws and instructions are obeyed at the local level. We are giving a lot of publicity and it needs publicity. Normally government gives publicity about the political achievements of what the government has done in two or three years. We had a series of advertisements saying that this is the true copy of the government order which entitles you to select the beneficiary in a proper manner, which entitles you to see the accounts of a public work and the like. All these are recorded and given in a Government Order. It is not propagandist. It is pure information. But we do link all decentralization advertisement consciously from propaganda and put accurate Government Order Number and use layman language to enable public to understand and access.

8. Democracy Wall

We had a series of training programmes. There are at least hundred persons in each Panchayat who knows all these things. About a hundred thousand people were trained under the leadership of the State Planning Board on what is the Plan, what are the rights of the Grama Sabha etc.? So at least hundred on an average in a Panchayat having fairly large population of say thirty thousand, know what are the things that matters in decentralized planning and development. Now we want to expand. This year we have built upon an idea of a democracy wall in each Panchayat wall that is one big notice board where everything is written down before it happens and confirmed after it happens. It is mandatory. We have given the design just two weeks back to Grama Panchayats. It is a mandatory kind of thing. Now everything will be there in the democracy wall or notice board if you call it so. When the atmosphere is there lot of innovations come. One Panchayat on its own published in its democracy wall every financial transaction it did. A Panchayat gets fifty to sixty lakh rupees. Its budget will be about seventy-eight lakh rupees of public money.

They decided to publish every single item of expenditure. How much they purchase for the big shop, what was the cost? Each transaction of the fifty lakhs was printed and circulated in the village. We thought this as great. Now we are going to include this in the Statutes so that every Panchayat will be able to do this. Who are the persons they gave assistance to, how much they gave for purchase of a cow, to whom, the address should be there. It is a bit costly; the printing and circulating of all this. But it is now being made mandatory.

Then some of the negative things; things which are disconcerting and even saddening. As I said the number of people whose access is far less than we would have liked to have. Keralites have a place of activism. But the activism is not seen to the extent desirable in this. Non-governmental organizations, political parties, even the press have not been active to the extent we anticipate. To go to the Panchayat, refer the documents which are there, know the laws concerning them, get required information and come to a conclusion you don't have to really do any investigation. All the records are open to you. Press persons can go and get it from the Panchayat. But not many people have done it. Again most of the demands for information came from groups. People demand information as a group and that also through a formal group. We go to the Grama Sabha; then people say give this information. Outside the group a person going and asking for information, an individual seeking information at his own initiative is not seen very common here. The other thing is common. And people are more interested in oral information and not in getting a hard copy. Tell me how much? It may be because this system is new. We realize that legal barriers can be easily broken. But psychological barriers and extra legal barriers are a little bit difficult. It will be very slow; but breaking them will be the ultimate in carrying out our programme.

9. Grandeur Plans

So we have grandeur plans of using information technology, linking all the Panchayats with computers in two years for a two-way communication and hopefully people also accessing it from the Panchayat computer. This year we are providing photocopiers. Cost price of copying only will be charged and photocopies of documents will be given on request by any. We are trying to device new Panchayat budgeting, auditing and accounting systems which are more friendly for information access formal social audit. So let us take some names which are accepted by all groups. Let them go and access and let them give there comments. So it will be smaller groups accessing information and giving there comments. So they can express their opinion boldly. Then we are organizing neighbourhood groups. We expect to achieve it in six months. Through these neighbourhood groups the entire poor of the state will get organized. It was started in one district. We hope to cover all 14 districts, so that poor are ordained and they are trained. Volunteers will be trained and they will act as co-ordinators and also for more awareness creation and now an initiative is being launched jointly by Kerala Institute of Local Administration and Integrated Rural Technology Centre nearby so that we can have a citizen training programme where all the participants will be made enlightened citizens. They can go and access any information they want. Everything is open and waiting for them. So this is in brief the attempt Kerala is making to ensure people's right to information and transparent functioning at the local government level.

5

Transparency in Local Governments with Special Reference to Public Works

T.R. CHANDRADATH

The Central, State and Local Governments have to fulfil the desire of the Indian people to give to themselves the highest standard of living and superior access to essential services through rapid economic growth and social justice. This, in the present context requires a model of governance based on cooperative federalism, decentralization, accountability, social justice, economic reforms, respect for citizens' rights and transparency, all of which will benefit both the nation and the individual citizen. As emphasized by the latest Human Development Report of the UNDP, progress cannot be measured only in terms of growth in the GNP or the per capita income. The attributes of human development as are reflected by the seven basic human needs as well as poverty alleviation, have to be given due importance.

1. Concerns of Unserved Sections

The new model of participative governance will require the government to become more caring and responsive both to the needs of a growing economy and to the concerns of the relatively unserved sections. The popular references to a non-interventionist and smaller government cannot be taken to imply the abandonment by the central and state governments of the fundamental obligation of a democratic government to provide an administration which is efficient, effective, clean, corruption free, freely accessible to the people, and based on simple and transparent procedures.

Despite the recognition of th: critical role of a responsive administration for achieving the goal of growth with equity, the public administration and the civil services at all levels are passing through difficult times in terms of eroded credibility and effectiveness of the civil service, growing public perception of an unholy nexus between certain elements among politicians and civil servants and criminals as elaborated in the Vohra Committee Report, and increasing criticism of the low level of honesty, transparency and accessibility to the political and bureaucratic elements in charge of administration.

2. Areas to be Reformed

The message underlining the political consensus on reforms is that Government at all levels must reinvent themselves and must redefine their roles and responsibilities, and that reform is needed in all areas which have an impact on the lives of the people. This would involve areas relating to:

- precise role of the government as an enabler and facilitator;
- the reforms in the structures of ministries/departments and work organization in Government, including the scope for the separation of policy formulation from implementation;
- delineation of the functions of the central, state and local governments in the context of cooperative federalism and the 73rd and the 74th Constitutional Amendments, accompanied by steps to avoid parallel and overlapping functions, and devolve resources commensurate with the assigned functions;
- objective analysis of the functions of different departments in order to identify areas and activities which could be vacated by government, constituted into autonomous entities, entrusted to the private sector, or shared with voluntary agencies and community organizations as attempted successfully by a number of common wealth countries and China;
- introduction of consumer orientation and quality management through citizens charter and training;
- harnessing information technology for improved data storage and retrieval, monitoring, support to decision-making and communication with the public.

3. Restructuring of Civil Service

Since the civil service in India, constituted into All India and State level services, is the major instrument of the government for the implementation of policies for economic growth and the delivery of services, the restructuring of the civil service, and thc reorientation of its attitudes and value systems are essential components of a responsive administration. While there are striking examples of officials with demonstrated excellence, motivation and commitment to the cause of the under privileged, these have been perceived by the public as outnumbered by inaccessibility, indifference to the public, undue emphasis on procedures and regulations, lack of quality and promptitude, proneness to corruption, and the lack of accountability for results. The associations of civil servants, on the other hand, complain about demoralization, political interference and lack of motivation. The assumption of an executive role by the judiciary in recent years is seen as arising from the failure of the civil service in different levels of government in the proper and responsive performance of assigned functions, and in conforming to the code of conduct.

4. Accountability of Officials

The question of accountability can no longer be interpreted narrowly as the responsibility for the achievement of assigned tasks within a department/agency. It is, in fact, an integral part of the broader aspect of governance and civic society, and involves the pro-active participation of difference stakeholders of the society in the provision of various services and the performance of tasks. Recent judgements of the High Courts, the MRTP Commission and the consumer courts hold the officials accountable to the public and the clients for effective service delivery according to well-publicized quality and standards. More fundamentally, accountability requires consumer orientation to administration and the assessment of the obligation of public agencies to conform to principles like published standards, information and openness regarding operations, provision of choice and consultation to the consumers, courtesy and helpfulness, well publicized and easy to use systems of complaints and redressal, and ensuring value for money.

5. Transparent Civil Service

In terms of concrete actions to ensure an accountable and open civil service, the following measures can be considered:

- introduction of greater transparency in the functioning of government and public bodies, including procedures for various statutory approvals, allotment of land and property, systems of assessment and levy of taxation, award of work tenders, procurement of goods and services, delivery of services, identification of beneficiaries under various government schemes, etc.;
- widespread and easy access of citizens to all information relating to government operations and government decisions, as well as the performance of the government, except to the extent specifically excluded by law or considerations of national security. For this purpose a legislation for Right to Information could be introduced after suitable public consultation on the proposals of the government;
- strengthening the grievance redressal machinery at all levels, accompanied by close monitoring of delays and punishment of the delinquent officials on the one hand, and steps to remove systematic causes for grievances and delays on the other;
- involvement of citizen's groups and consumer associations in providing information to consumers on services, in the monitoring of public services, as well as the distribution of benefits under government schemes; and the close interaction of the media, community associations and local agencies in prompt attention to various local problems, including those connected with the police;
- ensuring the effective empowerment of urban and rural local government bodies, with adequate resources for the delivery of services and administration of income support schemes, in response to needs articulated at the neighbourhood level, with the full involvement of community organizations, as envisaged in the Central Government schemes for poverty alleviation, and as already practiced in a number of States;
- encouragement to the widest possible awareness and participation of citizens in decision-making, plans and delivery of schemes affecting their living standards and quality of life.

6. Responsive Administration

The sustenance of responsive administration depends on:

- the devolution and delegation of responsibilities,
- adherence to clear ethical standards, and
- consultation and participation.

7. Kerala Experience

In this connection the Kerala experience of people's planning is worth mentioning. About forty per cent of the total plan outlay has been given to three-tier panchayat samitis to implement developmental project as per their choices. The panchayat samitis are empowered for the following :

- to identify projects and programmes so as to fill up the gaps in local level development.
- to implement the projects and programmes so identified with people's participation and assuring transparency.
- to strengthen Grama Sabhas.

Moreover clear guidelines and criteria are fixed for selection of beneficiaries and transparency in this process is ensured.

8. Criteria for Funding

For devolution of funds also some criteria has been fixed. But these criteria are to be upgraded and made more scientific taking into account the levels of development and location specific issues. COSTFORD has attempted for assembling as much data as possible on different aspects of the Grama Panchayat economy with respect to all the Grama Panchayats in Thrissur District using available secondary sources. But it is found that reliable and accurate data are not available at Grama Panchayat level with respect to a number of sectors.

The most unfortunate fact is that the data on agricultural sector, the development of which is mostly the responsibility of the Grama Panchayat are extremely poor. It would be a surprise to know, just to cite one example, we do not have reliable data on irrigated area, area under high yielding varieties, fertilizer use, cropped area (gross or net), etc. in most of the Grama Panchayats. We are of the opinion that appropriate development indicators at local level should be constructed so as to devolve funds, functions and functionaries to the local government. Database and Information systems at local level should be developed so that transparency and participation of people could be assured. The question of panchayat level data and information system should be addressed in the context of the 73rd and 74th Constitutional Amendments.

9. Transparency in Public Work

COSTFORD is implementing a number of public works as part of people's planning which includes construction of District Panchayat Offices, Block Panchayat Offices, school buildings, Primary Health Centres, Anganwadis etc. COSTFORD is following innovative strategies in order to enforce transparencies at all stages. COSTFORD follows the principles mentioned below:

- preparation of plan and design with participation of all stakeholders, determination and identification of materials and techniques for construction with community participation.
- publication of all documents before the commencement of the work.
- access of all documents to all.
- publication of the details of materials and labour for each item of the work.
- access to the measurement book of work.
- subject to social audit.
- making all documents public.
- use of locally available materials and workers.
- innovations of traditional technologies.
- use of energy efficient materials.

REFERENCE

Social Indicators of Development for India in *Economic and Politica Weekly*, May 14, 1994 and May 21, 1994.

6

Information for Development Status Assessment of Grama Panchayats

P.P. Pillai

Decentralized planning for development has come to stay in Kerala. The "People's Plan Campaign" started in 1996 with the three-tier Panchayat Raj Institutions in the State has made the Grama Panchayat; the bottom-most unit of planning. The basic principles of this decentralized planning with people's participation in Kerala is the optimum use of available local resources for the all round sustainable development of the Grama Panchayat as conceived and desired by the people of the panchayat. The formulation and implementation of such development projects as necessary to meet the felt-needs of the local people, expressed through the Grama Sabhas in the territories and functional areas assignment to the Panchayats, has now become the responsibility of these Panchayats. During the Ninth Five Year Plan, 30 to 40 per cent of the state plan outlay is being used for development projects formulated by the people at the three levels of the Panchayat Raj system. There are, of course, other State/Central schemes, supplementing the development efforts of the Panchayats.

1. Assessment of Development

When development activities are planned and implemented at the local levels, there arises the need for assessing the aggregate outcome of all these development efforts at the local level. Also, there would be need for assessing the levels of development or development status at Grama Panchayat level, not only to understand the temporal changes in the level of development but also for knowing the spatial disparities in development and the relative position of any Grama Panchayat with reference to other Grama Panchayats or Block Panchayats or District Panchayat. Appropriate measures or indicators of development are required for this.

In the absence of decentralized planning, till now there did not arise any need for looking at development at the disaggregate local level. The measurement of the level of development or disparities in development were relevant only at the aggregate (state) level. Attempts to measure development were, therefore, confined to this aggregate level and very seldom they were extended to district level.

2. Development Indicators

Measures of development at the aggregate (National and State) level still continue to be an interesting subject of attraction to both researchers and policy makers. Apart from the widely used index of development, the GDP or per capita income, there are several other alternative indicators of development such as, PQLI, HDI, GDI etc. Numerous studies are available in this area at the national or state level. But similar studies at the district, block or taluk level are very few. No attempt so far seems to have been, however, made to assemble data at the Grama Panchayat level for working out development indicators. This is true at least in the case of Kerala. A study recently made at the instance of the Royal Netherlands Embassy on development status of districts in six states in India has covered Kerala also, along with Andhra Pradesh, Gujarat, Haryana, Maharashtra and Uttar Pradesh.

3. Aggregate and Sectoral Levels

In study on Kerala, districtwise development indicators are worked out at aggregate level and sectoral level for three sectors, agriculture, manufacturing and social sectors, making a distinction between 'input' indicators and 'output' indicators. Ranking, indexing and principal component methods are used. The aggregate index of development at the district level is obtained by simple addition of sectoral scores. The districts are then classified as less developed, moderately developed and developed. The report highlights the salient features of the development profile of the districts with the help of sectoral and aggregate composite indicators. Also, in the appendix to the report, there is a brief note on the sources, quality and limitations of the data used, which points towards the limitations of a study of this type at the district level, caused by the non-availability of data and lack of quality of data. The present exercise, the first of its kind in Kerala, is attempted in this background, knowing very well that: the data position and the quality of data at the Grama Panchayat level are precariously poor and in many strategic areas the data simply do not exist though India as a whole and Kerala in particular has one of the best statistical systems among the developing countries. The results from this study have only limited use at present, mainly because of the gaps in the data and the incomplete nature of the results, and despite these shortcomings, as a first exercise it provides an opportunity to know the gap as well as the inconsistencies in the data and the poor quality of statistics at the Grama Panchayat level which is true of statistics at the Block level also.

4. Objective

The objective of the study is limited to:

- assembling as much data as possible on different aspects of the Grama Panchayat economy from immediately available secondary sources and preparing a table of basic statistics relating to Grama Panchayat in Thrissur District;
- work-out as many indicators as possible to represent the level of development in various sectors, sub-sectors and areas of the economy from the basic statistics;
- assessing, through the use of raining method, the relative development status of Grama Panchayats in Thrissur district with respect to each of the indicators worked out; and
- identifying and bringing to the attention of the authorities concerned and others who are genuinely interested in the successful continuation of people's planning with Grama Panchayat as basic unit, the existing gaps in the data, the inconsistencies in the data, the poor quality of the data and the immediate need for systematic collection, updating and assembling of data at the Grama Panchayat level.

5. Methodology

The methodology adopted is simple and direct. No rigorous technique is used due to various reasons. First, the reliability and quality of basic data used in the exercise are not beyond doubts. Secondly, this exercise is meant also for the benefit of numerous people's representatives, volunteers and officers in the Grama Panchayats. Thirdly, this exercise does not aim at any composite index, either at the aggregate or sectoral level, by combining the individual indicators. Fourthly, some earlier studies have shown that simple method of ranking, indexing and rigorous methods of Factor Analysis or Principal Component Methods, all lead to almost identical conclusions with regard to the relative positions of various spatial units. For example, the Uttar Pradesh study on the district level development status compares the results arrived through different methods, simple and complex, and finds them more or less identical, with rank correlation more than 0.80.

We may also point out in this context that we do not attempt to select any particular indicator(s) or to prepare any composite index and then classify the Grama Panchayats on the basis of such indices, as developed, moderately developed or less developed. Instead, the individual indicators, worked out, are left as they are for the users to choose any of them or a group of them, according to their purpose and the relevance of various indicators in each case.

6. Exercise Done

Data for, Table 1 attached to this paper are prepared by collecting Grama Panchayat level data drawn from different sources. The two main sources for this are: Panchayat Level Statistics of Thrissur District, published by the Directorate of Economics and Statistics (1995) and 'Vikasana Reports' of various Grama Panchayats prepared in connection with the people's planning. Data for items 1 to 27, 40 to 48, 54 to 65, 69 and 70 in Table 1 are from first source that is Panchayat level statistics. Items 28 to 39, 49 to 53, 67 to 68 and 71 to 75 are from Vikasana Reports. The data on item 66 are from the District Credit Plan (1997-98) for Thrissur District (Canara Bank). Data for items 1 to 27 relate to the year 1991 and all others to the years 1993-95.

TABLE 1 : Development Profile of Grama Panchayats: Selected statistics

No.	Indicators	Chalakudy Block Athirappally
1.	Total geographical area in ha	
2.	Total population numbers	
3.	Density of population (person/sq.km)	
4.	Total male population	
5.	Total female population	
6.	Sex ratio	
7.	Total SC/ST male population	
8.	Total SC/ST female population	
9.	Total literacy rate	
10.	Total male literacy rate	
11.	Total female literacy rate	
12.	Total workers	
13.	Total male workers	
14.	Total female workers	
15.	Total work participation rate	
16.	Total male work participation rate	
17.	Total female work participation rate	
18.	Total workers in primary sectors	
19.	Total male workers in primary sectors	
20.	Total female workers in primary sectors	
21.	Total workers in secondary sector	
22.	Total male workers in secondary sector	
23.	Total female workers in secondary sector	
24.	Total workers in tertiary sector	
25.	Total male workers in tertiary sector	
26.	Total female workers in tertiary sector	
27.	Total cropped area in ha	
28.	Total area irrigated (in ha)	
29.	Total area under H.Y.V. (in ha)	
30.	Total number of pump sets	

(Contd.)

Table 1 : *(Contd.)*

No.	Indicators	Chalakudy Block Athirappally
31.	Total number of tractors/tillers	
32.	Total number of sprayers	
33.	Total fertilizer consumption (tonnes)	
34.	Area under Mundakan paddy in ha	
35.	Area under Virippu paddy in ha	
36.	Area under Puncha paddy in ha	
37.	Productivity of Mundakan crop in kg/ha	
38.	Productivity of Virippu crop in kg/ha	
39.	Productivity of Puncha crop in kg/ha	
40.	Number of cattles	
41.	Number of large/medium industries	
42.	Number of workers in large/medium industries	
43.	Number of small/household industries	
44.	Number of workers SSI/household industries	
45.	Length of PWD roads	
46.	Length of Panchayat roads	
47.	Number of post offices	
48.	Telephone connections	
49.	Number of public telephone booths	
50.	Number of electrified houses	
51.	Number of houses with toilet facility	
52.	Number of houses with safe drinking water	
53.	Number of Balawadis/Anganawadis	
54.	Number of Primary schools	
55.	Number of students in primary schools	
56.	Number of Upper primary schools	
57.	Number of students in Upper primary schools	
58.	Number of Secondary schools	
59.	Number of students in secondary primary schools	

(Contd.)

Table 1 : *(Contd.)*

No.	Indicators	Chalakudy Block Athirappally
60.	Number of Primary schools	
61.	Number of primary health centres/sub-centres	
62.	Number of dispensaries	
63.	Number of hospitals	
64.	Number of doctors	
65.	Number of buses	
66.	Number of commercial banks	
67.	Number of co-operative banks	
68.	Number of co-operative societies	
69.	Number of libraries	
70.	Number of clubs/cultural societies	
71.	Total internal income of panchayat in rupees	
72.	Professional tax income in rupees	
73.	Building tax income in rupees	
74.	Total number of buildings	
75.	Total number of storied/terraced buildings	

Basic data collected for Table 1 are then used to work out 83 different indicators presented in Table 2, in most of the cases, these indicators are computed by relating the absolute values either to the corresponding values at the district level or to the total value of the item concerned at the Grama Panchayat level and expressed in percentages. In some cases the absolute values are expressed in relation to the population or geographical area of the Grama Panchayat. In a few other cases, the absolute figures (sometimes they are 'rates') in Table 1, are retained as such in Table 2 also, as they themselves could be used as indicators on certain occasions. A comparison of Table 1 and Table 2 can brings out clearly the type of calculation adopted in each case.

Table 3 gives the ranking of the Grama Panchayats on the basis of each indicator given in Table 2. This again is left open-ended without working out any overall ranking of the Grama Panchayats, mainly because we do not have indicators with respect to a number of items in many of the Grama Panchayats, as could be seen from the numerous blank cells in Tables 1 and 2.

7. Ranking of Grama Panchayats

Table 2 provides 83 separate indicators. The use of these indicators varies according to occasion and purpose. Despite all the shortcomings of the data as mentioned above these indicators provide a basis for understanding the level of development of any Grama Panchayat or the disparity in development among the Grama Panchayats in Thrissur District, measured in terms of any chosen indicator(s). For example, Indicator 1 tells the relative position of a Grama Panchayat in Thrissur district in terms of its geographical area, which may be useful, if we want to take geographical area as a criteria for plan fund allocation, either total or sectoral. Similarly, Indicators 2 to 27 represent various characteristics of population and labour force, which again could be used for a variety of purposes. From this table we can choose indicators that could be related to the level of development in education and culture, health, habitat, economic infrastructure, agriculture and industry. There are some indicators that can tell us about the relative overall economic affluence, degree of urbanization, performance in income mobilization etc. of the Grama Panchayat.

TABLE 2 : Development Status of Grama Panchayats: Selected Inidicators

No.	Indicators	Chalakkudy Block Athirappilly
1.	% of geographical area with Dt.	
2.	% of population with Dt.	
3.	Density of population	
4.	Total male population	
5.	Total female population	
6.	Sex ratio	
7.	% of SC/ST population	
8.	SC/ST male population	
9.	SC/ST female population	
10.	Total literacy rate	
11.	Male literacy rate	
12.	Female literacy rate	
13.	% of workers with Dt.	
14.	% of male workers with Dt.	
15.	% of female workers with Dt.	
16.	Total work participation rate	
17.	Male work participation rate	
18.	Female work participation rate	
19.	Total workers in primary sector	
20.	Male workers in primary sector	
21.	Female workers in primary sector	
22.	Total workers in secondary sector	
23.	Male workers in secondary sector	
24.	Female workers in secondary sector	
25.	% of workers in tertiary/seco. sector	
26.	% of male workers in tertiary/seco. sector	
27.	% of female workers in tertiary/seco. sector	
28.	Total croped area in ha	
29.	% of gr. cropped area/total geographical area	
30.	% of area under H.Y.V. to geo. area	
31.	% of net area irrigated to total geo. area	

(Contd.)

Table 2 : *(Contd.)*

No.	Indicators	Chalakkudy Block Athirappilly
32.	Number of pump sets/sq. km of geogram area	
33.	Number of tractors/tillers/sq. km of geo. area	
34.	Number of sprayers/sq. km to geogram area	
35.	Amt. of fertilizer/sq.km of geo.area	
36.	Number of cattle/sq.km	
37.	Area under Mundakan paddy in ha	
38.	Area under Virippu paddy in ha	
39.	% of gr. area under Puncha paddy with Dt.	
34.	Productivity of Mundakan crop	
41.	Productivity of Virippu crop	
42.	Productivity of Puncha crop	
43.	No. of large/medium industries	
44.	No. of workers in large/medium industries	
45.	No. of small/household industries/1000 pop.	
46.	% of small/household industries with Dt.	
47.	% of workers in SSI/Household industries with Dt.	
48.	No. of workers in SSI/H.hold indu/1000 pop.	
49.	Length of P.W.D. roads (in km)	
50.	Length PWD road/sq.km	
51.	Length of Panchayat roads	
52.	Length of panchayat road/sq.km	
53.	No. of people served by post office	
54.	Telephone connections	
55.	Tel.connections/1000 population	
56.	No. of public telephone booths	
57.	No. of peoples served by Tele.booths	
58.	No. of electrified houses	
59.	% of houses with safe drinking water	
60.	% of houses with toilet facilities	

(Contd.)

Table 2 : *(Contd.)*

No.	Indicators	Chalakkudy Bolck Athirappilly
61.	No. of people served by a Balwadi/ Anganwadi	
62.	No. of peoples served by a primary school	
63.	Number of students in primary school	
64.	No. of peoples served by a UP school	
65.	Number of students in Upper primary schools	
66.	No. of peoples served in secondary schools	
67.	Number of students in secondary primary schools	
68.	No. of libraries	
69.	No. of people served by library	
70.	No. of people served by a clubs/cul.soc./library	
71.	No. of people served by P.H.C./Sub-centre	
72.	Number of people served by a dispensary	
73.	Number of people served by a hospital	
74.	Number of people served by a doctor	
75.	Number of people served by bed	
76.	Number of commercial banks	
77.	Number of people served by a co-operative/ Comm. banks	
78.	Number of people served by a co-operative societies	
79.	Number of libraries	
80.	Total internal income of panchayat	
81.	% of professional tax income to total income	
82.	% of building tax income to total income	
83.	Total number of buildings	
84.	% of storied/terraced building to total buildings	

(Contd.)

TABLE 3 : Development Status of Grama Panchayats: Ranking on the Basis of Selected Indicators

No.	Indicators	Chavakkad Block Kadappuram
1.	% of geographical area with Dt.	
2.	% of population with Dt.	
3.	% of SC/ST population	
4.	Density of population	
5.	Sex ratio	
6.	% of SC/ST population	
7.	% of total workers with Dt.	
8.	% of workers in Sec/Ter. sector to total workers	
9.	% of male workers with Dt.	
10.	% of male workers in sec/Ter. sectors	
11.	% of female workers with Dt.	
12.	% of female workers in sec/Ter. sectors	
13.	Work participation rate	
14.	Female work participation rate	
15.	Total literacy rate	
16.	Total female literacy rate	
17.	No. of people served by a Balwadi/ Anganwadi	
18.	No. of peoples served by a Primary school	
19.	No. of peoples served by a UP school	
20.	No. of peoples served in secondary schools	
21.	No. of people served by a clubs/cul.soc./ library	
23.	No. of people served by P.H.C./Sub-centre	
24.	Number of people served by a dispensary	
25.	Number of people served by a hospital	
26.	Number of people served by a doctor	
27.	Number of people served by bed	
28.	Number of commercial banks/Co-op. bank	
29.	Number of people served by a co-operative societies	

(Contd.)

Table 3 : *(Contd.)*

No.	Indicators	Chavakkad Block Kadappuram
30.	% of P.W.D. roads with Dt.	
31.	Length PWD road/sq.km	
32.	% of Panchayat roads with Dt.	
33.	Length of panchayat road/sq.km	
34.	No. of people served by post office	
35.	No. of post offices/sq.km	
36.	% of storied/Terraced building out of total buil	
37.	% of Electrified houses	
38.	% of houses with drinking water facility	
39.	% of houses with toilet facilities	
40.	% of cropped area of Geo. area	
41.	% of net irrigated are a to total geograph area	
42.	% of total gross area under paddy with dt.	
43.	% of area under H.Y.V. to geograph area	
44.	No. of pumpset/sq.km to geographical area	
45.	No. of tractors/sq.km to geographical area	
46.	No. of sprayers/sq.km to geographical area	
47.	Amount of fertilizers/ sq.km to geog. area	
48.	No. of cattles/sq.km	
49.	% of small/household industries with Dt.	
50.	No. of small/household ind./1000 population	
51.	% of workers in SSI/Household industries with Dt.	
52.	No. of workers small/household ind./1000 pop	
53.	Total income of panchayat	
54.	Professional tax income of panchayat	
55.	% of professional tax income to total income	
56.	Building tax income of panchayat	
57.	% of BT income to total income of panchayat	

8. Aspects Indicated

From the 83 indicators given in Table 2, we have chosen 55 indicators in Table 3, in which the ranking of Grama Panchayat is attempted. We have to limit it to 55, because in the case of many indicators we do not have data for a large number of Grama Panchayats. Those indicators for which we have data only from a few Grama Panchayats have been left out in Table 3. Thus, the indicator 1 on Table 3 refers to the relative position in terms of geographical area (the land resource). Indicators 2 to 27 refer to population and labour force characteristics. Indicators 14 to 20 relate to the status of education and cultural development. Health status is brought out by indicators 21 to 25. The development in economic infrastructure is captured in indicators 26 to 33 and that of habitat status by indicators 34 to 37. But it may be noted that these indicators are not available for many of the Grama Panchayats. The level of development in agricultural sector is brought out by the indicators 38 to 36 and in the industrial sector by 47 to 50. The last indicators from 51 to 55 tell something about the financial status as well as the relative contribution of various sources of income of the Grama Panchayat.

In fact, these indicators when considered in suitable combinations can be used to understand the level of development in terms of different norms or criteria we choose. For example, the efforts of the Grama Panchayats in mobilization of income from various sources can be examined in terms of indicators 51 to 55. The nature and extent of urbanization in various Grama Panchayats can be compared with the help of indicators like 4, 7, 12, 26, 27, 28, 29, 32 to 35 etc. Similarly, the gender related development status could be assessed using the indicators 5, 10, 11, 13 and 15. Again, the structural characteristics of the Grama Panchayat economy as revealed in terms of the labour force in each sector could be examined with the help of indicators 6, 7, 12, 47, 48, 49 and 50. In short, the indicators could be put to numerous uses. They could be used also for a number of further studies, seeking explanations for the correlation, if any, among the indicators and for the disparities in development status as brought out by individual indicators.

9. Information Development

The most important lesson that follows from this exercise, of course, is about the non-availability of essential data at the Grama Panchayat level. A great deal of effort is called for in improving the data base, if we want to work out reliable indicators that could be used with confidence for policy purpose and for further studies on development at the local level. The data on some of the most important aspects are at present either do not exist or incomplete and unreliable. The most unfortunate fact is that the data on agricultural sector, the development of which is mostly the responsibility of the Grama Panchayat are extremely poor. It would be a surprise to know, just to cite one example, we do not have reliable data on irrigated area, area under high yielding varieties, fertilizer use, cropped area (gross or net), etc. in most of the Grama Panchayats. We do not elaborate on this now. We conclude this note by emphasizing the fact that this exercise is just a beginning in search of appropriate development indicators at the local level in Kerala. We also observe that elaborate arrangement for refinement of data base and for studies in development indicators including the compilation of GDP at Grama panchayat level at the local level is called for in the context of the people's planning under execution at present in the state.

REFERENCES

Giri Institute of Development Studies, *Socio Economic Development Status at the District level in Uttar Pradesh (India)*, 1997, p.150.

Indian Journal of Regional Science, No.2, 1984 (pp.108-120), No.2, 1985 (pp 17-22; 35-46; 87-94), No.1, 1988 (pp.11-28; 81-86; 87-98), No.2, 1989 (pp.47-56), No.1, 1991 (pp.41-52), No.1 1992 (pp.27-36), No.1, 1953 (pp.81-85).

KRPLLD, *Development Status of Districts;* Kerala; CDS, 1998.

Social Indicators of Development for India in *Economic and Political Weekly*, May 14, 1994 (pp.1227-1240) and May 21, 1994 (pp. 1300-1308).

7

Information and Socio-Economic Equality

T. K. RAMA KRISHNAN

With the advent of people's campaign for planning considerable developments have taken place in application of Information Technology for governance and by linking different administrative units; Panchayats, the blocks and the districts as well as for provision of various services to the people especially in the areas of information collection and dissemination. Developments are occurring in science and technology fields in an unprecedented speed particularly in the areas of computer and communication technologies which opens before us immense possibilities for the upliftment of the downtrodden. Information is the most important wealth of the present day and for an individual or a group or a country the information and knowledge it possesses determines the economic and cultural gains the individual or group can achieve. In a democratic state everyone should have equal right to utilise the information that society holds. People should have equal right to access any information which is essential for their success in their life and activities. Information technology permits distribution of this wealth in an equitable manner; cost effectively and efficiently. Therefore the context of the seminar is very important.

1. Dissemination of Knowledge

We may recall some of the observations which our late Prime Minister Jawaharlal Nehru has made on the need for transmitting new scientific knowledge to the people. Unfortunately many of the information of public interest does not reach the people. In many fields people with expertise and devotion are out of place. Outside world is ignorant of what is happening due to lack of publicity and transparency. So it has become difficult to protect the public interest in the activities in many organisations. The situations are such that many of our scientists and technologists have to leave the country seeking deserving existence and acceptance. Information systems, and law protecting peoples right to know can prevent such things and contribute to our development.

2. Wealth of the Tribals

Today with the internationalisation and liberalisation a new context is also emerging specially with patent laws and related developments. The traditional knowledge of our rural folk and tribal people had for centuries have already been understood to be the knowledge for sustainable development. Various incidents of cheating them by the patenting of their knowledge by scientists and multinational groups have come to light. The poor have been deprived of their right. Main reason for this is lack of information systems that record such knowledge and the details of those who contributed it to humanity as well as the availability of information on patenting and such procedures to these people who really own it. A bill has already been presented in the Parliament. It should be noted to what extent the new Bill, presented in the Parliament, would permit the information to reach the ordinary people and particularly the poorer section of the community.

3. Breaking the Restrictions

In our country the access to information was limited only to the elite for a long time. If we examine through history we can see that the rich always were clever to limit access to knowledge; access to education within themselves. They knew that if that is done material wealth and power will surely remain with them. So the most important struggles; the revolutions that changed humanity and uplifted the down-trodden were struggles for equal right to knowledge. Once when knowledge; information is with the people they will know what is to be done for protecting their rights, for getting hold of the material resources for which they are entitled to. In modern times also to ensure people's participation in framing policies that affect them, in taking decisions on their development; information availability is very important. People should have access to all informations so that they are well aware of the pros and cons of programmes in which they involve. One of the related issues which the seminar should discuss is that how information can reach the relatively poorer section of the society.

4. Computers for People's Welfare

Changes are taking place in the information technology scene particularly in the use of computers for the people's welfare measures and for extending information services of high quality to remote areas. IT gives us the power to access any huge libraries existing in any part of the world. In the present situation we can reach any part of the world through Internet facilities and we can interact literally person to person seeing and hearing each other but sitting in different corners of the earth through the modern Internet based communication systems. Such facilities should not be confined to the elite but also it should be accessible to relatively poorer sections of the society. IT makes all these possible without much extra investments for that. Emphasis should be given in the seminar on the importance of the Bill on Right to Information. The information of government's action should reach the people. New opportunities which has been coming through the new technology, the problems arising from them and extending information services to one and all transcending urban, rural, rich poor, differences should form part of the discussion of the present seminar. On behalf of the government, I thank the organisers for finding Thrissur and Kerala as venue of the seminar.

8

Information Access and Empowerment

K.N. SHYAMASUNDARAN NAIR

The Kerala Agricultural University community indeed feels privileged having the honour to host the National Seminar of the prestigious organization IASLIC and I would like to avail the opportunity to place our grateful thanks to the organizers for their consideration.

The role of libraries is increasingly becoming complex both in contents and the means of performing the multiple functions of providing information and it acts as repository of knowledge more so in case of academic institutions such as the universities. In case of agricultural universities this function is far more demanding with their multiple mandates including teaching, research and extension. This is demanding because we have not only to cater to teachers and researchers and students but also to the farming community who are our principal client.

In this age of information explosion it is an enormous task to keep pace with these developments. Gone are the days when libraries were storehouses and repository of knowledge in the print media of books and journals.

1. Digital Library

The marshalling of electronic media have revolutionised the access and dissemination of information. We in this university are trying to keep pace with these developments. We have already assembled in digital storage systems, the major sources of information required for agricultural education, research, extension and development activities. We have completed the digital library system to store and networks to access information stored in electronic media from any place. Already we have good repository of CD-ROMs and other modern electronic facilities for information transfer.

2. Information as Power

The National Seminar of IASLIC has chosen the very important topic 'Right to Information'. All through the history of human civilisation it has been recognised that information is power. But the developments in last two decades of this century have amply demonstrated the power of information. There have never been so much concern of empowering the deprived and the rich. Enabling access to information is the first step for empowerment. Our nation is wedded to democracy. At very stage of civil life democratic institutions are built and stengthened. The latest being the 73rd and the 74th Amendments of Constitution ushering in democratic institutions down to the level of villages. The practice of democracy in its true sense is not just participation of people merely to periodical exercises of right to franchise although that is one of the most vital components of the process. Participation of people at all levels of the process of government both in administration and development is an important component of democracy. Only a well informed citizen can ensure effective participation.

3. Access to Government Documents

Access to information is vital to be informed. Here comes the criticality of right to information as the most crucial input to our informed participation in a democracy. Notwithstanding the well established democratic institutions and their functioning have become a part of civil life in our country.

By and large government is shrouded in secrecy. Under such an environment accountability and access to government information and transparency are primary determines of successful functioning of democracies. The access to government information is regulated by the Official Secret Act of 1923 of Government of India. What is generally found is that the spirit of the Act is diluted in respect to access to information while issuing government orders, government notifications, proceedings and memos by the bureaucracy. Reconsideration of the provisions of the Act is a significant step in ensuring access to information. As normally bureaucracy plays greater role than the legislature and judiciary in the governance of our country. It is heartening to note that the government both at the centre and the state themselves are taking some initiatives in opening free access to information. The setting up of the Working Group of the Department of Personnel and Training, Government of India in terms of reference among others for the examination of feasibility and the need to introduce a full-fledged 'Right to Information Act' in 1997 is an evidence of governmental initiative in this regard. Other governments which have taken initiative include Tamil Nadu, Madhya Pradesh and Rajasthan. What is more heartening is the initiative such as women's movement in Rajasthan and others for the right to information.

4. Tradition of Openness

We in this state have small experience of the evidence we have earned through openness. As part of the people's campaign the government declared that all documents related to implementation of the plan are open and any document in the respective area can be accessed by the people in lieu of a small payment. Information open to public scrutiny include estimates of accounts of construction works, criteria for selection of beneficiaries, the list of beneficiaries selected etc. Needless to say such openness has generated much enthusiasm and confidence among the participating communities. With these few words by way of backdrop to this national seminar on 'Right to Information', let me go on my pleasant duty of offering welcome.

We could not have a better person than the Honorable Minister for Cultural Affairs, Fisheries and Rural Development in inaugurating the function. He is a well-known freedom fighter and has been in the forefront of the democratic struggles for securing the rights of the oppressed and the suppressed. He is acclaimed as one of the erudite persons in our language. To you Sir, I offer the warmest welcome. I welcome warmly Dr. Prithvish Nag, President of IASLIC and Director, NATMO, who is presiding over this function. I offer my warm welcome to all delegates who have come from all corners of the country to participate in this seminar. In this meeting a few other important events are taking place. We have also the unique opportunity to release a resource atlas of Thrissur district which is going to be released by Sri K.P. Aravindakshan, a member of the executive committee of the

Agricultural University. I offer him my warm welcome. I welcome all those who have assembled here in this function. Thank you all.

(Welcome Address at the Inagural Session of IASLIC 98 Conference 21st December, 1998.)

9

Community Development Information System : A Technocratic Neo-Gandhian Model

S. VENUGOPAL

Community development may be defined as conscious acceleration of economic, technological and social change by combining outside assistance with organized local self-determination and effort. This is UNO's widely accepted concept. Arthur Dunham looks upon community development as organized efforts to improve the conditions of community life and the capacity for community integration and self-direction. As these statements imply, many community development programmes are national in scope and are geared to overall governmental plans. The Government of India (1958) has been quite specific in treating community development as a method designed to initiate a process of transformation in the social and economic life of the Indian village. Gandhian economics stresses on community development.

1. Human Development

Development *per se* cannot be equated with accelerated economic growth, as progress cannot be done with civilization. As consistently argued the goal of development is the expansion of human 'capabilities' that will give people the freedom to do things that they value. Human Development should be the focus of Community Development, as yellow yolk of an egg. The Human Development Report (first) explicitly emphasizes the three basic elements "people to lead a long and healthy life, to acquire knowledge and to have access to resources needed for a decent standard of living." The absence of an automatic connection between per capita income and human development is a reflection of the fact that the government and countries do not always use the resources at their command to achieve the kind of human development that is possible for society.

2. Need for CDIS

The need for Community Development Information System (CDIS) arises from the last two basic elements: to acquire knowledge, and to have access to resources/information. Information should be recognized as an important resource. Resource Management System should include Management Information System. Vital statistical data, and project details are prerequisites for model planning. Progress reports, seasonal agricultural predictions, and Farmers' Frequently Asked Question (FAQs) have to be updated periodically. As recently warned by the Director, NIC, the non-updated websites would be deleted.

3. Functioning of CDIS

Self-governing is the best form of government. Voluntary cooperation is the hallmark of community development. The first and foremost factor responsible for successful development is the local leaders who will act out of a spirit of public service. Real leadership quality is more important than charismatic quality. Normally, four types of functionaries are identified. The first two are local leaders as mentioned above and Community Organizer or Block Development Officer. By working with local leaders, he initiates, motivates, guides, and educates, supposedly taking into account the goals of the local people as well as the goals of the larger programme. Next type is subject-matter specialists: agriculturists, sanitarian, literacy expert, and the like. A community development professional should not compete with others. And the last type, administrative machinery, is also a critical factor.

4. National Development Information System

The Government of India has already established National Informatic Centre (NIC) at New Delhi. The network system connects all State

Capitals (State Informatic Centres). Each SIC will, in turn, have a cluster of District Headquarters (District Informatic Centre) under the control of Collectorate. It will further be extended to community informatic centres (CICs). Though the Network system has been designed, maintained and monitored in a top-down fashion, building information system should follow bottom-up approach. The strength of the community nodal point is the strength of the total network system. The design and development of local databases may follow a proto-type. Even the Website of each community informatic centre may follow a uniform pattern with some local flavour.

5. Profile of CDIS

A sample profile of Community Development Information System will be as follows. If we apply modular design, we could divide the whole system into five sub-systems: Basic Details, Resources, Projects, Health and Education. Details of each module may be summarized as follows:

Basic Details

- Area
- Population
- Literacy
- PC Income
- Employed/unemployed
- Children

Resources

- Wells
- Canals
- Lands
- Industries
- Minerals
- Institutes

Projects

- Agriculture
- Industrial
- Public Road

Drinking Water
Irrigation
Literacy

Health

Primary Health Centres
Dispensaries
Hospitals — Government Private
Nursing Homes

Education

Schools
Colleges
University
Non-formal institutes

6. Neo-Gandhian Model

The relevance of Gandhian thoughts has, time and again, surfaced for public analysis on the eve of Gandhi Jayanthi. It is an irrefutable fact that real India lives in villages. Self-reliance at the village was his pet project. Resources, environment and socio-cultural milieu are different from village to village, and from time to time. No single model developed at the national level could be adopted at every village. Mr. C. Subramanian, the former Union Minister responsible for Green Revolution, has put it in a nutshell a conceptually sound strategy for rural development: "a strategy of rural development, based on a comprehensive survey of national resources, their exploitation based on technologies appropriate to the local environment, mass mobilization through a process of education, all with a view to a scientific utilization and equitable sharing of available resources." Though Gandhi was not in favour of capital-intensive industrialization, he was not at all against modernization. Technology has become a vital factor for accelerated economic growth. So community development should absorb appropriate technology or rural technology. Rural reconstruction programed should naturally involve active local participation. The participation of the local force becomes an integral component of whatever methodologies being evolved. A neo-Gandhian model with technology overcoating may be designed so as to be easily adaptable to varied forms of community development projects.

7. Need for Values

Perhaps the greatest tragedy of the human experience is that our understanding of man and his behaviour has not kept pace with our knowledge of how to control nature. We have now reached the point where from a technological point of view starvation and misery in the world are inexcusable. We can mobilize our genius to fly to the moon. But somehow we are unable to mobilize that same genius to build a world in which all people who care to do so can lead free, abundant and even creative lives. (Brown)

Finally, a human society without a system of values shared by its members is highly unstable, but conflicting values operate in our world, and impede progress towards a global society. Hence human development should be the focus of community development as yellow yolk of an egg.

REFERENCES

Brown, Harrison. (1969) "Resource Needs and Demands." In *The Place of Value in a World of Facts*. Ed. Arne Tiselius and Sam Nilsson. New York: Wiley Interscience Division.

Raju, K.A. (1998) "Socio-economic Development through Harnessing Information and Communication Technologies." In *Towards the New Information Society of Tomorrow*. 49th FID Conference and Congress, 11-17 October, 1998, New Delhi.

Rammanohar Reddy, C. (1998) "The Idea of Human Development." *The Hindu Magazine*, 25 October.

Sanders, Irwin T. (1968) "Community Development." In *International Encyclopedia of the Social Sciences*.

10

Role of Micro Level Social Institutions in Participatory Planning

V.R. RAGHUNANDANAN

A pioneering model building exercise in micro-level planning in the form of an action research programme entitled, "Programme for Participatory and Sustainable Panchayat Level Development Planning" (PLDP), was undertaken by Integrated Rural Technology Centre, Palakkad and brought out some interesting findings on the role of social institutions in participatory planning. Panchayat (Local Body), Development Societies (PDS), Neighbourhood Groups (NHG) and Technical Support Groups are the three institutional forms hitherto unknown to our society, and emerged under PLDP initiative, in five of its experimental Grama Panchayats (GP). These institutions are not independent entities and in fact both PDS and TSG are born out of and controlled by NHG.

1. Neighbourhood Groups

NHG is a unit of 50-60 households in a locality. On an average there can be about 10 NHGs per ward and 100-140 NHGs per GP (In the case of municipalities and corporations, the number of NHGs will be still larger). NHG is a sort of permanent areawise social set-up convenient for ensuring people's participation in decision making, development planning and implementation. The constitutional powers developed at present to Grama Sabha can be taken as an umbrella protection to safeguard the rights and responsibilities of citizens comprised in an NHG and also their collective decisions and actions.

NHG provides a convenient platform for empowerment of citizen in people centred development process. It can also ensure true democracy, cutting across the barriers of party and religious differences in our society. Experience so far shows that women empowerment and their involvement in developmental activities have tremendously improved under NHG system.

2. New Development Culture

In a system where participation is at the same time both an end and a means for achieving progress, NHG can function as a very effective social institution. NHG system can inculcate a sense of social responsibility in every citizen and sustain it. It can form various sub-committees in order to ensure real involvement of people. Among the activities that NHG can identify from its own locality include data collection with regard to status of poverty, education, health, hygiene, drinking water availability, shelter, women's status, employment, infrastructural facilities, etc. Knowledge about the actual conditions of living situation will naturally lead to suitable local initiatives for improving the situation. This would ultimately lead to a new development culture where the citizen identifies and undertakes one or other community responsibility. The PLDP experience in Kumarakom panchayat in the case of thrift societies managed by women is only an example to illustrate the potential of NHGs in decentralised planning.

3. Sustainable Development

Our Constitution has recommended the Panchayat Raj Institutions as the basic unit for decentralised planning and development. The formulation, implementation, monitoring and evaluation of annual and five-year plans have become mandatory functions of local governance in a new environment of functional and financial autonomy in Kerala. Hence the PLDP action research has tried a model, introducing Panchayat Development Societies, basically to facilitate integrated and perspective planning in local bodies which do not have any previous experience in planning at all. PDS was contemplated as a registered society to be constituted democratically through representative participation (one woman and one man) from NHGs to the general body of PDS. Elected panchayat council members become ex-officio members both in the general body as well as executive committee of PDS, with president of GP as chairperson. Collectivism, transparency, equity and competency in local planning process will be ensured by offering participation of eligible and capable persons from all walks of life including scientific professional communities. Feeder units such as sub-committees at NHG, Ward and GP levels will establish a network which in turn ensure effective interaction and exchange of ideas from among the NHGs in the panchayat. The system emerged in PDS for formulation, implementation and monitoring of development plan in PLDP panchayats are better and stable compared to other panchayats. They have acquired relatively better insight in perspective planning, integrated planning and spacial planning. They have already developed a social system for data generation, processing, documentation and updation. These panchayats are now preparing their Master Plan for development, based on the local information system in conformity with regional and district plans. PLDP panchayats have already taken a headway in bringing out innovative, production-oriented and environment-friendly development projects and implementing them through NHGs. Local initiatives in the form of voluntary labour finance, expertise and consultancy services are effectively mobilised in these panchayats. The NHG-PDS network system has proved its effectiveness in ensuring local sustainability to the planning process to a certain extent.

4. Making Citizens Informed

Continuous education of citizens and quality improvement of local planners are perhaps the two most important aspects of participatory planning. PLDP experience have shown that the conventional training programmes and interactions are far from satisfactory in effecting desirable changes in the attitude and perception of the people. This is mainly because majority of them see "people's planning" only as a new way to do old things to 'distribute benefits and favours'. There are other problems like data gap, concept poverty, lack of expertise and inertia that prevail in our society. The old type of professionalism still hold 'technology transfer' and 'blue print approach' as their paradigm of development. The reorientation contemplated in the bottom up planning process therefore requires proper animation, structuring and facilitation to take its root in an entirely new development culture. Technical Support Group is a team of local experts developed organically in every panchayat, who participate voluntarily as an intermediary in leading the reorientation process ahead. The TSG training programme developed under PLDP has been found very successful in realising the said objectives. The TSG teams that has been developed in the PLDP panchayats are now engaged in a continuous process of self-learning and aided learning as well as Citizens' Education Programme adding further dimension to the prospects of NHG-PDS social institution network.

5. Equity and Sustainability

Development planning essentially has to be a process of utilising human and material resources in the most efficient manner so that the wealth of the society increases continuously in conformity with equity and sustainability. Ideally the entire process should lead to visible improvement in employment, in production and in the quality of life of the people. The social institutions evolved under PLDP intervention have been proved effective and capable of dealing with the challenges of decentralised planning.

11

Library Movement and Development Process in Kerala

P. GOVINDA PILLAI

As is now widely recognized the world over the development pattern in Kerala is unique. It is unique not only in India but also in the third world as a whole. Though according to conventional standards of development measurement Kerala is still very backward — for example, the field of per capita investment in industry, per capita savings, level of unemployment etc. — the quality of life in Kerala is regarded as better than not only in other parts of India but of most parts in the third world. Dr. Amartya Sen thinks that in certain respects the development and quality of life in Kerala compares favourably even with that in China. Kerala has the highest literacy rate in India (100 per cent), the lowest child mortality rate, highest life expectancy, high level of women's literacy and education, much better health standards, etc. This fact of the high quality of life in Kerala in India and perhaps in the third world, is acknowledged even by international bodies like UNDP and World Bank.

1. Cause and Result of Development

How this remarkable development has come about and how the remaining drawbacks could be overcome are all subjects which cannot be dealt with in the scope of this paper. But speaking about the development of library movement in Kerala we cannot avoid connecting it with the economic, social, political and educational development of the State because all these dovetail each other so inextricably that advanced library movement in Kerala is both a cause of social and economic development and also a result of that.

Kerala has the largest number per head of the rural libraries in India. Kerala has 900 and odd villages and 160 townships and cities. If the number of the public libraries in Kerala go upto 4000 and odd then on an average Kerala has almost 4 libraries per village. This compares very favourably with other states in India.

2. Effort of the People

It is not in the number alone that Kerala libraries excel. It is in their quality of service and functioning that Kerala libraries claim their uniqueness. Though the first public library in Kerala or perhaps in India, was established way back in 1828 by an enlightened monarch of the erstwhile State of Travancore, generally speaking, Kerala library system owes less to the Government sponsorship and aid and more to voluntary effort of the people. The 4000 and odd libraries in Kerala affiliated to the Kerala Granthasala Sangham which was founded way back in 1945 as the Travancore Granthasala Sangham, were all the result of local voluntary efforts.

3. Constructive Social Work

Though the Kerala Granthasala Sangham as an organized body began only in 1945 the library movement was there for many decades before this crucial date. In Northern Kerala of the Indian National Congress; outstanding leaders of the freedom struggle likes Shri E.M.S. Namboodiripad, K.Kelappan, Mathruravanam Krishna Kurup, K.P. Kesava Menon and others were actively involved in the movement. Once when Shri E.M.S. Namboodiripad was the General Secretary of the Kerala Pradesh Congress Committee, he issued a circular to all Congress Committees to take up library work as part of the constructive social service programme of the Congress at the grassroots. Whenever there was a wave of repression against popular movement the hammer always fell on the libraries first. From 1940 onwards left wing groups like the Socialists and Communists and the nascent Kisan and Workers organizations also took up organization of libraries as part of their mass education programme. In the erstwhile native State of Travancore and Cochin the pioneers of the national movement were associated with the library work. It is in this background that network of rural libraries came into existence. The present massive movement of the libraries spread out over 900 and odd villages are the successors of this movement.

4. Centres of Community Life

The rural libraries in Kerala besides collecting and distributing books and periodicals, conducted evening and night classes for the spread of literacy. They also organized groups of talented villagers for the performing arts. Many libraries have had separate corners devoted to children, women and such specialized groups. Many libraries also have sections devoted to agriculture. The libraries also conducted nursery schools; for children from weak sections of society. Since nursery schools and kindergartens are often very costly outfits to cater to the needs of the elite and upper sections of society, the library nursery schools, then called Balakairali were a boon to the poorer sections. This is yet to be strengthened and increased manifold.

5. Non-Govenmental Organizations

In Southern Kerala, i.e. the erstwhile native state of Travancore, government accepted from 1945 onwards that libraries are non-governmental organizations (NGOs) and it is better to keep them so. Therefore the government did not interfere in the day-to-day activities of the libraries and the government grants to the libraries were disbursed with the collaboration of the Kerala Granthasala Sangham. Needless to say that the grants were only a small part of the expenses of the individual libraries. The major chump of their expenses for day-to-day running of the library, purchase of books, payment to librarians, and the construction of buildings etc. were made by the voluntary donations collected by the activists concerned.

6. Semi-Government Organizations

In Malabar District directly under British administration, the pattern of library movement was quite different. There were, of course, libraries built, kept and run by the voluntary efforts of nationalist youth and leaders as we have mentioned earlier. There were another set of libraries established by the semi-governmental organization called Local Library Authority (LAA), established under the Library Act of erstwhile Madras Presidency. With the help of the government, many local authority libraries had land, buildings, furniture and also books. But in the long run because of the lack of people's participation and initiative they were declining. Buildings often remained closed and books in the shelves ill arranged and getting spoiled. There was a library cess in Malabar collected for the maintenance of the libraries. More often than this cess was not collected regularly and even the amount collected were disbursed in a haphazard manner. Therefore when the Kerala State was formed in 1956 the library scene in the northern part of Kerala was a dismal one in contrast to the vibrant movement in the southern districts of erstwhile Travancore. Then Travancore Cochin Granthasala Sangham was expanded to form all Kerala Granthasala Sangham comprising the entire state of Kerala as organized by the States Reorganization Act of 1956.

This contrast between the popular democratic libraries of the South and the quasi-governmental libraries under the LAAs in the North brought up many new lessons for the further development of the library movement to the newly formed united Kerala.

7. Attempts for Reform

One of the first steps taken by the first government of united Kerala under the leadership of Shri E.M.S. Namboodiripad was to reorganize the library movement in Kerala and give it a new fillip for advancement. For that the government invited famous Indian library scientist Dr. S.R. Ranganathan to visit Kerala and make a study of the library movement here and propose steps for its advance and reform. He came here and after a few months of deliberations produced a master plan for the reorganization and strengthening of the libraries in Kerala. Though Dr. Ranganathan was a great pioneer and expert in the field of library movement and science he failed to take into consideration the specific character of library movement in Kerala. His recommendations were more or less on the lines of library movement in many other states of India where the initiative for starting and funds for running the libraries came mainly from the government — more or less as it was in the northern district of Kerala, as we have seen. The library activists, the functionaries and the people in general in Kerala strongly opposed all LAA system because in Malabar it was a standing witness of the drawbacks of making libraries government outfits. The Kerala Granthasala Sangham objected to the bureaucratization aspects of Ranganathan's recommendations.

Thus began a long drawn out struggle between the library movement in Kerala and the Kerala Government. Though the colour of the Kerala governments kept on changing from Congress to Communist, from right wing to left wing, they all seemed to be unique in their policy regarding libraries. They all wanted some sort of bureaucratization and governmental control over the libraries. They held that the money from the exchequer cannot be thrown out to non-descript organizations of volunteers and social workers, unless sufficient guarantees is there for accountability at the Government. So many bills were brought up by the successive governments and were thrown out by the assemblies due to opposition of the movement.

8. Legislation and After

In 1977 another hurdle also fell upon the library movement in the dark days of the Emergency. The government dissolved the Kerala Granthasala Sangham and the administration of 4000 and odd libraries were entrusted to a government committee with hand picked members who had little to do with the popular base of the movement. Naturally the library activists opposed this and called for redemocratising the Kerala Granthasala Sangham and reviving it on the founding principles of democracy, but at the same time they also wanted a statute to be passed by the assembly to confer legal status on the democratic structure and procedure of the libraries. Again precious time was lost and almost 12 years were taken to bring around the Government to the views of the democratic library movement. Kerala Public Library Act, 1989 though it took 3 years to be implemented, inaugurated a new chapter in the history of Kerala library movement and perhaps also in the history of library movement in the country as a whole. The unique feature of this Act is that it gives same legal status and authority of the elected library to the block library level, Taluk level, District level and finally at State level. The highest authority of the State library movement is the State Library Council consisting of a representative each of the every Taluk Council which is elected by representatives of individual libraries. There are a minority of government representatives on the State Council and its executive. This executive of the library council which meet every month runs the organization as a whole and implement the system of the State Library Council which must meet at least once a year. The funds for its functioning are given by the Government as grant. The Government also gives grants to be distributed to every affiliated library in the State. The libraries are differentiated and graded into 7 categories and they get grants ranging from Rs.10,000 to Rs.1,000 per year. Separate grants are given for construction or development of buildings and payment of librarians. The libraries purchase books from funds collected by them and grants by the Government.

The perspective for the libraries as centres of village people's enlightenment and entertainment are spelt out in the Act. This perspective is the guiding line for the libraries but they have total freedom to chart out their own lines of activities and the libraries are not owned by the Government but by its members and leaders represented by elected committee of each library.

The 100% literacy achieved by the Kerala was with the participation and initiative of the 4000 odd libraries in the State. Now the Kerala Government has launched the celebrated decentralized planning process and development and the libraries have a great role to play in it.

Now the libraries utilize new methods of communication especially the electronic media. Many libraries have their own TV sets and some libraries have been experimenting with the use of computers. This era is called the era of Information Technology and libraries at the grassroots level are the instruments of this great endeavour in communication. The developmental effort of the society are accelerated by this information exchange through wide network of libraries in the State. Kerala's unique development is intertwined with development of libraries and system for exchange and delivery of knowledge and information.

9. Improving the System

Though the claims made above are valid there is a great weakness in the library movement in Kerala. That relates to the lack of advanced libraries that can support other libraries as with common resource of costly materials and which can be the reliable source for any information which local libraries are not having. Many of our colleges have advanced libraries and the State has a State Central Library in Trivandrum and almost a similar type of library at Kozhikode. And many districts also have district libraries, but all these are not integrated into a cohesive system for which the library movement has to be hierarchical. Some of the major libraries have not been admitted to the library system under State Library Council and a large number of rural libraries are still at primitive level and there are school libraries and college libraries which also should somehow be connected to the village libraries and its resources made available to the people. Also a device has to be evolved for the utilization of Internet facilities and other computer and electronic facilities. The Kerala Government has already presented an information technology policy in which all these are included. It is for the library profession to come forward with the concrete proposals before people at the Government for advance of the library movement in Kerala as a whole. As I have stated, there are many unique and admirable aspects in the movement of Kerala, but at the same time there are few hurdles or weaknesses to be overcome before long.

12

Participatory Approach and Information Access : Steps to Development Planning

PADMA V. UPADHYA AND I.K. RAVICHANDRA RAO

In the information age there is no argument regarding the importance of information and its role in the development of the individual, society and country. Similarly there is also no doubt about the fact that we are in the dilemma of unbalanced development in our society where one part of the society is enjoying all the available amenities and the other part is struggling to get the minimal facilities. Strictly we are not able to cope up with the different crisis. We are proud to declare that ours is a nuclear country and also do agree that yet large percentage of the people are still below poverty line, literacy level and unemployed. All facilities, which are made available in the urban area, are at the cost of the others. Sherlin Madon (1997) in her case study reports that

- Indian society at large remains biased in favour of main cities and professional worker society.
- There is a distinct bias towards establishing access to information for urban inhabitants at the cost of the others.
- The information infrastructure in urban area appears to be the inequality of its development.

1. Balanced Development

To over come this situation explained above that is to have a balance in the national development with regard to urban and rural areas, the only solution is to encourage participatory approach between and among people and make them aware of the different activities by providing information. This will enhance people's ability to actively participate in the developmental activities. Both Government and Non-Government organizations have to work on this task to realise the dream of self-sustained society. Since the Non-governmental Organizations (NGO) and local voluntary organizations are more easily approachable to the people more importance and consideration has to be given to them. Here an attempt is made to study the role of participatory approach, importance of voluntary/NGO and need for the information provision in planning process.

2. What is Participatory Approach

Participatory approach assumes an activity in which the community takes part with the involvement of at least one other party usually a government or non-government organization. Participatory approach concept otherwise is also known as 'popular participation', 'grass-root development' or 'development from below'. The literature available on participation centres on 'potential representations'. It is a channel through which people ensure their effective role and influence on the decision making process at all levels of social activity and social institutions. Further it can also be defined as 'organised effort' to increase control over resources and regulative institutions in a given social situation on the part of the groups and movements of those hitherto excluded from such control.

Thus the participation converge on two key concepts, viz. taking part and influence. The concepts of the participation process are Decision and Action. All decision making processes are to decide upon what is to be achieved and what action process can realise the objectives decided upon. We can say that participation leads to 'Collective Action'.

3. Why Participatory Approach

The capacity to manage and utilise the national resources depends on each country's ability to identify the course for solving its problems. Here the participatory approach is perhaps the only solution. This will enable us to overcome the problems of man and material and time resources. From the point of view of Government/N.G.O./

agency, Participatory Approach (PA) can be deemed desirable for the planning of development activities. Participatory approach is necessary because

- community participation enable the people to have the right to participate in the development process which directly affects their living conditions.
- helps to promote social development by increasing local self-reliance.
- enables to achieve better project results and then satisfy the needs of both the community and authorities.
- enhance the effectiveness of the project by giving assistance to project experts.
- enables to improve the relation between the people and the government and make them realise that people and government are working hand in hand.
- helps to achieve political and social control by increased co-opting of strong but manipulable community leadership.
- helps to move to sustainable development.

Since the achievement of sustainable development requires a substantial capital investment in the developing country the participatory approach can assert the project experts to some extent to cope up with financial crisis. The participatory approach will enable agencies

- to have transparency of their programmes.
- to mobilise people's participation.
- acquire the people's confidence.

These factors to a large extent make the programme success and also help to have sustainability in future.

4. Participatory Approach in Planning

Planning is defined as an organised process by which a society achieves its developmental goals. It is a means to achieve development. In the planning process it is necessary to :

- specify quantified target.
- specify potential of reaching such target.

- find out the resources available to reach the target.
- find out alternative approach in case the resources are insufficient.
- specify implementation process.

It is also necessary to understand that plan should not be reinforced on other and for which understanding the need and problems of the people is necessary. To know the problems of the people they have to be involved in the process. This indicates that planning is not a task of only professional planners at top level. Therefore involvement/ involving of the people is participation and participatory approach in planning is very much essential and is the need of hour.

Normally we find that while planning these concepts are not considered. It deals with the bureaucratic and technocratic exercises. To overcome this, Participatory Approach is the only way to achieve success in a real sense. Participatory planning presupposes planning by people. Then the bureaucracy, technocracy and voluntary agencies are to participate in what people want to do. Then here people become the centre of attraction. This can be represented as follows:

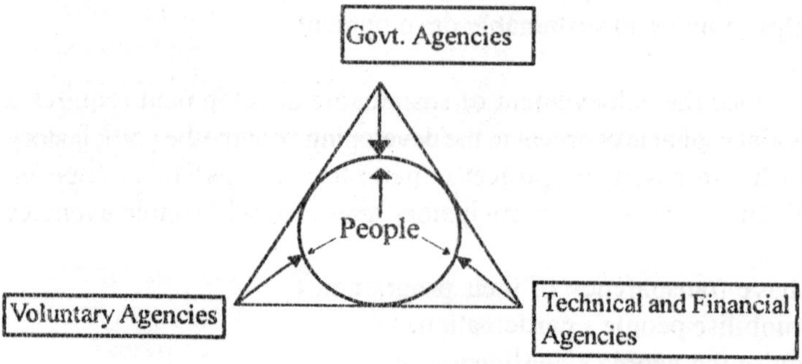

To make this model a working model there is a need for the sharing of information/knowledge; between/among people and the agencies. According to the information related to planning, projects and people; problems and needs will certainly narrow down the gap between the people and the professional planners. The problem and access to information will make the people actively participate in the activities.

5. The Way of the People

Emphasis should be given to Non-Governmental organizations and voluntary agencies of the area. It is observed by the author during the survey made for the recent work that people have more tendency to approach these organizations and they prefer these organizations.

It was found that among the 756 people of 21 villages in two Districts, 503 (66.5%) of the people were members of one or other local voluntary and non-governmental organizations. The following table can give an approximate picture.

Table 1

Members	Male	Female	Total
Yes	251	252	503
No	146	107	253
Total	397	359	756

The above table indicates that men and women equally represent themselves in the organizations. 251(49.90%) were men and 252(50.10%) were women representatives. The equal participation by men and women indicates that the development is equally important to them. Though 503 people were members of the various organizations, only 311 were actively involved in the activities. Their involvement was either as field workers, communication officers and organizers (Table 2).

Table 2

Role	Male	Female	Total
Field work	143	101	244
Organisers	25	6	31
Communications Officers	21	15	36
Total	189	122	311

The above table indicates that large number of people were field workers. The study also revealed that people's interest in development activities depend on their gender but there is no difference in the role played in the development activities. Since we observed that a large percentage of the people are involved as field workers and they worked voluntarily we can exploit their capabilities to make them participate in the developmental activities. This is a sign of mark to participatory approach. Proper attention and interest will help to make them participate. The enrolled people as member of various organizations clearly indicate that non-governmental and voluntary organizations play a key role in the development activities. Both facts, i.e. people's enrolment and agencies/organizations intent to take part compliment each other.

Manipal Industrial Trust in collaboration with IDRC, Canada conducted a survey at village information centres. This is the only project where a NGO has taken interest to promote the facility of information access to the rural people. Apart from this it has several other projects. In all the projects it has adopted the participation approach. The field workers worked voluntarily for the projects. This is an example for participatory process in development.

The outputs of the entire project except the vieing project are quantifiable. The benefits of the vie is subjective in nature. Since the funding is stopped the vie are still providing services to the people, with the help of the volunteers. Efforts are to be made to make people aware of the benefits of knowing all the activities and the importance of information centres.

6. Information as Key Component

All these factors reveal that participatory approach and access to information are the key components of planning process. Participatory approach can be made successful venture only if the people have access to varieties of information at their disposal. The information which are to be made available to people can be grouped as follows :

- survival information — information related to housing, financial assistance etc.
- citizen action information — information related to people's role in social and political activities.

Or information related to

- general information awareness
- professional activities
- governmental activities
- organising activities
- cultural/ethical activities etc.

7. Information Services

The information that an information centre can provide are listed below based on the survey made by the author :

- demographic features.
- village profile, company, population of the village, preference of the people and their activities, land use pattern, agricultural products cultivated, problems faced by the people.
- socio-economic data.
- trade information.
- social amenities available.
- departmental activities and projects.
- educational and counselling information.
- rural media and health.
- professional activities and improvements.
- NGOs and voluntary organization's activities.
- women and children health problems.
- rehabilitation work.
- social security.
- environment and protection.
- law regarding consumer health, trade etc.
- any other information which may be useful to the people.

Immediate action on enactment of Access to Information Act,1996 will certainly make the people to have their right of access to information.

8. Planning Process

The model shown in the figure clearly indicates the role of information, people and agencies in the planning process.

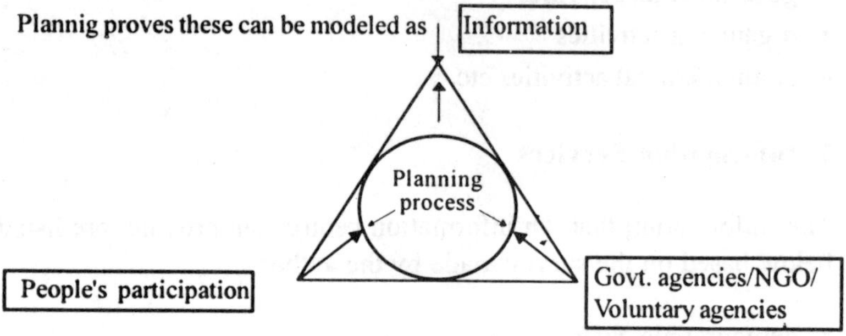

Provision of information will increase the social responsibility, individual integrity, personal credibility, professional competence, participating process, freedom of communication, dignity of the individual, equitable opportunity, cultural quality of life, individual choice of different activity and team approach.

9. Findings and Conclusions

To achieve, success in planning we have to give due importance to many aspects. Since people have more tendency to approach the Non-Governmental Organization's and voluntary organization's efforts are to be made

- to identify such organizations in the area,
- to identify their role in the village, and
- to incorporate these organizations in the planning process to achieve success and sustainability in the developing new projects.

Provision has to be made for the disposal of information to the people and keep the people well aware of the activities. This will enhance the participation activity among the people. It will enable the government officials to acquire the confidence of the people. Identification of indigenous technologies which will help the technocrats in fulfilling their role will become possible. Participation process and provision of information/access to information are the two ends of the planning process. Unless they are merged properly there is no chance of success in planning.

REFERENCES

Consumer Education and Research Centre, Ahmedabad. *Access to information bill,* Ahmedabad, the author, 1998.

Madam, Sherlin. *Information based on Global Economy and Socio-economic Development: The case of Bangalore City.* Bangalore, Information Society, 1997.

Misra, P.P. *Development issues of our time.* Delhi, Concept, 1985.

United Nations Centre for Human Settlements. *Community participation in the execution of low-income housing projects.* Nairobi, 1963.

Updhya, P.V. *Development information support to rural endues* (Thesis) guided by Prof. L.K. Ravichandra Rao, DRTC Bangalore (Subnitted to Mysore University

13

Information for Participation of Ethnic and Rural People in Planning and Development

C. PYTHAL AND A. VARADARAJAN

India, a vast country in the Indian sub-region of the Oriental Zoogeographical Region, had been a natural-resources-rich land that cradled one of the few cultured civilizations of human history. Stretching north-south from the unsurmountable ice-clad Himalayas to the enchanting solar-rise and - set birth of Cape Comorin thrusting into the Arabian Sea as also east-west from the long coastal edifices of the Eastern Ghats percolated by the Indian Ocean to the Western Ghats at the frills of the Pacific Ocean, this land had been endowed with perennial life-supporting natural resources of water, soil, flora and fauna. This immense wealth of resources supported a substantial population divided in anthropological, religious as well as cultural sects, but unified in harmonious cults of life style, work, social decorum, knowledge and sustainability. The latter depended on a rather extant fuller existence intricately woven out of the ever-sustainable renewable rich natural resources of the locality. Having been shackled into colonialism but had the break of freedom therefrom for the past more than 5 decades, our people of poverty in plenty now stand historically at the cross-roads of the laborious process of bridging the strifes between the eliteness of a powerful sector enjoying the fruits of development on 96% of the landmass and the under-development of a rather poor as also ignorant huge ethnic rural sector on the remaining 4% area, which almost exclusively constitutes the protected preserves that presently provide whatever remains of the once plentiful life-sustaining natural resources of the country.

1. Rights of Ethnic Rural Communities

The dilemma constitutes one of the world's serious internal contradictions characterized by fragmented sectoral thinking, wholly inappropriate disjunction of conservation and development, ignorance of developmental aspirations of majority consisting of millions of people as well as ruthless devastations of the precious natural resources and comprising the wrath of unreckoning the right to information of the major ethnic rural community. The right would have effectively made them intimate participants and valuable contributors of the universallyrecognized sustainable natural resources-utilization for development planning and implementation process that has taken nations of both the other continents and even Asia which historically supported several materially and idealistically abundant podiums of wealth and civilizations.

The present study endeavours to provide a humble effort to unravel the probable causes and solutions of this tragical dilemma mostly in the perspective of the information aspect.

2. Peep on the Myopia

The more acclaimed development planning process of the colonialism-shattered independent India of the present had forsaken to break away from the programme of alienation from the natural resources-preservation commitment of establishing protected areas that had taken root by the end of the 19th century in colonial India itself. This had been in vogue for correcting the natural-world-devastation that had been unleashed in the American New World by Europeans for over three centuries. However, this National Parks movement of the United States had ample bases in vast land tracts having very little human presence and summary decimation/displacement of ethnic populace under bureaucratic administration answerable only to wilderness enthusiasts. This myopic West-borrowed System — only transplantable unsuccessfully into a basically natural-resources-subsisting, rural-predominant, extremely inequitable society governed by bureaucracy refusing acceptance of accountability to people, dismissing its indigenous traditions and slitening the tremendous aboriginal sustainability against immense adversities has miserably been inadequate in leading the colonialistically shattered glorious land of ours to the posterity of wealthy welfare society. As the Father of the Nation, the great Mahatma had been quoted in 'I Go West' by its learned British author, "we do not want or need European Machine civilization .... our people are an inherently simple folk ...... I want to take them to their ancient simplicity ....", a grassroots' perspective was vital for the Indian development planning and implementation process. Instead a flawed approach, monopolisedly conceived, decided and conducted by self-centred politicians as well as arm-chair bureaucratic and technocratic experts, lacking location specific information, grounded on inappropriate assumptions, insensitive to the traditional knowledge and aspirations of the massive ethnics, bent on vested interests as also having least little understanding of the inherent natural and social systems and unreckoning the people's right to information has been thrusted on to the land, which inevitably had rebounded with vehement no-confidence and non-commitment in the formal machinery at both the centralized and decentralized levels.

3. Ancient Indian Sensibility

A "Yajur Veda" poem invokes universal peace with special mention of the "peace of air, peace of earth, peace of waters, peace of plants, peace of trees ....", which reveals how responsible was the ancient Indian sensibility to the benediction of nature and wildlife including the ethnics in the milieu. The American philanthropist forester Aldo Leopold in his book "A Sand Country Almanac" proclaimed the "Land Ethic" concept, contening that the path of social expediency is not discernible to the average individual, that all the then prevalent ethics rest on the single premise of the individual, being a member of a community, is instinctly prompted to compete for his place but ethically prompted also to co-operate. The Land Ethics simply enlarges the boundaries of the community to include soils, waters, plants and animals, or collectively the "Land".

Indira Gandhi, in her serial talks to the diverse people of the nation as also the world, had urged them to reckon the cultural and material umbilicus from nature and sustain the latter for more meaningful and equitable life, enabling sustainable use of the renewable natural resources of the nation, and the world. Mehr Homji, the Professor of the Centre of Ecology of Pondicherry University, also elucidated the need for the sustainable use of the renewable natural resources for the posterity and prosperity of our people.

4. Ecological Refugees

Professor Madhav Gadgil of the Centre for Theoretical Studies of the Indian Institute of Science, Bangalore has spoken much more than anyone in the country on the need and advantages of sustained use of renewable natural resources. He had delineated the people of the land into those who are ecosystem (Biosphere) people, ecological refugees etc. on the basis of the relative degree of contact and extent of dependance people have with the ecosystem. He has also dwelled very deeply with the role of the administrators in the degeneration of the biosphere and habitat and also on the imminent fate of the people of becoming slaves to administrative as well as academic fallacies. He has, *inter alia*, exposed the utter wrongness in the context of pleading for the removal of the buffalo herds of the Maldwaris of the Gir Lion Sanctuary, which led to clogging of the marshes with weeds and failure of the prey-predator relationship to the dismal debacle faced ultimately by the uncrowned king of the forest, namely the Asiatic lion, whose only and last remnants were in the Gir Lion Sanctuary.

Pythal (1987) had established on the basis of ample evidence that the conservation of nature and natural resources, especially in the wildlife preserves could well be attained by allowing controlled (guided) tourism into the closed preserves so that the appreciation of the beauty and the inevitability of the so called beasts could be made the responsibility of the general public also. He (1988) further suggested that renewable natural resources utilization of the wilderness areas would go a long way in attaining conservation of wildlife, including even the vulnerable and threatened species.

5. Developmental Impoverishment

The denial of the right to information and managemental sovereignty over the traditionally entitled natural resources systems has pushed the inherently strong ethnic rural majority through unending poverty, lack of basic resources, shelter, nutrition, helplessness and perverseness into the fathomless abysses of disenchanted disintegration. The appalling, miserable subversion of a historically aloft wonderful, prosperous matrix of racially and culturally diverse but ethnically and compassionately united community that gifted covetous fruits of earning, learning, co-existing mutually for creating and flourishing innumerable nation states is most baringly traceable to the deprivation of informational involvement of our gigantic rural populace in the essential provincial as well as national developmental planning and implementation processes. The reasons involve not only the carelessness regarding the needs and aspirations of the poor but also the unrecognition of the useful role of appropriate information as well as the negligence of the unforgettable role of participatory involvement of the poor in national development. Education invoked Swami Vivekananda at the first World Religious Congress "is not the amount of information that is put into (one's own) brain and runs riot there, undigested all (the) life ......" but should be "........ man-making, character making assimilation of ideas ....". The rulers have been utterly incapable to stretch out not only the real ends for good livelihood but also the proper means for accreditable citizenship to our vast poor populace.

6. Empowerment of Ethnic Populace

Across the world several ethnic tribal, rural races like the Antarctic Eskimos and Inyiuts, various American Indians, Mayas, Aztecs and so on of the New World, the African Pygmies, Watusies and Bushmen as well as the Australian Aborigines and others who were inheritors of wholesome, independent, meaningful life have, on account of foreign colonization of their home lands, been constrained to border line sustenance of impoverishment on account of the alien encroachments, plundering and consequent disintegration of their natural resources-full habitats. However, the 20th century has witnessed at least their empowerment as free people, although confined to 'reservation', and thus entitled to lead original type of crude, nature-dependent yet full life.

7. Indian Situation

In stark contrast, the many ethnic communities of the Asian continent and particularly the innumerable tribal communities of the Indian subcontinent have been relieved beyond even such 'reserved redemption' from the shackles of alien domination and disruption of self-sustained, proud, untarnished existence, due to the wholesale uprooting removal and deprivation of the renewable natural resources as well as the more deteriorative denial of provisions of justifiable, apt community development programmes implementation. This has in fact been especially the fate with respect to the ethnics of India, particularly the unduly heavily populated province of Kerala. Thus the Nagas and Bodos, the Mundas, Oraons and Santhals, the Bishnoi, the Andaman's tribes like Onge, the Solliga of Mysore as well as the many ethnics such as the Kurichiars, Malampandarams, Adiyars, Koragars, Kattunaickans, Kurumars and so on of Kerala have all been left in the unfathomable potholes of poverty, diseases, uneducatedness, expulsion from homelands and so on. The plight of the innumerable small communities have been not significantly different. Non-availability of the appropriate rightful information has further dealt severe blows on the resilience of these poor people. The colossal chunk of the people of the nation have been thus made helpless and left to rot amidst the rest of the insensitive planned revamping and development of free India. A most important single reason for such rather irretrievable tragic plight of our huge ethnic populace could very well be traced out to the deprivation of the right to information.

8. Conservation Conundrum

The ethnic, tribal upliftment propelled to help sustain the vast ethnic communities in various ecosystems has never reckoned the fundamental fact that in the Biosphere these poor marginal ethnic communities originally constituted the ecosystem people and that those of them who got displaced as ecological refugees for establishment of so called preserves for sustaining the biotic wealth especially the threatened species such as the African and Asian elephants, the Cheetah in Africa, the lion in India as well as Africa and the eight thriving sub-species of tiger including Bengal tiger of India, have actually been subserved to disintegration especially with denial of the vital right of information. The insensible wildlife and forestry scientists and technocrats and the ruthless bureaucratic administrators have miserably failed to reckon the fundamental facts of allowing the ecosystem people to be not merely the refugees in the system but most essentially the partakers and participants of the natural system inclusive of the valuable threatened biota. In the African continent, in which 90 countries supported a gigantic population of about 1.5 million elephants in the 70s, the Ivory ban and consequent poaching decimated the majestic animals into a meagre cluster of less than one lakh merely in a decade. The Species Survival programmes of the International Union for Conservation of Nature and Natural Resources (I.U.C.N) for the threatened species, clearly brought out as the Project Tiger and the Project Elephant and so on have miserably failed in reaching their goals. These tragic experiments at the conservation of valuable species of the Biosphere constitute stark examples of the failure to reckon and entrust the ecosystem people their role necessarily in the vital programmes.

9. An Effective Wayout

In the above contest, Marshall Murphies's Campfire (Communal Areas Management for Indigenous Resources) Programme has succeeded in turning out the ethnic Masokas of a Zimbabwean village from poachers to protectors of the natural resources including wildlife, which could provide an increment of 18,000 in the elephant population of the province over the past 15 years. Here the ecosystem people had been just provided informed participatory involvement in the development of the system as a whole.

There are hundreds of thousands of such examples of the ravage, disruption and destruction of the natural wealth and communities of ecosystem in every part of the world, merely attributable to the deprival of the right of information and attendant effective participation of the tribal rural populace in the development planning implementation process. This grave shortfall warrants most urgent attention for corrective approach by the bureaucrats, technocrats and administrators. Hopefully, such a change in the perception is slowly but surely reaching into the arena of conservation and all other efforts for development in almost every part of the world although the steps are very much slower.

REFERENCES

Dyson, J. (1998). "Hope for Africa's Wildlife". *Reader's Digest*. 153(20): 154-161.

Gadgil, M. (1998). Let the People Speak. *The Hindu Survey of the Environment*, 1998.

Leopold, M. (1972). *A Sand Country Almanac*. Smythsonian Institution, Washington.

Pythal, C. (1987). *Recent Trends in Wildlife Conservation*. Lecture delivered at the National Workshop for Senior IFS officers, KAU (mimeograph).

Pythal, C. (1988). *Resources and Development*. Paper presented in the KAU Workshop for Forestry and Wildlife, KAU (mimeograph).

14

Information Centre for Regional Planning and Development

M. PARAMESWARAN AND A.B. GEORGE

Area studies is a post-world war development. According to Chauney D. Harris area studies encompass several social sciences in a multi-disciplinary approach to the understanding of contemporary society in some special area. Acquaintance with the cultures of other peoples have been promoted as an important element of training for potential Government officials selected for the programmes of technical and educational assistance to developing countries. This is currently an explicit justification for area studies in developed countries. All the major countries of the world are today engaged in area studies keeping in view their policy implications. However, in the developing countries area studies has a new dimension. It is used for the study and research of the various aspects of the society in which we live in. Thus the problem of area studies collection development has a special significance at the regional, linguistic or state level in India.

1. Area Studies in India

Reyaz Rufai has identified sixteen area study centres in India. The Centre for South and South East Asian Studies, University of Madras and Kerala Studies Centre, University of Kerala are worth special mention, because these are relevant to the present study. Further there are research studies on a linguistic basis such as Tamil studies, Telugu studies, Kannada studies etc. Thus there is somewhat a coincidence between area studies and language based studies.

Kerala studies is the term used to refer to the branch of area studies with Kerala as core entity. The International Congress on Kerala Studies held at Thiruvananthapuram in 1994 and the setting up of Kerala studies centre in the University of Kerala are indirect evidences of the emergence of Kerala studies.

2. Malabar Studies

We take Malabar as example for this study. Malabar which forms northern most areas of the northern Kerala is a historically important region having geographical, ethnic and social conditions that are peculiar to it. Hence the region requires special attention. Use of the term Malabar studies has not got acceptance. However there are indirect evidences to show the emergence of this new branch of area studies. There are several agencies other than the Departments of the University or the Government which are engaged in the study and research on fragments of knowledge which may be considered as parts of Malabar studies. Mappila studies (studies on Muslims of Malabar), Nila studies (Studies on River Bharathappuzha), studies on Northern Ballads (Vadakkanpattu) may be cited as examples. This list is not exhaustive. Thunchan Patana Gaveshana Kendram (The Centre for Study and Research on Thunchattu Ramanujan Ezhuthachan, the author of Adhyathma Ramayanam Kilippattu) located at Tirur is notable among such agencies.

3. Need for Co-ordination

Thus there are evidence of fragments of knowledge which may be considered as components of Malabar studies. What is needed is coordination of efforts in library activities such as collection development, interlibrary loan and bibliographical control so that an integrated view in study and research will slowly evolve.

A perusal of ongoing research topics of the University of Calicut show that many topics are exclusively on Malabar area. A scrutiny of the topics included in the publication of Abstracts of the International Congress on Kerala Studies held at Trivandrum in 1994 shows that many topics are exclusive studies on Malabar area. These are indications that a new branch of area studies is emerging. This new branch of area studies, namely Malabar studies is to be considered as a branch of the broader field Kerala studies.

The development of Malabar studies as a branch of Kerala studies due to fission (repeated subdivision) of the original universe, viz. area studies, may be diagrammatically represented as shown below:

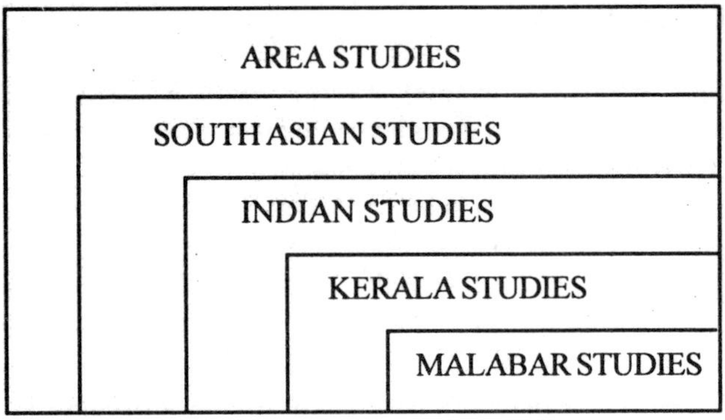

The Hierarchical relationship of area studies

Malabar Studies may be considered as the last link of the chain derived from the original universe Area Studies.

4. Facets of Area Studies

According to Indian School of thought in library classification area studies are subjects developed due to cluster mode of formation. Inputs, viewpoints or works on an area come from diverse field of study. These fields of study may be considered as facets of the particular area studies. Newly emerging Malabar studies can be envisaged to have the following facets :

- Science and technology
- Agriculture and agrarian movements
- Transport and industries
- History and political developments
- Folklore and arts
- Religion and philosophy
- Literature and linguistics

- Castes and tribes
- Society and culture

5. Importance of Malabar Studies

Kerala consists of three regions, namely Travancore, Cochin and Malabar. Malabar is at the Northern region of Kerala and is away from Thiruvananthapuram, the capital city of the State. Due to these reasons it is less developed compared to the other regions. Clamor for special programmes for development of Malabar is well reflected in the headings of the daily newspapers.

It has been accepted that Malabar requires a master plan for the development of transportation, communication, education and other facilities. Area studies and research programmes with Malabar as the nodal point can contribute much to such development programmes. Various departments of the University of Calicut have undertaken several such research projects. The establishment of Kannur University for the development of Northern Malabar only strengthen our argument that intensive studies on Malabar should be anticipated in future.

6. Maintenance of Collection

A comprehensive library collection and compilation of bibliography are prerequisites for all such study groups, research projects and development programmes. Such library and information services will provide an integrated approach and holistic view to the entire research programmes.

Malabar has its own folk tradition which is evident in the ritualistic arts like thira and theyyam and in the Northern ballads such as those describing the heroic acts of *Chekavas*. Studies on such cultural aspects will enable us to understand our tradition and preserve them. The folk literature is written in vernacular and not available from standard publishers. Special efforts are needed to acquire them and organize them as a library collection.

The recent celebrations of the Platinum Jubilee (75th year) of the Mappila rebellion or Malabar rebellion of 1921 has provoked lot of discussions, seminars etc. on this topic of historical importance. Lot of historical evidences are available on this historical event which should be preserved in lasting media and made available for study and research.

The historical record of the royal dynasties such as the Arakkal dynasty and Zamorrins (Samuthiris) are to be collected and preserved. Considering all these a Malabar studies collection should be maintained in a prominent library of the region.

7. Malabar Information

A Malabar Information Centre (MIC) should be set up with the special aid of the State government. It can be established either in the C.H. Mohammed Koya Library (i.e. Calicut University Library) or in the Calicut University Study Centre Library at Calicut city. Calicut Public Library at Mananchira, Calicut city is another place which deserves consideration in this regard. The Malabar studies collection described earlier can be housed in the MIC. However MIC as a regional information centre will have several other functions in addition to maintaining an area studies collection. CHMK Library will have the advantage of an academic environment. CHMK Library being located at the centre of Calicut University Campus it will be possible to bring together the materials relating to Malabar from various departments and organize them at a central place. Nevertheless, the other two places will have the advantage of being situated in the heart of the city.

8. Functions of Malabar Information Centre

The proposed Malabar information centre will have the following functions:

- to serve as a depository for all kinds of documents relating to various aspects of Malabar.
- to maintain an electronic/microfilm/microfiche collection of old and valuable documents and other records relating to Malabar studies.
- to provide reference service, i.e. providing answers to queries on all aspects of Malabar; to maintain facts on file.
- to provide career information service, i.e. to provide information about job opportunities.
- to provide educational guidance, i.e. to provide information about

courses and mode of selection.

- to provide tourist information service, i.e. to provide information about places of tourist importance with details about transportation and accommodation.
- to provide health information guidance, i.e. to give information about hospitals and specialists and to provide general awareness on health hazards.
- to provide bibliographical service on Malabar studies. A quarterly periodical bibliography has to be regularly published scanning the current periodical articles on varius aspects of Malabar. *Ad hoc* bibliographies on specific topics also have to be compiled from time to time.

9. Planned Regional Development

MIC should have facility for microfilming old records. There should be audio-visual facilities including television, video cassettes and video cassette player. Lot of studies and researches are being done on various aspects of Malabar. Development of a document collection on Malabar and setting up of MIC can contribute positively to the overall development of Malabar region.

REFERENCES

Gopinath, M.A. and Seetharama, S. Interdisciplinary subjects and their classification. Neelameghan, A. (ed.). *Ordering systems for global information networks:* Proceedings of the Third International Conference on Classification Research, Bombay, 6-11 Jan., 1975. Bangalore: F.I.D./C.R. & Sarada Ranganathan Endowment for Library Science, 1979.

Harris, Chauncy D. Area studies and library resources. In: T.H. Sien and Kh.W. Winger (eds.). *Area studies and the library.* The Thirteenth Annual Conference of the Graduate Library School, May 20-22. Chicago. University of Chicago Press, 1965.

Parameswaran, M. Libraries for socio-economic development: Proposal for Malabar Studies Collection. Kumar, (R.P.) [*et al.*] (eds.). *Role of libraries in national development*: Papers of the 42nd All India Library Conference, Calicut, Dec. 21-24, 1996. Delhi: ILA, p.89.

Reyaz, Rufai. The scope of a specific area study: a reference framework for information service professionals. *Indian J. of Information Library & Society*, 6 (1993): p.245.

Trikha, Sudha. National information system for South Asian Studies (NISSAS). Navlani, K. and Satija, M.P. (eds.). *Library and information systems: Emerging challenges.* Jaipur. RBSA Publications, 1996.p. p.189-200.

15

Information Technology in Governance: Opportunities

NARESH REDDY

When challenges are met with inspiration and resolve they become opportunities. Information Technology puts forward hitherto untapped possibilities to the government to increase its efficiency and meet the challenges in all aspects of its activity. Access, storage, processing, organization and transfer of information and data to various levels of administration and to people as well as cost effective and speedy discussions and meetings, quick and speedy action based on timely reliable information etc. are also some of the advantages provided by application of Information Technology in governance. Transparency is made possible which enables participation of the people in development and it makes democracy meaningful.

1. Electronic Government

Inter-networking government departments using information and communication technologies forms an "electronic government". It also includes the concept of providing automated services to organizations, businesses and the public as and when they are required, and in forms convenient to them, through various delivery channels including the telephone, the Internet and public access information kiosks. Electronic Government aims to use IT in all aspects of governance to maximize efficiency, transparency, convenience and accessibility.

The key to transforming government is to build a customer-oriented government; based upon business management principles, with the citizens as customers of the government. The political governance will change from the mode of operator and controller of the economy, to facilitator and catalyst for overall development, from being intrusive to enabling. Information Technology can help governments build up a more efficient administration, which is workflow oriented to reflect the needs of the public, whereby, information and services may be made available to the public more extensively, and more speedily. The paradigm shift from desktop to pervasive computing is driving this citizen interface improvement focus of government applications of IT.

2. Information Services

The essence of an electronic government is to make integrated information and services readily available to all, as opposed to controlled releases through bureaucratic operations. The traditional structure requires citizens to seek information through government departments, which control the information sources. With the assistance of information technology, an electronic government will respond to the needs of the public with the offer of a variety of services as and when they are required, and in forms in which they are required.

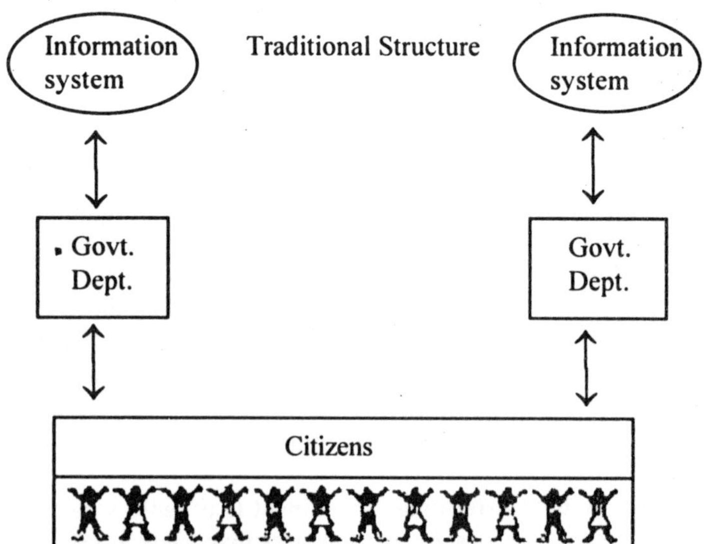

The future structure will provide transparent access to the same information sources that the government departments have access to without having to route their requests through the government departments.

Interface in the Future

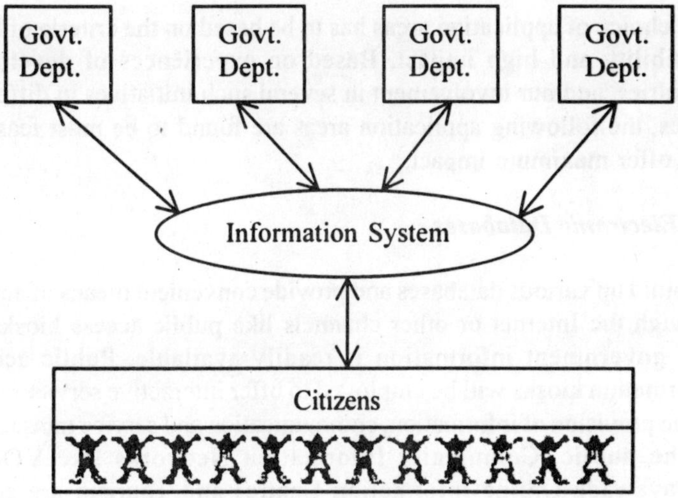

3. Communication Infrastructure

The cornerstone of an electronic government is a communication infrastructure. That, in effect, consists of "guided channels" for the flow of information, which include copper cables, fibre optic cables and other facilities or tools for the transfer of information, plus the controlling software that facilitates end-to-end delivery of information. The Governments must study the establishment of communication network infrastructure for an electronic government, which will serve as a platform for exchanging and sharing government information. The study should look at the application of Internet technology as a basis for interconnecting the existing Information Systems which are already in place, and other Intranets under construction.

The service delivery could be using multiple channels. They include telephones and data service, personal computer and workstations, automatic teller machines and "public access information kiosks", which will be distributed over homes, public venues, offices and government departments, offering a variety of channels for people from all quarters to access information and services provided by the electronic government.

4. Application Areas

The choice of application areas has to be based on the criteria of high feasibility and high impact. Based on experiences of developed countries, and our involvement in several such initiatives in different states, the following application areas are found to be most feasible and offer maximum impact.

4.1 Electronic Databases

To build up various databases and provide convenient means of access through the Internet or other channels like public access kiosks so that government information is readily available. Public access information kiosks will be employed to offer interactive services such as the provision of information, communication and service transaction to the public. Community Information Networks like VOICE (Vijayawada Online Information Centre) and Tourism are some examples of such initiatives.

4.2 Police Applications

To apply wireless communications and digital technology in a public, secured information network, GIS based vehicle tracking and finger print recognition systems, and to strengthen crime detection and fighting capability of law enforcement departments. CMC has provided solutions to a number of state governments.

4.3 Intranets

An Intranet linking all government departments can be established, which will provide e-mail addresses, electronic directories, electronic news and electronic mail boxes to various levels of staff. These Intranets will exploit the communication infrastructure to link all departments.

A Collector's Information System initiative is underway in Andhra Pradesh.

4.4 Electronic Benefits Transfer

This represents the processing of the government's social welfare operations using electronic data interchange, magnetic cards and smart cards, whereby government welfare benefits will be processed and transferred directly to the recipients.

4.5 Electronic Document Management

This is used to computerize documentation and management processes, and to provide facilities for the exchange of documents over the information network. Computerization of Land Records is a major initiative in this area. Inter-departmental information systems can be established to facilitate the implementation of electronic documentation exchange. Through on-line data interchange, duplication of data input is avoided and administration efficiency is enhanced.

4.6 Electronic Taxation

Electronic Taxation is applications providing filing of returns and assessments electronically and is a very promising application area. Commercial Tax application have been taken up in several states.

4.7 GIS Applications

Remote sensing and Geographical Information System (GIS) can be applied in environmental and transport planning. While GIS applications have long implementation cycles, the potential benefits are large. Several state governments have undertaken such applications for public utilities.

4.8 Electronic Commerce

With security provided by electronic signature and public key technology, communications and transaction processing by electronic data interchange can be implemented among government departments and between government departments and business enterprises. Cyber laws being passed will give a boost to such applications.

4.9. Electronic Procurement and Tendering

In the secured environment of electronic commerce, government departments and suppliers should implement electronic on-line procurement, transactions and payments.

5. Innovative Services

Electronic government is not just about replacing manual work by information technology. What is more important is that these innovative services will strengthen coordination or cooperation between departments. Traditional ways will give way to new workflow processes, and re-appropriation of duties and responsibilities will lead to a restructure of human resource planning. Eventually professional expertise of government departments will be strengthened, casting a new image for the government. The anticipated benefits of an electronic government are many. A few of them are discussed below.

6. People's Participation

Empowering citizens through Information is the most important benefit. Electronic Government provides convenient, immediate and innovative services to the people. Through the electronic window of Internet, people will have faster and better access to more updated information.

New processes and improved administration workflow becomes possible. Besides information enquiries, Internet is also good for service application. For example, the Income Tax Department can study the use of the Internet in filing tax returns.

Electronic Governance can establish feedback mechanism and strengthen interaction between the public and the government: While the public can access government information and services on the Internet and public access kiosks, the government can also make use of electronic mail boxes to receive public opinions and to reply immediately, so as to expand public participation.

Electronic Governance can expand public participation and

consolidate common consensus: With government information readily available for public reference on the Internet and various information kiosks, we can aim to achieve consensus, seek public support and expand public participation.

7. Improved Quality of Life

With drastic reduction in amount of superfluous documentation, human resources can be re-directed to more value-added services and improving the quality of work life to government employees. Information Kiosks can reduce the number of times a citizen has to visit government offices, and the time he spends there. For example, lakhs of copies of certificates of caste and nativity are issued every year. If government departments can identify each citizen uniquely via the information network, the public will not need to spend time on applying for duplicates, which will help reduce social and transport costs.

Improved Policy Planning and decision support becomes possible. For example, the Treasury Network can provide real-time information about government revenue. The Employment Services Information System can reflect the current employment market and computerized statistics of other industries. All of these will help improve the quality of government's decisions.

8. Open and Transparent Administration

Computerized and networked operations cannot only simplify workflow but also protect against corruption. This will facilitate for a more open, transparent government. An example is Procurement Information System, whereby government departments' procurement information is made known to the public on the Internet. This can achieve a fully transparent process. In future, award of contracts and public tenders can be processed over the information network to minimize untoward occurrences. All departments of public services will employ the computer for registration and controlling workflow. That will speed up processes and reduce the number of times a member of the public needs to visit government offices, whereby a greater degree of transparency is achieved.

9. Intelligent State

The government should embrace competitiveness as the focus of the state's effort to change and aim to strengthen competitiveness. Starting with a corruption-free and capable government, the state should strive to fulfil the needs of the public. The state should employ information technology to step up service efficiency and quality.

Administration's performance and efficiency is the primary engine in driving us forward in the global race of competitiveness. In view of progress made in information technology, the government can apply new concepts and new ways of doing things to boost administration efficiency and service quality, so as to enhance competitiveness.

Judging by the above parameters, India has a long way to go to become "Intelligent". However in recent years, development of applications of information technology has picked up in pace. Given our resolve, we can employ a frog-leap strategy to stride forward. Union and State governments are taking steps in that direction and we can hope that we are now on the first firm step in the direction of ushering in an "Intelligent" State.

Obstacles are those frightful things you see when you take your eyes off your goal.

16

Strategic Plans for Designing Information Systems Under Local Government

R. RAMAN NAIR

Now local bodies which are concerned with various administrative educational and development issues, and the planning for use of technology have started to recognize the value of information. This study attempts to evolve technical guidelines for building up an information system under local government that provides networking services by connecting various offices and institutions like Block Panchayat Office, Village Panchayat Office, District Educational Office, schools, colleges, and other organizations existing in the geographical jurisdiction under District Panchayat.

1. Technical Model

The concept of a modern information system serving all educational research and development institutions and offices has been a serious topic of discussion in many forums. In developed countries most of the local governments have efficient information systems. In India also in geographical areas coming under local governments many institutions have implemented information systems and networks in response to their own perception of the importance of this resource. It is better that a standard network implementation model to assist local governments in their planning may be designed by NIC or other National or State level government agencies so that all such implementations will be compatible with each other and with any national level information system plans.

The possibilities offered by current information technology for materialising an integrated voice, data, and video network extending to every institution, offices and home is very exciting. But the investment in money and time will be beyond the powers of the local bodies unless there is a strong awareness of its importance as well as careful planning and provisions from higher levels of government. But local bodies can do a great deal within the limitations of resources under their control if the network and communication facilities of institutions in the locality can be pooled and shared by providing possible support also to them.

National policy should be to define a highly functional, homogenous, and well supported network system that could interconnect all districts, states and nationvide institutions and departments to enable everyone to use new communication tools and network based information resources. It will take considerable time to adapt the procedures and activities of the institutions and offices at various levels to take full advantage of the current information technology. Using standard models for implementation of information systems District Panchayats can begin the process. Many institutions existing in various districts have already developed information systems and services which can be shared under the support and cooperation of District Panchayats. This can also enable extracting the maximum utility of the systems developed.

Modem accessible systems are available in many district headquarters. They serve to encourage people to become familiar with network resources and capabilities. But they will always be limited in functionality and capacity. Considering the emerging bandwidth intensive information resource applications and the functionality that they will require, it is essential to provide direct access to Internet from computers in every office and institution in the district.

TCP/IP which the Internet communication protocol will allow all computers to communicate. Softwares that implement this protocol is available with most of the present packages. This protocol supports vide variety of applications, from electronic messaging to client server data access. The use of this protocol will ensure that all networked computers will have direct access to the vast range of existing information on the Internet as well as the National and State Information Infrastructures that are coming up.

2. Implementation

Current proven and cost effective technology which would be expandable and up-gradable to later technology with minimum additional investment should be used. This study proposes a modular design to meet the criteria :

- physical infrastructure development that will be general and flexible enough to be reused as technology improves.
- integrating as much as possible the existing equipments and systems in various offices and institutions into the information system.
- locating the network server in a place where it can be efficiently managed and supported.
- using inter-connect topologies that will be both cost effective and manageable.

In many institutions that come under the local government or the geographical area under its jurisdiction already there are some form of network and communication infrastructure. While implementing a district level information system in some cases such infrastructures can be adopted to newer technologies and in other cases they are to be replaced within a span of time.

2.1 Implementation Model

No single design for an Information System can be considered to be fit for every District Panchayat. Location, physical constraints functional needs, existing technology base, funds, opportunities for sharing resources with major institutions or organizations existing in the region etc. will necessitate major modifications. Hence at national or state level a set of general guidelines that can be followed for the planning of an information system under local government at District Panchayat level can be formed. Using Internet protocols in developing local information systems can enable avoiding the major expenses of building new backbone infrastructure at district and state level for the time being. Inter-connection of institutions, offices at district level to district headquarters and then to departments and headquarters at state level can be achieved by getting Internet connection services from Department of Telecommunications (DOT) or Videsh Sanchar

Nigam Limited (VSNL) which has established Gateway Internet Access Services (GIAS) and hubs in most of the district headquarters as well as from other Internet Service Profiders. Connection to Internet service will provide communication capability to all local bodies and institutions subscribing to and from within the state and country. Internet technology is designed to allow very flexible intensity topology. A hierarchical topology is the simplest to develop. This means hierarchical connection of facilities at offices and institutions from institution to Panchayat level which will be further aggregated at district headquarters and finally a link to VSNL hub in the district.

Circuit services coordination and a single point of connection to GIAS enables minimising overall costs and increasing of chances to use current technology. The basic network implementation under District Panchayat is not a complicated process. A LAN is to be created within each institution, office or cluster of buildings with one network server for that LAN. Such LAN's can be interconnected with a similar LAN existing at the District Panchayat Office. The centrally managed information resources will exist there. This LAN at district headquarters is to be connected to the nearest GIAS. Primary technical support for network monitoring and solving problems should come from the district head quarters to avoid unnecessary duplication at the institutional/office level. When expertise is developed at the local level more of the responsibility for daily operation and problem solving can be undertaken at the institution, office level. It will be impossible to cover all conceivable scenarios for implementation of information networks under District Panchayats. But general principles can be given which should be followed in designing and implementing information networks under local governments in any region.

3. LAN Implementation

An institution or office mean a building or a cluster of buildings that are managed as a unit under District Panchayat or one existing in the geographical area under the jurisdiction of the local government. Here the wide meaning of under local government is taken which include institutions existing in that locality also. LAN implementation in this setting will include installation of a cabling system to distribute the network throughout the building or cluster of buildings, installation of premise wiring to support connections of computers and terminals to the network distribution system, installation of one or more network server machines in a central location and provision of network router and telecommunications circuit or radio link to connect that office to the district headquarters. Popular LAN technology is Ethernet. It is cost effective and easy to install and maintain. Ethernet is adaptable to most modern computers and is now built into high performance workstations available in Indian market also. Hence it is good for all computer connections and for network distribution system and LAN backbones.

Individual computer will need network or communication adapters and necessary softwares. Basic communication software is available free of cost for most computers. Software packages with advanced facilities for applications such as e-mail, distance learning, multimedia database access etc. are also available from many software solution providers. LAN developers should look at all available software and base choices on required functionality and support costs. In locations where computers will be purchased the choice of computer type should be driven by the availability of software for the particular applications to be supported. Most of the computer systems presently available in the market can be attached to all networks.

3.1 LAN Cabling

One important work for the LAN implementation will be installation of cabling to connect individual computers or group of computers to the LAN. The advisable topology is a star type where each computer is wired directly to a hub site within the building. A cluster of computers to be placed in a single room can be interconnected there itself and the cluster can be connected to the hub site with a single cable. UTP wire that meets category 5 standards for high speed data communication service should be utilised. Their ends will terminate on a standard 110 distribution block at the hub site utility closet. Installation and wiring in a building is to planned and installed professionally after considering both current and future requirements. It will be cost effective to install premise wiring to as many locations as might ever serve a computer. In high density locations consideration should be given to installation of two UTP cables to each outlet location in order to provide the potential for several computers or workstations. Terminating both cables on the same wall plate will add little to the overall wiring project costs and will add greatly to the flexibility of the system. Premise wiring that is not to be used initially will not be connected to any electronics in the hub site. Hub sites should be utility closets or other protected, non-occupied areas. Hub sites can be created by construction of small closets or cabinets in low use areas. A hub site must be located within three hundred feet of any connection. Multiple hub sites will be required in large or multi-story buildings.

4. Interconnections

The hub sites within an institution or office must be interconnected to complete that institution's LAN. The design of such network will depend mainly on the physical layout of the buildings of the office or institution. If all hub sites are within 300 cable feet of a central location, then 10-base-T wiring can be used from a central hub to connect each hub site. If distance is longer thin-net or standard thick ethernet can be used. Fibre optic cable can be used if distance necessitates it and resources are available. If fibre optic cable is used; multimedia fibre for current and future data requirements and single mode fibre for video and future high speed data systems should be kept in mind. Specific design of the backbone network distribution system will depend on the layout of the buildings to be served. Many computers can be connected to a single ethernet segment.

Each institution should install a network server to support local storage of commonly used information, files, software, electronic mail and other functions that may require high-speed communication to the users computer. The connection to the outside network will be much slower than the institutional LAN. Hence it will be very efficient to access information locally. The software that is to be shared among the institutions computers must be stored locally since it will be very difficult to transmit it through the slower external link. The network server will be connected directly to the ethernet network. The location of the server should be chosen carefully to ensure its protection from abuse and environmental damage. Traditionally most offices and institutions coming under local bodies are doing the information gathering and storage activities. Examples are the records section of the present collectorates, plans and documents section of the village offices, information about houses, residents etc. in panchayat offices and the files and document collections in various other offices, organizations and institutions as well as records in panchayat and district libraries. Many institutions like village offices, libraries of educational and research institutions etc. have already installed cluster of computers or terminals. The libraries in the institutions or offices are the most logical place to locate the network server computer. The network router also should be located in the library.

The network server will be a small but powerful computer with large amount of disk storage capacity, typically of ten to forty GB. It will run software capable of supporting access by a large number of user simultaneously. It could also support dial-in access from officers homes using standard inexpensive modem. Access control with user authentication is essential when dial-in-service is also provided. If dial-in access is to be provided to more than a few institutions within a district, a single central modem pool maintained at the district office will be cost effective.

4.1 External Connection

One communication circuit will connect the institutional LAN to other local offices and institutions. In the institution or office there will be a network router attached between the LAN and this circuit. On the LAN side, the connection will be a typical ethernet cable. On the external side the connection will depend on the communication circuit used.

All the offices and institutions within a district should be connected individually to the network router at the district panchayat office. This star topology will be much easier to manage and the capacity of each institution or office connection can be increased appropriately as needs change. A standard communication circuit service may be used to effect this connection. Where limited use only is there dial up using high speed mode is advisable. This is not apt for heavy and serious use because of its limited capacity.

Most offices receive telephone service under business tariffs. Hence usage will be measured and the cost will be dependent on how long the connection is used. Dedicated communication circuits are good because they will allow unattended access to and from the institutional network at all hours. This will be particularly important if information files are to be loaded during the night to local network servers or officers and users have access to the institutions information resources from home.

5. Communication Options

For communication, frame relay communication service can be used. It is a shared, packet-based data transport service. An office site would contract for frame relay service as part of a larger service group that includes the District Panchayat Office and may include the Internet service provider. All members of that group could share the communications capacity. This enables each member to order a connection to the common service and the capacity offered to each member can be upgraded independently. The cost of frame relay service will not be dependent on distance to the service provider which can make the service to Grama Panchayats, Village Offices, schools etc. much less expensive than any equivalent services. Overall system costs can be minimised since the central router at the District Panchayat Office will need fewer connections. Frame relay necessitates careful planning of overall services. As all institutions, offices in the locality will share connection to the District Panchayat and possibily to the VSNL; that must be a high capacity connection. Initially the aggregate capacity of all office/institution links should not exceed the capacity of the District Panchayat Office by more than a factor of three. The virtual connection topology, the connection to VSNL etc. also should be considered while designing the system. Future options for such information systems will include Community Access Television Cable System offering either share or dedicated bidirectional data communication services, fibre optic communication service providers, Asynchronous Transfer Mode connection services supporting voice data and video communications at high speed etc. As demand for network speed will increase due to heavy use of multimedia and other band width-intensive applications, high-speed communications circuits can replace the initial circuits with minimal change in the equipment or LAN. This can enable flexibility necessitated by finance and applications.

6. District Panchayat Office LAN

The District Panchayat Office should form the focal point for interconnection of all offices and institutions in the District. Within the District Panchayat Office LAN network operations can be monitored and problem solution managed. One or more network servers can provide essential network support as well as central archiving of common information and software. An important work of the District Panchayat Office LAN will be to manage Internet Domain Name System service for the Block Panchayats, Grama Panchayats and other offices and institutions in the district. This is defining of the basic network level identity of each computer, workstation, server and active network component. The GPO should be wired in a manner similar to the offices/institutions in the district described earlier. This will allow Block Panchayats, Grama Panchayats and other offices and institutions in the district to share information easily. Network Access Server connected to the Central Pool of modems can provide dial-in-access to the District Panchayat Network.

7. Internet Connectivity

Internet connection of the entire district should take place through the District Panchayat Office interconnect site. This hierarchical model can be extended another level to inter-connection of the District Panchayat Offices through the State Headquarters to national level systems. Many administrative information resources could be located at the state level and there might be cost savings if the entire state connects to VSNL through a single point. But, the bandwidth required for this single connection will be higher than that required for each District Panchayat Office since traffic will be aggregated. This hierarchical topology also provides a logical model for network support and information resource management. District Panchayat Offices or State headquarters can provide continuous monitoring of the network and provide high level technical expertise for problem resolution, relieving the individual District Panchayat Office's of this burden. Interactions with Internet service providers will be more effective if handled through state headquarters. Network users should get a single reliable point of contract in case of problems or questions. Connection will require a high quality router that can be configured to interact correctly with the VSNL's routers. This can be the same router used to support District Panchayat Offices connections.

Village offices, libraries and many other institutions would already have developed LANs to support of their specialized activities or administrative functions. The technologies used may be obsolete or different. If they are capable of transporting Internet protocols they can be integrated into the new LAN system and upgraded or replaced later.

8. System Management

All information systems require some level of network management to ensure reliable and efficient service. Monitoring the functionality of the network can help to identify problems before they became detrimental to network users. It also can help predict trends in traffic patterns and volume. Network management consists primarily of determining the proper routing parameters for optimal and reliable network operation, assignment of network Internet Protocol(IP) addresses and maintenance of a network-accessible database of node names corresponding to each address and monitoring the daily operation of the network. These functions are to be performed by staff of a network operations centre.

8.1 Domain Name System

Domain Name System (DNS) is the mechanism for documenting and distributing information about the name and address of each computer attached to the network. DNS service is provided by software that runs on the main network server. An Internet address is the numerical identifier for a node and it must be unique among all nodes associated with the network. DNS node names are hierarchical and by appropriately using this hierarchy sub-domains can be assigned to each Block Panchayat Office, Grama Panchayat, Village Office and other institution sites or District Panchayat Office.

While planning network installation a norm for assignment of IP network addresses and mode names should be developed. At first the database serving DNS should exist on the District Panchayat Office server so that there is one site at which all assignments are officially registered. As the network grows and expertise is developed, secondary DNS service can be run on the servers at sites of big institutions or offices. The main DNS server for the District Panchayat Office should be located close to Internet connection so that network problems within the district will have minimal impact on access to the server. Associated with the assignment of node names and addresses there should be a database of specific information about the computers connected to the network. When resolving problems this can help to know where the computers and other nodes are located in the district, what type of computer and software are in use and what type of network connections are installed.

Network monitoring serves three basic purposes. Firstly, it helps constant observation of the proper functioning of the network, its components and external connectivity. Standard simple network management protocol support is built into most active packages available these days. Network servers and workstations also can be monitored in this way. Secondly, it collects statistics on the performance of the network and patterns of traffic in order to identify needed enhancements or re-engineering. Thirdly, it enables more rapid problem resolution. When problems occur simple network management protocol tools can help to pinpoint the source of the problem. Since network management and monitoring is a technically demanding task and requires special equipments and softwares it should be a centralised function in the initial design of information networks under District Panchayat.

9. Conclusions

District Panchayat Information system proposed here is based on various documents proposing such systems, as well as technical designs of such systems prepared by the Library and Information services unit in Kerala Agricultural University and other institutions. Such a system can be a leap towards bringing information resource to bear for enriching all the District Panchayat Offices' programmes. The design suggested here can be the foundation at the district level in preparation for future high capacity networks and information systems for the people.

REFERENCES

Berridale, A.K. National Policy on information for India. In *National Information Policies and Programmes*, ILA, 1991.

Carole Teach. *Building the future: K-12 network technology planning guide.* Barkley, CDER, 1994.

David, P.S. Inter-connecting the LANs. *Computers Today*, 1995.

Lacy, Dan M. *Freedom and equality of access to information: A report to the ALA*, London, ILA, 1986.

Padma V. Upadhya. Information Technology and Community Development. *In Role of Libraries in national development.* New Delhi, ILA, 1996.

Raman Nair, R. Resource Sharing Networks for Higher Education at State Level. *Computerisation and Library Network*, December 1990, New Delhi, ILA, 1990.

Raman Nair, R. Gramangalil Vijnanavitharanam. *Information Service to the Villagers*. Trivandrum, Vijnanakairali, Vol. 9, No. 8, August 1988.

Sarista Sharma, Scope and challenges of networking libraries in India. In *Role of libraries in national development.* New Delhi, ILA, 1996.

17

Digital Local Government Information Centre for Democratic Decentralisation

K. RAJASEKHARAN

Democratic decentralisation is the process of devolving more functions and resources to the local bodies. Through this process, the local bodies in Kerala have become substantially powerful institutions with more powers, functions, functionaries, and funds. Each local body is now nucleus of developmental and regulatory functions in that region.

Decentralisation involves numerous changes in administrative structure, allocation of functions and control of resources. Decentralisation brings the task of decentralised local planning to the local bodies. So each local body shall have to prepare a comprehensive area plan as part of the 'bottom-up' planning process. The bottom-up planning process requires the involvement of elected representatives, voluntary agencies, non-official experts, ordinary people assembling in the grama sabhas, etc. in formulating projects and drafting the final plan. The redeployment of staff from various government departments to the local bodies is on progress and many of them are professionals like medical officers, veterinary doctors, agricultural officers, and so on. This has restructured the manpower profile of the local bodies, making them so complex. The decentralised development initiative of invigorated local bodies require technical skill and that is a challenging task. In short, the process of decentralisation has made the management of local bodies a very complex task. The ever increasing complexity of managing a local body demand an array of various kinds of information by all the actors involved in the management of local bodies. But the demand for diverse kinds of information required for effective governance of local bodies can only be met speedily and cost effectively by application of emerging information technologies.

In this context, there has been an attempt as part of Information Kerala Mission (IKM) to establish an extensive computer network connecting all the local bodies numbering 1214 in the state. This provides an excellent environment for creating a digital local government information centre. Kerala Institute of Local Administration (KILA) is the right place to have such a centre on many counts.

1. Position of KILA

Kerala Institute of Local Administration (KILA) is an autonomous training and academic institution with excellent infrastructural facilities and an exclusive focus on 'local governance'—both rural and urban. KILA has been elevated as a nodal agency functioning with the twin objectives:

- to act as a catalyst for formulating policy decisions on local governance at the governmental level.
- to engage in research, training, information dissemination, consultancy etc. for enhancing the performance of local bodies in Kerala.

KILA is now undergoing a revamping and relaunching process in its organisational development with view to groom it as a designated lead organisation for design, organisation and co-ordination of all capacity development activities in the area of local governance in the State. Increasing accessibility to information, ideas and knowledge has a very crucial role to play as a capacity building measure in invigorating the local bodies in the state and hence KILA can be the right place to have such a digital information centre as part of its library and information activities.

1.1 *Vital Resource for Local Development*

Information, ideas and knowledge have turned out to be the most vital resource for local governance. Real empowerment of the functionaries of local self-government institutions (LSGIs) shall begin with ensuring free accessibility to relevant information needed for their day-to-day development activities. Right and appropriate decision making process is possible only when actors engaged in the mission of bringing about decentralisation are fed with right information expeditiously as needed. Availability or insufficiency of information of technical, procedural or legal nature can make or mar the local planning and development more than anything else.

2. Digital Information Centre (DIC)

Digital information centre is expected to be the most widely used information dissemination system of the next century. Across the world more and more documents are appearing as digital or hypertext documents. DIC is an information storage and retrieval system, which can store a large amount of multimedia information including text, pictures, sound and video in digital form and distribute such information across the network. DIC shall consist of digital information storage and retrieval servers and client nodes connected to it. In a digital information centre all kinds of information are in digitised form as a set of bits and bytes. Digitisation is a process through which information is converted into digits for computer use.

DIC, for our purpose, is defined as electronic information collections containing large and diverse repositories of digital objects, which can be accessed by a large number of users, geographically distributed. Digital information centre would be very relevant in any environment where people have to spend more time to reach the library than to access and acquire the information.

2.1 *Objective of DLGIC*

Digital Local Government Information Centre (DLGIC) is proposed as a computerised information storage or databank facility maintained for the purpose of providing diverse types of information on local self-governance and planning, to all actors connected with it. Specific objectives of DLGIC are:

- to collect all primary and secondary information, data and documents required for local planning and governance in electronic form.

- to organise all such collected data or information for its easy access and retrieval by local functionaries and other users through computer networks.
- to disseminate appropriate information and data on its demand and in anticipation.

The precise objective of DLGIC is to create a comprehensive electronic database of already existing and emerging body of knowledge, ideas and information on all aspects of local governance with a view to ensure easy accessibility to it by the policy makers, researchers, trainers, functionaries of local bodies and the public through on line or other digital means.

3. Information Needs for Local Governance

3.1 *By Policy Makers*

Policy makers require information on all aspects of procedures and practices of decentralisation in order to achieve it and new innovative happenings occurring in other regions of the country and the world. Such information needs can possibly be met from a wide variety of documentary sources like authoritative reports, standard books, local government acts of other States in India and other countries, commission reports on local governance etc. Intellectuals, researchers and trainers concentrating on this field also require similar information to bring about a vibrant local government system.

3.2 *By Local Government Functionaries*

The local government functionaries including elected representatives are expected to know about panchayati raj acts, other related acts, numerous rules framed under them and various orders issued by diverse governmental agencies. The collection of all these documents together is certainly an uphill task for any local body in our beurocratic environment. Non-accessibility to such updated documents and resultant ill-informed decision-making may lend many of our functionaries in trouble.

In the process of local planning, the local government

functionaries would require a fairly comprehensive data on land, water, natural resources, climatic conditions, availability of human resources etc. for drawing up the integrated area plan for their local body.

3.3 *By Others*

The public, who are the members of the grama sabha, also need many of the above said information to keep track with and participating in the development activities. Journalists and newspaper offices require such information for preparing analytical write-ups on local development initiatives. The teachers in the educational institutions and the opinion makers in the society also require such updated information, at times, for their academic activities.

This indicates that there is great demand for local government information for diverse kind of users. Now no single information centre could provide all needed information to such diverse categories of local government information seekers, nor any other co-ordinated agency can satisfy all the dispersed information seekers.

3.4 *Need for a DLGIC*

As said earlier the main rationale for establishing DLGIC is the scattered availability of local government information and the complexities in its easy accessibility to policy makers, local functionaries, media persons, researchers etc. Local governance and planning are interdisciplinary and complex activities, which require knowledge and information from diverse disciplines and sources. A huge body of such basic development information emerges from research and development institutions like Centre for Water Resources, Development & Management (CWRDM), Centre for Earth Science Management (CESS), Centre for Development Studies (CDS), Kerala Forest Research Institute (KFRI), Tropical Botanical Garden Research Institute (TBGRI), Kerala State Land Use Board (KSLUB), Kerala Agricultural University (KAU) etc. But because of the non-availability of such information in a digestible and comprehensive manner at any centre, the local development functionaries many a times cannot have access to the required information. As well, the form of those information materials may not be understandable to a layman. So such information and knowledge need to be collected and made available to the local functionaries in a manner easily usable by them. In short, the DLGIC will act as a facilitator, which bridge the gap between the available body of information and its users.

The ongoing computerisation of local bodies is another strong reason that substantiates the need to have a digital information centre for local governance in Kerala. The DLGIC is also expected to collect all other information on local bodies obtainable from State Election Commission (SEC), State Finance Commission (SFC), Directorate of Panchayat, Directorate of Municipalities, all local bodies in the state and other relevant organisations.

4. Components of DLGIC

DLGIC shall have the following four sub-systems.

Media Conversion System : Media conversion sub-system digitises various kinds of information and stores in digital databases. Media conversion operation consists of scanning, digitising, compressing using different coding methods and indexing and hyper linking for easy retrieval.

Storage and Retrieval System : Digital storage and retrieval sub-system shall be able to store variety of information containing millions of data items and hence require large storage capacities preferably using optical disks.

Location Service System : Location service sub-system shall have pointers to identify other libraries having similar information and will be able to mediate between the users and real digital libraries that hold information.

Offline Retrieval System : Offline retrieval is also essential for a digital library, as it would help to those who have no time or online connection to the networks. In such cases the information pertaining to their search can be obtained as a batch job and can be delivered to the users E-mail box.

4.1 *Equipment and other infrastructure required*

The equipment and other infrastructure required for the information centre are :

- Copy stand with dimming fluorescent fixture.

- High resolution digital camera (1600 X 1200) 24 bit colour SCSI - 2 connector.
- Custom mounts for different materials to position the document without irrelevant motion.
- Spot colorimeter or photometer.
- Windows 98 workstation with large capacity storage with Ethernet.
- Adobe Photoshop machine with 128 MB RAM high storage and with Ethernet.
- Server class Unix/Linus SCSI machine with RAID having 20 GB.
- Fijitsu 3990, full duplexing, 600 DPI page feed scanner attached to Pentium II PC.
- Database management system software.
- Webserver.
- CD-ROM writer for Back-ups.
- Adobe captura for machine conversion software.
- Exclusive Internet connectivity using VSAT.
- Large storage back-up device.

4.2 *Structure of DLGIC*

The DLGIC can function as part of KILA library, which may contain printed documents as well as electronic information. The DLGIC shall have connectivity with the Internet and the proposed computer network of local bodies and shall function as a facilitator of information among these networks.

5. Creation of DLGIC Database

DLGIC rely mainly on secondary information sources available as text in various centres. The textual materials to be included in DLGIC can be scanned by high quality digital scanners and be included in the server in digital form. These textual materials shall be made easily searchable by using powerful search software.

5.1 *The Information or Database Contents of DLGIC*

Panchayats Raj and Nagarpalika Acts amended up-to-date.

- Rules framed under the above Acts.

- Other Acts connected with local government and related rules.
- All orders issued by various governmental agencies in an easily searchable form.

Authoritative reports on decentralisation :

- Balwant Rai Mehta Committee report.
- Ashok Mehta Committee report.
- Administrative Reforms Commission Report of 1957.
- State Finance Commission Reports.
- Naik Committee Report of Karnataka.
- Sen Committee Report etc.
- Panchayat and Nagarapalika Acts of other States.

Statistical Documents :

- Census - wardwise.
- Statistics for planners.
- Annual Economic Review.
- Statistics relating to local bodies collected from directorates.
- State Election Commission etc.

Technical documents prepared by various institutes in Kerala :

- Resource atlas of Kerala (CESS).
- Agricultural Atlas of KAU (if completed).
- Water resource atlas (CWRDM).
- Documents on Forests by KFRI.
- Consolidated micro watershed atlas of KSLUB.
- Steering Committee Reports of State Planning Board.
- Other similar information materials.

Some basic documents on sustainable development :

- Agriculture: organic agriculture, vermi-composting etc.
- Industries: Village industries, Khadi etc.
- Low cost house construction technologies, sanitation etc.
- Water conservation, environmental protection etc.
- Development reports of all local bodies.

- A database on all court-decisions relating to local bodies.
- All publications of KILA including reading materials prepared for training.
- A comprehensive collection of best practices in the local bodies all over the country and, if possible, from across the world. For example "Singapore — clean city project" is a best practice worthy of emulation.
- Collection of all newspaper items on local administration using digital scanner.

The above listing is only a tentative one and the essential items need to be worked out in detail after a wider discussion.

6. Services from DLGIC

In addition to providing online access to all the information contained in the DLGIC, it can provide the following services too.

Article alert service on decentralisation : This service shall contain listing of articles on decentralisation appeared in various subject journals, with a short descriptive abstract. This is useful for researchers.

Information package to policy makers : The DLGIC can provide tailor-made information services to policy makers, at times. The package shall contain diverse information and ideas on the specific topic that will serve as a base to take policy decisions. It can be in the form of "background materials" given to MLA's along with the bills for legislation by the legislature secretariat. Hard copy of this can also be brought out and that can be made available to users not accessible to network.

Online newspaper clipping service : The newspaper cuttings collected and composed into pages can be released over Internet and even hard copy can be printed and distributed for others. This can be an excellent saleable publication.

Electronic publication of documents: DLGIC can prepare and distribute copies of documents such as rare reports, acts, etc. in CD-ROM, in case copyright violation is not involved. It can, as well, prepare many status reports on specific topics concerned with local governance.

Online public access catalogue : Online Public Access Catalogue of books, journals reports standards etc. of the KILA library with access points like authors' name, title, publication year, subject and title key words and abstract of the documents. This will enable the users to have document search to be done by author's name, title, publication year, keywords etc., sitting at their nodes.

7. Resources Required

Since this is a very complex task, it is necessary to engage a consultancy organisation to prepare a detailed project report for planning and operationalizing this digital information project. Indian National Scientific Documentation Centre (INSDOC) is a suitable consultancy organisation for the purpose.

7.1 *Human Resource*

The project may require:

- two development specialists as Research Associates.
- two EDP Assistants for computer work.

It is necessary to have an expert having development knowledge and information technology perspective as project adviser during the gestation period of the project.

7.2 *Estimated Expenditure and Source*

- KILA's own funds and facilities.
- Specific project fund available for the purpose.

The exact details of estimated expenditure could be worked out only after preparing a detailed project report utilising an established consultancy agency.

Recurring items :

- Salary for project staff.
- Administrative support services.

- Training for project staff.
- Information Technology consumables.
- Stationery and Printing.
- Software packages.

Non-recurring items

- Equipment.
- Furniture.
- Packages.
- Storage facilities.
- Physical facilities.

7.3 *Development Phasing*

Phase I	Preparation of project report by consultants.
Phase II	Purchase of equipment. Appointment of staff. Creation of physical facilities. Development of software. Creation of database. Operationalising the project.
Phase III	Continuance of the information services.

9. Conclusion

In the area of local governance, information activities have become a vital capacity building measure in our knowledge-based society in these years. KILA can revolutionalise the process of local governance and implementation of local planning in a big way by creation of DLGIC which provide pinpointed, exhaustive and expeditious information service to the local functionaries. Thereby KILA can become an active partner in the process of local level development of the State.

REFERENCES

Borgman and Bates, *et al. Social Aspects of Digital Libraries*. Final Report to the National Science Foundation, Computer, Information Science, and Engineering Directorate. Available at http://www.gslis.ucla.edu/DL.

Clifford Lynch and Hector Garcia-Molina, *Interoperability, Scaling, and the Digital Libraries Research Agenda:* A Report on the May 18-19, 1995 Information Infrastructure Technology and Applications Digital Libraries Workshop. National Science and Technology Council. Available at http://walrus.stanford.edu/diglib/pub/reports/iita-dlw/main.html.

Definition and purpose of a digital library (URL;http://sunsite.berkely.edu).

Donald Waters, *The Digital Library Federation*: Program Agenda. Washington, D.C.: Council on Library and Information Resources, 1998.

Drabenslott, Karen M. *Analytical review of the library of the future*, Washington : Council Library Resources, 1994.

Preserving Digital Information. *Report of the Task Force on Archiving of Digital Information*. Washington, D.C.: Commission on Preservation and Access and Mountain View, CA: The Research Libraries Group, 1996. Available at http://www.rlg.org/ArchTF.

Venkadesan, S. and A. Narayanan. *Digital library initiative in an Indian Research Library:* An experience report. Proceedings of the Conference on Recent Advances in Information Technology October 28-29, 1999.

18

Scope and Challenges of Geo Information Management for Decentralized Planning

RADHAKRISHNAN NAIR AND HARIDAS P. NAIR

Development of a region depends largely on its strategy for effective management and utilization of natural resources, both renewable and non-renewable. To accomplish this, reliable and accurate spatial and non-spatial information on the land and land resources and various processes involved in the evaluation, upgradation and degradation of these resources is a basic requirement. This information constitutes the 'geo information' which has a wide spectrum of application in resources evaluation, development and management. The economic growth of the State depends largely on the wealth of its natural resources and the manner in which those resources are developed and managed to meet the growing demands of its population. The land and biomass resources of the State with its very high density of population is under tremendous pressure. The competing and often conflicting demands for its natural resources has led to frequent non-judicious use of its resources, which in turn has resulted in severe damages to the environment in many parts of the state. This situation is manifested in the degradation of land and its resources. In this context optimal management of our resources becomes crucial. This calls for the collection, processing and dissemination of the geo-information on the desired manner and usable form. The policy makers, planners and mangers of development programmes should have facility to access these information.

1. Geo Information Usage in Kerala

Systematic efforts have rarely been made so far to collect, process and store the spatial information on the land resources in the State. Many departments and agencies in the State work to generate data in their respective area, more or less in an isolated manner. The scale and coverage and mode of collection of data are also not uniformed in nature. No efforts are seen made to integrate these studies. The decision makers and planners are depending mostly on the non-spatial, statistical data for their needs in development planning. As a part of the national programme of Integrated Mission for Sustainable Development (IMSD) in Phase I and II the erstwhile Remote Sensing cell which now stands upgraded to Kerala State Remote Sensing and Environment Centre of the Land Use Board in collaboration with the National Remote Sensing Agency, Government of India, have completed the systematic survey and data collection in three districts and three water sheds in other three districts. The scale of spatial data in this programme is 1:50,000. Of these six regions two of the districts are included in the National Natural Resources Information System (NRIS). The target for phase III of the Integrated Mission for Sustainable Development Programme is yet to be fixed. However, it is believed that some more areas in the State would be covered under the phase III of the IMSD. The spatial information with the 1:50,000 scale is capable of providing data support for regional planning purpose.

2. Panchayat Resource Mapping

The Panchayat Resource Mapping Programme of the State which was started during 1990 with a target of building up database for geo information in a large scale format for the entire state within a period of three years could not achieve the target and was discontinued. The programme which was initially carried out by the Centre for Earth Science Studies is being re-organized to be implemented by the State Land Use Board. The project designed as a participatory programme would collect spatial data of land resources on a 1:4000 scale. The data collected in three layers on completion would provide the database for micro-level that is de-centralized planning.

The status of geo-information in the state is summarized in Table 1.

Table 1

Location	Mode	Scale	Themes	Status	% area to state
District		1,50,000	6	Hard copy	5.1
Kasaragod	Remote Sensing				
Palakkad	—	—	—	Digitised	11.2
Thrissur	—	—	—	To be digitized	7.8
Watersheds					
Thrikkulam	—	—	—	Hard copy	.31
Perambra	—	—	—	—	1.1
Ranni				Hard copy partial	2.9
Panchayat	Partici-patory				
167 CESS	Ground survey	cadastral	2	—	5.8
	—	1:4000			
10 LUB (Recognized)	—	—	3	—	.97

3. Information for Decentralized Planning

In the context of the decentralized planning in Kerala need for sound geographical information system is very high. The nature of requirement of the scale and pattern are also varying in the context of three-tier Panchayats and statewide planning. For state and district level planning spatial information on 1:50,000 is an acceptable scale whereas the Block and Grama Panchayat would need a scale of 1:4000 or 1:10,000, and not one smaller than that. This would necessitate generation of twotier information system one with the state and districts and other for Block and Grama Panchayat.

The potential of GIS as Management Information System and Satellite Remote Sensing as a tool for gathering information is not fully explored in our state. Both these fields are closely connected with development of information technology (IT). Here we will discuss: how best these technologies can be applied in our context? Since Satellite Remote Sensing technology generates information rather than analyzing it, we have to first consider the potential of the remote sensing for resource mapping and how closely it is connected with developments in information technology.

4. Satellite Remote Sensing

It is an accepted fact that the only constant thing in information technology is change and to stand firm we have to run fast. This is somewhat true in remote sensing field. Ten years back digital image processing was a tool of few privileged groups. We needed to have very costly and powerful mini computers and proprietary software to utilize it. The resolution of data was very low making it useful only for macro level application. The availability of data was also not very easy. We have to depend on foreign satellite for imageries. The whole concept has been changed by IRS series of satellites and advancement in IT. The digital image processing is now very much possible on desktop machines.

The data from Panchromatic band has a resolution of 5.8 metres and LISS III has 23.5 metres. The PAN data is considered as one of the best resolution civilian satellite data available in the world. These high resolution indigenous satellite data can be extensively utilized for collecting information on land use/land cover, geology, geomorphology, groundwater, potential soil conservation, forest mapping etc. With the present status of data and technology available this is best suited for regional, district and state level planning. In the era of decentralized planning micro level information gathering is very important. By the launch of next generation satellites with resolution less than 2 metres our dream of preparing cadastral maps directly from satellite data would be fulfilled. With the available image resolution it is now possible to create maps of various themes in the scale of 1:15,000. The digital image processing of these high resolution data is the contribution of the technological advancement in IT. As the resolution comes down the data become so voluminous. The processing and storage would become costlier. But the many-fold increase in the processing speed of the machines and the nose-diving in the price of front of the desktop machines brought down the cost of data processing and thereby afford the ability of the satellite imagery technology.

5. Geographic Information System

The value of information has a time tag on it. If the information we are getting is delayed the subsequent action will also be delayed, which may negate the whole concept of information gathering. Once the planning process is in micro level the data incoming are inexhaustible. They need to be classified and analyzed and must be put across to the decision makers in the most comprehensive manner. GIS has a role to play as a Management Information System (MIS) with facilities for spatial operation on data. Queries like : Which are the hospitals lie within 1 km of each other, or what is the shortest route connecting two locations? need the help of a GIS package to answer. The concept of GIS to supplement Remote Sensing can be applied to three major sections, viz. inventory, analysis and planning. Initially the application of the technology could be mainly to a complete inventory of the resources available, man made as well as natural.

The advantage of GIS is that we can visualize only required layers of maps and use it for analysis. With the database of geo information integrated with socio-economic input various models can be created in GIS analysis much in advance of actual implementation so as to enable an evaluation by the decision makers. It also can be utilized to create an action plan to improve the productivity of the land, provide information service to farmers on best crops, market potential and various similar matters.

GIS and remote sensing are closely linked with the advancement in IT industries. The leapfrogging in processing speed, networking and telecommunication made things much faster and easier. This advantage which we harvested from developments in IT must be passed to the common man for his welfare. Then only we can claim that the mission of IT is fulfilled.

6. Resource Management

Resource management is a great task which require intelligent integration of different components. Most important components of significance are generation of database, its processing and data upgradation to make it computer compatible for storage, value addition and dissemination of informaion. It is important that these are accomplished speedily and in a cost effective manner. Tools like remote sensing can be effectively used for collection of data as described earlier. The data from new generation satellite of IRS.1C provide vide variety of applications.

Data base required for regional planning up to district level could be generated in a time effective manner with the help of the LISS III, PAN and WiFS data of IRS 1C. Besides these data from other source such as LANDSAT, ERS, NOAA etc. are also available. The data collected in different layers could be digitized and processed in a GIS environment to make required value additions and work plan extraction. Through data linkage and suitable networking the data and information could be disseminated. This can be accessed by the planners and decision makers in the District and State levels. The NRIS programme make this concept operational in two districts in Kerala — Palakkad and Thrissur.

7. Data on Block Panchayat

The Kerala State Remote Sensing Environment Centre has created the geo information on a scale of 1:50,000 for Attappady Block of Palakkad District. The different themes of land use, slope, drainage density, and hydro geomorphology, soil and land capability, transport network etc. were prepared and interpreted. The data digitized for interpretation and action plan was generated in a GIS environment with a powerful package. Through this it was made possible to access, analyze and visualize the information of the study area. Map 1 & 2 show an action plan on land and water resources of Attapady Block, Palakkad District.

The data needed for micro-level planning would be managed by the resource maps prepared under the Panchayat Resource Mapping Programme through processing and value addition in GIS environment. Depending on the information need these maps can be enhanced with additional layers of information other than those included in the present programme.

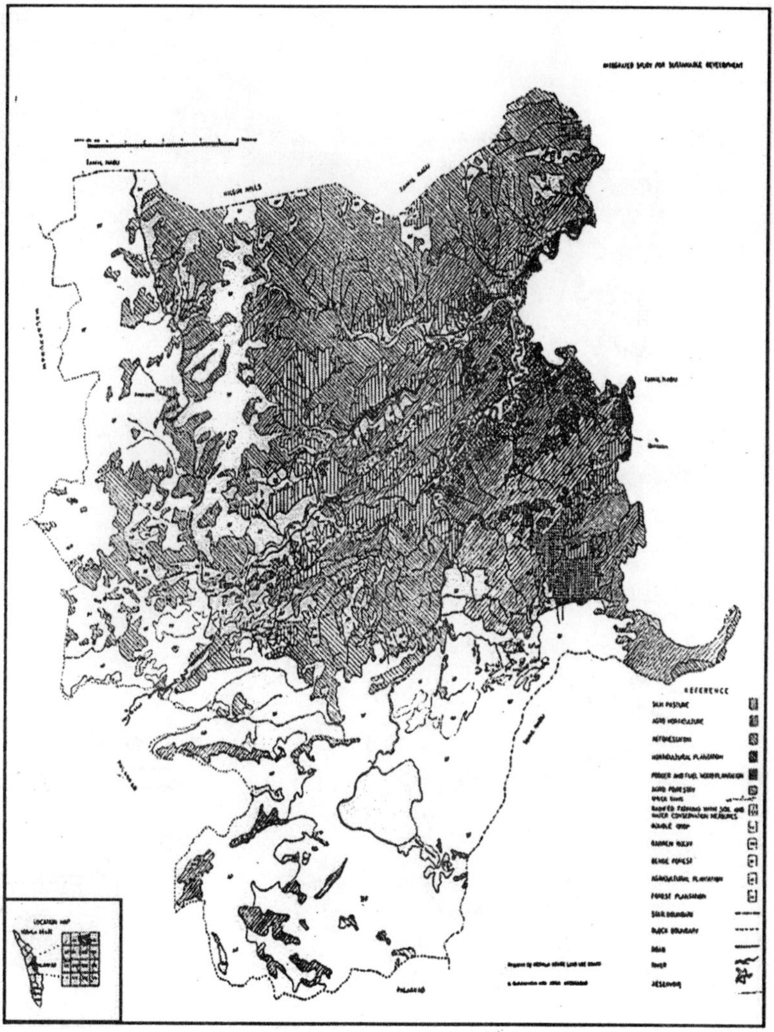

Map 1: Action Plan: At Toppody Block Palakkad District.

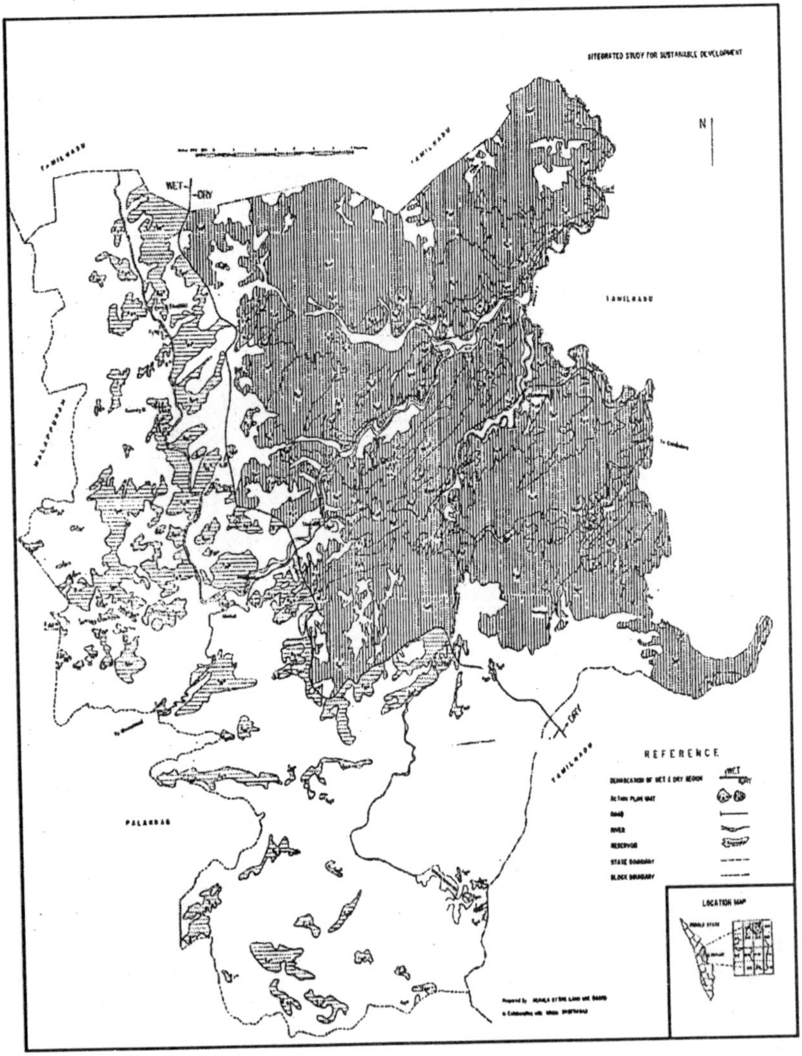

Map 2: Action Plan: At Tappadi Block Palakkad District

8. Immediate Concern

The challenges of immediate concern in the field are mostly the non-availability of a reliable spatial database of required scale for the entire State. There is a need to generate such spatial database without much loss of time. Data base on 1:50,000 scale for the remaining part of the State, other than IMSD areas has to be created. The status of large scale data is more pathetic.

The technology for processing, value addition and access to the database requires to be made in an easy to operate and customer friendly mode.

Facilities to impart required training is limited at present. This has to be adequately enhanced. Data linkage and networking; enabling easy access to end-users must be brought in. The need for making it more cost effective is also a very important need.

9. The Possibilities

A very favourable environment prevails in Kerala for providing a sound geo information facility. This could be accomplished in a phased manner starting with the District and State level. The database and geo information system in the Panchayat could be taken up in the next phase. Making optimum use of the potential of satellite image processing and analysis and value addition in the GIS environment; it would be possible to start building up of a sound geo-information system.

19

Geographic Information System for Soil Resource Analysis at District Level

N. SAIFUDEEN

A Geographic Information System (GIS) is a specialized data management system designed for the entry, analysis and display of the data commonly found on maps. This paper is meant to stimulate the delegates' interest in GIS/RS applications so that they can contribute to sustainable management of natural and built-up resources. Basic introduction of a GIS is provided. A case study conducted as part of a project titled "An assessment of stressed ecosystems of Thrissur district of Kerala" is presented. An indigenous GIS package and dBASE III plus software were used for preparation of a digital database (spatial and non-spatial) of the land/soil characteristics of Thrissur district and integrating the same into a Geographic Information System (GIS). SRI-Thrissur (Soil Resource Information of Thrissur district) is now ready for analysis and generation of thematic maps.

The management and development of any area (panchayat, district or state) requires a large amount of information for project planning, implementation, monitoring and evaluation, and the analysis and monitoring of natural resources. The application of Geographic Information System (GIS) and Remote Sensing (RS) technologies for the establishment of a district level natural resources database will help to integrate many/different sources of data that can be used for assessment and monitoring of natural resources in the area, and for analysis and formulation of appropriate solutions to different resource management and development problems. Access to results from these analyses, within the limits of time and resources, can lead to better decisions that will facilitate smooth implementation of the project and encourage wider participation of the people.

1. Concept of a Geographic Information System

A Geographic Information System (GIS) is a specialized data management system designed for the entry, analysis and display of the data commonly found on maps. This computer-based system requires special software, hardware and procedures to store and manipulate geographic information. This technology has developed so rapidly over the past three decades that it is now accepted as an essential tool for the effective use of geographic information in many areas. GIS has a crucial role in understanding and dealing with some of the most pressing problems of our time; problems like deforestation, climate changes, land degradation, land slides, natural resources depletion, urbanization, to name a few. GIS technology helps us organize the data about such problems and understand their spatial associations, and provides a powerful means for analyzing and synthesizing information about them.

Data on resources and environment are, in general, available, but they are dispersed among many agencies and cannot be quickly compiled for multi-sectoral, problem-oriented analyses. Thus, the ability to respond to the information needs of planners and decision makers is limited. The strength of GIS is its ability to integrate data from various resource disciplines, using a common geographical boundary of reference. These computerized systems which can store, manipulate, display, and produce geographic (spatial) information integrated with statistical and textual data, are becoming the most useful and powerful analytical tools for resource planners and managers.

2. Application in Regional Development

GIS and Digital Elevation Models along with GPS (Global Positioning System) are used for different types of applications, e.g. regional resource inventory, planning and management, hazard assessment, modelling of the ecology, climate or hydrology and geomorphology, in the sense that activities like location of a development project, construction of a road, harvesting of timber from forest plantations, or the location of a natural preserve can be better assessed and managed using GIS methods.

Remote Sensing (RS) is now playing an essential role in data gathering, rectification, and updating in many GIS applications. In fact most of the remotely sensed data are now used chiefly within the context of GISs. The information obtainable from remotely sensed data is not only more effective when used within a GIS, but the GIS can also be used to improve the accuracy of the remote sensing analysis.

As far as a soil resource inventory is concerned, the basic pre-requisite, i.e. a physiographic map of the area concerned, is prepared usually with the help of satellite imageries. Moreover, real time data of land use patterns, which are included in soil surveys, can also be derived from an imagery. The application of GIS for soil resource management studies has opened a new era in cartography, database management and integrated analysis systems in India.

3. Land Resources of Kerala

Kerala state presents a great challenge for the application of GIS because of its diversity in landforms, as well as its uniqueness in physical, biological and societal systems. The physical characteristics of Kerala's environment (hills, midlands, plains) are more complex than many other states and need to be analysed using three-dimensional approach or similar methodology in order to arrive at an appropriate representation of the aspect, slope and topography.

Lessons of the past have shown that the strategy for agricultural growth has to be based on the conservation and improvement of soil productivity. Soil is one of the most important factors in maintaining ecological balance and so sustainable development. Soil is characterized by the manifestation of the effect of all other natural resources, viz. vegetation, climate, physiography, geology, hydrology, etc.

Though the term "soil resource" has a restricted meaning compared to "land" or "natural resource", every crop growing on the "land" is planted or sown into the "soil" and it makes a big difference whether the soil is good or bad. That is why the International Society of Soil Science was given the mandate for land resource research (following UNCED of 1992), and the NBSS & LUP and other soil science research centres are doing the same in India.

Scientific appraisal and analysis of available land resources are prerequisites for their rational utilisation. ICAR (NBSS & LUP, AISLUS, etc.) and the Kerala Government (Soil Survey Wing of DOA, KSLUB, CWRDM, CESS, etc.) has institutional arrangements for this and for the study of various components of the ecosystems that are supported by these resources. Nevertheless the disciplines under land resource research in the state is not yet streamlined to suit the kind of technological advancements and research systems achieved by developed nations/states.

4. Land Resources Information

A project entitled "An assessment of stressed ecosystems of Thrissur district of Kerala" was sanctioned by the Department of Science and Technology, Government of India under the Natural Resource Data Management System (NRDMS), for implementation in the Kerala Agricultural University. The project activity started with effect from 1st July, 1996.

The scope of the project is to build up part of a district information system (soil-related land resources) that would enable the decision makers, and private organisations to better visualise existing natural and infrastructural situations; integrate natural science and socio-economic data and use the information thus gained for improved area-specific planning, programme monitoring and monitoring of natural resources.

5. District Taken for Study

Thrissur is known as the cultural capital of Kerala State. Geographically the district is centrally located and occupies an area of 3030 km^2 out of the total 38,863 km^2 of this state. Population of the district exceeds 27 lakhs, with a density of 903 per km^2.

Physiographically, the district comprises land features ranging from sea coast to high ranges. Taluk-wise distribution of natural regions is given on next page.

Consequent to the variation in land forms, the land use patterns in the district is diverse; ranging from mixed-cropped homesteads to large plantations and undisturbed forests.

Taluk	Area in hectares		
	Low land	Mid land	High land
Talappally	—	48650	17650
Thrissur	10811	40912	11844
Chavakkad	20183	3243	—
Kodungallur	12512	1978	—
Mukundapuram	3038	59897	68663
Total (Thrissur district)	46544	154680	98157

6. Resource Materials on the District

GIS is capable of holding and using data describing places on earth's surface, and are characterized by two forms of data: geographic information, spatial or locational, contained in various kinds of maps and attribute data, e.g., statistics or textual, contained in tables, lists, catalogues, etc. Basically a GIS differentiates between geographical information of three different types; areas/polygons (e.g., land use, soil units), lines (e.g., rivers, roads, drainage systems), and points (e.g., houses, markets, schools) which are then connected to the attribute data. The major group of spatial data set identified for the current project is the distribution of soil-related land resources.

6.1 *Soil Map and Reports*

A soil map of Kerala at scale 1 : 250,000 which has been completed by the National Bureau of Soil Survey and Land Use Planning (NBSS & LUP) was the base resource material for digitizing and assessment. The map and accompanying reports were collected and the data pertaining to the present project were extracted. Descriptive legend and the area covered by each soil map unit in the district are given in Table 1.

Out of the 38 map units identified in the said soil map of Kerala, 16 are present in Thrissur district. The 16 soil map units are distributed in 50 polygons in different parts of the district. Morphological description of typifying pedons of the dominant and subdominant soils of the 16 map units as well as site descriptions have been collected. Chemical analysis data of these pedons were also tabulated. Altogether there are 30 sets of data (32-2 rock lands) available for the 16 map units. However, only the data pertaining to dominant soils were used for generating GIS database.

Since this particular map was intended to analyze soil resources of Kerala at a small scale (1:250,000), this is more useful for interpretations at a macro level. The present project was initially prepared to cover the state of Kerala as a whole, for which this map is very useful. However for interpretations at a district level as approved by the DST, a soil map at a large scale would be a better resource material. But we have to initially depend on this map since it is the only completed document available.

6.2 *Secondary Data*

Survey of India toposheets, maps provided by the department of Survey and Land records, Kerala, and the publications of various organizations like Kerala State Land Use Board, Centre for Earth Science Studies, etc. were other resource materials for the study.

6.3 *Primary Data*

Soil profiles were examined and samples were analyzed to fill data gaps and to collect additional data.

7. Geo Referenced Area Management

Although there are several software available for GIS activities (PC ARC INFO, MAP INFO, SPANS, IDRISI, etc.) the present project activities are undertaken with an indigenous software — GRAM (Geo-Referenced Area Management Version 2.0). This is a PC based and raster based software package which runs on personal computers, and developed by the Centre of Studies in Resource Engineering, IIT, Mumbai, under the Natural Resources Data Management System (NRDMS) of the Department of Science and Technology, Government of India.

7.1 *Map Digitization*

The analog soil map of Thrissur district, which was extracted from the soil map of Kerala, was converted to digital format, using the GRAM-software, and a Summagraphics — Summagrid IV digitizer. There were fifty polygons where the spatial dimensions of the sixteen map units were distributed within the district. The digitized map was corrected for digitization errors, and then rasterised, using the POL-FORM and POL-RAS modules of GRAM. Each polygon in the map was assigned a number which would facilitate linking of attribute data to the polygons. This computerized map formed the spatial database for the project.

8. Database Design and Development

An attribute database on the soil and land qualities pertaining to the sixteen map units (50 polygons) were prepared. The development of a format for digitisation of available data, coding of the different parameters, and preparation of soil resource databases were major tasks accomplished. The description of various attributes (land and soil qualities) pertaining to the map units were organised as relational tables using dBASE III plus software. These information layers include site descriptions, general soil features, taxonomic classification, physico-chemical characters, etc. Tentative formats have been developed for collection and compilation of data under different headings. Guidelines developed by the NBSS & LUP, ISRIC and the NIC have been consulted for this exercise. There are certain variations in the method of rating and coding between NBSS & LUP and ISRIC. Sample codes being followed are presented in Appendix I of this paper. Such ratings were developed for several attributes describing soil/land qualities. These are being refined and perfected.

9. Soil Resource Information of Thrissur District

The project envisaged preparation of a digital data base (spatial and non-spatial) of the land/soil characteristics of Thrissur district and integrating the same into a Geographic Information System (GIS). Necessary databases are now ready for effective land resource analysis. The GIS components will be used to make an assessment of soil and climatic stresses in different parts of the District, to demarcate areas with specific stress conditions for crop production and other land uses (salinity, acidity, drought, flood, laterisation, etc.) and to provide early warning indicators. Land evaluation techniques will be used to measure the extent of degradation and to suggest mitigatory measures to retard or reverse soil degradation in the district. Field checks will be conducted on the stress conditions identified. Maps showing potential land use for Thrissur District will be prepared.

Considering the present initiative of the Government of Kerala on decentralized planning at Panchayat level, an attempt will be made to organize the data bases at Panchayat level so that the products of the project will be available in the region on demand after completion of the project.

GIS technology has already become in developing countries a part of the decision support environment of everyone who makes decisions that affect either the natural world or the built-up world. If our country also is to harness GIS that technology must be more widely known, more widely understood, and more widely appreciated.

Table 1 : Soils of Thrissur District of Kerala

Map symbol	Description	Area ha (%)
	SOILS OF THE LOW LANDS	
K01	Very deep, moderately well drained, sandy soils with moderately shallow water table on very gently sloping subdued sand dunes, with very low AWC and slight erosion *(Mixed, Aquic Ustipsamments)* association with very deep, moderately well drained, sandy soils *(Mixed, Typic Ustipsamments)*	24303 (8.02)
K02	Very deep, some what excessively drained, sandy soils with moderately deep water table on very gently sloping beaches, with very low APC and slight erosion *(Mixed, Typic Ustipsamments)* associated with very deep, moderately well drained, sandy soils with moderately shallow water table *(Mixed, Aquic Ustipsamments)*	7069 (2.33)

(Contd.)

Table 1 : *(Contd.)*

Map symbol	Description	Area ha (%)
SOILS OF THE LOW LANDS		
K03	Very deep, very poorly drained, clayey soils with moderately shallow water table in nearly level broad valleys, with high AWC and slight erosion *(Fine, mixed, Typic Tropaquepts)* associated with very deep, imperfectly drained, clayey soils with moderately deep water table on very gently slopes *(Fine, mixed, Eric Tropaquepts)*	37274 (12.31)
K05	Very deep, imperfectly drained, clayey soils with shallow water table on level lands with valleys, with high AWC and slight erosion *(Fine, mixed, Typic Dystropepts/Aeric Tropaquepts)*	10852 (3.58)
K07	Very deep, imperfectly drained, clayey soils with shallow water table on level lands with valleys, with high AWC and slight erosion (Fine, mixed, Typic Kandiustults) associated with very deep, well drained, gravelly clay soils with moderate surface gravelliness (clayeyseletal, kaolinitic, Typic Kandiustults)	39071 (12.90)
SOILS OF THE MIDLANDS		
K08	Very deep, moderately well drained, clayey soils with moderately shallow water table in nearly level narrow valleys, with high AWC and slight erosion *(Fine, mixed, Typic Dysropepts)* associated with very deep, imperfectly drained, clayey soils with moderately shallow water table on nearly level lands *(Fine, mixed, Typic Tropaquepts)*	6873 (2.27)
K09	Very deep, well drained, gravelly clay soils with moderate surface gravelliness on moderately steeply sloping laterite mounds, with low AWC and moderate erosion *(Clayey-skeletal, kaolinitic, Ustoxic humitropepts)* associated with deep, well drained, gravelly clay soils on gentle skioes *(Clayey-skeletal, kaolinitic, Ustic haplohunults)*	23.40 (0.77)

(Contd.)

Table 1 : *(Contd.)*

Map symbol	Description	Area ha (%)
	SOILS OF THE MIDLANDS	
K11	Very deep, well drained, gravelly clay soils on gently sloping midland laterites with valleys, with low AWC and moderate erosion *(Clayey, kaolinitic, Ustic Kandihumults)* associated with deep, well drained, clayey soils with coherent material at 100 to 150 cm on gently slopes *(Clayey, kaolinitic, Typic Kanhaplustults)*	16784 (22.66)
K17	Very deep, moderately well drained, loamy soils with moderately shallow water table on very gently sloping lands of Palghat Gap with valleys, with high AWC and slight erosion *(Fine-loamy, mixed, Typic Ustropepts)* associated with deep, well drained, gravelly loam soils with coherent material at 100 to 150 cm on gently slopes, moderately eroded *(Fine-loamy, mixed, Typic Haplustalfs)*	9274 (3.06)
K31	Very deep, well drained, gravelly loam soils on steeply sloping medium hills with thick vegetation, with medium AWC and moderate erosion *(Fine-loamy, mixed, Ustic Humitropepts)* associated with very deep, well drained, clayey soils on moderate slopes *(Clayey, mixed, Ustic Palehumults)*	26410 (8.72)
K32	Deep, well drained, loamy soils on gently sloping low hills with isolated hillocks, with high AWC and moderate erosion *(Fine-loamy, mixed, Ustic Humitropepts)* associated with deep, well drained, loamy soils with coherent material at 100 to 150 cm n moderate slopes *(Fine-loamy mixed, Ustic Haplohumults)*	12723 (4.20)
K33	Deep, well drained, gravelly clay soils on moderately sloping medium hills with thin vegetation, with medium AWC and severe erosion *(Fine, kaolinitic, Ustoxic Humitropepts)* associated with rock outcrops	21960 (7.25)

(Contd.)

Table 1 : *(Contd.)*

Map symbol	Description	Area ha (%)
	SOILS OF THE MIDLANDS	
K35	Deep, well drained, gravelly clay soils with coherent material at 100 to 150 cm on moderately sloping isolated hillocks, with medium AWC and severe erosion *(Clayey-skeletal, maolinitic, Ustoxic Humitropepts)* associated with moderately shallow, well drained, gravelly loam soils with coherent material at 50 to 75 cm on very gently slopes, moderately eroded *(Fine-loamy, mixed, Ustoxic Humitropepts)*	855 (0.26)
K36	Very deep, well drained, clayey soils on moderately steeply sloping high hills with thick vegetation, with high AWC and moderate erosion *(Clay, mixed, Ustic Haplohumults)* associated with deep, well drained, gravelly loam soils on gently slopes *(Fine-loamy, mixed, Ustoxic Humitropepts)*	16784 5.54
K37	Very deep, well drained, clayey soils on moderately sloping foothills with high AWC and moderate erosion *(Clayey, mixed, Ustic Palehumults)* associated with very deep, well drained, gravelly clay soils on gently slpes *(Clayey, mixed, Ustic Haplohumults)*	615 (0.20)
K38	Very deep, well drained, clayey soils on moderately steeply sloping high hills with thin vegetation, with high AWC and moderate erosion *(Clayey, mixed, Ustic Palehumults)* associated with rock outcrops	13127 (4.33)
	Water bodies	4710 (1.56)

Table 1 : *(Contd.)*

Map symbol	Description	Area ha (%)

Soil classification according to Soil Taxonomy (USDA) is given in parenthesis. Soil temperature regime is isohyperthermic.

REFERENCES

FAO, *Geographic Information Systems in FAO*. Rome: FAO 1988.

Heywood, D.I.; Price, M.F.; and Petch, J.R., 1994. Mountain Regions and Geographic Information Systems: An Overview. In Price, M.F. and Heywood, D.I. (eds.), *Mountain Environments & Geographic Information Systems*, pp. 1-23. London: Taylor & Francis Ltd.

Nair, K.M., Shivaprasad, C.R., Nagabhushana, S.R., Srinivas S., Ramesh M., Raghumohan, N.G. and Sehgal, J. (1996) *Fertil. News*, 41, 21.

Appendix I : Sample Codes for Soil Attributes (Attribute : Diagnostic features of horizons)

No.	Code	Description	No.	Code	Description
1	at	abrupt textual change	27	NA	natric
2	al	albic material	28	FR	fragipan
3	am	amorphous material	29	PC	petrocalcic
4	fa	ferratic properties	30	PG	petrogypsic
5	fe	ferric properties	31	Pl	placic
6	gi	gilgai	32	SA	salic
7	or	high organic material content	33	SO	sombric
			34	SP	spodic
8	sa	high salinity	35	SU	sulfuric
9	hy	hydromorphic properties	36	AN	anthropic
10	if	interfingering	37	HI	histic
11	pf	permafrost	38	MO	mollic
12	sg	plinthite	39	OC	ochric
13	sl	slickensides	40	Um	umbric
14	sc	smeary consistence	41	PA	plaggen
15	k	soft powdery lime	42	DU	duripan
16	su	sufidic material	43	OX	oxic
17	ta	takyric	44	co	COLE
18	ir	thin iron pan	45	cl	paralithic contact
19	to	tonguing	46	cf	petroferric contact
20	ve	vertic properties	47	li	lithic contact
21	AL	albic	48	mo	mottles with chroma < 2
22	AG	agric	49	nv	n-value
23	AR	argillic	50	tx	thixotropy
24	CI	calcic	51	we	weatherable minerals
25	CA	cambic	52	du	durinodes
26	GY	gypsic	53	PE	petroferric

20

Role of Rural Libraries in Participatory Development

R.P. Alha

Rural libraries will be the centres of knowledge and information which can play a vital role in the development in the context of decentralized planning and development. The information required for the rural population like better health, water supply, sanitation, government policies, crops production, animal husbandry, natural calamities, culture, other social problems etc. will be provided by their rural libraries; for which in traditional societies or the expected networked society of the future no other alternatives are there. It is therefore very essential to establish rural libraries in each and every village of India for effective implementation of Rural Development programmes and all information technology policies and plans for establishing information infrastructures should see them as the most important development agencies.

1. Rural Development Initiatives

India is the 7th country in the entire northern hemisphere. The main land extends between altitude 8^0 4' and 37^0 6' north, longitudes 68^0 7' and 97^0 25' east and measures about 3,214 km. from north to south between the extreme altitudes and about 2933 km from east to west between the longitudes. It has a land frontier of about 15,200 kms. The total length of the coastline of the mainland, Lakshadweep islands and Andaman and Nicobar Islands is 75166 km. [India - 2001].

As per 1991 census the total population of India is 84630 million, out of which 629 million live in rural areas (74.3% of total population).

The total number of villages in India are 5,87,810. It is evident that the majority of the population live in rural areas. The overall literacy rate in India is 52 .21%. Among the population, male and female have 64.13% and 39.29% literacy rate respectively. 48 % people are living in illiterate conditions. Government of India implements Five-Year Plans for the rural development since independence. The different kinds of programmes that are implemented for the benefit of the rural population are Community Development Programme (1952), Intensive Agriculture District Programme (1960), Intensive Agriculture Area Programme (1964), and Small Farmer's Development Agency, Marginal Farmers and Agricultural Labour Rural Work Programme (1970), renamed as Drought Prone Area Programme (1973), Accelerated Rural Water Supply Programme (1972), Desert Development Programme (1977), Command Area Development Programme (1974), Tribal Area Programme, Hill Area Programme, Integrated Rural Development Programme (1980), Training of Rural Youth for Self-Employment Programme (1979), Crash Programme for Rural Employment Pilot Intensive Rural Employment Programme, Food for Work Programme (1997), National Rural Employment Programme (1988), Minimum Needs Programme, 20-point Programme, Western Ghats Development Programme, Special Programme for the North-Eastern Region, Special incentive programme for the industrially backward areas, Rural Labour Employment Guarantee Programme (1988), Development of Women and Children in Rural Areas, Wage Employment Programme, Jawahar Assurance Scheme (1989), Employment Assurance Scheme (1993), Supply of improved tool kits to rural artisans, Million Wells Scheme (1985), Members of Parliament Local Area Development Scheme (1993) and Ganga Kalyan Yojana (1997).

2. Uninformed Beneficiaries

It is an accepted fact that Information services is a most important factor that contributes to the speed, quality and appropriateness of any development programme. But no programme for the development of the information systems for the people at local level was initiated till now by government. All the above programmes meant for the rural populace went without sufficient information support and information dissemination services which hindered the benefit from reaching the aimed groups fully as envisaged. Due to the lack of information systems and libraries in rural areas the publicity on these programmes have not reached the beneficiaries so that intended population could not take the benefit of these programme.

Hence the concept of rural libraries as community information centres if properly understood and implemented in the present context of decentralized planning and development will be of great relevance in making people's participation real as well as bringing the over all literacy among the rural population which in turn also will influence the effectiveness of development programmes envisaged by the Government of India. Libraries, by their very nature are the centres for the spread of knowledge and dissemination and as such, they can play a very important role in supporting rural development by various means. The rural people needs relevant customized information support and assistance for a better health, water supply and sanitation. They also require continuous updating of their information on government policies, production of better crops, prevention and control of environment pollution, text books related to specific local literature and teaching aids, sports facilities, prevention and control of social problems and other community literature.

When a person living in a village requires some information he will go to his local library which is the easily accessible and nearest institution that can be approached without any procedural difficulties. It is the place where he expects to get most of the essential sources of information for satisfying his enquiry related to studies, profession, or anything. So all the information services of government including the government publicity mechanism for its projects and programmes should function through local libraries where people's information needs are attended. For these reasons it is very much essential to establish efficient reliable rural libraries in each and every village of India. Their should be good inter-linkages between libraries and organizations engaged in rural development.

3. Rural Library Scenario

To many rural people the concept of a library or information centre is somewhat misleading. Many of them even cannot make any difference between a library and a commercial bookstore. Even in states like Kerala were peoples planning and decentralized development are underway, having people with high literacy rate, and strong library movement, libraries are book collections or places meant for cultural activities or political training. In remote areas where the tribal people live the concept of library is allowed with fear and thought of as a demand of a different culture into the local social system. The tendency therefore in remote areas, is outright rejection of what to them is 'modern' which aims at changing their most common way of transferring information which is done by the word of their mouth. Information source originates from such traditional institutions and like the local tea stall, hat bazaar (the public market) and many other places where people gather and exchange information. The transfer of information is done informally with no definite pattern or direction. A considerable amount of information transaction takes place between the rural people households and this also act as a primary source of information. In other words, the information channel starts and terminates with in the supra locality. At present rural libraries are not effectively operated in most of the villages in India. In Kerala also even though 5000 and more village libraries exist which were established by people's own initiative' the people's planning and decentralization programmes have thought of establishing another parallel information system. Kerala's Information technology policy has envisaged nothing for developing the village libraries which have been for more than a century people's information sources; and bringing them into the State Information Infrastructure as local service outlets. Hence majority of the rural population will go on without the essential information on different aspects for development and their informed participation in planning and development.

4. Information for Development

If rural libraries are properly developed and brought into the State Information Infrastructures they can act as nodal centres for the development of rural people in the following ways:

- can create awareness among the rural people about different data sources and information available in the libraries which may help them in preparing local level development plans and encourage them to use such information for overall development of the region.
- can appraise the population and the local bodies regarding the

economic, educational, social, cultural and informational needs of the local people and develop information system for the community accordingly.

- can improve the literacy among the rural people and thus give them confidence and power to decide on their development.
- can provide the people information on agriculture, finance, public hygiene, family planning, legal matters etc. and thus improve the awareness of the people as well as quality of the development programmes.
- libraries in the rural areas will also help to create an awareness among village children and adults on the principles of basic education and increase their knowledge.
- can supply information and reading material directly related to the people's day-to-day activities as well as that required for local administration.

5. Channelizing Information

Since India is predominantly agricultural based nation, much emphasis is being given by Government for overall food security and nutrition to the entire population. This can be attained through the development of precision farming in the villages. The information generated in the research and development organizations and laboratories on agriculture/ animal husbandry/poultry etc. may be percolated to the rural areas through the rural libraries. This will help in increasing the income, jobs and food. Rural population needs local-specific information, which can be achieved through these rural libraries only. Now-a-days Information Technology is fast expanding in all the fields of developments. Thus the state and national level library network of which rural libraries have to become part of will enable access of any information stored in the country through the village libraries and by that they will play a vital role in overcoming the limitations in accessing information hindering the overall development of the rural areas.

6. Records of Information

The rural libraries have to collect information meant for the rural population available in the following types of documents published by government as well as private agencies.

Printed Reports

- Administrative Report
- Budget Report
- Research Reports
- Census Reports
- Statistical Documents
- Committees and Commission Reports
- Plans (Five year plans and annual plans)

Legal Documents

- Judicial Decisions
- Law Reports
- Codes
- Rules and Regulations
- Bills, Digests
- Parliamentary Proceedings (Including reports of Parliamentary Committees)

General Information

- Bibliographies
- Maps
- Periodicals/Magazines
- Leaflets/Pamphlets
- Brochures
- Commemoration and Centenary Volumes
- Tourist Guides
- Charts
- Collected Works
- Microfilms

Government Publications

- Economic Survey
- Gazette/Gazetteers
- Annual Report of Government Department of Public Enterprises
- Notes on Demands for Grants

- Reviews of Economic Trends
- Finance Commission Reports

Local Government Publications

- Report of Local Government—Panchayats
- Panchayat Samitis—Zilla Parishads
- Municipalities, Corporations, Urban Development Authorities etc.

The above literature may be made available to the rural population for their knowledge and improving their skills. Rural libraries can act as nodal centres for pooling all the information generated in that area.

7. Relevance of Information

A village library should be developed as the complete and most reliable collection on that village. It should be able to satisfy any information sought about that village by anyone from anywhere for any purpose; let it be for preparing the economic plan of that village or for doing academic research on that village. It should be able to satisfy any level of information requirement on that village or region. We cannot expect that information regarding the locality will be existing in printed or on any recorded form. Hence it is the responsibility of the village library to record all information on that locality remaining unrecorded and preserve it for the future generations. Now Information Technology provides cost effective and efficient solutions for fulfilling this objective.

8. Electronic Media

Electronic media especially TV/Radio may be popularized and the libraries should show the live demonstration of various agricultural operations, cultural activities, news—national and international, sports, events etc. The rural libraries can act as centres of knowledge dissemination on such aspects. While preparing the Plans for State Information Infrastructures; while formulating Information Technology Policies and while preparing Development Plans of the region the village library and the information system it has to maintain for the locality should be given due consideration. Village library should become the central hub of the information system for the village. All information systems and networks should reach the village library as the final service outlet where those huge expensive infrastructures are to contact people and become useful for them. In this regard it is to be watched with interest and curiosity that even in the highly literate state of Kerala which is proud of the people's library movement government has decided to put information service outlets and Intent Kiosks at panchayat offices and other government institutions in the locality. It will take years for them to realize that computers and communication systems are mere hardware and software and to make them information systems, information which our earlier rural librarians also used to serve with should be there. It should be information of local relevance. The villager will go to the library for information relevant to his needs; his locality. It will be there in the local library. Will it be there in the Information Kiosks provided at the Panchayat Office. If a villager goes there searching information on the colleges where the courses meant for his son will be available the terminal available at Internet service in Panchayat Office will place before him information on lakhs and lakhs of colleges in America or Australia. Not even information on a single college in his region, even in his state will be there. But the local librarian may be able to provide it even now with his broken chair and rat eaten books kept in the dark humble building which you call rural library. If he was provided simple training and if the concept of library was understood by the big men who devised plans, Information Technology could have yielded a thousand times more than what it gives at present.

9. People's Information System

Rural libraries can act as a nerve system of the Indian Societies. The information can improve the intellectual ability and power of the rural workers. The lack of correct information affects the decentralized development. The developments of information technology and electronic media can surely improve the efficiency of rural libraries and indirectly improve the people's health, financial powers, and so promote rural development and national integration. Therefore the main thrust of our development plans should be that the libraries must be established in all the rural areas and thereby bridge the information gap between urban and rural communities. Rural libraries can play a vital role to reduce the illiteracy among the rural people. Thereby, they can understand the provisions made in the government policies for there upliftment and fight for the effective implementation of the programmes. The quality of the rural libraries must be upgraded from time to time with the latest techniques. However, to achieve this gigantic claim, the government should support the rural libraries. There should be a proper coordination among all the libraries and professionals in India to bring success. It is finally opined that the quality of the rural people can be improved through the establishment of rural libraries, which will connect the rural people to the external world wherefrom they can derive the desired benefit. Finally, the rural libraries will improve the socio-economic conditions of the rural people. Participation of people in planning and development will become real only if there is an efficient mechanism for collecting, organizing and disseminating information to the people and for protecting their right to information. In the national, and regional level information infrastructures content relevant to the regions are to be developed in digital form for which there is no other alternative than libraries. In all these aspects and for enabling the harnessing of information which is the most important resource and power of the present and future no institution can replace a rural library.

REFERENCES

Balaji, V., Rajamohan, K.G., Pandey R.R. *et al.* The Information Village Experiment in Pondicherry. *Information Today & Tomorrow*, Vol. 19, No. 4, 2000.

India, *Govt. of India 2001: A reference Annual*, New Delhi: Publication Division, Ministry of Broadcasting, Govt. of India, 2001.

Md. Hanif Uddin: The Role of Rural Libraries in the Rural Development of Bangladesh. *IASLIC Bulletin*, Vol. 45 No. 3. September 2000.

Manalan, Jesudas and Swaroop Rani, B.S. (2001); "The Use Pattern of Government Documents". *University News,* Vol. 39, No. 7, 2001.

Sunder Raj, D. *People's participation in rural development,* Kurukshetra, Vol. 48, No. 5, Feburary 2000.

21

Information Management for Rural Development

SAJAL KANTI GOSWAMI

Rural areas account for nearly seventy-four per cent of India's population and have the largest concentration of the people living below the poverty line. Illiteracy rate is also higher in rural areas. Progress of the nation depends on all-round development and unless development plans and programmes consider the rural people also with the same importance given to others as well as provide the necessary facilities for people's participation in development we cannot achieve the nation's objectives. Improving the overall quality of life in the rural areas require effective and result oriented planning supported by proper management of information. For this information systems should be application oriented. This paper attempts to show the present information sources that can support rural development and the need to manage them effectively.

1. Development of the Weaker Section

Grassroots level is the primary unit of planning. Projects at this level are to be taken on systematic basis covering a specified area. Various operational programmes have been taken by the Government for rural development. There are presently a number of programmes for rural development run by both the Central and State Governments to provide better life and social justice. All the development progammes are designed aiming at maximum socio-economic benefit of the weaker section. Some of the programmes listed here are taken up by the Government during last five decades.

- Integrated Rural Development Programmes
- Jawahar Rojgar Yojana
- Indira Vikas Yojana
- Minimum Needs Programme
- Development of Women and Children in Rural areas
- National Rural Employment Programme
- National Rural Landless Employment Guarantee Programme
- Training of Rural Youth for Self-Employment
- Programme for Rural Education
- Small Farmers Development Agency
- Council for Advancement of People's Action and Rural Technology
- Rural Water Supply
- Integrated Rural Energy Planning Programme

2. Lack of Awareness

Due to lack of information on the above schemes it is found that the beneficiaries are hardly aware of these programmes. Publications and publicity materials that introduce these programmes are lacking or they are not reaching the expected beneficiaries who are to avail these programmes. Officials are also not aware of most of these programmes as well as they are not having information with them to provide on site when it is requested. Centres where people may go for getting information on such programmes, like village offices, Panchayat offices, rural libraries etc. are not supplied with sufficient information materials on these programmes. Basically we have no good information system to support the weaker section of the society. All these have hindered the above programmes achieving their objectives and the result was waste of resources or its mismanagement.

3. Project Implementation

In the Panchayat system Gram Sabha is the lowest level and the implementation of the schemes are started from this level. Grama Sabha has various powers and in certain fields of action they may exercise their own judgement, initiative and administrative skill.

Though government has taken so many rural development programmes, they have not fulfilled all requirements and also it was difficult to extend the plans and programmes to remote areas. So non-governmental organizations are engaged in various developmental works to fill the gap.

4. Information Requirement

Management of Information is also to be based on an action plan. An action plan is the primary prerequisite to plan and implement a programme. In order to increase the facilities an action plan is to be taken on the basis of the following aspects.

- Demographic feature
- Administrative division
- Occupational pattern
- Land reforms
- Land utilization
- Agriculture
- Irrigation
- Live stock and Fisheries
- Co-operative credit society
- Consumers co-operative society
- Education: primary, secondary and adult
- Health: primary, intermediate and hospital facility
- Veterinary
- Social welfare activities like child welfare
- Communication facilities, roads, transport, railways, telecommunications
- Financial Institutions: rural bank, land development bank
- Food and nutritional security
- Employment Generation etc.

5. Existing Information Sources

National Informatics Centre was established with a view to provide an effective information system for rural development. It provides information to Government Ministries and Offices to help them in decision making related to socio-economic development, planning and programme implementation functions. Census plays a vital role in the field of village level information. It provides demographic and socio-economic characteristics in each village and town and respective districts.

6. Systems that Need Reform

District information centres were launched by Planning Commission in 1987 to provide information link from State, district, subdivision, block, village levels for both way communication that makes managing development programmes possible. But could not reach the people or become useful for development programmes at lower levels because they are not connected to institutions in Panchayat or village levels or are accessible from village libraries or information centres. In this regard library and information centres play a vital role. Village library can act as a rural information centre. They supply both general information and technical information required specially by technical experts and professionals engaged at grassroots level development activities. The most effective unit that can collect, organize and provide information required for development of a locality is the village library of that locality.

Mass communication plays a vital role in creating among people awareness about the policies and programmes taken by the government for rural development. But its activities should be extended to grassroot level.

7. Rural Documentation

To fulfil the growing need for latest information, regional level information networks are very important. Systems like Centre for Rural Documentation can work as a database and network organization to provide an integrated information service on all aspects of rural Development. Centre for Rural Documentation in National Institute for Rural Development (NIRD) is a national level information centre. In the five-year plan minimum needs programme was introduced with an aim to setup a network of facilities and services in respect of selected items of social consumption within a timeframe. After review it was seen that there are significant differences between the states in this regard.

8. Managing Rural Information

Monitoring information is the main part of managing rural development. The data is to be collected, reports are to be compiled and they are to be analyzed at the district level itself. The findings of these analyses in respect of block and Panchayat have to support action taken at the grassroot levels.

The objective of the Ninth Plan is growth with social justice. Better management needs a hierarchy of information system from state level to village level. Delivering relevant information at the local level is very important. Simple information has no value. For example if a farmer wants maximum utilization of land he needs information on proper irrigation; that is water capacity, fertilizer proportion, high yielding seeds availability, methods of preservation, weather-crop correlation etc. So micro level development requires a system to gather, integrate, compare, analyze and disperse information—internal and external to the enterprise in a timely effective and efficient manner.

In decentralized planning and development it is necessary to establish village level data banks to facilitate proper development of rural people. It is also necessary to guide local library and information systems to develop competence to generate and utilize information at village level.

The concept of data bank or information resource centre at the village level is still missing in our local level development plans. Considering the emergence of various micro level development projects, their specializations and importance, information systems at local level have become very crucial to gear up these projects as well as overhaul their activities.

9. Need for Modernization

Information systems for development requires useful change and modernization in the present context of decentralized planning. Rural information systems will have to provide modern amenities and facilities to develop manpower and skill requirements and fulfil participative management. The administrative structure of monitoring of a system is to be built up at the various levels of the districts. Modern information systems and computer networks as well as access to outside information have become important for rural development. There should be a permanent financial allotment for rural information systems.

Information management for rural development has come to an important position at present. In the coming days electronic information centres at various levels have to play a leading role in development. They have to help to accelerate the concept of both decentralization and distributive justice. In rural areas by collecting, processing and disseminating right information to the right individual at the right time in the right form information support systems will increase the speed and improve the quality of development. It will enable real participation of the people in development.

22

Access to Government-held Information

V. SREENIVASULU AND DR. H.B. NANDWANA

The right to access government-held information is essential to protect democracy. The existing rules, procedures and attitudinal factors for limited access to government-held information sources indicates the types of government-held information required by the people that can be provided under various conditions. This paper will explain the need for giving exemption to restrictions in certain cases of public interest. Though there is a concern for transparency in administration, the bureaucracy considers secrecy a useful weapon to resist public pressure for right to information legislation and tries to dilute the issue by introducing weak classes in the law. The government agencies have also made no effort to publish the data and information held by it which is useful for non-official users and researchers. Information about all information held by government, should be available to the public at any time through government's public relations department or public library systems. Information technology can do a lot to organise government held information and also make it useful for development activities.

A popular government, without popular information, or the means of acquiring it is but a prologue to a farce or a tragedy. Knowledge will for ever govern ignorance, and people who mean to be their own governors must arm themselves with the power which knowledge gives said James Madison. The right to access government-held information is essential to protect the democracy. Government secrecy about its operations endangers individual liberty. There is an emerging campaign to pass laws that would enable citizens to 'know what their government is upto'. The culmination of the fight is the passage of the Freedom of Information Act.

1. Need for Transparency

The following can be considered as the reasons why people should get access to government-held information :

- to know about how government operates, what actions it has been taking, how it has been spending people's money, and what statistics and other information it has collected on development.
- for accountability of the government.
- to provide transparency in administration.
- to facilitate freedom of information.
- to know about the style of functioning of the government.
- to understand the national and regional issues.
- to know the performance of government as well as private agencies undertaking development activities
- to know the status of public issues.

2. Types of Government Information

- Citizens routinely request records relating to prices of agricultural products, pesticides, public health, environmental hazards, consumer product safety, government spending, labour relations, business decisions, taxes history, foreign policy, national defence and the economy.
- The second type of information that citizens often request is any records that the government has about them.
- Socio-economic data include government ministries, departments, offices, public undertakings, universities, research institutions, private firms, individual research workers, etc. and other supports.
- Statistical data, Current events and developments.

4. Sources of Information

Government-held information sources are, administrative records, official records, files, official documents, commission reports, government files, government notifications and circulars, gazetteers and gazettes, government laws and acts, government bills, records, archives, results—population census, agricultural census—census of factories/establishments, sample survey data, institutional sources, public interest documents, office manuals, procedures and rules, and commission reports, committee reports.

5. Access to Government Documents

The following government-held information sources and records must be available for public inspection and copying —

- final decisions in particular administrative cases.
- government's general policies and policy statements that the government uses, but hasn't been published.
- internal manuals written for the government staff that affect members of the public.
- index of the information that will be available to the public for reference.

6. Government Records to be Published

- description of government organisation's structure — Central as well as State government offices.
- description of procedures that are set-up to give the public access to the government records.
- general description of how the government functions and its decision-making process.
- government rules of procedure — including a description of government forms and where one can get them and exemptions.

7. Classified Documents

Government or its agency can refuse to release certain types of information on various grounds.

National security : Defence records which "reasonably could be expected to cause damage to the national security" if disclosed, are exempt. This kind of data usually covers, military plans, weapons and science and technology information that relates to national security.

Internal Agency Rules : Information related solely to the internal personnel rules of the government agency. This is not usually of great interest to the general public, but in some instances the courts have ruled that it is of interest to the general public, and has ordered its release, for example, training manuals.

Business Information : Trade secrets includes commercial or financial information, confidential information, processes or formulas, material protected by attorney-client.

Privileged or Confidential Information : The disclosure of which would make it difficult for the government to obtain necessary information in the future.

Internal Government Memos : Memos or letters concerning confidential communications between an attorney and a client or information compiled in preparation for a trial materials involving advice on recommendations or opinions which are part of the process of government decision-making.

Private Matters : Personal files, medical files, and other files that would lead to an invasion of personal privacy if released are exempted.

Law Enforcement Investigations : Any data that is compiled for law enforcement purposes, which if released, would interfere with enforcement proceedings, constitute an unwarranted invasion of personal privacy and disclose the identity of a confidential source.

8. Information Clearing House

An Information Clearing House should be set-up as a centre, which gives legal and technical assistance to public interest groups, journalists and individuals, citizens using the laws granting access to government-held information and make requests for government files, records as specific as possible.

The cost is the cost of searching for the documents, the costs of reviewing the documents to decide if they should be included in the response to request, the costs of duplicating the documents.

9. Change in Attitudes

The provision of access to information for the people in India will largely depend on the role and attitude of government, particularly the local bodies. The attitude of civil servants towards information should change for the better. Computers can be installed in village libraries, village offices, panchayat offices and administrative blocks of other departments. Softwares that enable digitising, storing and retrieving documents asked for by the people should be used. It is increasingly self-defeating for the government to try to control what information is released or available, and the real challenge is to provide leadership to the process by which people interpret and make sense of that information.

REFERENCES

Bunker Ray. "Where does all money go"? Peoples struggle for information. *Economic and Political Weekly*, 32 (July 12, 1997: 1688-1689).

Donals, C. Rawat. Need for a right of access to administrative information. *Indian Journal of Public Administration*, 36 (July-September, 1990), 603-609.

Noorani, A.G. "The Press Council's Bill on Right to Information". *Economic and Political Weekly*. 31 (December 21, 1996), 3283.

Rawat Need for a Right to Administrative Information. *Indian Journal of Public Administration*. 36 (July-September, 1990), 603.

Steren A. Rossell. Governing in an Information Society. *Technical Forecasting and Social Change* 54 (January 1997), 29-35.

23

Integrated Information Systems for Development

M.A. PRODHANI

Information is considered as the "building block" of the universe of knowledge. In any field of human knowledge information plays the pivotal role if it is available to the information seekers exhaustively, efficiently and timely with full accuracy. The existing information systems in North East India does not serve different categories of people efficiently. There are many reasons for the inefficiency of the system. The primary reason is the inadequate budget and inefficient management system. Information generated in different Central and State Governments and private organizations is not being properly brought to usable forms due to many reasons, specially the financial provisions for the purposes in these organizations. This has direct effect on libraries and information centres in the region. They are unable to provide services to the user community from different fields like agriculture, public works, and allied activities. Moreover, these libraries and information centres are using traditional methods for organizing and managing various information sources available to them. The present study finds out ways and means for solving these problems judiciously.

1. Information Poor

Information is dynamic. It is the life-blood of any system which develops with the flavour of nature. It is the culmination of "mind" over the existing knowledge-base in the "brain" of a human being. Any piece of work done by any human being is dependent on his/her own knowledge-base, and the available formal and informal sources of information. It has been observed that despite the multiplicity of electronic media and improvements in communication facilities, information access in India has not improved considerably. Increasing cost of information products and services, and low buying capacity of libraries and institutions are the major reasons for this deplorable situation. These factors, coupled with a low degree of information awareness, have led to a state of information poverty and this affects areas of human activities including education, research, administration, development, culture etc.

2. Development Information Systems

Information system as a whole consists of many sub-systems related to all possible fields of activities of human being concomitant to nature and its vast resources. These information sub-systems are individually systems by themselves. The present study has been undertaken to examine the agricultural information system in North East India with a view to depicting the status in terms of information resources, organizational aspects, management of information, barriers of free flow of information, and ways and means for improvement of the system for their optimum utilization by all categories of user communities in the region. The North Eastern region of India has vast biotic and abiotic resources. In order to manage the resources for balanced development of the region it is extremely important to organize and manage the huge information generated in different government and private sectors everyday in different formats. Information generated in different information systems have to pass through different stages before being received by the user community.

3. Status of Agricultural Information System

Agricultural information is generated by two groups of people. One group consists of agricultural research personnel, research workers for Ph.D. degree, students for Master's degree, research guides/ teachers and agricultural field workers. Another group consists of the officials of Central and State government departments, and NGOs who have been engaged in many plans and schemes under agriculture and allied fields.

Information generated in agriculture and allied fields are available both in formal and informal mode. Formal mode of information is public and are available through printed and electronic media. Informal mode is private which is based on personal communication with different persons, groups of persons, different organizations both government and non-government, etc. In North East India agricultural information generating system consists of many government and private organizations. Under government organizations, all the agricultural universities, affiliated colleges, research organizations, different research stations/centres on specific fields, Departments of Agriculture, Animal Husbandry, Fisheries, Horticulture, Forest and Environment of all the seven states and expert groups who have taken up various projects/schemes on various selected problem solving fields under Central and State governments, and private sectors, non-government organizations (NGO), many expert groups getting financial support from national and international organizations operating in the region etc. are the generators and sources of information in the field of agriculture and allied activities.

4. Barriers to Flow of Information

In North East region status of agricultural information is very poor in terms of usability, availability and accessibility. Agricultural Information is available in all fields but due to many barriers they are not being utilized by the information seekers of the region. The major barriers to the flow of information in North East region are the following:

- language
- cost of publication
- geographical location
- political interference
- postal communication
- time lag for publication
- lack of transparency of information
- level of understanding

5. Measures for Proper Utilization

Information is dead if it is not utilized by the people and not referred frequently by many. Hence, information generated by the agricultural research systems is practically dead due to its limited utility and non-accessibility of user communities in the region. In order to make the information dynamic it is high time to restructure the system in such a way so that at least 90% of the "gray literature" could be utilized by all categories of user community.

6. Need for Connectivity

The Government should frame some policy which will guide all the information generating systems to make information public in any form and to deposit it compulsorily in accessible places. At least one copy of publications of the agencies referred above in any form should be made available at all the State and Central libraries, university libraries, prominent research organizations, etc., where maximum number of user groups visit for collecting information pertaining to the region. These libraries/information centres should have separate sections for all these publications and they are to be organized region-wise so that whoever wants to get information in any field of activity relating to their region should get them in one place. Presently, almost all the eleven universities in the region are linked up with ERNET (Educational and Research Network) nodes. Information could be used and exchanged with the help of e-mail facilities available with these universities. Many research organizations, government departments, etc. are also having these facilities through NICNET (National Informatics Centre Network) connectivity which helps to utilize these vast sources of information very easily, exhaustively and timely. However, the State Central Libraries in the region are not in a position to have the facility due to very conservative perceptions of the government and the library personnel working in the region.

7. Awareness of the Power of Information

It is high time for the government and all the intellectual groups of the region to understand and realize the value of information. The government should put libraries in the priority list for development so that automated library infrastructure could be implemented. The manpower also should be properly trained to run the system smoothly and efficiently. People should realize that 'information' is power. Any individual or group of people, organization or government, who have huge information base both current and retrospective in any areas of human activity, will be powerful in these aspects. The most prominent and live example is USA. This is the first country in the world which understood and realized the importance and value of 'information' in this electronic age. As a result they developed their information infrastructure very strongly after World War-II. Today, it is surprising to know that for collecting information on multi-farious human activities in almost all the countries in the world, they have more than one thousand spy satellites which are placed in different orbits at various attitudes with different wave bands. Each satellite has its own 'command area' and due to powerful remote sensing capabilities of the satellites they can collect all possible information of various resources both biotic and abiotic of different countries. Moreover, they have a very strong net of spies working in all the countries of the world. They are collecting and passing information continuously to the different expert groups who are analyzing, processing and distributing information very secretly to expert groups in different fields supporting decision makers. Over and above, they have many communication satellites for speedy and instant flow of information to different corners of the world. India is very poor in terms of information generation, information processing and information utilization for even development activities of the country.

Position of other information generating sub-systems in industry, transport and communication, post and telecom, education, tourism, forestry, defence, mining, power, etc. are the same. They do not have any information system in real sense, for proper management of information, which helps to provide information to all categories of user community.

8. Cooperation and Coordination

A system may be open or close. When a system is open it will have links with other systems operating in nearby and remote areas. All the information generating sub-systems must be open so that they are linked up with one another in such a way so that they cooperate with each other in sharing information for speedy development in their own areas. It has been observed that individual sub-systems are not linked up with the different components or sub-sub-system and there is no free flow of information from top-downward, down-upward, laterally and diagonally. As a result all these sub-systems are practically closed. In order to develop them into a viable open system it is very essential now to make them linked up permanently for free flow of information in all the sub-sub-systems in the sub-system. Thereafter, all the identified sub-systems must be linked up for developing a total information system for the region. After having developed such a system, it would be necessary to develop it as a viable well managed regional information system which will able to provide all categories of information to all the information seekers of north-east.

9. Integration and Cooperation

It has been observed that in any sub-system, there is no cooperation and coordination among the sub-sub-systems. As a result flow of information is delinked and all the sub-systems become unaware of individual activities. One of the prominent examples is the continuous digging of roads in Shillong town. It has been observed that if Telecom Department digs road for laying telephone cables and after completion of their work the MSEB starts to dig the same road for laying electric cables. The work of PHD starts immediately after the MSEB work. The same road is dug many times round the year. This kind of activities of various Departments have not only duplicated the same digging work but also spent huge amount of money, manpower and labour. And at the same time these activities put the public in inconvenience. This is one example. The same thing happens in many areas of activity in every region of the country. Crore and crore of rupees is wasted daily for their labour as well as the cost of hindrances to movements and expenses on fuel caused by this duplication of work. There are hundreds of examples like this in all the fields of government operation. This is due to poor flow or non-flow of information from one department to another and the non-cooperation and coordination of these departments. An information system can support government on avoiding similar waste of resources.

REFERENCES

Galinski, Christian. Information and Documentation in Science and Technology in Japan. *Journal of Information Science*, 5, 1982, 63-77.

Ramesh Nair, R. *Priorities in information management systems for agricultural research and development in India.* In proceedings of ILA Conference, 1996, New Delhi, ILA, 1996.

24

Kerala's Unique Contribution to Information Handling in Agriculture

KRISHNAN KANIYAMPARAMBIL

Presently Information Technology and people's right to information are much discussed topics in this country. I understand from the summary of deliberations on Right to Information conducted here presented to me that transparency in administration and using the power of IT to enable that are very important in the present day to maintain democracy in its true sense.

If we refer back to the experience of the past in Kerala we can see that Kerala in a sense missed the bus. The contribution of late Minister T.V. Thomas was very significant in this aspect. He was the person who set up the electronic industry. In fact, he was a pioneer and perhaps only Uttar Pradesh Government was competing with us earlier. But some how Kerala missed the bus. We could not go forward. It is because of the lack of awareness of IT and defective strategy at decision making levels in organizations and government.

Even though a bit late the Government has recently constituted an IT Department and we can hope that we will be able to catch up. Information Technology will be used to protect people's right to know also. Right to Information is fundamental. It is true that information is not accessible to a vast majority of people who need it. But there is nothing new about it. It has been there for thousands of years because those who possessed information deliberately kept it to themselves and never allowed it to pass on to those who needed it. We have to break this nexus between information accessibility and possession and the denying of information to those who need it. A massive struggle is to be organised on this aspect. When we consider the widening gulf between use of IT and facilities for access to information available at the developed nations and the developing world we can see that a new hegemony of information is arising and we have to be vigilant about it. Developed countries know the value of information and they are now trying to hold control of information and knowledge. In any institution or project in any sphere of activity what they do first is to build up an information system specialising on that activity which contributes to their speed, efficiency and quality. We still do not have that nature.

1. Information for the Poor

A massive struggle has to begin, to be launched against the denial of information to those who need it, the masses. Without efficient information dissemination systems at the villages people's participation in planning and development activities will be meaningless. True participation is informed participation. We have to be vigilant about the dangers lurking in the patent bill, which is now currently being discussed in the parliament. There is a need to organise a massive awareness programme and open discussion so that patent bill can be reformed and ensured that it is not affecting the ordinary people adversely. I have listened with interest to the report presented by Prof. Narasimha Raju on the deliberations of this seminar and the conference on Right to Information conducted here during the last four days. Let me congratulate all those who have participated and let me hope that the findings of this deliberations would enable to build up or reform our information systems that can enable the people who are toiling, to have access to information they require, in time when they need it. I am very happy to note that KAU has conducted this four-day programme which included, different seminars, exhibitions, technical demonstrations etc. on the possibilities of IT and how IT can protect peoples right to information; in an apt time. Right to Information Bill is now under consideration. Kerala and other States are establishing Departments of Information Technology. The findings of the seminar can surely guide these developments. The various exhibitions, demonstrations and other programmes conducted here have given an exposure to possibilities of IT in different spheres of activity.

2. Agricultural Information System

At this instance KAU is entering into a new era with the commissioning of the library services we have started from here. The new facilities we have built up at the University Library at Vellanikkara will provide to the university the necessary power to perform well its leaderships role in information handling in agriculture in India. The library that is being dedicated now is one of the foremost in Asia when the facilities, and technology used are considered. In India there is no equivalent to this system. It was designed in a way in which it can harness all possibilities offered by current information technology. It can support the scientist, the teacher, the student and the farmer in their work and improve the efficiency and quality of work by providing required information on current research in agriculture. Its one important division is for farmers; with a huge collection of literature specially prepared for them, exhibitions, video programmes and interactive multimedia programmes that can help them to adopt sustainable methods in farming and animal rearing.

The uniqueness of the facility is that it is not only confined to the elite but also to the masses particularly the farmers and the rural people. With the providing of Vsat connectivity to this library the video films, interactive agricultural training programmes and all the information stored here in the digital library will become accessible to the farmers throughout the state.

3. People's Libraries

We have an unique library movement. Library movement was always in the forefront of the freedom struggle in the state as well as also in the social revolution which has today given an equitable society. In our earlier days the workers of the library movement used to carry literary books on their shoulders and reach out every household. This has played an important part in the revolutionary process by enabling people to have more awareness about the freedom movement. These workers who devoted most part of their life to the movement are responsible for the equalisation society we are having now as well as the high literacy rate about which we are proud of.

The library is a university in itself it is told. This library with facilities for accessing information from the whole universe of knowledge is to be considered university within a university with unlimited powers. It is great asset which can progressively transform the state's agriculture. With the power of IT, it is having to store and disseminate knowledge, this library will be an asset to the agricultural sector not only of the State but of the whole nation. It can by making available latest knowledge from agricultural research conducted all-over the world speed up invention and adaptation of required technology, boost up production and improve quality in all aspects related to agriculture and animal husbandry. More than that it can become a model for university libraries in the country and can take up a leadership role in modernising our libraries and library systems.

Much work remains to be done in many areas. One is in the area of Bio-technology. Bio-technology opens up immense possibilities. With such an unique information system that can support bio-technology research and development also, university is in an apt position to play an active role in this area of research. On behalf of the government I offer all support to the university to play its rightful role in promoting and developing biotechnology and for building up information resource on that specialised area at this centre. Government is confident that Kerala Agricultural University will bring over agriculture to the forefront.

The present government in which I am a member is the most open government. There is nothing to hide and this government is very particular that right to information is ensured. Members of the Legislative Assembly present here will be knowing that I am very particular that within the time limit prescribed the proper answers are given to the questions you make in assembly and Agriculture Department was complemented for this by Hon'ble Speaker.

4. Current Technology

Long delay occurred in establishing this library. In the very basic classes of the Kerala Agricultural University Act of 1971 and Statutes Government has visualised the establishment of a planned Library and Information System headed by a Statutory Officer with specialization to manage it. We could not establish this unit for the last twenty-five years since establishment of the university and the making of the provision in the Act. But the delay in establishing it had in a way done something good also. The curse of Urvasi had turned out to be a boon for Arjuna at a propitious movement. Since we have developed the library recently we were able to make it a high tech system from its base itself which we all can be proud of.

From this library, information on agricultural research kept at any library anywhere in the world can be accessed within seconds. ICAR has in its annual report accepted Kerala Agricultural University Library as the biggest multimedia library coming up in the country. The digital library of KAULIS which is also going to be commissioned here can store in its computer systems 6 crore printed pages as well as educational video and audio programmes of about 60 hrs duration at the first instance. In the library while explaining its configuration Librarian Sri R. Raman Nair has demonstrated to me how 65 students can at a time use this digitally stored information that is text, video, animations and sound files from different parts of the three floors of the building as well as teachers can mix them with their lectures when library network extends through the campus to the class rooms. More access terminals can be provided at the library, class rooms, staff rooms, hostels etc. according requirements of increasing usage. When the university completes its campus Network the information stored here can be used by scientists and students from all institutions and also libraries and hostels of the university in the main campus without visiting the central library. When the VSat and other communication links forming part of KAULIS project are also installed at the library building the information stored here can be used from the eight college campuses and 40 research stations under the university existing throughout the State as well as from any Krishi Bhavans where minimum access facilities are available.

5. Access to the Farmer

My view is that access to this valuable a store of knowledge in agriculture should be open to all people of the State and the country. As State Information Infrastructure is coming up; computers and communication equipments will become available at Krishi Vigyankendras, the Panchayat offices, village offices, village libraries and also at many other local level institutions. Our farmers and people at remote corners of the State will get the power to access this knowledge base. Hence the information stored here in farmer's division and computers of KAULIS should be made accessible online to all the people. This IT based system has the power to extend services to all at all time of the day without any additional expenses and hence this resource should be kept accessible 24 hours a day, seven days a week, 365 days a year so that all the ways through which this knowledge can flow to the farm are not hindered.

6. Agricultural Research Information

I am happy to understand that KAULIS has already acquired in digital form information on agricultural research conducted from 1972 all over the world published in 8500 or more journals, complete publications of 16 international agricultural research institutions from different countries and also many databases. Librarian has explained that the library is having a very good IT training facility where all the possibilities like interactive multimedia etc. will be used for training; and teachers, students and extension activists will be provided training in using IT for their work. This can surely help the university and state to harness the possibilities offered by IT. I know that university could avail technical support for developing this system from national and international organisations specialising in IT aspects. This is surely one the most important contribution of our State to national agricultural research system.

7. Facility for Farmers

For ever we can be proud of designing this unique agricultural library and information system. Let me congratulate Prof. R. Raman Nair and compliment at this instance all those who have contributed to the development of this unique project and managed its successful implementation in this way. It is an entirely new venture for no such big IT projects with similar facilities have ever been implemented earlier in the State or elsewhere. The villager and the farmer should be able to come here and use the literature and interactive multimedia programmes meant for them. They should feel no psychological barriers in using this system. Unless this facility respects the farmer and cares him it will be of no value. Library is not only an institution which transmits knowledge it also helps transparency in everything. The answer to the question in the legislature come to the table in the library. I hope the seminar on this aspect has become fruitful and I hope the findings will guide the university and the nation in various IT aspects.

Let me wish you all a happy and prosperous new year. I have to congratulate all those people who have toiled for developing this library and also complement all those who have worked to make the National Conference and Seminar on Right to Information a great success.

12.11.99 (Minister for Agriculture)

In this occasion (by activating the network system installed here) let me declare that the Kerala Agricultural University Library and Information System is formally commissioned.

25

Information Should Flow to the Farm

K.P. RAJENDRAN

Honourable Minister for Agriculture has mentioned the need for making available the result of research conducted at the university to the farmer speedily and effectively. It was Sri C. Achutha Menon the earlier Chief Minister of Kerala who took initiative in establishing an Agricultural University in the State. Three decades have passed. Situations have changed. At that time there was severe criticism against the establishment of this institution that is Kerala Agricultural University. But people were able to understand the concept and think of the development of such an institution can bring into the agricultural sector of the State. Sri Achutha Menon has conceived every aspect of this university including this library which we are materializing about four decades after it was planned. The Act and Statutes of the University very clearly provides for a unit which will coordinate library and information services provided through the service outlets existing in colleges and research stations at distant campuses of the university. The high tech system we have built up now fulfils his vision. We have to remember him on this occasion.

This library which can transcend the boundaries of time and space to extend knowledge based service should function as an open university, a centre of learning for the rural and farming community. Whatever the system lacks for fulfilling this objective will be provided. Executive Committee and Government will take this matter seriously and will do all that is essential to make the system useful to the people. I am also a library activist. Public Library systems of this region have started using Information Technology for its operations. Trichur Public Library is one which has computerized most of its functions. I remember at this occasion the guidance Prof. R. Raman Nair, Librarian of this university has provided for computerization of Trichur Public Library which is at present ahead of all other Public Libraries in the State in application of IT.

The five thousand and more libraries existing in the villages of Kerala are preparing themselves for modernization. We have the necessary leadership in this sphere of activity. In every remote corner of Kerala you will find a library. These libraries should be interlinked. As Vice Chancellor has stated this university library is having very valuable and costly documents and information resources which an ordinary library cannot afford to acquire and store. We should take initiative to make such information available here accessible to the people. For this, this library should be linked to the village library systems and networks. We should install V-sats and other facilities at the library where information is stored and develop necessary communication links that can facilitate connectivity to this library throughout day and night through Internet etc. so that the resources become useful to the state and information flows to the farm from here through village library networks or State Information Infrastructure.

We know that the system requires at least a minimum number of staff for its functioning. The Executive Committee of the University and Government will surely consider it with all seriousness and we hope proposals for staffing the system if submitted will be considered favourably by government.

This agricultural university is entering into a new phase of development with the inauguration of this library, a facility for bringing information on worldwide agricultural research to our scientists as well as disseminating our research results to the farm. The system will surely facilitate informed decisions and development and hence is to be considered a milestone in the progress of the university to a great institution of the State. The four-day seminar on Right to Information and other programmes on Information handling in Agriculture etc. conducted here has enabled us and the people to view these developments in their right perspective.

26

Protecting Farmer's Right to Information

C.N. Jayadevan

Kerala Agricultural University which is a pride of the State has become the venue for this programme which brought in information scientists from all over the country. On this final session of the four day conference on Right to Information which dwelt mainly upon the role of IT in protecting people's right to information, this prestigious institution the library of the university is going to be dedicated to the nation. It was the wish of all of us that the commissioning of this information system should be on an occasion in which representatives from all educational and research institutions of Kerala is present and the incident gets attention of the people of State for it is an information system that should support the activities and development of our farming community and of the rural people. But being able to commission it in an occasion like this, during a national event on which library activists and information technology experts from all-over the country is present is really a blessing.

1. Reliable Source

If we consider the library facilities in the state as well as the country in comparison with the configuration of this system as Vice Chancellor has pointed out we can find that it is going to be one of the best library and information system in the country. Being a system using current IT, it has the power to provide information services to those from all the institutions in the State. On our areas of specialization and on topics related to the agro-climatic regions covered by the university the information that can be collected and organized at this centre will be a unique reliable and complete source for scientists from all over the country.

It was pointed out here that even though the working of such an institution requires minimum 30 staff members, only four is provided for this institution at present. I hope that Kerala Agricultural University Executive Committee and Government will see to it that necessary minimum staff is provided so that the resource developed is brought into full use.

I understand that different sessions of the last four days have discussed various aspects of people's right to know and the role of Information Technology to make government transparent as well as to make access to information speedy and efficient. Right to Information is very basic for making a democratic system real. India is a democratic country. But still the control of the press and media rests with various interest groups. Hence my view is that the right of the majority of people to know and take informed decisions is not protected.

2. Authentic Information

Discussion on many things of interest to the people reach the people in a distorted version according to the interest of the groups who control the media. Let me cite an example. The views expressed in a recent speech of Hon'ble Minister for Agriculture of Kerala; Sri Krishnan Kaniyamparambil on Mandari delivered at this university reached the people in a totally distorted way to mean the opposite of what he intended. I have listened to his whole speech and it was surprising for me to read as his speech in many papers, what he never told. People of a country have the right to know what those at the helm of power, those at different levels of government, and the organisations in a democratic set-up, and noted people and movement speak, their activities and their views without any distortions.

3. Systems for the People

The government also has the responsibility to let people know in time the developments in science and technology that will affect their life, the changes it brings into different spears of activity. It is government's duty to maintain systems which can disseminate such information and knowledge in a way in which the common man can understand and benefit from it. The lack of this in the present governing systems is a fact. So we have to concentrate more on developing information systems for the people. Unless all views and information on all aspects about a development activity reaches the people concerned, even with their involvement participation is not real. In our country in all fields more transparency requires to be achieved.

Let me express my happiness to be present in this occasion which is to dedicate to the nation this library and information system which is going to be one of the most valuable assets of the university and the country. Let us hope that this system will contribute for protecting the right of our farmers to get timely relevant information for their day to day life and work. Thanks. Namaste.

27

IT Application Crucial in Agricultural Development

JAYA SOORYA

This is really a very auspicious most solemn occasion. Kerala Agricultural University is taking a very long stride in its path of progress by the inauguration of this unique information system. As you all know, in the present world application of information technology is most important factor in the case of scientific research and development. The institution today formally dedicated by our Honourable Minister is one on the best of its kind in the whole world. It is an occasion of grate pride for everybody associated to this project. The discussions and deliberations that took place during the last four days have really helped to find out solutions to the problems faced in managing information as well as disseminating it, protecting people's right to know and for evolving recommendations on applying it for these functions and for ensuring legislation to protect the right to information. About 300 experts on different aspects of Information Technology application, from various institutions in the country have participated in this programme which is a matter of pride to the organizers. At this occasion, being a member of Executive Committee, I have a humble request to Hon'ble Minister. Under the able guidance and leadership of our present Agricultural Minister, not only the Agricultural Department but all the portfolios handled by him and the Agricultural University is making sharp progress in all aspects. It is a fact admitted by everybody. In the case of Agricultural University even though it is an autonomous institution, for financial matters it is having no autonomy. That is a sorry state of affairs. About this institution commissioned today, I am told that there are only five junior library assistants in entry cadre as staff to man this huge institution. If we consider libraries of similar type in other universities of Kerala minimum 25 staff members will be required. There is a total ban on creation of posts. That is applicable to all departments. In the case of research and development especially in cases like that of this system of agricultural university certain leniency is most desirable. More than six crore rupees had been spent to develop this facility. But it is working from 10 a.m. to 5 p.m. like an ordinary office. If the facility and the resources collected here are to be fully utilized by the state this system should function 24 hours a day, 7 days a week. With five staff members, offering any services expected from such a huge system will be difficult. I wish to bring to the notice of the Hon'ble Minister that in such matters a liberal attitude is essential. If Minister thinks, this problem can be solved. Hence, I hope Minister will give help to staff this system on which more than 6 crore had been spent to enable extracting its optimum utility.

Usually Government policies are penny-wise and pound foolish. Money will be there for purchasing elephants but the hook to control it cannot be purchased. This six crore Information Technology project requires only an annual expense of ten lakhs to staff it and generate products and services. I hope our most beloved Minister respected and loved by all will kindly consider my humble suggestion for providing necessary staff to make this resource useful to the people.

Let me once again extend my hearty greetings to the delegates who have visited our State. I hope you will return with sweet memories of this land.

Reply from Honourable Minister for Agriculture

I can understand the staff requirement for this system. You know the difficulties in immediately providing that. Till a proposal could be discussed and approved by Executive Committee and given to Government, for that period my view is to utilize voluntary and temporary service by giving some nominal remuneration. University should immediately do the needful for such an arrangement for the interim period. Students also can be trained and utilized during their leisure time. As Agricultural Minister all my support will be there to find a permanent solution.

28

India's Largest Digital Library to Support Agricultural Sector

K. N. SYAMASUNDARAN NAIR

Hon. Minister for Agriculture, Sri Krishnan Kaniyamparambil who is to inaugurate the plenary session of the All India Conference of Indian Association of Special Libraries and Information Centres and the National Seminar on "Right to Information" and also to dedicate to the nation one of the most advanced Library and Information Systems and certainly the foremost among those in the State Agricultural Universities in this country, respected Chairperson of this session, Sri C.N. Jayadevan, MLA, who is also the Executive Committee Member of the University, Dr. G.S.L Narasimha Raju, who is also to present and brief the Minister on the findings of the Seminar, Dr. Subratta Datta, Secretary, IASLIC, Sri Rajendran, MLA, and Dr. M.L. Jaya Surya who are also the Members of the Executive Committee.

It is with grate pleasure, sense of pride and gratitude that I stand before you to welcome you all to this function. IASLIC has honoured this university by allowing us to host its Eighteenth Conference and National Seminar on Right to Information. After me Professor Narasimha Raju will be presenting the findings of the conference and the national seminar. So I will not dwell upon it. But for the kind information of the Hon. Minister, Sri Krishnan Kaniyamparambil; let me say that over 300 delegates specialising on Information Technology, Information Science, Computer Applications, Library Science and related fields trom all over the country have been assembled here and they have been debating and crystallising some of the vital issues related to the Right to Information. Sir I hope you will agree with me that 'Right to Information' is fundamental to the substances of democracy in this country. Hence we consider this as an important occasion which can contribute to the improvement of the Right to Information Bill which is under consideration of Government. Hon'ble Minister has to perform also another momentous task of dedicating the Central Library of the Kerala Agricultural University.

This Library's facilities are considerable. To those who are looking at libraries only in the traditional manner, perhaps the figures which I doll out will be mind boggling. Sir, this library has a capacity to store 60 million pages of information material on its computer and its digital storage systems. It is a multi-media system in which directly you can interact, you can get pictures, you can get the sound and you can really feel that you are part of the discussions or activities you are viewing from the system, and we have provision for plugging in 65 terminals, so that 65 persons can at a time use this facility and even one page of a document or 65 pages of the same or different books or other documents can be simultaneously used by 65 people. Video programmes and sound files stored here also will be available in the same way.

Sir, We also have during the last three years built up one of the largest digitised information resource collection in the country. We have complete agricultural databases of Centre for Agriculture and Bio Sciences International and National Agricultural Library of USA. We have also the complete publications of such international organizations like I DRC, and the entire CGIAR organizations which consists of seventeen massive institutions all the world over. Now we are also wanting to hook up this facility so that probably with your kind support Sir, in another two three years we will be linking all the forty and odd institutions under KAU from the last village in the Karnataka border Vorkady down up to Balaramapuram. For developing this library and information system we have so far spend about 6 crore rupees on this facility perhaps somewhere about 3.5 crore on the buildings, about 1.5 crore on the materials like digitised documents and what we call the software, as well as 1 crore for hardware needed for this project. Almost 1 crore we have literally got free because the information material we got free has information value of Rs.1 crore. We are also trying to reach out to as many people as possible.

Now with this brief introduction let me now formally welcome our Hon'ble Minister for Agriculture who by his sheer dint of dynamism has helped to provide new dimensions to the activities of KAU. On behalf of the KAU community and also the members of the IASLIC, Sir, I offer you our welcome most warm. Our warm welcome also goes to Sri Jayadevan, MLA,who is presiding over this function, Dr. G.V.S.L. Narasimha Raju and Sri Subrata Datta from IASLIC as well as Sri K.P. Rajendran MLA, Dr. Jayasurya who are members of our Executive Committee.

Sir, seeking your indulgence, may I mention few words. I will be failing in my duty if I don't place on record the monumental work done by my colleague Prof. R. Raman Nair, and his band of dedicated people, but for their enthusiastic and dedicated work probably what we have seen today would not have been realised. I want you sir to place this on record.

Sir, with all this huge building you might be knowing probably, perhaps wondering, that we are managing it with only five library assistants. I am sure our Executive Committee Members, Sri Jayadevan, MLA, Sri Rajendran, MLA and Dr. Jaya Surya would be briefing you Sir, the problems we are facing in managing this massive institution. On this occasion on behalf of all of you I request that we continue to receive your valuable support in really making the full use of this great facility we have created. Once again, I welcome you all; the delegates who have assembled, who have come over here. We are not sure, we have reached up to the expectations but as I told on inaugural day itself we were doing our best possible but we have our limitations. I also welcome to this august occasion the press people here who have been always giving us ample support. Once again I offer my warmest possible welcome. Thank you.

(Welcome Address to the Validictory Session of the IASLIC Seminar and National Conference on Right to Information. 24.12.1998.)

29

Networking of Agricultural Information Centres at State Level

K. VEERANJANEYULU

The library network aims at providing documents, information and services from different types of libraries through participating libraries to the needy users. These libraries may be in different jurisdictions but agree to serve through participating libraries one another on the same basis as each serves its own constituents. Computer and telecommunication are the tools used for facilitating communication among them.

The information is a vital resource for agricultural development also. Its importance to scientists and farmers cannot be overemphasized when we consider the increasing number of information generators and users in the field. We can visualize to a certain extent the magnitude of the problem of collection, organization, and dissemination of agricultural information. Agricultural libraries in Andhra Pradesh are playing a vital role in this direction. However, with the growth of agricultural information, there are very often delays in providing service to the end-users. The cost of providing service is also rising, mainly because of adoption of manual methods and duplication of investments in library holdings.

It has become imperative to share information resources and to go in for networking of agricultural information systems, in Andhra Pradesh. This is possible only by the application of modern information technology. The need for networking of agricultural information systems for Andhra Pradesh has been well recognized but the technology options available till now are limited. This study proposes a network called AP Network.

The AP-AGRINET will cover six Agricultural University Libraries, 6 Regional Agricultural Research Stations, 49 Agricultural Research Stations, 8 major Agricultural Research Institutes established by Indian Council of Agricultural Research and Government of India on specific disciplines of Agriculture and one International Agricultural Research Institute, namely ICRISAT.

1. Existing Agricultural Information System

In the present set-up, the services of several agricultural libraries have been found to be far from satisfactory. The shortcomings observed mainly relates to two aspects. They are : insufficient reading materials, services and funds.

1.1 Insufficient Reading Materials and Services

Most of the complaints received from the users are lack of easy access to information. The problem of providing the required reading materials or sources of information to the readers, with limited financial resources of libraries, is now almost universal.

1.2 Insufficient Funds

Almost all agricultural information centres in Andhra Pradesh are facing financial constraints. Due to lack of sound financial position of the centres they could not provide the required information to the users. The escalation cost of the reading materials, and huge cost of the infrastructure make the agricultural information centres suffer due to scarcity of funds.

The various information services that can be employed in the centres also depend on their sound financial position. The existing information services available in the agricultural institutes of Andhra Pradesh are not adequate and sufficient.

To improve the existing condition of the agricultural information services effectively, it becomes necessary to design a networking model for agricultural information centres situated in Andhra Pradesh.

AP-AGRINET will evolve as a state network of the library and information service centres of the agricultural colleges and research institutions with the following objectives :

- to develop a state resource collection of agricultural literature accessible to agricultural professionals.
- to identify all the potential users of the programme and to be responsive to their scholarly needs.
- to encourage the participants to pool and share their resources so that a usable and exhaustive knowledge resource base required in the field of agriculture and related areas is built-up and the limited funds are thus made to go a long way.
- to facilitate access to other related national and international databases, information centres and networks in India and abroad.
- to overcome time and space barriers in accessing and obtaining the desired document or information through compilation of union catalogue; and promoting faster modes of document delivery.
- to evolve standard and uniform guidelines in techniques, methods, procedures, hardware, software and services to promote adoption.

2. Governing Board for AP-AGRINET

AP-AGRINET is to be housed in Acharya N.G. Ranga Agricultural University, Hyderabad. It will act as Central Information Facility (CIF) which controls other participating libraries. It can be formed with the representatives of agricultural college libraries, Agricultural Research Institution/Station libraries. A fifteen-member Governing Board with the Vice-Chancellor of Acharya N.G. Ranga Agricultural University as the Chairperson and atleast two Principals on rotational basis, for two years, five members from the Agricultural Research Institutes on rotational basis for two years and 4 Senior Librarians from different colleges on rotational basis again for two years, a representative from National Informatic Centre, Hyderabad and the University Librarian of Acharya N.G. Ranga Agricultural University who will act as Member-Secretary for AP-AGRINET governing is to be constituted. The main function of this governing board is to see that the objectives of AP-AGRINET are fully implemented.

3. Hardware and Software

Ideally AP-AGRINET participants may have to go in for Computer system which, have minimum hardware redundancy, have scope for up-gradation, have high computing facilities, are compatible to improved software, and are compatible with other Computer systems.

Exact configurations will, however, depend upon the size of the participant library or information centre. Software required for AP-AGRINET can be grouped under : system Software, Applications Software and Networking Software.

4. Information Communication in AP-AGRINET

There are many options available to connect the different nodes in the network AP-AGRINET participants fall in the Wide Area Network (WAN), where the data transmission rate envisaged is 100 K bps. The appropriate channels of communication could either be dedicated telephone lines or satellite links. The main advantages of the satellite based networks are: reliability, high transmission rate and economy in access to remote locations, etc. AP-AGRINET, being a statewide network may ultimately go in for both satellite as well as leased DOT lines although it could begin its operation with dedicated telephone lines. The exact choice will, however, depend upon the actual traffic flow in the AP-AGRINET.

Until the telecommunication support is made available, the libraries equipped with computer facilities should find alternative to interact with each other through fax, telex, telephone and speed post. The participant libraries of AP-AGRINET may extend off-line bibliographic services to each other based on their local databases. The off-line facility should enable them to enjoy various benefits that includes: consolidate reference service and co-ordinated selection and acquisition.

5. Topology

The nodes, when linked together will form patterns that are classified as star-like topology; tree-like topology; ring topology and meshed topology. The successful topology for AP-AGRINET depends on several factors like funds, trained personnel, hardware, software and communication facilities that continually influence their growth. The number of terminals in AP-AGRINET that have to be connected, can be as follows:

- Agricultural libraries in Hyderabad
- Agricultural college libraries in Andhra Pradesh
- Regional Agricultural Research Stations
- Agricultural Research Institutes/Stations

6. Coordination

The basic configuration of network exhibits a federal one with a decentralized system. The nodes that are Agricultural Colleges and Research Centres act as vital gatherer, store retriever and disseminator of information. Co-operative linkages having electronic communication facility with high degree of co-operation with information professionals, provides scope for Conducive Network for Information Service.

Information resource centres are the heart of information networks. Hence the basic technology required to support an information network is to create in-house database in various institutions. This involves getting compatible record formats and adopting the common communication format, imputing records for various types of information sources and developing search strategies, and vocabulary control for this purpose. On the basis of the examination of facilities available within the State a set of standards in organizing agricultural information retrieval services through AP-AGRINET can be commenced.

7 Standardization

Adherence to standard techniques, procedure and methods is an essential pre-requisite for the effective functioning of an information network. Participating libraries will have to follow certain procedures and practices without which the resources held by them cannot be effectively and meaningfully shared. In the context of library networking standardization in areas like classification, subject indexing and cataloguing of various kinds and types of library materials, bibliographic description, interchange of bibliographic data, search command etc. are very necessary.

7.1 Training

For better results, AP-AGRINET should offer continuous training to librarians in the use of software, hardware and networking techniques. The training process should start as soon as the work on the network begins.

8. Cost-benefit Analysis

By sharing its resources, libraries of AP-AGRINET will benefit a lot. Now-a-days, the cost of the various automation parameters are decreasing day-by-day. So, it is not difficult for any library to buy a computer. Overall, the cost of agricultural libraries in Andhra Pradesh will be reduced by adopting automated systems. The tangible and intangible benefits of the network suggested are listed below:

- the quality and reliability of the database will improve as new entries would be inserted immediately and deletions/updating would not get into backlog.
- due to comprehensive and prompt user services, such as automated SDI, CAS and resource availability through serials control there would be an increase in the utilization of library holdings and reduction in the turn around time for requests.
- resource sharing due to efficient and reliable means of communication would lead to reduced investment in multiple subscriptions.
- improved utilization of the library management's time for planning, organizing, directing and controlling investments and requirements of the user based on availability of timely data and information will become possible.

9. Action Plan

In the first phase the following will be the action plan of AP-AGRINET:

- several on-line access systems should be established in agricultural colleges and agricultural research stations/institutions.
- databases should be steadily augmented for future link with international and national databases, i.e., FAO, CAB, ICAR and IARI.
- the main activity of this phase should be supported by the following steps.
- identifying potential users for each database by institution

designations and names.

- preparing literature on each database, clearly setting forth the scope, coverage and usage characteristics of each database.
- disseminating this information to individual users.
- conducting training and user education programmes for the advantages of accessing database.
- providing cost-efficiency and effectiveness to the end-users and information centres.

In the second phase network can be spread through modem computer, terminal and other network devices to have access at multiple places such as agricultural colleges and agricultural research institutions/stations.

In the third phase end users may compose a target of farmers, policy makers, and scientists to have access to the system. This calls for user-friendly system development. Indigenous databases may have to include a variety of interfacing devices.

In fourth phase information included in the databases should take care of non-published data also such as on-going research, details of survey and official data system as well as CD-ROM and other compact devices may be used.

In last phase development of intelligent knowledge base systems (Expert system) in specified agricultural areas more applicable in specific situations can be designed and provided.

REFERENCES

Akopov, A. Regional Information Network for South and Central Asia (RINSCA). *NISSAT Newsletter* 9(4). 1990.

Borchard, B.H. The three aspects of Library Resources Sharing. *Herald of Library Science* 17(23). 1978.

Bose, Kausik. *Information Network in India: Problems and Prospects*. New Delhi, Ess Ess Publications, 1994.

Dhir, S.C. Network and resource sharing in family planning libraries and documentation centers, *International Library Review*. 12(3). 1980.

Gennaro, Richard De. Library automation and networking perspectives on three decades. *Library Journal* 108, 1983.

Guha, B. A Report on the feasibility study on automation and Networking of Delhi Libraries, New Delhi, *NISSAT*. 1991.

Kalla, Jaagadesh. *Management information systems for agricultural research*, Hyderabad, NAARM. 1991.

Kaul, H.K. *Library Networks: An Indian Experience*. New Delhi, Vurgo Publications. 1992.

Martin, Susau K. *Library Networks. 1986-87*. New York, Knowledge Publications. 1986.

Martin, Susau K. Technology and co-operation: the behavior of networking. *Library Journal*. 112(16): 1987.

Mohan, Surendar. Agricultural Information Networks in India. *Annals of Library Science and Documentation*. 25(1-4). 1978.

30

Information Support for Health Care Under People's Plan

M. CHANDRAKUMARAN NAIR

Although Kerala has achieved considerable strides in health sector, increasing morbidity rates, resulted from increase in life expectancy and low mortality rates, creates problems in health care delivery and planning. The resources are limited and we have many other constraints. This situation warrants need based planning and it is felt that only through an administrative and financial decentralization of health care system, an equitable, efficient and quality health care services can be achieved. People's participation and community oriented approach will be a solution for the need based reallocation of resources and for generating possible local resources. However, efficient working of the health care system very much depends on how comprehensive the data and information are available, accessible and made use of. The main focus of the paper is the establishment of an integrated oncology information system to provide an efficient information support for the successful planning, control, and management of cancer in the state of Kerala in the context of the health care through decentralization under the people's plan.

Health and development as envisaged in the Constitution of India are to be achieved only through eradication of poverty, ill health, malnutrition, poor standard of living, ignorance on the health care issues and by comprehensive management of diseases using modern techniques and methods. Improvement of the quality of life of the society by and large depends heavily on the development of socio-economic living conditions, sanitation, housing, nutrition intake, education, health awareness, etc. Adequate health care has been a priority area of our Governments.

1. Decentralized Health Care

Efficient working of a health care system very much depends on how comprehensive the data and information are available, accessible and made use of. World Health Organization defined the term health as a state of complete physical, mental and social well being not merely the absence of disease or infirmity. If we look at this definition in its true perspective, it can be seen that the health should be viewed as not merely a matter of medical care but the overall care and development of the society in economic, social, cultural, political and other spheres. In this process, the main task is the integration of all the issues with a wider perspective to have an entire transformation of the society. It is at this transformation process that the people's participation becomes an inspiring force and complementary in all respects. Health care activities of the state can very well be initiated and implemented in planning and development through decentralization process. Communities can be mobilized for making improvements not only in the curative process but also in the prevention and control of diseases and for health education. Information is the key resource, which effectively promotes for the success of the entire system.

Cancer is a priority area in any country's health agenda. It is a serious public health problem particularly in developing countries as it forms one of the most common causes of death. It is of special health concern because of its increasing incidence, incurability beyond certain stages, difficulties in early detection, inability to control certain risk factors and high expenditure for the treatment. At the same time one can observe spectacular initiatives in prevention and control of the diseases. As reported by WHO, it is possible to prevent as many as one-third of cancer cases and to cure a similar proportion. Primary prevention focuses on controlling the exposure to cancer risk agents such as tobacco, carcinomic chemicals and certain environment and viruses. One-third of cancer cases can be prevented in secondary level which warrants early detection of the disease through screening camps, mass screening, etc.According to WHO statistics almost two-third of all cancer cases will occur in the developing countries, but they have only 5% of the resources for cancer control. At present, of the estimated 9 million new cancer cases a year, 4 million are in developed and 5 million in developing countries. Our country is also very much concerned of the problems in spite of constraints. Implementation of necessary measures such as education, health awareness, prevention and control, palliative care etc. requires the formulation of appropriate health policies, mapping of local resources, people's participation and community oriented approach. A thoughtfully organized oncology information system is an essential tool for the planning, control and management of cancer and to achieve the government commitment to improve the quality of life of cancer patients and health care.

The establishment of an integrated oncology information system to provide an effective information support for the successful planning, control, and management of cancer in the state of Kerala is essential in the context of the health care through decentralization under the people's plan of Government of Kerala. At present there is a library and information centre attached to RCC and oncology information system will be established here for wider network use.

1.1 Health Crisis and People's Plan in Kerala

Despite the economic backwardness, Kerala enjoys a sound health status. This may be due to the high literacy, achievements in family welfare programmes, maternal and child health activities, irradication of diseases and above all, the social setup and physical environment prevailing in most parts of the state. Kerala's infant mortality rate was 16 in 1995 which is far below the national figure which is 74. The birth rate per thousand in 1995 was only 17.7 as against the national figure 28.8. This is directly linked to high female literacy rate, 86.3 per cent which must have been inspiring force for dissemination of such information. At the same time, the per capita income of Kerala is Rs.2363 in 1996-97 which is behind the National per capita income which stood at Rs.2761. The death rate stood at 6.0 in 1995 against the all-India rate 9.0. The per capita expenditure on health was only Rs.163.12 in 1996-97 which is very high in developed countries. This high health profile of Kerala compared to developed countries prompted the economists to call it as 'Kerala model of health'. However, the morbidity rate is high compared to other Indian states in spite of all health care achievements. This crisis in the health scenario has been rightly pointed out by Panikar and Soman (1984) in their study (Health status of Kerala) who called it as

'Low Mortality High Morbidity Syndrome'. Another disturbing trend is the phenomenal growth of private sector without any standardization in charges and poor quality of service in the public sector.

Improving the quality of health standards is the government policy. The major problem is the shortage of resource constraints. At this stage, the people's plan has significant role to play. The Panchayat Raj now provides ample scope for community participation. Kerala has a three-tier system of health care facilities. As part of the decentralization, Primary Health Centres (PHCs), Community Health Centres (CHCs), and taluk hospitals are handed over to local bodies who can now initiate a number of programmes with the active participation of people and local resources.

Paradoxically to the development indicators such as high level of literacy, health awareness and long life expectancy, low mortality, low birth rate, Kerala faces a problem of high rate of incidence of cancer. It is true that as the proportion of elderly people increases, tobacco use and exposure to carcinogens, certain food habits, changing life style and environment are prevalent, the burden of cancer also will rise. In Kerala, the life expectancy of the males was 67 years and females 72 years in 1995.

2. People's Health Policy

Records reveal that head and neck cancers, lung cancer, breast cancer and cancer of the uterine cervix are the commonest cancers of the males and females. With the active participation of communities and utilization of all the available local resources, it is possible to strengthen the activities for tackling the magnitude of the problem. State Planning Board is in the process of formulating a people's health policy considering availability of resources and health status of the State. The scope of the health sector in the changing administrative and financial decentralization under the people's plan campaign will be multi-focal. They are :

- Mapping of potential resources available in the state.
- Determining the breadth of the cancer spectrum.
- Effective organization of early detection camps and centres.
- Organization of cancer awareness programmes.
- Health education.

- Reallocation of resources and identification of new local resources through direct people's involvement.
- Efficient implementation of Centre's National Cancer Control Programmes (NCCP).
- Collaboration with primary health care workers to facilitate primary prevention and detection.
- Attainment of cordial relationship among health professionals, health workers, patients and people's representatives.
- Cost effective use of Government machinery and financial resources.
- Listing the priority requirements and identification of real beneficiaries of services and resources.
- Control of the growth of private sector and provision of overall equity and healthcare.
- Strengthening the services of the Public Sector.
- Effective utilization of PHC and CHC workers for Community Cancer Control activities. The availability of grassroot level health workers spread over the entire state would be the most appropriate group for this. They just need to carry one more kit to give this message too and for this the local bodies will be the policy making agencies.

Being the key resource for the accomplishment of the above prospects, it is necessary to strengthen the information systems. Information pertaining to all these aspects are to be stored in a usable form.

3. Integrated Health Information System

The genesis of the term 'oncology' refers to 'oncos' the Greek word which stands for 'lump or mass and logos'. The cancer, the malignant growth comes under the broad term 'oncology' which is a science of new growths. Because of its special nature, the treatment policy covers from the diagnosis and initial treatment to terminal care and rehabilitation. Even educating the patient and family members is part of management of cancer. The oncologist include all the five categories, namely radiation oncologist, medical oncologist, surgical oncologist, radiologists and cytopathologists. Apart from the oncologist in general, reliable information is required by the planners, administrators, health workers, patients and people's representatives for planning, evaluation and for other specific requirements.

Cancer centres are few and far between. Because of this the medical community in general is not aware of the developments in cancer management and prevention and control measures. Updating information on cancer is important for cancer control. A variety of valuable information is currently generated on cancer and related facilities, research, prevention and control programmes, epidemiological aspects, patient service and vital statistics which are of immense use in planning, cancer control, research and education. In this proposed set-up, both professional and public collated information from various sources are to be stored in an appropriate format.

The system will have a central server at the RCC library which may function as an apex body as far as the oncology information is concerned. This server can be linked to the Local Area Network at the RCC. The library resources and all the databases to be created in the new set-up will be in the server. The information generated here is to be made available online from the three sub-centres of RCC,viz. Karunagappally, Ernakulam, Palghat and later on from other district head quarters. Another network having Intranet based solution, called, CancerNET-Kerala, is proposed for Cancer Care and Control. Once that is established the information resources at RCC can be linked to that. RCC has the state of art facilities for comprehensive cancer care which is described briefly below.

Regional Cancer Centre, Trivandrum is one of the leading regional centres in this country for comprehensive cancer management and research. The main objective in forming such a centre were to provide referral service for comprehensive cancer management in this part of the country, to conduct basic, applied and epidemiological research in various specialities of oncology and to generate technical and scientific power in all branches of oncology. The centre has several outreach programme which include the Early Cancer Detection Centres (ECDC) in Ernakulam and Palghat and the community oriented programmes, cancer detection camps, anti-tobacco activities, professional awareness programmes among clinicians and other paramedical communities. In collaboration with several national and international agencies like WHO, UICC, IAEA, ICMR, DOE, IARC,

John Hopkins University, many research projects have been taken up by the Centre. The sub-centre established at Karunagapally focuses on studying the health effects of natural background radiation which is high on the population of that region. Now the centre has been designated as WHO collaborating Centre for Cancer control in Developing Countries. RCC is in the process of establishing another Centre for Epidemiology, Surveillance and Preventive Oncology (RESPO) which is the first of its kind in South Asia.

4. Services to Medical Sector

The centre maintains a resourceful research and reference library as one of its divisions. The library houses more than 6000 books and monographs, 3000 reprints and reports, subscribes to as many as 110 journals (mostly foreign), 100 audio video cassettes etc. The collection also includes some of grey literature like pamphlets, small bulletins and other materials being the patient information materials. Apart from the conventional services, the library provides the following services to cater the information requirements of the heterogenous group of users.

- Current awareness services like fortnightly RCCL current contents and quarterly onco news.
- CD-ROM based databases search services.
- Online search facilities in the NICNET.
- Internet search facilities.
- Selective Dissemination of Information.
- Reprint Services.
- Document delivery service.
- Photocopying service.
- Training.
- Compilation of bibliographies on demand.
- RCC publications database.

The infrastructural facilities consists of three computer systems, two photo-copiers including one heavy duty machine, various projection equipments, facilities for audio video cassette screening etc. This information system will contain the following databases.

- Database of monographs, journals, statistical series, reports and other documents and Union catalogue of journal holdings.
- Directory of specialized cancer treatment centres and institutions in India.
- Database of ongoing cancer research studies and programmes in India.
- Patient information service.
- Directory of cancer control programmes at regional levels.

NCCP Centres : Information such as the population covered, various activities and facilities available in connection with the District Cancer Control Programmes (DCCP) being conducted in Medical Colleges, Regional Cancer Centres and other private cancer hospitals.

Public Education Materials : Various Centres have produced useful public education materials in print, audio and video forms.

Professional Education Programmes : Regular training programmes are conducted by many institutions for clinicians, health workers and other professionals and the procurement of related literature.

Non-Governmental Organization efforts : A number of voluntary agencies and organizations are engaged in cancer control, health education and other programmes. Information on these agencies and related literature will be collected.

Hospices and Palliative Care Centres : Terminal care is one of the important health care activities in the Cancer management and on the quality of life of cancer patients. A number of such Centres are working sponsored by local bodies, RCCs and many other agencies.

Early Cancer Detection Centres (ECDCs) : As part of the cancer control programmes, ECDCs are working attached to DCCPs, RCCs, Hospitals, Medical Colleges and other organizations. Information on these aspects will be collected.

Cancer Registry : Information on cancer incidence is collected by the RCC with the help of Hospital based cancer registry funded by ICMR and two population based cancer registries funded by IARC/WHO. The registry in the RCC has generated a host of information from the patient records, which are in the form of case sheets. The salient objectives of this patient data collection are to provide :

- Description of the patient; such as socio-economic background,

family history, food habits, life style, etc.
- Description of the extent of disease. It gives detailed description of symptoms, diagnostic procedures, staging, classification, etc.
- Description of the therapeutic procedures, follow-up results including the quality of survival.

The information generated out of this data will be very much useful for clinical research, basic research, clinical trials, and planning and implementation of prevention and control programmes.

6. Objectives and Methods

How to achieve sufficient health care of a society. What are the barriers? How to manage the disease. The problems are many. In order to tackle this, the medical professionals, researchers, health workers and planners are to be exposed to all the advances and information generated in oncology. The objective of such efforts are to :

- Provide cancer related information to clinicians, researchers, health planners, health workers, administrators and patients.
- Enhance the productivity of health care professionals and reduce administrative costs of health care delivery and financing.
- To provide overall support to cancer research and achieve equity in health care delivery methods of data collection.

Various methods will be used to gather data relating to cancer and its centres :

- Scrutiny of published materials and reports of hospitals, research centres etc.
- Sending questionnaires to various centres and to concerned users.
- The retrieval of relevant information using remote data bases and from relevant websites.

A fully integrated multiuser library software will be used for the computerisation of these activities and services.

7. Client Oriented Information Service

Providing access to information is the main task of a modern library and information centre. Strengthening the information transfer, by making bridges between those who generate the information and those who really require it, is one of the greatest problems faced by the information world. Today information generated at local, regional, state and national level are equally important and in the context of decentralization, the need for local information is growing. In order to handle the issues like cancer, there should be an integrated approach as it necessitates a collective effort of various groups. It includes clinicians, nurses and midwives, medical students, health workers and para medical professionals, teachers, researchers, people's representatives, administrators, planners, patients and family members. Every client needs information which may relate to patient, disease, region, people, health status, food habits, environment, socio-economic background or any other similar aspects. The information system should be capable of answering all such quarries. Delivering effective information service to the client, at the grassroot level should be the task; since at policy level and execution level they may need up-to-date information. Only an integrated oncology information system will be able to respond to cancer information requirements from these various clients.

8. Ideal State for Tele-medicine

1998 is a very special year for the World Health Organization. It was exactly 50 years ago, countries in the world came together and signed a charter which led to the formation of this prestigious organization. In order to fulfil the aims and objectives of the organization, every nation should adopt all possible technologies being emerged from time to time. With wide applications in developed countries, Tele-medicine facilitates access to timely, quality and special medical care available at cities for those who are living in rural and remote areas where, as we all know, health care facilities are inadequate. Kerala is ideal state for introducing such a setup as all districts are being connected together. ISDN service is about to be introduced in Kerala which is required for the efficient functioning of Tele-medicine. VSNL is going to extend a leased line from their Cochin server to Trivandrum for facilitating 24 hours Internet connectivity and high speed data transmission. C-DIT is also in the forefront to provide Internet facility in association with DOT who proposed to set-up 64 KBPS line in each district. Unlike other states, where these developments are prevalent only in major cities, Kerala is far ahead for such applications. It would be highly helpful and exciting if a patient at a remote area get his case reviewed or get his disease diagnosed or get online access to a distant server where all information required by him is stored. It may become a reality in Kerala soon and this will boost the use of oncology information also.

9. Reaching Health to the Poor

The magnitude of the diseases like cancer is a challenge to the society and to face this challenge a number of health care activities are being undertaken at regional, state, national and international level. Still there is tremendous growth in the incidence of Cancer as we found in a recent press report. A group of epidemiologists in Bombay carried out a study and recorded an alarming rise in the case of oral sub-mucous fibrosis (OSMF), a pre-cancerous condition particularly in younger age group. They attributed the rampant use of tobacco in various forms for this condition. This finding corroborates the studies conducted at RCC also. This is a piece of information which, indeed, is an eye opener to any section of the community. Information like this should be disseminated at the right time up to the grassroot level. To make the health care centres work, to evolve an appropriate strategy, and to execute the things in the proper manner, the information, one of our vital resources, should reach them. This is more relevant in the context of people's plan which take up the issue of resource constraint as a major challenge. Recently emerged technologies have a wide range of applications to improve the transfer of information. Kerala is on a fast forward since the Internet is accessible in almost all districts with a local call. Further, it is proposed to set up two 64 kbps terrestrial telecommunication (DOT) lines in each district to facilitate high speed data transmission and for the high quality uninterrupted image transfer. Steps are being taken to link together the village, block, district, panchayat, municipalities and corporations to district/state headquarters for the efficient functioning and monitoring of the people's plan and other programmes. For the comprehensive Cancer Care, the oncology information system at RCC will be more accessible in the above set-up for any remote user which will have significant implications in future, particularly in reaching health to the poor.

REFERENCES

Alarming rise in oral cancer cases. *Indian Express,* November 29, 1998.

Chandrakumaran Nair, M. Management of oncology patient information : application of CD-ROM technology for its optimum use. In *Information technology and health science libraries* : papers presented at MLAI-93 National convention and workshop. New Delhi, MLAI, 1993. pp. 29-39.

Ekbal, B. Decentralised Planning and health sector. In *The people's plan : a debate on Kerala'sdecentralised planning experiment,* ed. by N. P. Chekkutty, Kozhikode : Calicut Press Club, 1997. pp. 3-70.

Gulati, I.S. and Thomas Issac,T.M. *People's campaign for decentralised planning : an experiment in participatory development.* Trivandrum, State Panning Board, 1998.

Kannan, K.P. *Health and development in rural Kerala : A study of the linkages between socioeconomic status and health status.* Trivandrum, Kerala Sastra Sahitya Parished, 1991.

Krishnan Nair, M. and Sankaranarayanan, R., Epidemiologic leads to cancer control in India. *Cancer Cases and Control* 2(3) 1991: 263-65.

Panikar, P.G.K., and Soman, C.R. *Health status of Kerala : the paradox of economic backwardness and health development.* Trivandrum, Centre for Development Studies, 1984.

Kerala. *Economic review 1997.* Trivandrum, Superintendent of Govt. Presses. 1998.

Peoples involvement in health and development of women and children: Proceedings and recommendations of third Regional conference of SEARB, IUHPE, Madras, 1994.

Prabha Chandran. Treating Cancer: the hope and the hype : special survey: *India Today Plus Fourth Quarter,* 1998 : 110-131.

Regional Cancer Centre : *Report of activities,* 1996-97. Trivandrum, RCC, 1998.

World Health Organisation. *World Health Report 1998.* Geneva : WHO, 1998.

APPENDICES

Appendix–I

Report of the Working Group on Right to Information and Promotion of Open and Transparent Government

Introduction

1.1 The working Group was set-up under Government of India, Department of Personnel and Training Office Memorandum F. No. 34011/1(s)/97-Estt.(B) dated January 2, 1997. The terms of reference of the Group included the examination of feasibility and need to introduce a full-fledged Right to Information Act so as to meet the needs of open and responsive Government. The Group was also asked to examine the rules framework with particular reference to the existing Conduct Rules and Manual of Office Procedure with a view to introducing greater openness and transparency in Government working including dealings with employees. A copy of the Government Order dated January 2,1997 is at Appendix A.

1.2 The following officials and non-officials were nominated to the Group :—

Chairman: Sri. H.D. Shourie, Chairman, Common Cause, Members: Sri. Soli J. Sorabjee, Senior Advocate, Supreme Court; Sri S. Narendra, Principal Information Officer, Ministry of Information & Broadcasting; Sri A. Sinha, Joint Secretary, Department of Legal Affairs; Sri R.N. Verma, Executive Director, Railway Board; Sri S.P Ojha, Senior Deputy Director General, Department of Posts; Sri Ashok Kumar, Joint Secretary, Department of Telecommunications; Sri Shashi Prakash, Joint Secretary, Ministry of Home Affairs; Sri N.S. Madhavan, Joint Secretary, Ministry of Information and Broadcasting; Sri Harinder Singh, Joint Secretary, Department of Personnel & Training. Consequent on his transfer Sri Ojha was replaced by Sri V. Saksena on the Group.

1.3 The Working Group was given a time of two months to give its report. However, taking into consideration the complexities of the issues involved, the time given for submission of its report was extended to May 31,1997.

1.4 The Group held six meetings. The Chairman of the Working Group also called on Justice P.B. Sawant, Chairman, Press Council of India to appraise him of the tentative views of the Working Group and to elicit his views on the subject. Similarly Dr. Sundaram, Additional Secretary, Department of Administrative Reforms also called on Sri A.K. Venkat Subramanian, Secretary, Department of Consumer Affairs, to appraise him of the proposals of the Working Group as regards use of the machinery under the Consumer Protection Act, 1986 as an appellate forum under the proposed Freedom of Information Act and to seek his informal views.

The Context

2.1 It is now widely recognised that openness and accessibility of people to information about the government's functioning is a vital component of democracy. In all free societies, the veil of secrecy, that has traditionally shrouded the activities of governments is being progressively lifted and this has had a statutory effect on the functioning of governments. In most democratic countries, the right of people to know is now a well established right created under law. It is a right that has evolved with the maturing of the democratic form of governance. Democracy is no longer perceived as a form of government where the participation of people is restricted merely to periodical exercise of the right of franchise, with the citizens retiring into passivity between elections. It has now a more positive and dynamic content with people having a say in how and by what rules they would be governed. Meaningful participation of people in major issues affecting, their lives is now a vital component of the democratic governance and such participation can hardly be effective unless people have information about the way government business is transacted. Democracy means choice and a sound and informed choice is possible only on the basis of knowledge.

2.2 Modern democracy embraces a wider and more direct concept of accountability — a concept that goes beyond the traditionally well established principle of accountability of the Executive to the Legislature in a parliamentary democracy. Increasingly, the trend is towards accountability, in terms of standards of performance and service delivery of public agencies to the citizen groups they are required to serve. Such accountability is possible only when public have access to information relating to the functioning of these agencies.

2.3 Finally, transparency and openness in functioning have a cleansing effect on the operations of public agencies. As has aptly been said, sunlight is the best disinfectant.

2.4 It bears mention that it is not only the developed countries that have enacted freedom of information legislation. Similar trends have appeared in the developing countries as well. In our neighbourhood, Pakistan recently promulgated a Freedom of Information Ordinance. The new South African Constitution specifically, provides the right to information in its Bill of Rights — thus giving it an explicit constitutional status. Malaysia operates an online data base system, known as Civil Service Link, through which a person can access information regarding functioning of the public administration. There is thus a broad sweep of change towards openness and transparency across the world.

2.5 In our own country, we have not been immune to these winds of change. There have long been demands for greater openness and transparency in administration which have gained momentum in the recent past and a consensus has evolved among the political parties on the need to legislate the right to freedom of information. The Common Minimum Programme of the present Government specifically mentions its commitment to introducing a Bill on Freedom of Information. In their 38th Report on demands for grants of the Ministry of Personnel, Public Grievance and Pensions, the Parliamentary Standing Committee on Home Affairs has strongly recommended that the ministry may take up the matter urgently to facilitate early enactment of a Right to Information. The Government of Tamil Nidu has recently passed an Act for Right to Information. Some other state governments have also taken administrative steps to make information available to public. The Governments of Gujarat, Rajasthan and Madhya Pradesh may be mentioned in this context.

2.6 The Courts too have, in a series of judgements, declared that the right to know is a facet of the fundamental right to freedom of speech and expression enshrined in Art.19(1) of the Constitution— a landmark judgement on the subject being the judgement of the

Supreme Court in *S.P. Gupta* vs. *Union of India* (AIR 1982 SC 149).

2.7 In bureaucracy also there has been an increasing awareness of the importance of openness and transparency. A consensus emerged in the Conference of Chief Secretaries, held in November, 1996, on the need for an early enactment of a law on Right to Information. We also note with satisfaction the various steps taken by the Government such as the issue of instructions on transparency to all Ministries/Departments of the Central Government and a request for similar action to the State Governments, the incorporation of a specific provision relating to transparency in the Draft Code of Ethics for the Civil Services and the initiative to formulate Citizens' Charters in various organisations under the Government.

Freedom of Information Bill

3.1 Even though the need for right to information has thus been widely recognised in the country, and the right has also received judicial recognition, there is no specific law which assures the public access to information. In many quarters apprehensions are expressed about the possible impact of such a law and the costs it might impose on public-agencies in terms of time and money.

3.2 We are of the view that the fears expressed in this regard are often exaggerated. It needs to be remembered that bulk of information that they may have to be supplied under the proposed enactment would already be getting compiled in the public agencies. Secondly, a substantial portion of the costs involved could be recovered in the form of fees to be charged for supply of information. With improved management of information and through adoption of appropriate technology, no public agency should face insurmountable difficulties arising from demands for information.

3.3 We are, therefore, convinced that a legislation for freedom of information is not only feasible but is also vitally necessary.

3.4 We are also of the view that the legislation should be enacted by the Parliament in order to ensure uniformity of its application throughout the country. The question whether Parliament has the legislative competence to enact the proposed Freedom of Information Bill was examined by us. We find that the subject does not fall under ambit of any of the entries in the State List (List II) in the Seventh Schedule to the Constitution. It would, therefore, be covered by entry 97 in the Union List (List I) of the Seventh Schedule — it being the settled legal position that the only limitation on the legislative competence of the Union is that the subject matter of the legislation should not be within the exclusive competence of the State Legislature in terms of List II of the Seventh Schedule.

3.5 Having elaborated on the importance of openness in Government, it is also necessary, to recognise that there would always be certain kinds of information which has of necessity to be kept secret in public interest. In deciding what to disclose and what to withhold from the public, one has to balance the public interest in disclosure with public interest in secrecy on the one hand and public interest in disclosure with legitimate private interest in secrecy on the other. This has been the approach of the countries having legislation on freedom of information.

3.6 In this background, we decided that our approach to the proposed legislation should be governed by the following broad principles:

(a) disclosure of information should be the rule and secrecy the exception;
(b) the exceptions should be clearly defined; and
(c) there should be an independent mechanism for adjudication of disputes between the citizens and public authorities.

3.7 With this approach in mind, we undertook a detailed study of the relevant material made available to us and suggestions received from various quarters. We also studied the legislation in certain other countries. Notably, the laws studied included the Freedom of Information Act, 1966 of the United States of America, Freedom of Information Act, 1982 of Australia, Access to Information Act, 1980 of Canada, the Official Information Act, 1982 of New Zealand and the Code of Practice on Access to Government Information (1997) of the United Kingdom.

3.8 After a detailed study of these documents, we have finalised a draft Freedom of Information Bill, 1997 which is annexed to this report.

3.9 A few remarks may be made about some of the important features of the Bill.

3.10 At the outset, we decided that the most appropriate title for the Bill would be "Freedom of Information Bill". The right to information has already received judicial recognition as a part of the fundamental right to free speech and expression and the purpose in enacting the Freedom of Information Act is mainly to promise a statutory framework for this right. Therefore, in our opinion, the expression "freedom of information" fully reflects the spirit and intent in the proposed legislation. We accordingly decided that the Bill may be called Freedom of Information Bill.

3.11 We believe that there are certain kinds of information that public authorities should, *suo motu,* make available to public. This includes information relating to functions and responsibilities of the concerned organisation, a description of its decision making processes and the statutory/administrative framework within which it performs its assigned tasks etc. In order to facilitate access of public to their records, the concerned organisations should also be required to maintain such records in proper manner. Similarly, there should be a duty to give reasons for decisions and, in respect of major policy announcement, to disclose to public the relevant facts and analyses. The Bill accordingly seeks to cast such obligation on public authorities. We may clarify that, in respect of the obligation as regards maintenance of records, the provision only refers to records that are operationally required and does not seek to impose an obligation to create new records, solely for the purposes of the Act, that are not required for normal operations.

3.12 In view of the wide diversity of conditions of life of our people, we recognised the need to specifically, provide for a facultative function for the officers responsible for providing, access to information. Accordingly the Public Information Officer is enjoined to render reasonable assistance to persons requesting for information. Similarly, where a person is unable to make a written request, the Public Information Officer may either accept an oral request or assist such person to make a written request.

3.13 We also considered it necessary to define clearly the areas of information that should remain exempted from disclosure under the proposed Bill. In drafting the relevant provisions for this purpose, we have kept in view the overriding importance of public interest.

3.14 We also kept in view the possible adverse effect of an

overload of demand on administration and provided that requests for information can be refused on certain grounds such as their being too general or causing a disproportionate diversion of the resources of a public authority. However, a duty has been cast on the Public Information Officer to help the requester as far as possible, to reframe his request in such a manner as would facilitate compliance with it, where it is being refused as being too general.

3.15 While we have provided for charging of fees for access to information, we have also made a provision for waiver of fees where the disclosure of information is in the public interest in order that an individual may not have to bear the cost where the community at large benefits from disclosure.

3.16 While setting out these grounds for exemption from disclosure, we have also incorporated the principle of severability in the Bill. This would ensure that access would be given to non-exempted information contained in a document, which also contains exempted information, if such information can reasonably be segregated.

3.17 We felt that there was need to provide a departmental remedy to the affected citizens first before recourse to an external grievance redressal forum. This would enable quicker redressal in many cases and would also result in filtering of disputes before they reach an external appellate authority. Accordingly, a provision has been made for an internal review of decisions to refuse access to information taken by Public Information Officers.

3.18 As regards the appellate remedy, we felt that there was a clear necessity to provide for an independent machinery for this purpose. We examined the feasibility of providing for appeal to the Courts having jurisdiction over the concerned public authority. We, however, felt that this might not prove an effective appellate remedy considering the state of arrears in Courts and the high cost of litigation. At the same time, creation of a separate machinery would entail huge costs and would also take time. We, therefore, felt that it would be preferable to utilise an existing district level mechanism to ensure quick and economic grievance redressal for the affected citizens. In our view the most suitable institution for discharging the appellate function under the Act would be the machinery created under the Consumer Protection Act, 1986 and a suitable provision has accordingly been made in the Bill.

3.19 While recommending this, we are conscious of the

deficiencies that continue to affect the functioning of these forums in many States. It would be necessary for the Government of India and State Governments to take effective steps to remove these deficiencies, particularly in view of the additional functions proposed to be assigned to them.

3.20 We also discussed at length the question whether the provisions of the Freedom of Information Act should be given an overriding effect or its provisions should be made subject to those of other laws. This was particularly in the context of the fact that even in advanced countries like the United States of America, Canada and Australia, the provisions of such Acts are subject to those of other laws. We, however, felt that the Freedom of Information Act might be frustrated by resort to other legislation unless there is a *non-obstante* clause. Besides, we are convinced that, for freedom of information, it is the provisions of this Act that should be the litmus test since the information that needs to be protected from disclosure would, in any case, be covered by the exemptions provided in it. The Bill accordingly contains a *non-obstante* clause which seeks to give the Act an overriding effect.

Amendments to Other Laws/Rules

4.1 There are certain other laws and rules which may impinge on access of public to information. If Freedom of Information Act is to fully serve its intended purpose, it would be necessary to review all such laws to make them consistent with it in order to ensure that they do not impede flow of information to the public. While the scope of such a review is obviously too wide for us to cover, we reviewed a few important provisions. These were Section 5 of the Official Secrets Act, 1923, Sections 123 and 124 of the Indian Evidence Act, 1872 and Rule 11 of the Central Civil Services (Conduct) Rules, 1964.

4.2 It is the Official Secrets Act that has been regarded in many quarters as being primarily responsible of the excessive secrecy in government. Its "catch-all" nature has invited sustained criticism and demands for its amendment. Section 5 of this Act provides for punishment for unauthorised disclosure of official secrets but omits to define official secrets. We have proposed an amendment to this section which incorporates a definition of 'official secret' and thus remove its omnibus character. The draft of Section 5 proposed by us is at Annexure B.

4.3 As far as the Evidence Act is concerned, we took note of the amendments to the above sections recommended by the Law Commission in its Eighty-Eighth report. We have made a slight change in their formulation and the provisions proposed by us are at Annexure C.

4.4 There is a widespread feeling that the Central Civil Services (Conduct) Rules,1964, and corresponding rules applicable to Railways, Foreign Services and All India Services, inhibit government servants from sharing information with public. The accent in these rules is on denial of information to public. This situation has obviously to change if Freedom of Information Act is to serve its purpose and if transparency is to be brought about in the system. We have accordingly finalised two drafts for the amendment to Rule 11 of CCS (Conduct) Rules. The first can be adopted straightaway, while the other may be adopted once the Act comes into force. The proposed amendments are at Annexures D and E of the Report. The All India Services (Conduct) Rules, 1968, and other similar rules, would also need to be amended on the same lines.

4.5 We also recommend that the Government may entrust the task of comprehensive identification and review of the Central as well as State laws, which may impinge on freedom of information to an expert body, such as the Law Commission.

4.6 In order to make the Act fully operational and effective, it would also be necessary to frame rules to be notified under it. We have confined ourselves to drafting of the Bill. The Government may consider setting up a small sub-group to draft the necessary rules.

Classification of Information

5.1 A major contributor to the lack of transparency is the tendency to classify information even where such classification is clearly unjustified. There is also the tendency to accord higher classification than is warranted. The Manual of Departmental Security Instructions issued by Ministry of Home Affairs, and the Manual of Office Procedure, which incorporates some of these instructions to lay down the criteria and guidelines for classification and specify the authorities competent to authorise classification of grades, viz. Top Secret, Secret and Confidential.

5.2 While the criteria for classification have perhaps necessarily to be broad, it is desirable, in the interest of a proper approach to classification, that they should be backed up by suitable illustrative list for guidance of officers. While drawing up such a list, the principle to be adhered to is that ordinarily only such information, as would qualify for exemption under the proposed Freedom of Information Act, should be classified.

5.3 We also find that, among other things, "serious embarrassment to government" appear as criteria for classification of information as secret and confidential respectively. These are obviously too vague and general and need to be deleted.

5.4 We are also of the view that the level of authority for deciding classification grading should be raised by one level in order to ensure adequate application of mind and well considered decisions.

5.5 We also find that the present instructions do not prescribe any specific period for validity of classification and merely state that a document shall remain classified as long is required. We recommend that a specific limitation on such period may be prescribed and this should be twenty years, excepting cases where a particular information may require to be kept classified beyond this period for reasons of national security/national interest. In such cases the competent classifying authority should be required to record the justification in writing.

5.6 We also note that the Manual of Departmental Security Instructions is itself classified as Confidential. Consequently, it appears that it is not widely available to officers in the government which may be a contributory factor for lack of uniformity and proper application of the prescribed guidelines. We, therefore, recommend that its classification should be downgraded to "Restricted" and it should be freely available to officers at least of the rank of Under Secretary and above.

5.7 Our recommendations relating to amendments to Manual of Departmental Security Instructions are at Annexure F of the Report.

Administrative Measures for Making Freedom of Information Effective

6.1 The proposed Act will not be fully effective unless the Government takes steps to build capacity in its systems to cope with the expected demand for information. There will have to be a substantial upgradation of the management of information in the Government and other organizations covered by the Act. We are informed that the Government, as a part of its thrust in the direction of administrative reforms, have made plans for computerisation of operations. These plans will have to be pushed through with vigour. Similarly, it will need to be stressed to the concerned organisations that they must develop modern management information systems to ensure quick and easy access to information held in their records. We are informed that the Government have already launched a project for public facilitation counters in identified Ministries/Departments with public interface. This is welcome measure and its coverage may be widened as expeditiously as possible.

Training and Reorientation of Employees

7.1 The full potential of Freedom of Information Act would not be realised unless a culture of openness and transparency pervades the Government and its agencies. Such a culture cannot come about unless there is a fundamental shift in the attitudes and ethos among employees. It would be necessary for the Government to make this a central component of the training inputs that it provides for its employees. The experience in other countries which have enacted freedom of information legislation suggests that this is a specialised field and officers need to be properly trained to exercise sound judgement in interpreting the provisions of the relevant legislation while taking decisions relating to disclosure of information. Special skills and aptitudes would need to be developed among officers to ensure that the provisions of Freedom of Information Act are implemented in their true intent and spirit and without jeopardising public interest. It would, therefore, be essential for the Government to develop special training modules for this purpose.

Conclusion

8.1 It only remains for us to thank the government for having given us the opportunity to devote ourselves to such an important task. The Freedom of Information Bill, when passed, will without doubt be one of the most significant milestones in the history of our country. We are confident that the Government will take all necessary steps to bring forward the draft legislation before the Parliament as soon as possible and appropriately during the fiftieth year of our independence. Any measure of this nature requires the widest possible consultation and debate in the community. We, therefore, suggest for the consideration of the Government that they may give wide publicity to our Report and invite reactions from all sections of society. We are told that a Conference of Chief Ministers is being held on May 24, 1997. This may be a good opportunity for the Central Government to circulate this Report and elicit the views of Chief Ministers of the States.

8.2 We would like to place on record our special and profound appreciation of the work done by the concerned officers : Dr. P.S.A. Sundaram, Additional Secretary, Department of Administrative Reforms, and Sri Y.C. Parande, Director, Department of Personnel and Training.

Sd/- (H.D. Shourie), Chairman, Sd/- Soli J. Sorabji, A. Sinha, V. Saksena, Shashi Prakash, S. Narendra, R.N. Verma, N.S. Madhavan, Harinder Singh, New Delhi, 21 May, 1997

(The Freedom of Information Bill and other answers appended to this report are not included in this volume — *Editor*).

Appendix–II

Working Group on Information Technology for Masses Background Report

Background

The last decade of 20th century had witnessed Information Technology emerging as the most prominent technology to have a revolutionary affect on the lives of people across the world. During this period, Indian engineers and scientists have earned a high degree of esteem around the world for their highly professional and innovative contribution to the technological advancements in this field. Large number of Indians occupy senior positions in IT companies of developed countries like USA. Recognizing the contribution of Indian software professionals in USA, countries like Germany and Japan have recently shown interest in hiring Indian software processionals to their countries. On the domestic front also, IT industry has shown highest growth rate consistently over the last many years compared to any other industry. Software exports from India have risen from US$ 50 million to US$ 5 billion during the last five years. Recognizing such a vast potential of IT industry, government has set an ambitious target to raise India's contributions to the IT-industry to the level of US$ 50 billion per annum by 2008 and thus help the nation emerge as IT Superpower in the world. Government is aware that sustenance of such a high growth rate in the long run requires an equally strong and vibrant domestic IT market. Government has, therefore, decided to use Information Technology as a major vehicle for all-round socio-economic development in the country and thus, as a by-product, facilitate creation of a strong domestic IT market.

With a view to facilitate fast paced growth of IT industry in the country, Prime Minister had set-up a National Task Force on Information Technology and Software Development. Based on the recommendations of this Task Force, Government has already implemented number of regulatory and promotional measures to remove impediments and enable the growth of IT industry in the country. With the passage of Information Technology Bill recently in parliament, Government has put in place legislative mechanism in the country to enable large-scale applications of IT in various areas related to day-to-day lives of the people. The enactment of this legislation is expected to act as a major enabler for mass spread of Information Technology in the country.

While Government has been taking number of pro-active steps to promote the growth of IT industry, it is equally conscious that these developments do not create a new division in society, referred to as digital divide by some people divide between those who have access to IT based services and those who do not.

Government is, therefore, determined to see that the benefits of Information Technology do not remain confined to higher classes of Society. In fact Government intends to use IT as a major instrument to provide new opportunities to those segments of society who do not see opportunities to improve their quality of life and tend to reconcile to their fate. It is a firm view of the government that if any technology can create new opportunities to bridge the gap between haves and have nots in society in the present times, it is IT. With a view to give a concrete shape to this thinking, and recommend catalytic, proactive and enabling steps to be taken by the Government to convert this commitment into an operational mechanism, Government has constituted a Working Group on Information Technology for Masses.

Objective and Vision Statement

The overall objective and vision of the Working Group is to ensure that government play a catalytic role in marshalling all resources, including financial, administrative, policy, infrastructure etc. to ensure that the other half of the Digital Divide also enjoys the benefits of IT revolution and not gets left out because of benign neglect and in the process get alienated further from the national progress in IT. The Working Group perceives IT providing a unique and new opportunity to address age-old problems in the field of education, health, rural development, poverty alleviation, employment etc. and be a major facilitator for information transparency, good governance, empowerment, participative management and grassroot democracy. The overall theme of the Working Group, therefore, revolves around steps required to be taken by the government to ensure enabling and empowerment of masses to ensure mass scale spread of IT and its benefits in the country.

Terms of Reference

- To review various schemes and major initiatives taken by various government agencies for taking IT to masses.
- To identify potential areas and applications for deployment of IT for masses.
- To recommend development schemes/programmes for citizen participation for taking IT to masses.
- To prepare a comprehensive plan for taking IT to masses.

Deliberations of the Working Group

The first meeting of the Working Group was held on May 23, 2000. This meeting was planned to be a brainstorming session to freely elicit and discuss the views of the members and invitees to the meeting on various issues related to the theme of IT for masses.

Various Divisions/Groups and associated organizations of Ministry of Information Technology (MIT) have been engaged in number of programmes in collaboration with different Ministries/ Departments of Central and State Governments with a view to facilitate the setting up and utilization of IT based services in the country.

Accordingly, to seek larger participation of these Divisions/ Groups and associated organizations of the Ministry, a meeting with senior officers of MIT was held on May 24, 2000. In this meeting, senior officers of the Ministry had participated and expressed their views on the approach to be followed by the Working Group as well as gave a brief overview of various programmes/projects being undertaken by the Ministry in this direction. Subsequently, a meeting was held on May 26, 2000 with HODs/SIOs of NIC who are engaged in providing IT services to various Ministries of Central and State Governments respectively.

The Working Group plans to meet some of the major government as well as non-government organizations across the country in its regional meetings scheduled to be held during second half of June, 2000.

The Working Group also has carefully studied the recommendations made by the Working Groups on Citizen-IT Interface; Content Creation and Content Industry; and IT-Human Resource Development which were constituted as a part of Prime Minister's National Task Force on Information Technology and Software Development. Number of recommendations made by these Working Groups are relevant to the theme of the present Working Group, IT and masses. The perception of people with regard to term Information Technology and Masses varies from person to person in the country. With a view to provide an appropriate context for these terms, the Working Group had deliberated on the scope of IT for masses before proceeding further with the steps to be recommended for this purpose.

For quite sometime, in conventional terms, Information Technology has been used as synonymous to computers. However, with the rapid advancement towards convergence of various information delivery systems such as Radio, TV, Telephone, Newspapers, Fax and of course computers and computer networks, it has now become feasible to offer IT services using conventional forms of information delivery system. The last five years have seen phenomenal growth in the country with regard to spread of cable-TV network and mobile phones. Their integration with Internet has been a major facilitator of empowering people with information. Internet over mobile phones and cable-TV networks have ensured that the power of information delivered to people through Internet is available even in the remotest places in the country and that too without necessarily requiring computers which have all along been the only device to access Internet.

The Working Group, therefore, looks at Information Technology as a set of media and devices out of which proper solutions can be configured based on the needs and affordability of the target clientele in the country.

With regard to term masses, the Working Group is fully conscious of the extreme variations in classes based on economic status of the people in the country. While 40% of nation's population on one hand continues to live below the poverty line, only about 20% belong to higher and rich classes in the country. The remaining 40%

form a large middle class in the country. Irrespective of such class based divisions in the society, there are sections of people such as women and senior citizens across all classes who are not able to actively participate in economic activities of the country. The Working Group believes that while the needs of higher middle and rich sections of the society can be taken care of by emerging markets, there is an urgent need to examine catalytic and enabling role to be played by the government to ensure that while on one hand 400 million strong middle class people, who provide a very large domestic market for IT products and services, get the benefits of IT in their day-to-day lives, on the other hand for 40% of the people who are living below poverty line, government has to take steps so that IT could provide new opportunities for these people to be able to move above the poverty line.

IT Applications Relevant to Masses

The Working Group has classified IT applications which are likely to have direct relevance to large number of people at different levels in the country into the following categories:

- Electronic governance
- Enabling literacy and education for masses
- Fulfilling local information needs of people
- Enabling better economic conditions of people
- Educating citizens about their duties

Some of the major applications in these categories are described in this section.

1. Electronic Governance

Government and its numerous agencies are the largest service providers in the country. It is obvious that in order to have a visible impact of the benefit of IT on people, government must select major services at different levels such as Ministries/Departments of Central Government and State Governments, District Administrations, Municipal Services and services related to local governance at Block/ Panchayat level, and re-engineer them through extensive use of IT.

While over the years, there has been considerable progress in the use of IT in government services, most of these applications have been confined to back-office computerization. As a result, the improvement in quality of service to public has not made sufficient impact. It is, therefore, necessary that each one of the government agencies involved in providing public-oriented services should identify at least one area and use Information Technology in a highly intensive manner so that all aspects of delivery of service to people should transform into an IT based service. While doing so it would obviously be necessary that for sustainability of good quality of service to citizens, back-office component of the concerned agency for the identified application is fully computerized. However, the approach for computerization and IT induction should be from front-office applications to back-office and not the other way. This will ensure that there is sufficient pressure on the government agencies from public to sustain the quality of service using IT. Back-office computerization alone, which has very little impact on the public interface, is not sustainable in the long run due to lack of such public pressure. Some of the applications, which Working Group would like government agencies at different levels to undertake on priority are:

- Computerization of land records all over the country with computerized land/property documents to be made available to people at all levels including in villages in a time bound manner.
- Payment of bills/municipal taxes.
- Computerization of information related to court cases particularly the ones related to land/property disputes and extensive use of computers in courts at all levels in the country for office-automation and judicial applications.
- All government regulations, notifications and forms for various services at all levels of government up to municipal/local government agencies to be made available to people on Internet.

2. Enabling Literacy and Education for Masses

In spite of Literacy Mission launched by the Government more than a decade ago, India continues to have largest population of illiterates in the world. The percentage of illiterates is considerably higher amongst women in the country. In an information driven society where socio-economic growth depends on capability to acquire and effectively utilize information, it is necessary that citizens not only be fully literate but also be educated in true sense (not just limited to formal education) so that they could fully exploit the benefits of technological advancements in various fields. Information Technology with convergence of various technologies related to communication and delivery of information such as video, audio, telephone, television, newspapers, computers etc. into one unified framework, provides for the first time a unique opportunity to spread literacy and education at a mass scale in the country at affordable cost. The convergence enables ease of providing educational material, which is one of the pre-requisites to spread literacy and education in the country. We need to look at the concept of Community Information Centres, Community Library Centres and Panchayat Centres across the country in a completely new way with the availability of IT tools and services. These community centres could be major hubs of educating (not just providing information to) people on a mass scale. Unlike the earlier SITE experiment using television as a means of educating people, the convergence of IT tools enables interactive learning along with broadcasting medium such as television and radio. Experience has shown that any exercise for educating people necessarily requires interactivity.

3. Fulfilling Local Information Needs of People

One of the major drawbacks of IT based systems developed in many areas is that its information content is generally not directly relevant to people for whom these are developed. The contents are generally planned by people who have themselves not lived in those areas particularly in semi-urban/rural areas. As a result, these systems have a heavy urban-bias. Such systems, therefore, have limited utility and soon become commercially unviable. It is a myth that people in rural areas like to have free delivery of information. Some of the surveys have shown that if information has direct relevance to people even in rural areas and will result in commercial gains and thus improvement in their economic conditions, people will be willing to pay for such services. We need, therefore, to launch a scheme, which would enable the process of large-scale self-employed youngsters across the country to set up and develop contents for Information Kiosks, particularly for rural areas. It has to be ensured that such schemes have large scale private participation and are not dependent on government funding alone. From the government side, we have to ensure that anyone who wants to set up Information Kiosk at any place in the country is not only freed from all government regulations and licences but also is encouraged through evolving simple and attractive financing schemes offered by banks and financial institutions.

The model of growth evolved in the country by Cable TV operators could be used as a base for evolving such a scheme where initially for many years government had not at all intervened. The sector grew with large number of cable operators operating in neighbourhood.

Enabling better Economic Condition of People

The Working Group feels that in the ultimate analysis Information Technology must ensure improvement in economic status and purchasing power of the people at all levels. Some of the areas which have direct relevance/impact on economic status of the people and are expected to be addressed by IT in a big way are as follows:

Employment Generation

Large scale utilization of Information Technology in a manner that it will facilitate its reach to masses will result in massive new opportunities for employment generation. Some of the indications in this direction are already available in the manner in which two major industries have grown in the country in the last few years.

Cable industry, where large number of operators operate in the neighbourhood to solve any problem faced by the users. Each one of these operators employ a small number of people who are generally semi-skilled and learn on-the-job.

The other area is the offshoot of large scale spread of cable TV reaching 30 to 40 million homes in the country. This has resulted in large number of TV channels with multilingual programming. As a result of such a massive programme requirements, the demand of TV programmes and as a result that of professionals who could work in various areas related to production of TV programmes such as journalists, music artistes, visual designers, scripting, acting etc. The success of TV channels depends directly on the viewer ship of its programme in the country. As a result TV programming has to cater to the taste of its target viewers, an issue which is not that well understood by IT industry yet. This development has resulted in large-scale employment generation in areas which were earlier not considered even employable. With the growth of Internet and its reach to masses in the country, such opportunities are expected to grow manifold. Millions of students and youngsters who remain jobless in spite of doing graduation and post-graduation could be made employable by making them capable of handling IT tools. The technological developments in IT are ensuring that such tools do not require extensive knowledge of computer science. Moreover, as these tools become available in Indian languages with at least as much ease of operations as presently in English, the application development in IT would become very widespread and thus create massive employment opportunities.

Direct Marketing of Rural/Agro Products

One of the important components of improving the socio-economic status of people in villages is to ensure that their products find right kind of markets and reach these markets in minimum time without number of middle men involved in it. The reach of IT to rural areas will provide unique opportunities to producers of rural products, agricultural/agro-processing products, rural handicrafts etc. to have direct access to markets. Internet will enable advertising of rural products produced even in the remotest villages to global markets.

5. Educating Citizens about Their Duties

Internet based information delivery systems in combination with conventional broadcast media, TV and Radio, could act as a major vehicle to educate citizens regarding their duties to the nation. This will immensely help in peopole's participation in programmes, like family welfare, conservation of environment, preservation of ethical, moral and cultural values.

Issues in Taking IT to Masses

For IT applications relevant to masses to be implemented in the country following major issues require to be handled on priority:

- Establishment of IT Infrastructure including communication network of good quality and at affordable prices with its reach up to rural areas.
- Government regulations and procedures to be recast in a manner that IT infrastructure and services to be established by people at any place in the country and with whatever capacities be not only allowed but facilitated by the government without requiring to go through complicated procedures of approval.

Over the last few years, government has taken number of steps to enable private sector participation in telecommunication which happens to be the most important prerequisite for Internet based IT services. However, the progress on this front has been considerably slow as a result of which we have only around 0.7 million Internet users in the country. We need to ensure that a clear objective of achieving a target of 150 to 200 million Internet connections in the country is set to be achieved in next three years. All government policies/procedures have to be worked backwards to ensure realization of these targets instead of conventional systems of working other way around where government procedures are simplified in a stepwise manner, its impact on the markets is studied and further simplification/ liberalization is introduced.

Government Funding

Government funding for new programmes has severe limitations. In many programmes, government is not able to even fund reasonable sized pilot projects. Such situation is not likely to significantly improve in the next 2-3 years within which this report suggests a target of 150-200 million Internet connections. The only way, then, for the government is to initiate enabling processes which will ensure large scale participation of self-employed people in unorganized sector. Attractive and easy financing schemes without commercial terms need to be launched by banks to make this happen.

Enabling and Empowering Masses Through IT

The basic theme of the recommendations of the Working Group to realize the dream of taking IT to the masses in the country is built around the concept of enabling and empowering the masses. Government has to set in motion the processes which will enable anyone anywhere to set IT based services even if this results in excess supply of the services. The current practice built around the concept of controlled supply of services and resources through licensing and regulations should be completely done away within this field. Having enabled people to enter the field of providing services, it is essential that government empowers its citizens to demand services not only from government but service providers in general. Government has to play a significant role in this area and in fact should focus on ensuring as to how people could be empowered more and more to demand and get best of services in the market. Empowerment will require complete transparency in procedures to be followed by service providers in government as well as in private sector. These service providers should, by adequate laws, be asked to make information about their rules and procedures available to public. As a first step, and to set an example and create a role model, government has to get into a massive exercise of re-engineering of its own procedures by making extensive use of Electronic Governance. The same should be done for other service providers. Consumer protection laws and consumer courts must be sufficiently empowered to deal with complaints of consumers. Mechanisms should also be set in motion to ensure that these consumer courts do not get over-burdened with the complaints and end-up facing the same problems of large numbers which are being experienced by courts in the country. Consumer courts must themselves make extensive use of IT to resolve the disputes in reasonable time.

Awareness regarding government rules, regulations, programmes and services is essential aspect of empowering the people. Till such time, IT infrastructure reaches the masses through Info-Kiosks and other means, Working Group recommends launch of IT Yatras across the country to be launched by NGOs, educational institutions and corporate sector.

Initiatives Already Taken by Central and State Governments

Over the years, Ministries/Departments of Central and State Governments as well as number of associated agencies have been taking various initiatives to implement people-oriented IT Applications. The Working Group has noticed that in spite of considerable work done by the government in this area, tne awareness regarding these is highly deficient at the level of people for whom these services are meant. Some of the major IT Applications in Central and State Governments are given at Annexures V and VI. The Working Group recommends that a massive awareness campaign must be launched by concerned ministries/departments of Central/State Governments to make public aware of these services and be able to extract best of the services from the government in these areas.

Conclusion

The Working Group in its deliberations has extensively analyzed the current level of IT Applications in the country and its future potential. The Working Group is convinced that IT is probably the only solution for the fast paced socio-economic development in a country like India where the population of one billion could be converted into largest pool of human asset to fully exploit the benefit of technology to uplift their socio-economic conditions. Unlike conventional strategies of services being planned around government schemes and funding, the Working Group recommends that government should confine its role to set in motion enabling processes to facilitate mushrooming of large number of self-employed people and groups in small and unorganized sector to develop and provide IT enabled services unto the remotest places in the country. On its part, government has to ensure that its presence becomes a facilitator and not a bottleneck. Towards this end all licensing provisions with respect to IT services should be removed completely making the market completely open for people in the country. Mass scale education and literacy programmes should be lunched through self-employed people in unorganized sector as well as by corporate sector to enable people to take informed decisions. The Working Group has identified some applications of higher priorities to be undertaken at different levels in the country at the earliest. Pursuing such applications by the government following the recommended model of enabling large-scale participation of people in its implementation will go a long way in taking the benefit of IT to masses in the country.

Annexure-V

Major IT Applications in Central Government Relevant to Masses

Agriculture

Department of Agriculture and Cooperation has accepted the IT-PLAN submitted by NIC and formulated (i) Central Sector Scheme to strengthen IT both in the Department and its Attached/Subordinate offices at a Project Cost of Rs.25 crores, (ii) a Centrally Sponsored Scheme for establishing "NICNET based Agricultural Informatics & Communication (AGRISNET)" in 25 states and 520 districts, one NCT and 6 UTs during Ninth Plan with the Project Cost estimate (both Non-recurring and Recurring) of Rs.155.74 crores. Revised project proposals for the both schemes were submitted for getting EFC approval. As suggested by the Department of Expenditure, establishment of AGRISNET Nodes in 6000 Block Agriculture offices, as stipulated in the IT- PLAN with the cost estimate (Non-recurring) of about Rs.255 crores and Recurring Cost of Rs.44 crores, is to be taken up during Tenth Plan.

Project review of the National Project on "Computerization of Agricultural Census (1995-96) and Input Survey (1996-97)" on turn-key basis with a cost estimate of Rs.9.40 crores was undertaken. A project Proposal for establishing "NICNET based Agricultural Marketing Informatics Network (AGMARK-NET)" in 710 Agricultural Produces Marketing Committees (APMCs), on a turn-key basis with the project cost estimate of Rs.10 crores was submitted and an EFC Note to this effect was on circulation for approval. Computerization and Networking projects in APEDA, NHB, TMOP, Crops Directorates, Trade Division and CDB were completed. Computerization and Networking project in MPEDA was taken up as a paid project. Project study Report on "GIS for Watershed Management" of the Department of Agriculture and Cooperation, in 5 pilot districts were submitted. LAN with 450 Nodes was established in Krishi Bhawan and Shastri Bhawan Wings of the Department.

As the Member-Secretary of the Core-Group (V) "Agricultural Resources Information System" of the NNRMS Standing Committee on Agriculture and Soils of Department of Agriculture and Cooperation, the draft report was prepared and submitted to the Principal Adviser (Agriculture), Planning Commission and Chairman of the Core Group (V). As desired in the meeting of Core-Group (V), the draft report has been sent to ICAR Institutes, State Agricultural Universities, NABARD, and Department of Land Resources, for their suggestions. Review meetings of ICAR Task Force on "Digitization of Databases" under NATP were undertaken twice under the chairmanship of the Director General (NIC).

IT-PLAN for the Animal Husbandry Sector was presented in a seminar "IT for Dairy Research" organized by National Dairy Research Institute (NDRI). This IT-PLAN envisages establishment of a NICNET based Animal Production and Health Informatics Network (APHNET) in the country. Project proposal to strengthen IT component of National Rinderpest Eradication Programme was submitted to the Department. NICNET based Animal Disease Surveillance Information System (ADSIS) was continuing. NICNET services were continued to NDDB Regional Offices. Presentation of the IT-Plan on Fisheries Sector (Fisheries Informatics Network) was presented in a seminar organized by the Central Institute of Fisheries Education (CIFE), Mumbai.

Agricultural Research and Education

NICNET based Agricultural Research Information System (ARISNET) of the Indian Council of Agricultural Research (ICAR) is equipped with about 80 NICNET VSATs installed at ICAR Institutes and State Agricultural Universities, to strengthen Agricultural Research and Education in the country. About 100 ARIS Nodes have been connected to NICNET via dial-up lines for Internet services. ARISNET envisages to link 4 Deemed Universities (IARI, IVRI, NDRI & CIFE), one Central Agricultural University, 85 ICAR Institutes/Directorates, 28 State Agricultural Universities, 107 Agricultural University Colleges, 261 Krishi Vigyan Kendras, and about 850 Agricultural Research Stations located through out the country.

NIC executed an order worth of Rs.1.5 crores to provide computer systems to further intense computerization in ICAR Hqrs.

Under a Consultancy Service contract, about 2000 Computer systems procured under the World Bank aided Resources Development (AHRD) Programme of ICAR, were tested and handed over to ICAR. Value-added services were provided to ARIS centres with respect to SUN Solaris System for using it as an Intranet server which was made operational and integrated with NICNET VSATs for Internet services in the State Agricultural Universities at Akola, Hissar, Jabalpur Ludhiana, Palampur, Samastipur and Solan, and ICAR Institutes (CIAE, CIFE, CIFT, CRIDA, CSWRTI, DRR, IASRI, IVRI, NBAGR, NBPGR, NBSS & LUP and NDRI).

Proposals for establishing LAN under paid projects were submitted to Indian Veterinary Research Institute (Izatnagar & Mukteshwar), Krishi Anusandhan Bhawan (I & II) and ICAR Hqrs., Jawaharlal Nehru Agricultural Universiry (Jabalpur), Birsa Agricultural University (Ranchi). A web-enabled applications on library system for ICAR were made operational.

Arts and Culture

Feasibility report on the development of computerized documentation of art objects and antiquities preserved in Museums, viz. Allahabad Museum (Allahabad), Indian Museum (Calcutta), National Museum (New Delhi), Salar Jung Museum (Hyderabad), and Victoria Memorial Hall (Calcutta), was submitted for approval.

Audit

Implementation of AGNET over NICNET, linking the offices of the Accountant Generals & Auditor Generals, Principal Directorates of Accounts of the Indian Audit and Accounts Department, was on-going. NICNET services were continued for the office of CAG and its field offices. NIC has deputed one officer at the level of Deputy Director General to the office of the CAG, as Adviser (IT). An intranet web site was created with the audit reports of the years 1996-97 and 1997-98.

Central Vigilance Commission

NICNET services were provided to Central Vigilance Commission at

Satarkta Bhavan. Databases on vigilance cases and Chief Vigilance Officers (CVOs) related to more than 600 organizations of the Central Government Ministries and Departments, Public Sector Units and Public Sector Banks, were updated. CVC Web Site (http://www.nic.in/cvc) was launched and instructions were issued by the CVC to lodge vigilance complaint through the web site. This web site has details on instructions, circulars, and notes issued by the CVC, for access. Project consultations to establish "CVCNET — An Intranet over NICNET", linking Chief Vigilance Officers of the Central Government, were held.

Civil Aviation

A comprehensive computerization plan was prepared in consultation with the Bureau of Civil Aviation Security (BCAS) for automation of photo identity cards being used for entry to various airports. The system has been implemented at four regional offices of BCAS in Calcutta, Chennai, Delhi, and Mumbai. It is proposed to develop web enabled applications for DGCA MIS applications. Commerce and Supply Web enabled application for licence processing and its electronic interface with trade and industry was made operational. The Export-Import Policy, procedure, ITC(HS) database and Rate Contract information were hosted on Internet. An Electronic Data Interchange based system for the benefit of Small and Medium enterprises were developed for interaction with Regional Offices of Directorate General of Foreign Trade. The major Regional Offices of Directorate General of Supply and Disposal have also been networked through NICNET. Structuring trade related documents under EDI was on-going.

Communications

NICNET services were provided to the Department of Posts and Department of Telecommunication, including Wireless Planning Cell. NIC implemented software packages for Telecom Accounting in 20 Circles and 4 Metros and demonstrated MIS software for installation at Telecom Hqs, 4 Metros, 20 Circles, and 321 Secondary Switching Areas (SSAs) of DOT. Computerization of Postal Life Insurance (for government employees) in 20 Postal Circles and Rural Postal Life Insurance in 20 Postal Circles and 25 out of 45 Regional Offices, sponsored by the Department of Posts, were completed.

Computerization of preparation of PLI schedules in 200 out of 865 Head Post Offices (HPOs) was completed so far and is on-going in the remaining HPOs, as per the schedule of the Department of Posts. Development of Software in NT Platform is on-going with respect to Savings Bank Accounting which was earlier implemented in Delhi (7 HPOs), Mumbai (2 HPOs), Punjab (1 HPO), and Army Postal Service (1CBPO and 99CBPO), under Oracle/Unix environment.

Implementation of Postal Accounting Computerization in 20 Postal Circles was completed. Pilot Project was undertaken to computerize "cash certificate", viz. Indira Vikas Patra, National Savings Certificate, Kisan Vikas Patra. In Tamil Nadu Circle, establishment of "POSTALNET" an Intranet over NICNET has been initiated.

Cooperatives

Ministry of Agriculture has decided to implement NICNET based Information system on Cooperatives throughout the country. Project on "Total-IT" solution for National Cooperatives Development Council (NCDC) and NICNET connectivity to its 15 Regional Offices, was implemented as a turn-key project. Project on "Cooperative Informatics" was under implementation in the state of Himachal Pradesh. Project Proposal on a countrywide network for IFFCO was submitted. An EFC Note has been circulated for computerization of Cooperative Statistics, as a turn-key project, with the project cost of about Rs.10 crores.

Courts Information System Programme (Courtis)

Interactive Voice Response System (IVR) for providing Supreme Court's pending/disposed cases information on telephone to the litigant/ advocates has been implemented. The second version of JUDIS-CD using Folio text based retrieval software has been brought out. Delhi High Court and Madhya Pradesh Case List has been made available on Internet on daily basis. Supreme Court Case List has also been made available on Internet for the benefit of advocates and litigants. The District Court Information System (DCIS) has been implemented in the District Courts of Haryana, Maharashtra, Karnataka, Delhi, Himachal Pradesh. The District Court Staff has been fully trained in the usage of the DCIS in almost all the District Courts. DCIS software has been implemented in most of the District Courts and these District Courts are taking out Daily Case List from the computer system provided by NIC. NIC conducted computer awareness courses for the District Judges of Andhra Pradesh, Kerala, Bihar, West Bengal, Maharashtra, Madhya Pradesh, Delhi, Himachal Pradesh, Orissa.

Economic Affairs

NIC has provided computerization support for the Budget 1999-2000 preparation. NIC has designed and developed the software for monitoring of Externally Assisted Projects (EAMIS) and made operational in the Ministries of Finance, Power, Agriculture, Surface Transport, Health and Family Welfare, and Urban Affairs and Employment, and also in 9 States. EAMIS software supports on-line monitoring of projects. Internet access has been provided 450 nodes with radio frequency link for Internet services in the North Block Wing of the Ministry of Finance. Budget Documents (1999-2000), Budget Speech (1999-2000) of the Hon'ble Finance Minister and Economic Survey (1998-1999) Report were available through its "NICNET website" to the Public. Project activities related to computerization of National Savings Organization (NSOs) were initiated in 6 states.

Education

An Internet web services (http://www.education.nic.in) and also an Intranet web server ("webedu") was developed over the NICNET LAN established in the Department. These sites were visited extensively by Indian Parents and Students, NRIs, and Foreign Students. "webedu" links to Central Universities, CD-ROM Series-I (Vols. I & II) and CD-ROM Series-II (Vols. I to XI) containing reports of the All India Educational Survey were released. NICNET services were continued to Copyright Office, Kendriya Vidyalaya Sangathan, Directorate of Adult Education, Navodaya Viadyala Sangatan, and NCERT. Web enabled applications were developed for various centrally sponsored schemes (Mid-day Meal schemes, Non-Formal education, Operation Black Board, etc.) of the Department. Technical report on creation of CD-ROM on Hindi Encyclopedia was submitted. The Department has formulated Central Sector Scheme on Information

Technology, viz. Induction of Information Technology in Kendriya Vidyalaya Sangathan (KVS) and Nayodaya Vidyalaya Sangathan (NVS), and Revised Class Scheme (Class-2000), with an outlay of Rs.200 crores during Ninth and Tenth Plans.

Energy

NICNET services and MIS support were provided to Central Electricity Authority (CEA), Ministry of Power (MOP), Ministry of Coal (MOC), Ministry of Petroleum & Natural Gas (MOP&NG), Department of Chemical & Petrochemicals (DC&PC) and Ministry of Non-Conventional Energy Sources (MNES). IT-Plan report has been prepared and submitted to MOP, MOC, MOP & NG, DC & PC and MNES. Implementation of POWERNET — An Intranet over NICNET — was taken up and VSATs were installed at 12 State Electricity Boards (SEBs). POWERNET is a sponsored project of Power Finance Corporation of India, funded by USAID. Implementation of Central Power Public Sector Units Network (CPSU-NET) with 64 KBPS SCPC VSAT was undertaken. NIC provided all necessary support services to the Power sector with respect to Y2K-Preparedness. Special training on "Rollover Test in Power sector" was conducted. NICNET support services for Y2K Rollover were made available to the Energy Sector. Project proposal for establishment of COALNET linking Public Sector Units of the Ministry was under preparation. Project activities related to bring 80 C-200 VSATs installed by VSNL for Coal India Limited (CIL) under NICNET were initiated. Establishment of NICNET based Renewable Energy Informatics Network (RE-NET) to link state nodal agencies, regional offices of the Ministry of Non-Conventional Energy Sources, State Electricity Boards, Manufactures and R&D institutions in the area of renewable energy, was on-going. MNES has allocated about Rs. 6.0 crores for the Information Technology Programme in the Ministry during Ninth Plan.

Environment and Forests

An Internet Server has been established in the Ministry. Environment and Forest Clearance for Development projects are being provided on-line in the web site of this Ministry. A decision support system for resource management and setting up research priorities related to Forest has been developed for the Indian Council of Forest Research and Education. Species Recognition System has been developed for Forest Research Institute for identifying the wood samples being provided by different organizations.

External Affairs

NIC has provided operational support for fully computerised Passport Offices at Ahmedabad, Bangalore, Bareilly, Bhopal,Calcutta, Chandigarh, Chennai, Delhi, Goa, Hyderabad, Jaipur, Jalandhar, Kochi, Kozhikode, Lucknow, Mumbai, Thiruvanthapuram, Tiruchirapalli, and Vishakapatinam, and other Ministry Divisions at Akbar Bhavan, South Block, Patiala House, ICCR, and ISIL Building etc. Passport Computerization Project was made Y2K compliant. New version of Tele-enquiry system has been installed to handle multilingual queries by the public. Web site (http://passport.nic.in) related to public services in the area of Passport, Visa and PIO card was launched. Database on NRIs was developed and installed in about 160 Missions abroad.

Expenditure

NIC has been actively working for the development and implementation of computer based information systems in the office of the Controller General of Accounts (CGA), Department of Expenditure. Enhancement of packages (IMPROVE, CONTACT, and GAINS) was undertaken. All accounting packages were made Y2K O.K. Office of the Controller General of Accounts has taken up development of PAO (PAO-2000) software on VB6/SQL server, for implementation in 272 PAOs. Under this project, NIC will undertake installation and training of officials in 272 PAOs. Design and Development of Computer based Financial Advisory System for decision support in various offices of Financial Advisers (FAs) of the Department of Expenditure, located in various Central Government Ministries/ Departments was initiated.

Fertilizer

The sponsored project of the Department of Fertilizers titled "Integrated

Fertilizer MIS [IFMIS]" with the cost estimate Rs. 1.99 crores was nearing completion. With the installation of LAN with UTP cabling, development of web enabled applications was initiated. An Intranet over NICNET for divisions of the Department located in various buildings was established. "Y2K Compliance in the Fertilizers Sector" seminar was organized in collaboration with the Department and the Fertilizers Sector participated. User manuals on various modules, based on IEEE standards, have been prepared and submitted to the Department. IT Plan for the Department was approved with an outlay of Rs. 3.85 crores during Ninth Plan. Fertiliser Informatics Network (FERTNET), which is an Intranet over NICNET, has been established by installing FTDMA VSATs at Department of Fertlizers and different sites of IFFCO, NFL, MFL, GNFC, along with dial-up connectivity to FCI and HFCL. FTDMA VSATs with voice to 8 NFL Plants/Zonal offices and dial-up connectivity to 30 NFL Area offices have been established to strengthen their decision support system. Project initiatives were undertaken to extend NICNET connectivity to other companies of fertilizer sector to strengthen FERTNET.

Food, Public Distribution and Consumer Affairs

FCI Intranet over NICNET was established linking FCI offices at districts, regions and zones. Business Information Management at Central Warehousing Corporation (CWC) was computerized. Web enabled programmes were developed for data access related to prices data, food-grain bulletins, directory of sugar factories, and directory of consumer forums. IT-PLANs submitted by NIC have been approved by the respective Ministries and Budget outlay was earmarked for 1999-2000 and 2000-01.

GISTNIC Informatics Programme

Design and development of the following information products were carried out :

- World Wide Web Based services
- Telne Services
- FTP Services
- GISTNIC Sandesh

- Lekha-G
- NICNET based Services
- Other Media based Services

The information contained include the demographic information, economic information, social information, business and industrial statistics, foreign trade information, banking and finance related information, agriculture statistics, universities information, the tourism information, agricultural commodities, prices information prevailing at 95 market centres in AP (which is being updated daily), etc. The URL for availing the service is http://gist.ap.nic.in/Design and development of Computer Telephony Integration (CTI) Technology based system for capturing price related information from remote markets, to update computerised data through an ordinary telephone instrument.

Health and Family Welfare

NICNET services were provided to Department of Health, Department of Family Welfare and Department of Indian System of Medicines & Homeopathy. NICNET website for the Ministry has been created for Internet access. NICNET services were provided to the Directorate General of Health Services (DGHS) for allotment of Medical/Dental seats under the Central Quota of Under Graduate and Post-Graduate Courses in India, as directed by the Hon'ble Supreme Court of India. Software programmes were implemented to computerize activities related to "Community Needs Assessment Approach in Family Welfare Programme", in project districts. Development of Web database on "traditional medicinal plants in India and their uses", to eliminate foreign patent on traditional knowledge resources of India, was on-going.

Home Affairs

NICNET services were provided to the Department of Internal Security, Department of States, Department of Jammu & Kashmir Affairs, Department of Home and Department of Official Language. NIC has provided advisory support for execution of IT projects in various Central Police Organizations, viz. Assam Riffles, BSF, CISF, CRPF, DCPW, ITBP, NCRB, and NSG. NIC has computerized and networked NSCBIA (Calcutta) and Land Check Post (Haridaspur) on Indo-Bangla Border on NICNET facilitating interchangeability of Port of Entry and Exit, as a part of Computerization of Visa Control Project for Bangladesh Nationals. Project activities related to the implementation of Visa Control System Project at High Commission of India (Dhaka) including NICNET connectivity to facilitate data interchange between HCI (Dhaka), NSCBIA (Calcutta) and Land Check Post (Haridaspur) on Indo-Bangla Border were undertaken.

Decision Support System , with input from "COURTIS" Project, was designed and implemented in the Department of Justice. An Internet site for the Ministry of Home Affairs (http://mha.nic.in) over NICNET is on-going. Software for Computerizing MHA Identity Cards for Government officials was developed and tested and handed over to MHA for implementation. A NICNET Training Centre was established in MHA for IT training. All systems including Immigration Control System were made Y2K Compliant ensuring smooth roll over on 1-1-2000. A Bilingual web site was designed and put into use over the LAN in the Department of Official Language. Promotion of bilingual computerization was undertaken in pilot departments.

Industry

NICNET services were provided to the Departments of Company Affairs, Heavy Industries, Industrial Development, Industrial Policy and Promotion, Mines, Public Enterprises, Food Processing Industries, Small Scale Industries and Rural Industries, and Steel, and BIFR, MRTP Commission and Tariff Commission. NIC has undertaken major turnkey projects which include computerization and networking of Registrar of Company Affairs (ROC) offices and computerization of District Industries Centre (DIC). As a result of success of Phase I of the ROC Project, Phase II dealing with process of registration was approved with the project cost of Rs.19.97 crores (non-recurring) and Rs.1.94 crores (Recurring). Under the DIC Computerization Project NICNET based Information System for smooth flow of SSI related data from DICs to State Directorates of Industries and DCSSI Headquarters and dissemination of information from States Directorates of Industries to DICs, was made operational. DCSSI has received monthly production data from about 20,000 Units manufacturing about 500 items over NICNET. Y2K Compliance reports on NIC Services and Systems were submitted and these reports were sent to other Ministries as "model document."

Annexure-VI

Major IT-applications & Other Services at NIC State/UT Centres

1. *NIC Andhra Pradesh State Centre*

Andhra Pradesh State Centre continued to provide NICNET services to the State Government with greater coverage, additional services and extension of the existing services to more users. Several turnkey projects were taken up. Some of the projects where NICNET services have been extensively used are :

- Software developed and implemented for the Mandal Level Computerisation Programme of Andhra Government covering the areas Land Records, Land Aquisition, Civil Supplies, Payroll. First Version Implemented in 308 Mandal offices. Implementation of Birth & Death Registration System in the Municipality. Web Site launched for the speedy dissemination of information like, Vacancy position in MBBS/BDS, Engineering Admissions, Common Entrance Test results, MCA, MBA etc.
- Web Sites launched for various Government departments like, Agriculture, Marketing, Education, Directorate of Economics & Statistics, Ground Water, DGS&D, AP Vaidya Vidhana Parishad etc.
- Development and implementation of the Property Tax Information System for the L.B. Nagar Municipality.
- Development of a District Accounting System for the Food Corporation of India. It is being implemented by all FCI-districts in the State. RF links established for various offices like High Court, CCMB, Kendriya Sadan etc.
- Implementation of District Accounting System (DAS) for Food Corporation of India. Training the staff of FCI on the above.
- FEM analysis of the Radial Gates of Singur Reservoir for the Irrigation Department.
- E-mail and Internet connectivity extended to various district offices and forest offices.

- 26 Training programmes were organized covering around 525 officials of the State Governments. Applications based training programmes also conducted and more than 1000 officials participated.

2. ***NIC Arunachal Pradesh State Centre***

NICNET facilities have been provided for development of Software for various State government departments. NICNET facilities are being used to exchange information between the State Secretariat and the districts of the State. Several application softwares have been developed for the State Government. Some of them are :

- Major Databases developed for 11th Finance Commission, Electoral rolls, Below Poverty Line Census (BPL).
- Software Packages for Targeted Public Distribution System (TPDS) for the Civil Supplies Department, File Management Software for the CM's Secretariat.
- Unified Fund Monitoring Package to monitor the expenditure incurred under various schemes.
- A file monitoring software was developed and implemented for the office of the Chief Secretary.
- MIS for the department of Education which manages all the requirements of the department.
- Computerisation support to various departments like Health Services, Rural Development, Agriculture, Planning and Urban Development.

3. ***NIC Assam State Centre***

NIC has been providing NICNET based services to all the State Government Departments. A video conferencing studio has been set up at the State Secretariat, which is being regularly used by various State Governments. NIC has helped in the study, design and development of several applications some of them are :

- Release of Regional Resource Database on the WWW.
- Software packages for various applications, like Revenue Collection.

- Public Distribution System, Crime Statistics and Registration of Births and Deaths etc.
- Computerisation of Treasury and Sub-Treasury. A detailed SRS is being prepared.
- Computerization support for the Election Management and Result Transmission during the Parliamentary Elections.
- Implementation of the Treasury Accounting Software.
- MIS developed for various Government schemes such as Shallow Tube Well, Welfare of Tribes and Backward Classes, State Human Riots Commission etc.
- E-mail and Internet access facility to Government Departments.
- Training programmes were conducted for the various departments of the state government.

4. ***NIC Bihar State Unit***

NICNET services have been provided for the computerization of various Government Departments. Computerization support has been extended for the following :

- GPF Computerization. A statewide GPF computerization is being done at all the districts after seeing the successful implementation of the GPF Directorate.
- Statewide District Treasury Computerization. It is proposed to implement district treasury computerization at 20 more districts and the plan proposal has been approved.
- Various packages developed for Bihar State Electricity Board (for billing) and Commercial Tax Monitoring System for the Finance Department and NICTRAN package for the Transport Department.
- Continued support to the High Court and District Court Computerization programmes.
- Public Distribution Monitoring system has been developed.
- Provide IT supports for the Enhancement of Computerization of Governor's office, Bihar Education Project Council.
- Database development for various sectors like Economy, Finance, Rural Development, Urban Development, Education, Transport and other sectors.
- A number of training programmes were organized.

5. *NIC Chandigarh (UT) Centre*

NICNET services are being utilised for the following :

- Web Site for Chandigarh, which includes planning and architecture, city government, city map, tourist information, Chandigarh police.
- Information Systems/Databases for PIS for the Chandigarh Administration.
- Industrial Electricity Billing.
- Motor Vehicle registration and Driving Licences.
- Budget Information System for the Engineering Department.
- Technical Services to various Boards, Corporations and Central Government Departments.
- Setting of UP Information Facilitation Counters at UT Secretariat and DC's Office.
- Development and hosting of a web page for the Chandigarh Housing Board.

6. *NIC Delhi NCT Centre*

NICNET Services are being used by large number of State Government Departments, viz. Food and Civil Supplies Department, Education Department, Office of the Chief Minister, Office of LG etc. NICNET services have been used for the following Information services :

- CM office's computerization has been accomplished, which involved implementation of various packages for file maintenance, public grievances, control room monitoring for DVB, CM Project Monitoring System.
- Computerization of Industry and Planning Department and Registrar of Cooperative Societies.
- Delhi Government WEB Site was created and hosted.
- Packages were developed for the Directorate of Family Welfare for Pulse Polio.
- Three district centres were made operational.
- Setting of computer network at different buildings of the Delhi Government.
- Various other packages like, Marriage Certificates, relief work, and expenditure statement.

7. *NIC Goa State Unit*

NICNET services have been utilized in the development and implementation of the following information systems :

- Implementation of Sales Tax Monitoring System, Registration of Births & Deaths, House Rent and Tax Collection, Trade and Occupation Licensing, Construction Licensing for Municipal Corporation, PIS for Police Department.
- Office Procedure Automation implemented in the Collectorate.
- Setting of NITPU.
- Implementation of the List of Business Information System at Panaji Bench of Bombay High Court.
- Implementation of the Land Records Information System in the State Collectorate.
- Implementation of RPLI and PLI in the Postal Department.
- Computerization of various censuses like Agriculture, Economic, Forest etc.
- Various training programmes were organized for officials of the Goa Government. Around 300 officials were covered during these programmes.

8. *NIC Gujarat State Centre*

Continued efforts are being put in making NICNET facilities available to all State Government Departments, several offices of the State Government located outside the Secretariat. Major achievements in providing informatics services include :

- Support in Implementation of Treasury Information System.
- LAN for the new High Court Building.
- Continued support for the High Court Computerization.
- Implementation of the District Court Information System at the District Courts.
- Training programme in the application pakages and general IT to various officials from state as well as district.

9. *NIC Haryana State Unit*

NICNET services have been provided to several government departments. Several information systems have been developed for the above mentioned departments. Some of the major achievements are :

- Full-fledged Intranet created in the Civil Secretariat and database access services were made available to the CM and others.
- Web Site hosted for many departments, like HSIDC,Tourism etc.
- Packages like Village Information System, Public Information Facilitation System, Project Progress Monitoring System.
- All the blocks of Fatehabad District linked to District HQ through Dial Up links.
- Web site hosting the Daily cases of the High Court.
- IT support to all the DRDAs.
- E-mail and Internet Services and support to various departments and district offices.
- Computerization support to the District Industries Centres in the State.
- Training programmes were organized at the State Secretariat and District Centres of NIC.

10. *NIC Himachal Pradesh State Unit*

NICNET facilities have been extended to various departments at the State Secretariat. NICNET services are being used for the following applications :

- Internet and E-mail services to various departments.
- Implementation office automation at the Chief Minister's office.
- Continued support for maintaining various databases at the State, which help the government in following areas :

    Vehicle expenditure Monitoring,
    Implementation of Cabinet Decisions,
    House Allotment,
    Personnel Management,
    Monitoring Court Cases,

Budget Information Processing System,
Support for Land Records Computerization,
Continued support for the District Treasuries Computerization in the State.

11. ***NIC Jammu and Kashmir State Centre***

NICNET services have been provided to the State Secretariat, all the Districts of the State, the High Court and several District Courts. NICNET services are being utilised for the following informatics services :

- Official Web Site of J&K Government.
- Video Conferencing, E-mail and Internet Access to the State Secretariat.
- Implementation of the Treasury Information System in several treasuries of the State.
- Computerization of various departments, like CPF organisation, Sales tax, GPF.
- File Monitoring System for the Secretariat has been implemented.
- Training and Workshops conducted in various fields.

12. **NIC Karnataka State Unit**

NICNET services have been provided for computerization of various state government departments. The major achievements are :

- Implementation of Accounting, PIS and letter monitoring package at Karnataka Neeravari Nigam Limited.
- Installation of Hardware/Software like, Pension Scheme, PF recovery etc. In the regional PF office.
- Service Rules were put on the net for instant and ready reference for the day to day operations.
- Computerization of various departments, like Agriculture, 3 Sub-registrar's officeS, Regional Transport Offices.
- Networking of Commercial Tax Assessment circles in Bangalore.
- Implementation of Permit Monitoring System for Commissionerates and District Excise Offices.
- Implementation of Public Grievance Monitoring System.

Computerized system for Classification, Control and Appeal for the staff.
- Web sites for various departments designed and launched.
- Various results like the SSLC, Common Entrance Test hosted on the Internet for public.
- Various Databases made for departments, like Education, Small Scale industries have been hosted on the Internet.
- Daily case list of the High Court published on the Internet with search facility.

13. ***NIC Kerala State Centre***

NICNET services have been provided to the State Government Departments, all the Districts, the High Court and several District Courts. NICNET facilities are being utilized for development of database and information system. Some of them are :

- Several packages developed and implemented, like Weights and Measures Registration & Verification System, Expenditure and Activity Monitoring System,LOC preparation System, Representation Monitoring System for the Backward Class Commission, Budget Monitoring System for the Finance Department.
- Implementation of PLI and RPLI in the Post Offices.
- Database creation for the Overseas Development & Employment.
- Promotion consultancy.
- Computerization of Passport office, Labour Commissioner's Office and High Court and district courts.
- Computerization of Land Records in the State.
- Development of MIS for the Public Works Department.
- Continued support to the computerization programme on Treasury Computerization in the State.
- Preparation of a proposal for extending NICNET Services up to the block and village level in the State.

14. ***NIC Lakshadweep UT Centre***

NICNET services are being utilised by the several islands in Lakshadweep, the Kochi office of the Lakshadweep administration and Liaison Officer, Lakshadweep, New Delhi. NIC, Lakshadweep UT Centre is providing Informatics support for the following :

- Computerized advance ship ticket reservation system introduced at Kochi, Calicut and all other major ports of Lakshadweep.
- Inventory Control Package for the Electricity Subdivisions at Minicoy, Kochi, Kavaratti and Beypore.
- Provided computer systems with multimedia and Internet facilities to teachers in all the high schools.
- IT supports to Chief Electoral Officer.
- Internet access facility to several government departments.

15. ***NIC Madhya Pradesh State Centre***

Video Conferencing, Internet access and E-mail services have been provided to Central Government Offices, State Government Offices, Public Sector Undertakings and State Government undertakings through NICNET. A Home Page for the State was prepared which has been hosted under the India Image Programme of NIC. Major achievements in providing informatics services include :

- Software package on Community Needs Assessment Approach completed and software to be implemented in all the other states.
- Retrieval system on Compendium of office orders, Circulars and forms.
- PIS for the panchayat inspectors of Social Welfare department implemented.Upgraded version of Treasury Accounting Information System (TRACIS Ver 3.0) to accommodate various other requirements of the department.
- Implementation of Pension Accounting and Management System (PAMS) for District Treasuries.
- Results of various competitive exams like Pre-Engineering, Pre-Medical, Pre-Pharmacy etc. were made available online for the benefit of public.
- Implementation of RF network setup to extend high-speed connectivity between Mantralaya, Vidhan Sabha, NITPU and NIC state unit.
- Work in progress for the establishment of 6 new tribal district centres.
- Implementation of Rate Analysis System completed for Rural

Engineering Services.

- Information exchange services through NICNET for the management of the Gram Sampark Abhiyan Programme of the State Government.
- Several training programmes for various departments of the Government. Around 500 officers and staff were covered in these programmes.
- Implementation of DRDA project in the state. Hardware, software and LAN facilities have been implemented in all the DRDAs in the state.
- Establishment of NIC District Court Centres and implementation of District Court Information system in the various district courts of the state.

16. ***NIC Maharashtra State Centre***

Maharashtra State Unit continued to provide NICNET service to State Government Departments and Central Government Departments, NGOs and Co-operative Societies in the State. The coverage of E-mail, Internet Access and Video Conferencing services were enlarged considerably. NICNET services were used for the following projects:

- Networking at the Mahrashtra Secretariat established and connected to NICNET via RF link and Video Conferencing setup established and made operational in the Secretariat.
- Various software packages were developed for various departments, like CM's information systems, Registry Computerization for Finanace Department, Ways and Means Monitoring System for Rural Development, Savings investment information system for Directorate of Small Savings.
- IT supports for various Central Government departments, like Zoological Survey of India, Central Poultry Board, Estate manager's office.
- Video Conferencing support to State Government.
- Implementation of District Court Information System (DCIS) for the district courts of the State.
- Training and Workshops on IT.

17. *NIC Manipur State Centre*

Continued support in providing NICNET connectivity to various state government departments and Deputy Commissioner in the districts. NICNET services are used for following information support for the State Government :

- Support to the SSI Registration Information System.
- E-mail connectivity to various state government departments.
- MEDLARS support to various institutions.

18. *NIC Meghalaya State Centre*

NIC has provided informatics support to various Central Government agencies and State Government Departments, which include the following :

- Web site creation for Meghalaya state and other departments, like Electricity Board, Industrial Development Corporation, Tourism etc.
- Implementation of Software Package for LOA and LOC in all the district treasury. First phase of treasury computerization project implemented.
- Loan Monitoring System for the finance department.
- Computerization support to the Public Health Engineering.
- Department for the management of the Rajiv Gandhi Drinking Water Mission.
- Computerization support in the preparation of the state budget.
- Establishment of Computer Centre at the Food & Civil Supplies department and networking it with the District office.
- Computerization of district rural development agency.
- Implementation of DRDA project in the state. Hardware, software and LAN facilities have been implemented in all the DRDAs in the state.
- Internet and E-mail connectivity to various state departments and corporations in the state.

19. *NIC Mizoram State Centre*

NICNET facilities have been provided to various departments of

Government of Mizoram. NICNET services are being utilised for the following projects :

- Implementation of the Land Records Information System for the Directorate of Land Records, Government of Mizoram.
- Computer based enumeration of State Government employees.
- Budget preparation for the State Government.
- Computerised assessment of financial resources for 1999-2000.
- NICNET support for the monitoring of developmental and social welfare programmes.

20. *NIC Nagaland State Centre*

NICNET facilities have been provided to several departments of the State Government :

- Transmission of monthly data for National Sample Survey Organisation.
- Continued support on the post Implementation of the Arms Licence Information systems at district level.
- Database to keep track of the Civil list of the State Government.
- MIS implemented for the departments in the state.
- Continued support to the NICNET based monitoring system for ICDS Project.

21. *NIC Orissa State Centre*

NICNET services have been provided to Departments of the State Government and District Administration. NICNET Services have been effectively utilised in the following areas :

- Coputerisation of Sales Tax for Circle COSTIC.
- Computerisation of various departments, like Finance, Industries.
- Various Packages and Databases developed like Budget Information System, Budget Forecasting and Analysis, Finance Commission Data Analysis System, Letter of Credit Monitoring system, Small Savings Deposit Scheme.
- Central Assitance Review and Monitoring System.
- Implementation of court case monitoring system in 10 districts.

- Implementation Pension Grievance Monitoring System.
- GIS application on Relief Monitoring in Orissa during Super Cyclone.

22. ***NIC Pondicherry State Centre***

NICNET facilities have been provided to the Government of Pondicherry and District Administration. NICNET services are being used to implement and to support IT in the key sectors of economy. Some of the achievements are :

- Exchange of information with the Central Government Department.
- Continued support in the implementation of the Birth and Death Information System.
- Computerization support to the Transport Department.
- Internet and e-mail access facility to the Government Departments.
- Imparted training in the field of IT to various officials.

23. ***NIC Punjab State Centre***

NICNET facilities have been upgraded at NIC District Centres in the state. A web-page of Punjab Government was launched on NIC web server. Internet connectivity was made available in 4 districts, State Centre and the State secretariat. NICNET services are being utilised for development of following databases and information systems :

- Web Site for Punjab Government and Overseas Cell of Employment, Punjab Tourism and ASUDA.
- Implementation of Land Record Computerization at various district levels.
- Development of software for treasury department.
- Computerization of District Rural Agency.
- Establishment of Punjab Secretariat.
- Technical Support to Passport Office, PIB, FCI, GPO, Central Excise and Customs.
- Implementation of District Court Project.
- Internet Access Facility to various Government Departments and at various districts.

24. ***NIC Rajasthan State Centre***

NICNET facilities in the state has been improved with the installation of IPA and Direc-PC V-SATs in all the districts. A new NIC District Centre is established at Karauli :

- Implementation of Treasury Software in all the districts.
- Implementation of New Judiciary System in 15 districts.
- Development and Implementation of Pension Revision System for Directorate of Pension.
- Implementation of Land Record Computerization in Tehsils.
- Execution of Phase III of assembled computerization.

25. ***NIC Sikkim State Centre***

The following are the some of the major achievements :

- Computerization of Sikkim subject certification.
- Computerization of NSSO Sample Survey.
- Computerization of House Hold Survey of Sikkim.
- Computerization of Agricultural census and input survey.
- Development of Departmaneal Expenditure Monitoring System.
- Computerization of All Sikkim Health Survey (ASHS - 1996).
- Computerization of Sukumbas; Survey (Sukumbasi i.e. Sikkimese citizen who does not own any land holding).
- Development of Motor-vehicle Registration System for the Motor Vehicle Department.
- Computerization of Chief Pay and Accounts Office.
- Ration Card Computerization.
- Computerization support to the Agricultural Department.
- Computerization of Food and Civil Supplies Department.
- Computerization of Urban Dev. & Housing Department.
- Rajiv Gandhi Drinking Water Mission computerization.
- Development of a GIS based Forest Information System.

26. ***NIC Tamil Nadu State Centre***

NICNET facilities have been provided to all State Government departments at the secretariat through 130 nodes. NICNET services are being used for the following :

- Web hosting for various departments like, TN State Government, Department of Tamil Culture and Development, Statistics etc.
- Dissemination of the results of the Xth Standard and Tamil Nadu Professional Courses Entrance Examinations etc. through WWW and GISTNIC booths spread all over the State.
- MIS for Women's Development Corporation and for IG prisons, Public Distribution System, Taluk Information Systems.
- RF connectivity established between Secretariat and other complex for data transfer.
- Computerization of all Sub-Treasuries and District Treasuries in the State.
- IT support to all the Export Promotion Zones.
- Under the District Courts Computerization Programme, Systems have been installed at 20 district courts.
- Various packages developed for Litigations monitoring, Teachers Recruitment Board and Online Bill Passing System for PAO's at Chennai.
- Creation and demonstration of Data Warehousing Application for the State with 7 (seven) Data Marks consisting of Village Amenities Data, India Economy Data, Rainfall Statistics, Prices of commodities, Agricultural Statistics, Material Statistics and School Statistics.
- Project Monitoring System for the PWD in Chennai.

27. *NIC Tripura State Centre*

NICNET services have been utilized in the State in providing e-mail, Internet Access, development of information system and IT related training. Some of the notable achievements of the state centre are :

- Establishment of LAN for the Main Secretariat.
- Inforamtion Facilitation Counter in the main Secretariat.
- Payroll Accounting System for the Secretariat.
- Personal Information System for the Secretariat.
- Web Site launched for the Tripura Government.
- Database created for the HRD having all the details like, number

of teachers, students enrolled, infrastructure etc.

- Several Packages like Certificate Issue and Monitoring System, District Administration Monitoring System, Pension Payment System.
- Database of Reang Migrants created to keep track of such migrants.
- Continued support for the implementation of schools information system.
- Schools Information System.
- Vehicle Master Database Maintenance System.
- Land Acquisition Monitoring System. etc.

28. ***NIC Uttar Pradesh State Centre***

The UP State Unit continued to provide information support to the State Government Departments, Central Government Departments, the Allahabad High Court and other organizations under NICNET service domain. The NICNET services have been used for the development and implementation of several information system projects. Some of them are :

- Ten important government buildings have been connected through a RF Link and LAN has been set-up in these.
- Computerization support to the Allahabad High Court.
- Implementation of the District Court Information System Software in the district court of the State.
- Computerization support to the various departments of the State Government at the State Secretariat, Divisional Offices and the District Level Offices.
- Software package for Employment Exchange was implemented in few districts.
- All the treasuries of UP have been computerized.
- Internet support and services to several government departments.
- Implemented Tube-well monitoring.
- Implementation of Land Records Management Information System (LRMIS) in all the districts of UP.
- Computer training was provided to many Government departments including officers of Secretariat, Employment Exchanges, and Treasury.

29. *NIC West Bengal State Unit*

NIC services are being used by all the State Government departments, for development of information system, communication between various departments, video conferencing and training in Information Technology. Some of the important projects implemented during the year are :

- PIS developed for Judicial Officers.
- Computerization of 16 District courts completed.
- Commercial Tax Information System implemented.
- Computerized system of land records maintenance has been implemented in 124 blocks.
- Treasury Information System has been implemented in 31 additional treasuries of the state.
- Computerization of Registrar Offices, Public Vehicle Department, Regional Transport Offices, State Transport Authority.
- PLI and RPLI computerization in Department of Post.
- MIS implemented for the Power Directorate.
- Digitisation of Mouza map is in progress.
- Computerization support to the Calcutta High Court.
- Implementation of the District Court Information system in the district courts of the State.
- Implementation of the computerized system for the preparation of the pension payment orders for the school teachers.
- A computerized system was developed for monitoring of the file movement for the Finance Department.
- E-mail and Internet Services to various State Government Departments.
- Video conferencing facility over NICNET to various state government departments.

30. *Andaman and Nicobar Islands Unit*

NICNET services have been extended to various departments. Some of the important ongoing computerization projects are :

- Computerization of the District Court.
- Internet and e-mail facility extended to various departments.

- Implementation of the Land Records Information System for the Directorate of Land Records.

31. ***Dadra and Nagar Haveli Unit***

NICNET Services are being utilized by several government departments. NICNET is being used extensively for exchange of information among government agencies. Some of the important projects implemented are :

- Implementation of Computerized Application Monitoring System in the collectorate.
- Revision of Electoral Works.
- Report Generation for various departments.
- Land Records Computerization.
- Computerization support to the DRDA.
- Training in area of use of computers and computerized system.
- Use of e-mail over NICNET.

32. ***NIC Daman and Diu Unit***

NICNET services are being used by the U.T. Administration for :

- Exchange of e-mail.
- LAN set-up at the secretariate.
- Electoral roll computerization.
- Exchange of data to the Central Government Departments.
- Development of MIS for government departments.
- Training on the use of IT and various other packages.

DISNIC Programme

IT Plan for the DISNIC-PLAN project has been submitted. Project discussion on Phase-II of the DISNIC Programme was initiated. Phase-II envisages an integrated system approach for development of informatics on agricultural development, rural development and backward area development, using Internet Technology Tools. Networking of about 65 Departments of Geography of various Universities and Institutions is considered to facilitate development of

GIS based DSS on backward area development. Project discussions were held to provide NICNET services for ATMA centres under NATP project in 6 Pilot districts, in order to strengthen DISNIC-AGRIS Database Project. IT-PLAN of Natural Disaster Management and Relief Programme envisages to strengthen the DISNIC-NCRMS project in districts, in the Ninth Plan. Strengthening of DISNIC-AGRIS, DISNIC-Fisheries, and DISNIC-APHNET Database Projects has been planned under the "NICNET based Agricultural Informatics & Communication" programme during 1999-2002.

Appendix–III

The Information Technology Act, 2000

(No. 21 of 2000) [9th June, 2000]

An Act to provide legal recognition for transactions carried out by means of electronic data interchange and other means of electronic communication, commonly referred to as "electronic commerce", which involve the use of alternatives to paper-based methods of communication and storage of information, to facilitate electronic filing of documents with the Government agencies and further to amend the Indian Penal Code, the Indian Evidence Act, 1872, the Bankers' Books Evidence Act, 1891 and the Reserve Bank of India Act, 1934 and for matters connected therewith or incidental thereto, whereas the General Assembly of the United Nations by resolution A/RES/51/162, dated the 30th January, 1997 has adopted the Model Law on Electronic Commerce adopted by the United Nations Commission on International Trade Law; and whereas the said resolution recommends *inter alia* that all States give favourable consideration to the said Model Law when they enact or revise their laws, in view of the need for uniformity of the law applicable to alternatives to paper-based methods of communication and storage of information; and whereas it is considered necessary to give effect to the said resolution and to promote efficient delivery of Government services by means of reliable electronic records be it enacted by Parliament in the Fifty-first Year of the Republic of India as follows:

Chapter I

Preliminary

1. Short Title, Extent, Commencement and Application.

(1) This Act may be called the Information Technology Act, 2000.

(2) It shall extend to the whole of India and, save as otherwise provided in this Act, it applies also to any offence or contravention thereunder committed outside India by any person.

(3) It shall come into force on such date as the Central Government may, by notification, appoint and different dates may be appointed for different provisions of this Act and any reference in any such provision to the commencement of this Act shall be construed as a reference to the commencement of that provision.

(4) Nothing in this Act shall apply to,

(a) a negotiable instrument as defined in section 13 of the Negotiable Instruments Act, 1881;

(b) a power-of-attorney as defined in section 1A of the Powers-of-Attorney Act, 1882;

(c) a trust as defined in section 3 of the Indian Trusts Act, 1882;

(d) a will as defined in clause (h) of section 2 of the Indian Succession Act, 1925 including any other testamentary disposition by whatever name called;

(e) any contract for the sale or conveyance of immovable property or any interest in such property;

(f) any such class of documents or transactions as may be notified by the Central Government in the Official Gazette.

2. Definitions.

(1) In this Act, unless the context otherwise requires,

(a) "access" with its grammatical variations and cognate expressions means gaining entry into, instructing or communicating with the logical, arithmetical, or memory function resources of a computer, computer system or computer network;

(b) "addressee" means a person who is intended by the originator to receive the electronic record but does not include any intermediary;

(c) "adjudicating officer" means an adjudicating officer appointed under sub-section (1) of section 46;

(d) "affixing digital signature" with its grammatical variations and cognate expressions means adoption of any methodology or procedure by a person for the purpose of authenticating an electronic record by means of digital signature;

(e) "appropriate Government" means as respects any matter,

(i) Enumerated in List II of the Seventh Schedule to the Constitution;

(ii) relating to any State law enacted under List III of the Seventh Schedule to the Constitution, the State Government and in any other case, the Central Government;

(f) "asymmetric crypto system" means a system of a secure key pair consisting of a private key for creating a digital signature and a public key to verify the digital signature;

(g) "Certifying Authority" means a person who has been granted a licence to issue a Digital Signature Certificate under section 24;

(h) "certification practice statement" means a statement issued by a Certifying Authority to specify the practices that the Certifying Authority employs in issuing Digital Signature Certificates;

(i) "computer" means any electronic magnetic, optical or other high-speed data processing device or system which performs logical, arithmetic, and memory functions by manipulations of electronic, magnetic or optical impulses, and includes all input, output, processing, storage, computer software, or communication facilities which are connected or related to the computer in a computer system or computer network;

(j) "computer network" means the interconnection of one or more computers through

(i) the use of satellite, microwave, terrestrial line or other communication media; and

(ii) terminals or a complex consisting of two or more interconnected computers whether or not the interconnection is continuously maintained;

(k) "computer resource" means computer, computer system, computer network, data, computer database or software;

(l) "computer system" means a device or collection of devices, including input and output support devices and excluding calculators which are not programmable and capable of being used in conjunction with external files, which contain computer programmes, electronic instructions, input data and output data, that performs logic, arithmetic, data storage and retrieval, communication control and other functions;

(m) "Controller" means the Controller of Certifying Authorities appointed under sub-section (l) of section 17;

(n) "Cyber Appellate Tribunal" means the Cyber Regulations Appellate Tribunal established under sub-section (1) of section 48;

(o)"data" means a representation of information, knowledge, facts, concepts or instructions which are being prepared or have been prepared in a formalized manner, and is intended to be processed, is being processed or has been processed in a computer system or computer network, and may be in any form (including computer printouts magnetic or optical storage media, punched cards, punched tapes) or stored internally in the memory of the computer;

(p) "digital signature" means authentication of any electronic record by a subscriber by means of an electronic method or procedure in accordance with the provisions of section 3;

(q) "Digital Signature Certificate" means a Digital Signature Certificate issued under sub-section (4) of section 35;

(r) "electronic form" with reference to information means any information generated, sent, received or stored in media, magnetic, optical, computer memory, micro film, computer generated micro fiche or similar device;

(s) "Electronic Gazette" means the Official Gazette published in the electronic form;

(t) "electronic record" means data, record or data generated, image or sound stored, received or sent in an electronic form or micro film or computer generated micro fiche;

(u) "function", in relation to a computer, includes logic, control arithmetical process, deletion, storage and retrieval and communication or telecommunication from or within a computer;

(v) "information" includes data, text, images, sound, voice, codes, computer programmes, software and databases or micro film or computer generated micro fiche:

(w) "intermediary" with respect to any particular electronic message means any person who on behalf of another person receives, stores or transmits that message or provides any service with respect to that message;

(x) "key pair", in an asymmetric crypto system, means a private key and its mathematically related public key, which are so related that the public key can verify a digital signature created by the private key;

(y) "law" includes any Act of Parliament or of a State Legislature, Ordinances promulgated by the President or a Governor, as the case may be. Regulations made by the President under article 240, Bills enacted as President's Act under sub-clause (a) of clause (1) of article 357 of the Constitution and includes rules, regulations, bye-laws and orders issued or made thereunder;

(z) "licence" means a licence granted to a Certifying Authority under section 24;

(za) "originator" means a person who sends, generates, stores or transmits any electronic message or causes any electronic message to be sent, generated, stored or transmitted to any other person but does not include an intermediary;

(zb) "prescribed" means prescribed by rules made under this Act;

(zc) "private key" means the key of a key pair used to create a digital signature;

(zd) "public key" means the key of a key pair used to verify a digital signature and listed in the Digital Signature Certificate;

(ze) "secure system" means computer hardware, software, and procedure that

(a) are reasonably secure from unauthorized access and misuse;
(b) provide a reasonable level of reliability and correct operation;
(c) are reasonably suited to performing the intended functions; and
(d) adhere to generally accepted security procedures;

(zf) "security procedure" means the security procedure prescribed under section 16 by the Central Government;

(zg) "subscriber" means a person in whose name the Digital Signature Certificate is issued;

(zh) "verify" in relation to a digital signature, electronic record or public key, with its grammatical variations and cognate expressions means to determine whether

(a) the initial electronic record was affixed with the digital signature by the use of private key corresponding to the public key of the subscriber;
(b) the initial electronic record is retained intact or has been altered since such electronic record was so affixed with the digital signature.

(2) Any reference in this Act to any enactment or any provision thereof shall, in relation to an area in which such enactment or such provision is not in force, be construed as a reference to the corresponding law or the relevant provision of the corresponding law, if any, in force in that area.

Chapter II

Digital Signature

3. Authentication of Electronic Records.

(1) Subject to the provisions of this section any subscriber may authenticate an electronic record by affixing his digital signature.
(2) The authentication of the electronic record shall be effected by the use of asymmetric crypto system and hash function which envelop and transform the initial electronic record into another electronic record.

Explanation. For the purposes of this sub-section, "hash function" means an algorithm mapping or translation of one sequence of bits into another, generally smaller, set known as "hash result" such that an electronic record yields the same hash result every time the algorithm is executed with the same electronic record as its input making it computationally infeasible

(a) to derive or reconstruct the original electronic record from the hash result produced by the algorithm;
(b) that two electronic records can produce the same hash result using the algorithm.

(3) Any person by the use of a public key of the subscriber can verify the electronic record.
(4) The private key and the public key are unique to the subscriber and constitute a functioning key pair.

Chapter III

Electronic Governance

4. Legal Recognition of Electronic Records.

Where any law provides that information or any other matter shall be in writing or in the typewritten or printed form, then, notwithstanding anything contained in such law, such requirement shall be deemed to have been satisfied if such information or matter is

(a) rendered or made available in an electronic form; and
(b) accessible so as to be usable for a subsequent reference.

5. Legal Recognition of Digital Signatures.

Where any law provides that information or any other matter shall be authenticated by affixing the signature or any document shall be signed or bear the signature of any person then, notwithstanding anything contained in such law, such requirement shall be deemed to have been satisfied, if such information or matter is authenticated by means of digital signature affixed in such manner as may be prescribed by the Central Government.

Explanation. For the purposes of this section, "signed", with its grammatical variations and cognate expressions, shall, with reference to a person, mean affixing of his hand written signature or any mark on any document and the expression "signaturc" shall be construed accordingly.

6. Use of Electronic Records and Digital Signatures in Government and its Agencies.

(1) Where any law provides for

(a) the filing of any form, application or any other document with any office, authority, body or agency owned or controlled by the appropriate Government in a particular manner;

(b) the issue or grant of any licence, permit, sanction or approval by whatever name called in a particular manner;

(c) the receipt or payment of money in a particular manner, then, notwithstanding anything contained in any other law for the time being in force, such requirement shall be deemed to have been satisfied if such filing, issue, grant, receipt or payment, as the case may be, is effected by means of such electronic form as may be prescribed by the appropriate Government.

(2) The appropriate Government may, for the purposes of sub-section (1), by rules, prescribe

(a) the manner and format in which such electronic records shall be filed, created or issued;

(b) the manner or method of payment of any fee or charges for filing, creation or issue any electronic record under clause (a).

7. Retention of Electronic Records.

(1) Where any law provides that documents, records or information shall be retained for any specific period, then, that requirement shall be deemed to have been satisfied if such documents, records or information are retained in the electronic form, if

(a) the information contained therein remains accessible so as to be usable for a subsequent reference;

(b) the electronic record is retained in the format in which it was originally generated, sent or received or in a format which can be demonstrated to represent accurately the information originally generated, sent or received;

(c) the details which will facilitate the identification of the origin, destination, date and time of despatch or receipt of such electronic record are available in the electronic record:

Provided that this clause does not apply to any information which is automatically generated solely for the purpose of enabling an electronic record to be despatched or received.

(2) Nothing in this section shall apply to any law that expressly provides for the retention of documents, records or information in the form of electronic records.

8. Publication of Rule, Regulation, etc., in Electronic Gazette.

Where any law provides that any rule, regulation, order, bye-law, notification or any other matter shall be published in the Official Gazette, then, such requirement shall be deemed to have been satisfied if such rule, regulation, order, bye-law, notification or any other matter is published in the Official Gazette or Electronic Gazette :

Provided that where any rule, regulation, order, bye-law, notification or any other matter is published in the Official Gazette or Electronic Gazette, the date of publication shall be deemed to be the date of the Gazette which was first published in any form.

9. Sections 6, 7 and 8 not to Confer Right to Insist Document Should be Accepted in Electronic Form.

Nothing contained in sections 6, 7 and 8 shall confer a right upon any person to insist that any Ministry or Department of the Central Government or the State Government or any authority or body established by or under any law or controlled or funded by the Central or State Government should accept, issue, create, retain and preserve any document in the form of electronic records or effect any monetary transaction in the electronic form.

10. Power to Make Rules by Central Government in Respect of Digital Signature.

The Central Government may, for the purposes of this Act, by rules, prescribe :

(a) the type of digital signature;
(b) the manner and format in which the digital signature shall be

affixed;

(c) the manner or procedure which facilitates identification of the person affixing the digital signature;

(d) control processes and procedures to ensure adequate integrity, security and confidentiality of electronic records or payments; and

(e) any other matter which is necessary to give legal effect to digital signatures.

Chapter IV

Attribution, Acknowledgment and Despatch of Electronic Records

11. Attribution of Electronic Records.

An electronic record shall be attributed to the originator

(a) if it was sent by the originator himself;

(b) by a person who had the authority to act on behalf of the originator in respect of that electronic record; or

(c) by an information system programmed by or on behalf of the originator to operate automatically.

12. Acknowledgment of Receipt.

(1) Where the originator has not agreed with the addressee that the acknowledgment of receipt of electronic record be given in a particular form or by a particular method, an acknowledgment may be given by

(a) any communication by the addressee, automated or otherwise; or

(b) any conduct of the addressee, sufficient to indicate to the originator that the electronic record has been received.

(2) Where the originator has stipulated that the electronic record shall be binding only on receipt of an acknowledgment of such electronic record by him, then unless acknowledgment has

been so received, the electronic record shall be deemed to have been never sent by the originator.

(3) Where the originator has not stipulated that the electronic record shall be binding only on receipt of such acknowledgment, and the acknowledgment has not been received by the originator within the time specified or agreed or, if no time has been specified or agreed to within a reasonable time, then the originator may give notice to the addressee stating that no acknowledgment has been received by him and specifying a reasonable time by which the acknowledgment must be received by him and if no acknowledgment is received within the aforesaid time limit he may after giving notice to the addressee, treat the electronic record as though it has never been sent.

13. Time and Place of Despatch and Receipt of Electronic Record.

(1) Save as otherwise agreed to between the originator and the addressee, the dispatch of an electronic record occurs when it enters a computer resource outside the control of the originator.

(2) Save as otherwise agreed between the originator and the addressee, the time of receipt of an electronic record shall be determined as follows, namely :

(a) if the addressee has designated a computer resource for the purpose of receiving electronic records,

(i) receipt occurs at the time when the electronic record enters the designated computer resource; or

(ii) if the electronic record is sent to a computer resource of the addressee that is not the designated computer resource, receipt occurs at the time when the electronic record is retrieved by the addressee;

(b) if the addressee has not designated a computer resource along with specified timings, if any, receipt occurs when the electronic record enters the computer resource of the addressee.

(3) Save as otherwise agreed to between the originator and the

addressee, an electronic record is deemed to be dispatched at the place where the originator has his place of business, and is deemed to be received at the place where the addressee has his place of business.

(4) The provisions of sub-section (2) shall apply notwithstanding that the place where the computer resource is located may be different from the place where the electronic record is deemed to have been received under sub-section (3).

(5) For the purposes of this section,

(a) if the originator or the addressee has more than one place of business, the principal place of business, shall be the place of business;

(b) if the originator or the addressee does not have a place of business, his usual place of residence shall be deemed to be the place of business;

(c) "usual place of residence", in relation to a body corporate, means the place where it is registered.

Chapter V

Secure Electronic Records and Secure Digital Signatures

14. Secure Electronic Record.

Where any security procedure has been applied to an electronic record at a specific point of time, then such record shall be deemed to be a secure electronic record from such point of time to the time of verification.

15. Secure Digital Signature.

If, by application of a security procedure agreed to by the parties concerned, it can be verified that a digital signature, at the time it was affixed, was

(a) unique to the subscriber affixing it;
(b) capable of identifying such subscriber;
(c) created in a manner or using a means under the exclusive control

of the subscriber and is linked to the electronic record to which it relates in such a manner that if the electronic record was altered the digital signature would be invalidated, then such digital signature shall be deemed to be a secure digital signature.

16. Security Procedure.

The Central Government shall for the purposes of this Act prescribe the security procedure having regard to commercial circumstances prevailing at the time when the procedure was used, including

(a) the nature of the transaction;
(b) the level of sophistication of the parties with reference to their technological capacity;
(c) the volume of similar transactions engaged in by other parties;
(d) the availability of alternatives offered to but rejected by any party;
(e) the cost of alternative procedures; and
(f) the procedures in general use for similar types of transactions or communications.

Chapter VI

Regulation of Certifying Authorities

17. Appointment of Controller and Other Officers

(1) The Central Government may, by notification in the Official Gazette, appoint a Controller of Certifying Authorities for the purposes of this Act and may also by the same or subsequent notification appoint such number of Deputy Controllers and Assistant Controllers as it deems fit.
(2) The Controller shall discharge his functions under this Act subject to the general control and directions of the Central Government.
(3) The Deputy Controllers and Assistant Controllers shall perform the functions assigned to them by the Controller under the general superintendence and control of the Controller.
(4) The qualifications, experience and terms and conditions of service of Controller, Deputy Controllers and Assistant Controllers shall

be such as may be prescribed by the Central Government.

(5) The Head Office and Branch Office of the office of the Controller shall be at such places as the Central Government may specify, and these may be established at such places as the Central Government may think fit.

(6) There shall be a seal of the Office of the Controller.

18. Functions of Controller.

The Controller may perform all or any of the following functions, namely:

(a) exercising supervision over the activities of the Certifying Authorities;
(b) certifying public keys of the Certifying Authorities;
(c) laying down the standards to be maintained by the Certifying Authorities;
(d) specifying the qualifications and experience which employees of the Certifying Authorities should possess;
(e) specifying the conditions subject to which the Certifying Authorities shall conduct their business;
(f) specifying the contents of written, printed or visual materials and advertisements that may be distributed or used in respect of a Digital Signature Certificate and the public key;
(g) specifying the form and content of a Digital Signature Certificate and the key;
(h) specifying the form and manner in which accounts shall be maintained by the Certifying Authorities;
(i) specifying the terms and conditions subject to which auditors may be appointed and the remuneration to be paid to them;
(j) facilitating the establishment of any electronic system by a Certifying Authority either solely or jointly with other Certifying Authorities and regulation of such systems;
(k) specifying the manner in which the Certifying Authorities shall conduct their dealings with the subscribers;
(l) resolving any conflict of interests between the Certifying Authorities and the subscribers;
(m) laying down the duties of the Certifying Authorities;
(n) maintaining a database containing the disclosure record of every

Certifying Authority containing such particulars as may be specified by regulations, which shall be accessible to public.

19. Recognition of Foreign Certifying Authorities.

(1) Subject to such conditions and restrictions as may be specified by regulations, the Controller may with the previous approval of the Central Government, and by notification in the Official Gazette, recognize any foreign Certifying Authority as a Certifying Authority for the purposes of this Act.
(2) Where any Certifying Authority is recognised under sub-section (1), the Digital Signature Certificate issued by such Certifying Authority shall be valid for the purposes of this Act.
(3) The Controller may, if he is satisfied that any Certifying Authority has contravened any of the conditions and restrictions subject to which it was granted recognition under sub-section (1) he may, for reasons to be recorded in writing, by notification in the Official Gazette, revoke such recognition.

20. Controller to Act as Repository.

(1) The Controller shall be the repository of all Digital Signature Certificates issued under this Act.
(2) The Controller shall

(a) make use of hardware, software and procedures that are secure from intrusion and misuse;
(b) observe such other standards as may be prescribed by the Central Government, to ensure that the secrecy and security of the digital signatures are assured.

(3) The Controller shall maintain a computerised database of all public keys in such a manner that such database and the public keys are available to any member of the public.

21. Licence to Issue Digital Signature Certificates.

(1) Subject to the provisions of sub-section (2), any person may make an application, to the Controller, for a licence to issue

Digital Signature Certificates.

(2) No licence shall be issued under sub-section (1), unless the applicant fulfils such requirements with respect to qualification, expertise, manpower, financial resources and other infrastructure facilities, which are necessary to issue Digital Signature Certificates as may be prescribed by the Central Government.

(3) A licence granted under this section shall

(a) be valid for such period as may be prescribed by the Central Government;
(b) not be transferable or heritable;
(c) be subject to such terms and conditions as may be specified by the regulations.

22. Application for Licence.

(1) Every application for issue of a licence shall be in such form as may be prescribed by the Central Government.

(2) Every application for issue of a licence shall be accompanied by

(a) a certification practice statement;
(b) a statement including the procedures with respect to identification of the applicant;
(c) payment of such fees, not exceeding twenty-five thousand rupees as may be prescribed by the Central Government;
(d) such other documents, as may be prescribed by the Central Government.

23. Renewal of Licence.

An application for renewal of a licence shall be

(a) in such form;
(b) accompanied by such fees, not exceeding five thousand rupees, as may be prescribed by the Central Government and shall be made not less than forty-five days before the date of expiry of the period of validity of the licence.

24. Procedure for Grant or Rejection of Licence.

The Controller may, on receipt of an application under sub-section (1) of section 21, after considering the documents accompanying the application and such other factors, as he deems fit, grant the licence or reject the application:

Provided that no application shall be rejected under this section unless the applicant has been given a reasonable opportunity of presenting his case.

25. Suspension of Licence.

(1) The Controller may, if he is satisfied after making such inquiry, as he may think fit, that a Certifying Authority has,

(a) made a statement in, or in relation to, the application for the issue or renewal of the licence, which is incorrect or false in material particulars;

(b) failed to comply with the terms and conditions subject to which the licence was granted;

(c) failed to maintain the standards specified under clause (b) of sub-section (2) of section 20;

(d) contravened any provisions of this Act, rule, regulation or order made thereunder, revoke the licence :

Provided that no licence shall be revoked unless the Certifying Authority has been given a reasonable opportunity of showing cause against the proposed revocation.

(2) The Controller may, if he has reasonable cause to believe that there is any ground for revoking a licence under sub-section (1), by order suspend such licence pending the completion of any inquiry ordered by him.

Provided that no licence shall be suspended for a period exceeding ten days unless the Certifying Authority has been given a reasonable opportunity of showing cause against the proposed suspension.

(3) No Certifying Authority whose licence has been suspended shall issue any Digital Signature Certificate during such suspension.

26. Notice of Suspension or Revocation of Licence.

(1) Where the licence of the Certifying Authority is suspended or revoked, the Controller shall publish notice of such suspension or revocation, as the case may be, in the database maintained by him.

(2) Where one or more repositories are specified, the Controller shall publish notices of such suspension or revocation, as the case may be, in all such repositories:

Provided that the data base containing the notice of such suspension or revocation, as the case may be, shall be made available through a web site which shall be accessible round the clock:

Provided further that the Controller may, if he considers necessary, publicize the contents of database in such electronic or other media, as he may consider appropriate.

27. Power to Delegate.

The Controller may, in writing, authorise the Deputy Controller, Assistant Controller or any officer to exercise any of the powers of the Controller under this Chapter.

28. Power to Investigate Contraventions.

(1) The Controller or any officer authorised by him in this behalf shall take up for investigation any contravention of the provisions of this Act, rules or regulations made thereunder.

(2) The Controller or any officer authorised by him in this behalf shall exercise the like powers which are conferred on Income-tax authorities under Chapter XIII of the Income-tax Act, 1961 and shall exercise such powers, subject to such limitations laid down under that Act.

29. Access to Computers and Data.

(1) Without prejudice to the provisions of sub-section (1) of section 69, the Controller or any person authorized by him shall, if he

has reasonable cause to suspect that any contravention of the provisions of this Act, rules or regulations made thereunder has been committed, have access to any computer system, any apparatus, data or any other material connected with such system, for the purpose of searching or causing a search to be made for obtaining any information or data contained in or available to such computer system.

(2) For the purposes of sub-section (1), the Controller or any person authorized by him may, by order, direct any person in charge of, or otherwise concerned with the operation of, the computer system, data apparatus or material, to provide him with such reasonable technical and other assistance as he may consider necessary.

30. Certifying Authority to Follow Certain Procedures.

Every Certifying Authority shall,

(a) make use of hardware, software and procedures that are secure from intrusion and misuse;
(b) provide a reasonable level of reliability in its services which are reasonably suited to the performance of intended functions;
(c) adhere to security procedures to ensure that the secrecy and privacy of the digital signatures are assured; and
(d) observe such other standards as may be specified by regulations.

31. Certifying Authority to Ensure Compliance of the Act, etc.

Every Certifying Authority shall ensure that every person employed or otherwise engaged by it complies, in the course of his employment or engagement, with the provisions of this Act, rules, regulations and orders made thereunder.

32. Display of Licence.

Every Certifying Authority shall display its licence at a conspicuous place of the premises in which it carries on its business.

33. Surrender of Licence.

(1) Every Certifying Authority whose licence is suspended or revoked shall immediately after such suspension or revocation, surrender the licence to the Controller.

(2) Where any Certifying Authority fails to surrender a licence under sub-section (1), the person in whose favour a licence is issued, shall be guilty of an offence and shall be punished with imprisonment which may extend up to six months or a fine which may extend up to ten thousand rupees or with both.

34. Disclosure

(1) Every Certifying Authority shall disclose in the manner specified by regulations

(a) its Digital Signature Certificate which contains the public key corresponding to the private key used by that Certifying Authority to digitally sign another Digital Signature Certificate;
(b) any certification practice statement relevant thereto;
(c) notice of the revocation or suspension of its Certifying Authority certificate, if any; and
(d) any other fact that materially and adversely affects either the reliability of a Digital Signature Certificate, which that Authority has issued, or the Authority's ability to perform its services.

(2) Where in the opinion of the Certifying Authority any event has occurred or any situation has arisen which may materially and adversely affect the integrity of its computer system or the conditions subject to which a Digital Signature Certificate was granted, then, the Certifying Authority shall

(a) use reasonable efforts to notify any person who is likely to be affected by that occurrence; or
(b) act in accordance with the procedure specified in its certification practice statement to deal with such event or situation.

Chapter VII

Digital Signature Certificates

35. Certifying Authority to Issue Digital Signature Certificate

(1) Any person may make an application to the Certifying Authority for the issue of a Digital Signature Certificate in such form as may be prescribed by the Central Government.

(2) Every such application shall be accompanied by such fee not exceeding twenty-five thousand rupees as may be prescribed by the Central Government, to be paid to the Certifying Authority: Provided that while prescribing fees under sub-section (2) different fees may be prescribed for different classes of applicants.

(3) Every such application shall be accompanied by a certification practice statement or where there is no such statement, a statement containing such particulars, as may be specified by regulations.

(4) On receipt of an application under sub-section (1), the Certifying Authority may, after consideration of the certification practice statement or the other statement under sub-section (3) and after making such enquiries as it may deem fit, grant the Digital Signature Certificate or for reasons to be recorded in writing, reject the application.

Provided that no Digital Signature Certificate shall be granted unless the Certifying Authority is satisfied that—

(a) the applicant holds the private key corresponding to the public key to be listed in the Digital Signature Certificate;

(b) the applicant holds a private key, which is capable of creating a digital signature;

(c) the public key to be listed in the certificate can be used to verify a digital signature affixed by the private key held by the applicant:

Provided further that no application shall be rejected unless the applicant has been given a reasonable opportunity of showing cause against the proposed rejection.

36. Representations upon Issuance of Digital Signature Certificate.

A Certifying Authority while issuing a Digital Signature Certificate shall certify that —

(a) it has complied with the provisions of this Act and the rules and regulations made thereunder;
(b) it has published the Digital Signature Certificate or otherwise made it available to such person relying on it and the subscriber has accepted it;
(c) the subscriber holds the private key corresponding to the public key, listed in the Digital Signature Certificate;
(d) the subscriber's public key and private key constitute a functioning key pair;
(e) the information contained in the Digital Signature Certificate is accurate; and
(f) it has no knowledge of any material fact, which if it had been included in the Digital Signature Certificate would adversely affect the reliability of the representations made in clauses (a) to (d).

37. Suspension of Digital Signature Certificate.

(1) Subject to the provisions of sub-section (2), the Certifying Authority which has issued a Digital Signature Certificate may suspend such Digital Signature Certificate,

(a) on receipt of a request to that effect from

(i) the subscriber listed in to Digital Signature Certificate; or
(ii) any person duly authorised to act on behalf of that subscriber,

(b) if it is of opinion that the Digital Signature Certificate should be suspended in public interest.

(2) A Digital Signature Certificate shall not be suspended for a period

exceeding fifteen days unless the subscriber has been given an opportunity of being heard in the matter.

(3) On suspension of a Digital Signature Certificate under this section, the Certifying Authority shall communicate the same to the subscriber.

38. Revocation of Digital Signature Certificate.

(1) A Certifying Authority may revoke a Digital Signature Certificate issued by it

(a) where the subscriber or any other person authorised by him makes a request to that effect; or
(b) upon the death of the subscriber, or
(c) upon the dissolution of the firm or winding up of the company where the subscriber is a firm or a company.

(2) Subject to the provisions of sub-section (3) and without prejudice to the provisions of sub-section (1), a Certifying Authority may revoke a Digital Signature Certificate which has been issued by it at any time, if it is of opinion that

(a) a material fact represented in the Digital Signature Certificate is false or has been concealed;
(b) a requirement for issuance of the Digital Signature Certificate was not satisfied;
(c) the Certifying Authority's private key or security system was compromised in a manner materially affecting the Digital Signature Certificate's reliability;
(d) the subscriber has been declared insolvent or dead or where a subscriber is a firm or a company, which has been dissolved, wound-up or otherwise ceased to exist.

(3) A Digital Signature Certificate shall not be revoked unless the subscriber has been given an opportunity of being heard in the matter.

(4) On revocation of a Digital Signature Certificate under this section, the Certifying Authority shall communicate the same to the subscriber.

39. Notice of Suspension or Revocation.

(1) Where a Digital Signature Certificate is suspended or revoked under section 37 or section 38, the Certifying Authority shall publish a notice of such suspension or revocation, as the case may be, in the repository specified in the Digital Signature Certificate for publication of such notice.

(2) Where one or more repositories are specified, the Certifying Authority shall publish notices of such suspension or revocation, as the case may be in all such repositories.

Chapter VIII

Duties of Subscribers

40. Generating Key Pair.

Where any Digital Signature Certificate, the public key of which corresponds to the private key of that subscriber which is to be listed in the Digital Signature Certificate has been accepted by a subscriber, then, the subscriber shall generate the key pair by applying the security procedure.

41. Acceptance of Digital Signature Certificate.

(1) A subscriber shall be deemed to have accepted a Digital Signature Certificate if he publishes or authorizes the publication of a Digital Signature Certificate

(a) to one or more persons;
(b) in a repository, or otherwise demonstrates his approval of the Digital Signature Certificate in any manner.

(2) By accepting a Digital Signature Certificate the subscriber certifies to all who reasonably rely on the information contained in the Digital Signature Certificate that

(a) the subscriber holds the private key corresponding to the public key listed in the Digital Signature Certificate and is entitled to hold the same;

(b) all representations made by the subscriber to the Certifying Authority and all material relevant to the information contained in the Digital Signature Certificate are true;

(c) all information in the Digital Signature Certificate that is within the knowledge of the subscriber is true.

42. Control of Private Key.

(1) Every subscriber shall exercise reasonable care to retain control of the private key corresponding to the public key listed in his Digital Signature Certificate and take all steps to prevent its disclosure to a person not authorized to affix the digital signature of the subscriber.

(2) If the private key corresponding to the public key listed in the Digital Signature Certificate has been compromised, then, the subscriber shall communicate the same without any delay to the Certifying Authority in such manner as may be specified by the regulations.

Explanation. For the removal of doubts, it is hereby declared that the subscriber shall be liable till he has informed the Certifying Authority that the private key has been compromised.

Chapter IX

Penalties and Adjudication

43. Penalty for Damage to Computer, Computer System, etc.

If any person without permission of the owner or any other person who is in charge of a computer, computer system or computer network,

(a) accesses or secures access to such computer, computer system or computer network;

(b) downloads, copies or extracts any data, computer database or information from such computer, computer system or computer network including information or data held or stored in any removable storage medium;

(c) introduces or causes to be introduced any computer contaminant or computer virus into any computer, computer system or computer network;

(d) damages or causes to be damaged any computer, computer system or computer network, data, computer data base or any other programmes residing in such computer, computer system or computer network;

(e) disrupts or causes disruption of any computer, computer system or computer network;

(f) denies or causes the denial of access to any person authorized to access any computer, computer system or computer network by any means;

(g) provides any assistance to any person to facilitate access to a computer, computer system or computer network in contravention of the provisions of this Act, rules or regulations made thereunder;

(h) charges the services availed of by a person to the account of another person by tampering with or manipulating any computer, computer system, or computer network, he shall be liable to pay damages by way of compensation not exceeding one crore rupees to the person so affected. *Explanation.* For the purposes of this section.

(i) "computer contaminant" means any set of computer instructions that are designed

(a) to modify,destroy, record, transmit data or programme residing within a computer, computer system or computer network; or

(b) by any means to usurp the normal operation of the computer, coputer system, or computer network;

(ii) "computer database" means a representation of information, knowledge, facts, concepts or instructions in text, image, audio, video that are being prepared or have been prepared in a formalized manner or have been produced by a computer,

computer system or computer network and are intended for use in a computer, computer system or computer network;

(iii) "computer virus" means any computer instruction, information, data or programme that destroys, damages, degrades or adversely affects the performance of a computer resource or attaches itself to another computer resource and operates when a programme, data or instruction is executed or some other event takes place in that computer resource;

(iv) "damage" means to destroy, alter, delete, add, modify or rearrange any computer resource by any means.

44. Penalty for Failure to Furnish Information Return, etc.

If any person who is required under this Act or any rules or regulations made thereunder to

(a) furnish any document, return or report to the Controller or the Certifying Authority fails to furnish the same, he shall be liable to a penalty not exceeding one lakh and fifty thousand rupees for each such failure;

(b) file any return or furnish any information, books or other documents within the time specified therefor in the regulations fails to file return or furnish the same within the time specified therefor in the regulations, he shall be liable to a penalty not exceeding five thousand rupees for everyday during which such failure continues;

(c) maintain books of account or records, fails to maintain the same, he shall be liable to a penalty not exceeding ten thousand rupees for everyday during which the failure continues.

45. Residuary Penalty

Whoever contravenes any rules or regulations made under this Act, for the contravention of which no penalty has been separately provided, shall be liable to pay a compensation not exceeding twenty-five thousand rupees to the person affected by such contravention or a penalty not exceeding twenty-five thousand rupees.

46. Power to Adjudicate.

(1) For the purpose of adjudging under this Chapter whether any person has committed a contravention of any of the provisions of this Act or of any rule, regulation, direction or order made thereunder the Central Government shall, subject to the provisions of sub-section (3), appoint any officer not below the rank of a Director to the Government of India or an equivalent officer of a State Government to be an adjudicating officer for holding an inquiry in the manner prescribed by the Central Government.

(2) The adjudicating officer shall, after giving the person referred to in sub-section (1) a reasonable opportunity for making representation in the matter and if, on such inquiry, he is satisfied that the person has committed the contravention, he may impose such penalty or award such compensation as he thinks fit in accordance with the provisions of that section.

(3) No person shall be appointed as an adjudicating officer unless he possesses such experience in the field of Information Technology and legal or judicial experience as may be prescribed by the Central Government.

(4) Where more than one adjudicating officers are appointed, the Central Government shall specify by order the matters and places with respect to which such officers shall exercise their jurisdiction.

(5) Every adjudicating officer shall have the powers of a civil court which are conferred on the Cyber Appellate Tribunal under sub-section (2) of section 58, and

(a) all proceedings before it shall be deemed to be judicial proceedings within the meaning of sections193 and 228 of the Indian Penal Code;

(b) shall be deemed to be a civil court for the purposes of sections 345 and 346 of the Code of Criminal Procedure, 1973.

47. Factors to be Taken into Account by the Adjudicating Officer.

While adjudging the quantum of compensation under this Chapter, the adjudicating officer shall have due regard to the following factors, namely :

(a) the amount of gain of unfair advantage, wherever quantifiable, made as a result of the default;
(b) the amount of loss caused to any person as a result of the default;
(c) the repetitive nature of the default

Chapter X

The Cyber Regulations Appellate Tribunal

48. Establishment of Cyber Appellate Tribunal

(1) The Central Government shall, by notification, establish one or more appellate tribunals to be known as the Cyber Regulations Appellate Tribunal.
(2) The Central Government shall also specify, in the notification referred to in sub-section (1), the matters and places in relation to which the Cyber Appellate Tribunal may exercise jurisdiction.

49.Composition of Cyber Appellate Tribunal

A Cyber Appellate Tribunal shall consist of one person only (hereinafter referred to as the Residing Officer of the Cyber Appellate Tribunal) to be appointed, by notification, by the Central Government.

50. Qualifications for Appointment as Presiding Officer of the Cyber Appellate Tribunal

A person shall not be qualified for appointment as the Presiding Officer of a Cyber Appellate Tribunal unless he

(a) is, or has been, or is qualified to be, a Judge of a High Court; or
(b) is or has been a member of the Indian Legal Service and is holding or has held a post in Grade I of that Service for at least three years.

51. Term of Office.

The Presiding Officer of a Cyber Appellate Tribunal shall hold office for a term of five years from the date on which he enters upon his office or until he attains the age of sixty-five years, whichever is earlier.

52. Salary, Allowances and Other Terms and Conditions of Service of Presiding Officer.

The salary and allowances payable to, and the other terms and conditions of service including pension, gratuity and other retirement benefits of the Presiding Officer of a Cyber Appellate Tribunal shall be such as may be prescribed:

Provided that neither the salary and allowances nor the other terms and conditions of service of the Presiding Officer shall be varied to his disadvantage after appointment.

53. Filling up of Vacancies.

If, for reason other than temporary absence, any vacancy occurs in the office of the Presiding Officer of a Cyber Appellate Tribunal, then the Central Government shall appoint another person in accordance with the provisions of this Act to fill the vacancy and the proceedings may be continued before the Cyber Appellate Tribunal from the stage at which the vacancy is filled.

54. Resignation and Removal.

(1) The Presiding Officer of a Cyber Appellate Tribunal may, by notice in writing under his hand addressed to the Central Government, resign his office :
Provided that the said Presiding Officer shall, unless he is permitted by the Central Government to relinquish his office sooner, continue to hold office until the expiry of three months from the date of receipt of such notice or until a person duly appointed as his successor enters upon his office or until the expiry of his term of office, whichever is the earliest.

(2) The Presiding Officer of a Cyber Appellate Tribunal shall not be removed from his office except by an order by the Central Government on the ground of proved misbehaviour or incapacity after an inquiry made by a Judge of the Supreme Court in which the Presiding Officer concerned has been informed of the charges

against him and given a reasonable opportunity of being heard in respect of these charges.

(3) The Central Government may, by rules, regulate the procedure for the investigation of misbehaviour or incapacity of the aforesaid Presiding Officer.

55. Orders Constituting Appellate Tribunal to be Final and not to Invalidate its Proceedings.

No order of the Central Government appointing any person as the Presiding Officer of a Cyber Appellate Tribunal shall be called in question in any manner and no act or proceeding before a Cyber Appellate Tribunal shall be called in question in any manner on the ground merely of any defect in the constitution of a Cyber Appellate Tribunal.

56. Staff of the Cyber Appellate Tribunal.

(1) The Central Government shall provide the Cyber Appellate Tribunal with such officers and employees as that Government may think fit.

(2) The officers and employees of the Cyber Appellate Tribunal shall discharge their functions under general superintendence of the Presiding Officer.

(3) The salaries, allowances and other conditions of service of the officers and employees of the Cyber Appellate Tribunal shall be such as may be prescribed by the Central Government.

57. Appeal to Cyber Appellate Tribunal.

(1) Save as provided in sub-section (2), any person aggrieved by an order made by Controller or an adjudicating officer under this Act may prefer an appeal to a Cyber Appellate Tribunal having jurisdiction in the matter.

(2) No appeal shall lie to the Cyber Appellate Tribunal from an order made by an adjudicating officer with the consent of the parties.

(3) Every appeal under sub-section (1) shall be filed within a period of twenty-five days from the date on which a copy of the order made by the Controller or the adjudicating officer is received by

the person aggrieved and it shall be in such form and be accompanied by such fee as may be prescribed :

Provided that the Cyber Appellate Tribunal may entertain an appeal after the expiry of the said period of forty-five days if it is satisfied that there was sufficient cause for not filing it within that period.

(4) On receipt of an appeal under sub-section (1), the Cyber Appellate Tribunal may, after giving the parties to the appeal, an opportunity of being heard, pass such orders thereon as it thinks fit, confirming, modifying or setting aside the order appealed against.

(5) The Cyber Appellate Tribunal shall send a copy of every order made by it to the parties to the appeal and to the concerned Controller or adjudicating officer.

(6) The appeal filed before the Cyber Appellate Tribunal under sub-section (1) shall be dealt with by it as expeditiously as possible and endeavour shall be made by it to dispose of the appeal finally within six months from the date of receipt of the appeal.

58. Procedure and Powers of the Cyber Appellate Tribunal.

(1) The Cyber Appellate Tribunal shall not be bound by the procedure laid down by the Code of Civil Procedure,1908 but shall be guided by the principles of natural justice and, subject to the other provisions of this Act and of any rules, the Cyber Appellate Tribunal shall have powers to regulate its own procedure including the place at which it shall have its sittings.

(2) The Cyber Appellate Tribunal shall have, for the purposes of discharging its functions under this Act, the same powers as are vested in a civil court under the Code of Civil Procedure, 1908, while trying a suit, in respect of the following matters, namely:

(a) summoning and enforcing the attendance of any person and examining him on oath;

(b) requiring the discovery and production of documents or other electronic records;

(c) receiving evidence on affidavits;

(d) issuing commissions for the examination of witnesses or documents;

(e) reviewing its decisions;
(f) dismissing an application for default or deciding it *ex parte;*
(g) any other matter which may be prescribed.

(3) Every proceeding before the Cyber Appellate Tribunal shall be deemed to be a judicial proceeding within the meaning of sections 193 and 228, and for the purposes of section 196 of the Indian Penal Code and the Cyber Appellate Tribunal shall be deemed to be a civil court for the purposes of section 195 and Chapter XXVI of the Code of Criminal Procedure, 1973.

59. Right to Legal Representation.

The appellant may either appear in person or authorize one or more legal practitioners or any of its officers to present his or its case before the Cyber Appellate Tribunal.

60. Limitation.

The provisions of the Limitation Act, 1963, shall, as far as may be, apply to an appeal made to the Cyber Appellate Tribunal.

61. Civil Court not to have Jurisdiction.

No court shall have jurisdiction to entertain any suit or proceeding in respect of any matter which an adjudicating officer appointed under this Act or the Cyber Appellate Tribunal constituted under this Act is empowered by or under this Act to determine and no injunction shall be granted by any court or other authority in respect of any action taken or to be taken in pursuance of any power conferred by or under this Act.

62. Appeal to High Court.

Any person aggrieved by any decision or order of the Cyber Appellate Tribunal may file an appeal to the High Court within sixty days from the date of communication of the decision or order of the Cyber Appellate Tribunal to him on any question of fact or law arising out of such order :

Provided that the High Court may, if it is satisfied that the appellant was prevented by sufficient cause from filing the appeal within the said period, allow it to be filed within a further period not exceeding sixty days.

63. Compounding of Contraventions.

(1) Any contravention under this Chapter may, either before or after the institution of adjudication proceedings, be compounded by the Controller or such other officer as may be specially authorized by him in this behalf or by the adjudicating officer, as the case may be, subject to such conditions as the Controller or such other officer or the adjudicating officer may specify :
Provided that such sum shall not, in any case, exceed the maximum amount of the penalty which may be imposed under this Act for the contravention so compounded.

(2) Nothing in sub-section (1) shall apply to a person who commits the same or similar contravention within a period of three years from the date on which the first contravention, committed by him, was compounded.

Explanation. For the purposes of this sub-section, any second or subsequent contravention committed after the expiry of a period of three years from the date on which the contravention was previously compounded shall be deemed to be a first contravention.

(4) Where any contravention has been compounded under sub-section (1), no proceeding or further proceeding, as the case may be, shall be taken against the person guilty of such contravention in respect of the contravention so compounded.

64. Recovery of Penalty.

A penalty imposed under this Act, if it is not paid, shall be recovered as an arrear of land revenue and the licence or the Digital Signature Certificate, as the case may be, shall be suspended till the penalty is paid.

Chapter XI

Offences

65. Tampering with Computer Source Documents.

Whoever knowingly or intentionally conceals, destroys or alters or intentionally or knowingly causes another to conceal, destroy or alter any computer source code used for a computer, computer programme, computer system or computer network, when the computer source code is required to be kept or maintained by law for the time being in force, shall be punishable with imprisonment up to three years, or with fine which may extend up to two lakh rupees, or with both.
Explanation. For the purposes of this section, "computer source code" means the listing of programmes, computer commands, design and layout and programme analysis of computer resource in any form.

66. Hacking with Computer System.

(1) Whoever with the intent to cause or knowing that he is likely to cause wrongful loss or damage to the public or any person destroys or deletes or alters any information residing in a computer resource or diminishes its value or utility or affects it injuriously by any means, commits hack;
(2) Whoever commits hacking shall be punished with imprisonment up to three years, or with fine which may extend up to two lakh rupees, or with both.

67. Publishing of Information Which is Obscene in Electronic Form.

Whoever publishes or transmits or causes to be published in the electronic form, any material which is lascivious or appeals to the prurient interest or if its effect is such as to tend to deprave and corrupt persons who are likely, having regard to all relevant circumstances, to read, see or hear the matter contained or embodied in it, shall be punished on first conviction with imprisonment of either description for a term which may extend to five years and with fine which may extend to one lakh rupees and in the event of a second or subsequent conviction with imprisonment of either description for a term which may extend to ten years and also with fine which may extend to two lakh rupees.

68. Power of Controller to give Directions.

(1) The Controller may, by order, direct a Certifying Authority or any employee of such Authority to take such measures or cease carrying on such activities as specified in the order if those are necessary to ensure compliance with the provisions of this Act, rules or any regulations made thereunder.
(2) Any person who fails to comply with any order under sub-section (1) shall be guilty of an offence and shall be liable on conviction to imprisonment for a term not exceeding three years or to a fine not exceeding two lakh rupees or to both.

69. Directions of Controller to a Subscriber to Extend Facilities to Decrypt Information.

(1) If the Controller is satisfied that it is necessary or expedient so to do in the interest of the sovereignty or integrity of India, the security of the State, friendly relations with foreign Stales or public order or for preventing incitement to the commission of any cognizable offence, for reasons to be recorded in writing, by order, direct any agency of the government to intercept any information transmitted through any computer resource.
(2) The subscriber or any person in charge of the computer resource shall, when called upon by any agency which has been directed under sub-section (1), extend all facilities and technical assistance to decrypt the information.
(3) The subscriber or any person who fails to assist the agency referred to in sub-section (2) shall be punished with an imprisonment for a term which may extend to seven years.

70. Protected System.

(1) The appropriate Government may, by notification in the Official Gazette, declare that any computer, computer system or computer network to be a protected system.

(2) The appropriate Government may, by order in writing, authorize the persons who are authorized to access protected systems notified under sub-section (1).

(3) Any person who secures access or attempts to secure access to a protected system in contravention of the provisions of this section shall be punished with imprisonment of either description for a term which may extend to ten years and shall also be liable to fine.

71. Penalty for Misrepresentation.

Whoever makes any misrepresentation to, or suppresses any material fact from, the Controller or the Certifying Authority for obtaining any licence or Digital Signature Certificate, as the case may be, shall be punished with imprisonment for a term which may extend to two years, or with fine which may extend to one lakh rupees, or with both.

72. Penalty for Breach of Confidentiality and Privacy.

Save as otherwise provided in this Act or any other law for the time being in force, any person who, in pursuance of any of the powers conferred under this Act, rules or regulations made thereunder, has secured access to any electronic record, book, register, correspondence, information, document or other material without the consent of the person concerned discloses such electronic record, book, register, correspondence, information, document or other material to any other person shall be punished with imprisonment for a term which may extend to two years, or with fine which may extend to one lakh rupees, or with both.

73. Penalty for Publishing Digital Signature Certificate False in Certain Particulars.

(1) No person shall publish a Digital Signature Certificate or otherwise make it available to any other person with the knowledge that

(a) the Certifying Authority listed in the certificate has not issued it; or

(b) the subscriber listed in the certificate has not accepted it; or
(c) the certificate has been revoked or suspended, unless such publication is for the purpose of verifying a digital signature created prior to such suspension or revocation

(2) Any person who contravenes the provisions of sub-section (1) shall be punished with imprisonment for a term which may extend to two years, or with fine which may extend to one lakh rupees, or with both.

74. Publication for Fraudulent Purpose.

Whoever knowingly creates, publishes or otherwise makes available a Digital Signature Certificate for any fraudulent or unlawful purpose shall be punished with imprisonment for a term which may extend to two years, or with fine which may extend to one lakh rupees, or with both.

75. Act to Apply for Offence or Contravention Committed Outside India.

(1) Subject to the provisions of sub-section (2), the provisions of this Act shall apply also to any offence or contravention committed outside India by any person irrespective of his nationality.
(2) For the purposes of sub-section (1), this Act shall apply to an offence or contravention committed outside India by any person if the act or conduct constituting the offence or contravention involves a computer, computer system or computer network located in India.

76. Confiscation.

Any computer, computer system, floppies, compact disks, tape drives or any other accessories related thereto, in respect of which any provision of this Act, rules, orders or regulations made thereunder has been or is being contravened, shall be liable to confiscation:

Provided that where it is established to the satisfaction of the court adjudicating the confiscation that the person in whose possession, power or control of any such computer, computer system, floppies, compact disks, tape drives or any other accessories relating thereto is found is not responsible for the contravention of the provisions of this Act, rules, orders or regulations made thereunder, the court may, instead of making an order for confiscation of such computer, computer system, floppies, compact disks, tape drives or any other accessories related thereto, make such other order authorized by this Act against the person contravening of the provisions of this Act, rules, orders or regulations made thereunder as it may think fit.

77. Penalties or Confiscation not to Interfere with Other Punishments.

No penalty imposed or confiscation made under this Act shall prevent the imposition of any other punishment to which the person affected thereby is liable under any other law for the time being in force.

78. Power to Investigate Offences.

Notwithstanding anything contained in the Code of Criminal Procedure, 1973, a police officer not below the rank of Deputy Superintendent of Police shall investigate any offence under this Act.

Chapter XII

Network Service Providers Not to be Liable in Certain Cases

79. Network Service Providers not to be Liable in Certain Cases.

For the removal of doubts, it is hereby declared that no person providing any service as a network service provider shall be liable under this Act, rules or regulations made thereunder for any third party information or data made available by him if he proves that the offence or contravention was committed without his knowledge or that he had exercised all due diligence to prevent the commission of such offence or contravention.

Explanation. For the purposes of this section,

(a) "network service provider" means an intermediary;
(b) "third party information" means any information dealt with by a network service provider in his capacity as an intermediary.

Chapter XIII

Miscellaneous

80. Power of Police Officer and Other Officers to Enter, Search, etc.

(1) Notwithstanding anything contained in the Code of Criminal Procedure, 1973, any police officer, not below the rank of a Deputy Superintendent of Police, or any other officer of the Central Government or a State Government authorized by the Central Government in this behalf may enter any public place and search and arrest without warrant any person found therein who is reasonably suspected or having committed or of committing or of being about to commit any offence under this Act.
Explanation. For the purposes of this sub-section, the expression "public place" includes any public conveyance, any hotel, any shop or any other place intended for use by, or accessible to the public.

(2) Where any person is arrested under sub-section (1) by an officer other than a police officer, such officer shall, without unnecessary delay, take or send the person arrested before a magistrate having jurisdiction in the case or before the officer-in-charge of a police station.
(3) The provisions of the Code of Criminal Procedure, 1973 shall, subject to the provisions of this section, apply, so far as may be, in relation to any entry, search or arrest, made under this section.

81. Act to Have Overriding Effect.

The provisions of this Act shall have effect notwithstanding anything inconsistent therewith contained in any other law for the time being in force.

82. Controller, Deputy Controller and Assistant Controllers to be Public Servants.

The Presiding Officer and other officers and employees of a Cyber Appellate Tribunal, the Controller, the Deputy Controller and the Assistant Controllers shall be deemed to be public servants within the meaning of section 21 of the Indian Penal Code.

83. Power to Give Directions.

The Central Government may give directions to any State Government as to the carrying into execution in the State of any of the provisions of this Act or of any rule, regulation or order made thereunder.

84. Protection of Action Taken in Good Faith.

No suit, prosecution or other legal proceeding shall lie against the Central Government, the State Government, the Controller or any person acting on behalf of him, the Presiding Officer, adjudicating officers and the staff of the Cyber Appellate Tribunal for anything which is in good faith done or intended to be done in pursuance of this Act or any rule, regulation or order made thereunder.

85. Offences by Companies.

(1) Where a person committing a contravention of any of the provisions of this Act or of any rule, direction or order made thereunder is a company, every person who, at the time the contravention was committed, was in charge of, and was responsible to, the company for the conduct of business of the company as well as the company, shall be guilty of the contravention and shall be liable to be proceeded against and punished accordingly :

Provided that nothing contained in this sub-section shall render any such person liable to punishment if he proves that the contravention took place without his knowledge or that he exercised all due diligence to prevent such contravention

(2) Notwithstanding anything contained in sub-section (1), where a contravention of any of the provisions of this Act or of any rule, direction or order made thereunder has been committed by a company and it is proved that the contravention has taken place with the consent or connivance of, or is attributable to any neglect on the part of, any director, manager, secretary or other officer of the company, such director, manager, secretary or other officer shall also be deemed to be guilty of the contravention and shall be liable to be proceeded against and punished accordingly.

Explanation. For the purposes of this section,

(i) "company" means any body corporate and includes a firm or other association of individuals; and
(ii) "director", in relation to a firm, means a partner in the firm.

86. Removal of Difficulties.

(1) If any difficulty arises in giving effect to the provisions of this Act, the Central Government may, by order published in the Official Gazette, make such provisions not inconsistent with the provisions of this Act as appear to it to be necessary or expedient for removing the difficulty:
Provided that no order shall be made under this section after the expiry of a period of two years from the commencement of this Act
(2) Every order made under this section shall be laid, as soon as may be after it is made, before each House of Parliament.

87. Power of Central Government to Make Rules.

(1) The Central Government may, by notification in the Official Gazette and in the Electronic Gazette make rules to carry out the provisions of this Act.
(2) In particular, and without prejudice to the generality of the foregoing power, such rules may provide for all or any of the following matters, namely :

(a) the manner in which any information or matter may be

authenticated by means of digital signature under section 5;

(b) the electronic form in which filing, issue, grant or payment shall be effected under sub-section (1) of section 6;

(c) the manner and format in which electronic records shall be filed, or issued and the method of payment under sub-section (2) of section 6;

(d) the matters relating to the type of digital signature, manner and format in which it may be affixed under section 10;

(e) the security procedure for the purpose of creating secure electronic record and secure digital signature under section 16;

(f) the qualifications, experience and terms and conditions of service of Controller, Deputy Controllers and Assistant Controllers under section 17;

(g) other standards to be observed by the Controller under clause (b) of sub-section (2) of section 20;

(h) the requirements which an applicant must fulfil under sub-section (2) of section 21;

(i) the period of validity of licence granted under clause (a) of sub-section (3) of section 21;

(j) the form in which an application for licence may be made under sub-section (1) of section 22;

(k) the amount of fees payable under clause (c) of sub-section (2) of section 22;

(l) such other documents which shall accompany an application for licence under clause (a) of sub-section (2) of section 22;

(m) the form and the fee for renewal of a licence and the fee payable there of under section 23;

(n) the form in which application for issue of a Digital Signature Certificate may be made under sub-section (1) of section 35;

(o) the fee to be paid to the Certifying Authority for issue of a Digital Signature Certificate under sub-section (2) of section 35;

(p) the manner in which the adjudicating officer shall hold inquiry under subsection (1) of section 46;

(q) the qualification and experience which the adjudicating officer shall possess under sub-section (3) of section 46;

(r) the salary, allowances and the other terms and conditions of service of the Presiding Officer under section 52;

(s) the procedure for investigation of misbehaviour or incapacity of the Presiding Officer under sub-section (3) of section 54;

(t) the salary and allowances and other conditions of service of other officers and employees under sub-section (3) of section 56;

(u) the form in which appeal may be filed and the fee thereof under sub-section (3) of section 57;

(v) any other power of a civil court required to be prescribed under clause (g) of sub-section (2) of section 58; and

(w) any other matter which is required to be, or may be, prescribed.

(3) Every notification made by the Central Government under clause (f) of sub-section (4) of section 1 and every rule made by it shall be laid, as soon as may be after it is made, before each House of Parliament, while it is in session, for a total period of thirty days which may be comprised in one session or in two or more successive sessions, and if, before the expiry of the session immediately following the session or the successive sessions aforesaid, both Houses agree in making any modification in the notification or the rule or both Houses agree that the notification or the rule should not be made, the notification or the rule shall thereafter have effect only in such modified form or be of no effect, as the case may be; so, however, that any such modification or annulment shall be without prejudice to the validity of anything previously done under that notification or rule.

88. Constitution of Advisory Committee.

(1) The Central Government shall, as soon as may be after the commencement of this Act, constitute a Committee called the Cyber Regulations Advisory Committee.

(2) The Cyber Regulations Advisory Committee shall consist of a Chairperson and such number of other official and non-official members representing the interests principally affected or having special knowledge of the subject-matter as the Central Government may deem fit.

(3) The Cyber Regulations Advisory Committee shall advise.

(a) the Central Government either generally as regards any rules or for any other purpose connected with this Act;
(b) the Controller in framing the regulations under this Act.

(4) There shall be paid to the non-official members of such Committee such travelling and other allowances as the Central Government may fix.

89. Power of Controller to Make Regulations.

(1) The Controller may, after consultation with the Cyber Regulations Advisory Committee and with the previous approval of the Central Government, by notification in the Official Gazette, make regulations consistent with this Act and the rules made thereunder to carry out the purposes of this Act.
(2) In particular, and without prejudice to the generality of the foregoing power, such regulations may provide for all or any of the following matters, namely:

(a) the particulars relating to maintenance of data-base containing the disclosure record of every Certifying Authority under clause (m) of section 18;
(b) the conditions and restrictions subject to which the Controller may recognize any foreign Certifying Authority under sub-section (1) of section 19;
(c) the terms and conditions subject to which a licence may be granted under clause (c) of sub-section (3) of section 21;
(d) other standards to be observed by a Certifying Authority under clause (d) of section 30;
(e) the manner in which the Certifying Authority shall disclose the matters specified in sub-section (1) of section 34;
(f) the particulars of statement which shall accompany an application under sub-section (3) of section 35;
(g) the manner in which the subscriber shall communicate the compromise of private key to the certifying Authority under sub-section (2) of section 42.

(3) Every regulation made under this Act shall be laid, as soon as may be after it is made, before each House of Parliament, while it is in session, for a total period of thirty days which may be comprised in one session or in two or more successive sessions, and if, before the expiry of the session immediately following the session or the successive sessions aforesaid, both Houses agree in making any modification in the regulation or both Houses agree that the regulation should not be made, the regulation shall thereafter have effect only in such modified form or of no effect, as the case may be; so, however, that any such modification or annulment shall be without prejudice to the validity of anything previously done under that regulation.

90. Power of State Government to Make Rules.

(1) The State Government may, by notification in the Official Gazette, make rules to carry out the provisions of this Act.

(2) In particular, and without prejudice to the generality of the foregoing power, such rules may provide for all or any of the following matters, namely :

(a) the electronic form in which filing, issue, grant receipt or payment shall be effected under sub-section (1) of section 6;
(b) for matters specified in sub-section (2) of section 6;
(c) any other matter which is required to be provided by rules by the State Government.

(3) Every rule made by the State Government under this section shall be laid, as soon as may be after it is made, before each House of the State Legislature where it consists of two Houses, or where such Legislature consists of one House, before that House.

91. Amendment of Act 45 of 1860.

The Indian Penal Code shall be amended in the manner specified in the First Schedule to this Act.

92. Amendment of Act 1 of 1872.

The Indian Evidence Act, 1872 shall be amended in the manner specified in the Second Schedule to this Act.

93. Amendment of Act 18 of 1891.

The Bankers' Books Evidence Act, 1891 shall be amended in the manner specified in the Third Schedule to this Act.

94. Amendment of Act 2 of 1834.

The Reserve Bank of India Act, 1934 shall be amended in the manner specified in the Fourth Schedule to this Act.

The First Schedule (See section 91).

Amendments to the Indian Penal Code (45 of 1860):

1. After section 29, the following section shall be inserted, namely:

   "Electronic Record.

   29A. The words "electronic record" shall have the meaning assigned to them in clause (t) of sub-section(1) of section 2 of the Information Technology Act, 2000."

2. In section 167, for the words "such public servant, charged with the preparation or translation of any document, frames or translates that document", the words "such public servant, charged with the preparation or translation of any document or electronic record, frames, prepares or translates that document or electronic record" shall be substituted.
3. In section 172, for the words "produce a document in a Court of Justice", the words "produce a document or an electronic record in a Court of Justice" shall be substituted.
4. In section 173, for the words "to produce a document in a Court of Justice", the words "to produce a document or electronic record in a Court of Justice" shall be substituted.

5. In section 175, for the word "document" at both the places where it occurs, the words "document or electronic record" shall be substituted.
6. In section 192, for the words "makes any false entry in any book or record, or makes any document containing a false statement", the words "makes any false entry in any book or record, or electronic record or makes any document or electronic record containing a false statement" shall be substituted.
7. In section 204, for the word "document" at both the places where it occurs, the words "document or electronic record" shall be substituted.
8. In section 463, for the words "Whoever makes any false documents or part of a document with intent to cause damage or injury", the words "Whoever makes any false documents or false electronic record or part of a document or electronic record, with intent to cause damage or injury" shall be substituted.
9. In section 464,

(a) for the portion beginning with the words "A person is said to make a false document" and ending with the words "by reason of deception practised upon him, he does not know the contents of the document or the nature of the alteration", the following shall be substituted, namely:

"A person is said to make a false document or false electronic record First Who dishonestly or fraudulently

(a) makes, signs, seals or executes a document or part of a document;
(b) makes or transmits any electronic record or part of any electronic record;
(c) affixes any digital signature on any electronic record;
(d) makes any mark denoting the execution of a document or the authenticity of the digital signature, with the intention of causing it to be believed that such document or part of document, electronic record or digital signature was made, signed, sealed, executed, transmitted or affixed by or by the authority of a person by whom or by whose authority he knows that it was

not made, signed, sealed, executed or affixed; or
Secondly Who, without lawful authority, dishonestly or fraudulently, by cancellation or otherwise, alters a document or an electronic record in any material part thereof, after it has been made, executed or affixed with digital signature either by himself or by any other person, whether such person be living or dead at the time of such alteration; or
Thirdly Who dishonestly or fraudulently causes any person to sign, seal, execute or alter a document or an electronic record or to affix his digital signature on any electronic record knowing that such person by reason of unsoundness of mind or intoxication cannot, or that by reason of deception practiced upon him, he does not know the contents of the document or electronic record or the nature of the alteration."

(b) after Explanation 2, the following Explanation shall be inserted at the end, namely:
'*Explanation* 3. For the purposes of this section, the expression "affixing digital signature" shall have the meaning assigned to it in clause (d) of sub-section (1) of section 2 of the Information Technology Act, 2000.'

10. In section 466,

(a) for the words "Whoever forges a document", the words "Whoever forges a document or an electronic record" shall be substituted;
(b) the following *Explanation* shall be inserted at the end, namely:

'*Explanation.* For the purposes of this section, "register" includes any list, data or record of any entries maintained in the electronic form as defined in clause (r) of sub-section (1) of section 2 of the Information Technology Act, 2000.'.

11. In section 468, for the words "document forged", the words "document or electronic record forged" shall be substituted.
12. In section 469, for the words "intending that the document forged", the words "intending that the document or electronic record forged" shall be substituted.
13. In section 470, for the word "document" in both the places

where it occurs, the words "document or electronic record" shall be substituted.

14. In section 471, for the word "document" wherever it occurs, the words "document or electronic record" shall be substituted.
15. In section 474, for the portion beginning with the words "Whoever has in his possession any document" and ending with the words "if the document is one of the description mentioned in section 466 of this Code", the following shall be substituted, namely: "Whoever has in his possession any document or electronic record, knowing the same to be forged and intending that the same shall fraudulently or dishonestly be used as a genuine, shall, if the document or electronic record is one of the description mentioned in section 466 of this Code.".
16. In section 476, for the words "any document", the words "any document or electronic record" shall be substituted.
17. In section 477A, for the words "book, paper, writing" at both the places where they occur, the words "book, electronic record, paper, writing" shall be substituted.

The Second Schedule (See section 92) :

Amendments to the Indian Evidence Act, 1872 (1 of 1872)

1. In section 3,

(a) in the definition of "Evidence", for the words "all documents produced for the inspection of the Court", the words "all documents including electronic records produced for the inspection of the Court" shall be substituted;

(b) after the definition of "India", the following shall be inserted, namely : 'the expressions

"Certifying Authority", "digital signature", "Digital Signature Certificate", "electronic form", "electronic records", "information", "secure electronic record", "secure digital signature" and "subscriber" shall have the meanings respectively assigned to them in the Information Technology Act, 2000.'.

2. In section 17, for the words "oral or documentary,", the words

"oral or documentary or contained in electronic form" shall be substituted.

3. After section 22, the following section shall be inserted, namely:

"When oral admission as to contents of electronic records are relevant.

22A. Oral admissions as to the contents of electronic records are not relevant, unless the genuineness of the electronic record produced is in question."

4. In section 34, for the words "Entries in the books of account", the words "Entries in the books of account, including those maintained in an electronic form" shall be substituted.
5. In section 35, for the word "record", in both the places where it occurs, the words "record or an electronic record" shall be substituted.
6. For section 39, the following section shall be substituted, namely:

"What evidence to be given when statement forms part of a conversation, document, electronic record, book or series of letters or papers.

39. When any statement of which evidence is given forms part of a longer statement, or of a conversation or pan of an isolated document, or is contained in a document which forms part of a book, or is contained in part of electronic record or of a connected series of letters or papers, evidence shall be given of so much and no more of the statement, conversation, document, electronic record, book or series of letters or papers as the Court considers necessary in that particular case to the full understanding of the nature and effect of the statement, and of the circumstances under which it was made."

7. After section 47, the following section shall be inserted, namely:

"Opinion as to digital signature where relevant.

47A. When the Court has 10 form an opinion as to the digital signature of any person, the opinion of the Certifying Authority which has issued the Digital Signature Certificate is a relevant fact."

8. In section 59, for the words "contents of documents" the words "contents of documents or electronic records"shall be substituted.
9. After section 65, the following sections shall be inserted, namely:

"Special provisions as to evidence relating to electronic record.

65A. The contents of electronic records may be proved in accordance with the provisions of section 65B.

Admissibility of electronic records.

65B. (1) Notwithstanding anything contained in this Act, any information contained in an electronic record which is printed on a paper, stored, recorded or copied in optical or magnetic media produced by a computer (hereinafter referred to as the computer output) shall be deemed to be also a document, if the conditions mentioned in this section are satisfied in relation to the information and computer in question and shall be admissible in any proceedings, without further proof or production of the original, as evidence of any contents of the original or of any fact stated therein of which direct evidence would be admissible.

(2) The conditions referred to in sub-section (1) in respect of a computer output shall be the following, namely:

(a) the computer output containing the information was produced by the computer during the period over which the computer was used regularly to store or process information for the purposes of any activities regularly carried on over that period by the person having lawful control over the use of the computer;

(b) during the said period, information of the kind contained in the electronic record or of the kind from which the information so contained is derived was regularly fed into the computer in the ordinary course of the said activities;

(c) throughout the material part of the said period, the computer was operating properly or, if not, then in respect of any period in which it was not operating properly or was out of operation during that part of the period, was not such as to affect the electronic record or the accuracy of its contents; and

(d) the information contained in the electronic record reproduces or is derived from such information fed into the computer in the ordinary course of the said activities.

(3) Where over any period, the function of storing or processing information for the purposes of any activities regularly carried on over that period as mentioned in clause (a) of sub-section (2) was regularly performed by computers, whether

(a) by a combination of computers operating over that period; or

(b) by different computers operating in succession over that period; or

(c) by different combinations of computers operating in succession over that period; or

(d) in any other manner involving the successive operation over that period, in whatever order, of on or more computers and one or more combinations of computers, all the computers used for that purpose during that period shall be treated for the purposes of this section as constituting a single computer; and references in this section to a computer shall be construed accordingly.

(4) In any proceedings where it is desired to give a statement in evidence by virtue of this section, a certificate doing any of the following things, that is say,

(a) identifying the electronic record containing the statement and describing the manner in which it was produced;

(b) giving such particulars of any device involved in the production of that electronic record as may be appropriate for the purpose of showing that the electronic record was produced by a computer;

(c) dealing with any of the matters to which the conditions

mentioned in sub-section (2) relate, and purporting to be signed by a person occupying a responsible official position in relation to the operation of the relevant device or the management of the relevant activities (whichever is appropriate) shall be evidence of any matter stated in the certificate; and for the purposes of this sub-section it shall be sufficient for a matter to be stated to the best of the knowledge and belief of the person stating it.

(5) For the purposes of this section,

(a) information shall be taken to be supplied to a computer if it is supplied thereto in any appropriate form and whether it is so supplied directly or (with or without human intervention) by means of any appropriate equipment;
(b) whether in the course of activities carried on by any official, information is supplied with a view to its being stored or processed for the purposes of those activities by a computer operated otherwise than in the course of those activities, that information, if duly supplied to that computer, shall be taken to be supplied to it in the course of those activities;
(c) a computer output shall be taken to have been produced by a computer whether it was produced by it directly or (with or without human intervention) by means of any appropriate equipment.

Explanation. For the purposes of this section any reference to information being derived from other information shall be a reference to its being derived therefrom by calculation, comparison or any other process."

10. After section 67, the following section shall be inserted, namely:

"Proof as to digital signature.

67A. Except in the case of a secure digital signature, if the digital signature of any subscriber is alleged to have been affixed to an electronic record the fact that such digital signature is the digital signature of the subscriber must be proved.".

11. After section 73, the following section shall be inserted, namely:

"Proof as to verification of digital signature.

73A. In order to ascertain whether a digital signature is that of the person by whom its purpose have been affixed, the Court may direct.

(a) that person or the Controller or the Certifying Authority to produce the Digital Signature Certificate;
(b) any other person to apply the public key listed in the Digital Signature Certificate and verify the digital signature purported to have been affixed by that person.

Explanation. For the purposes of this section, "Controller" means the Controller appointed under sub-section (1) of section 17 of the Information Technology Act, 2000. "

12. After section 81, the following section shall be inserted, namely:

"Presumption as to Gazettes in electronic forms.

81 A. The Court shall presume the genuineness of every electronic record purporting to be the Official Gazette, or purporting to be electronic record directed by any law to be kept by any person, if such electronic record is kept substantially in the form required by law and is produced from proper custody.".

13. After section 85, the following sections shall be inserted, namely:

"Presumption as to electronic agreements.

85A. The Court shall presume that every electronic record purporting to be an agreement containing the digital signatures of the parties was so concluded by affixing the digital signature of the parties.

Presumption as to electronic records and digital signatures.

85B. (1) In any proceedings involving a secure electronic record, the Court shall presume unless contrary is proved, that the secure electronic record has not been altered since the specific point of time to which the secure status relates.

(2) In any proceedings, involving secure digital signature, the Court shall presume unless the contrary is proved that

(a) the secure digital signature is affixed by subscriber with the intention of signing or approving the electronic record;
(b) except in the case of a secure electronic record or a secure digital signature, nothing in this section shall create any presumption relating to authenticity and integrity of the electronic record or any digital signature.

Presumption as to Digital Signature Certificates.

85C. The Court shall presume, unless contrary is proved, that the information listed in a Digital Signature Certificate is correct, except for information specified as subscriber information which has not been verified, if the certificate was accepted by the subscriber.".

14. After section 88, the following section shall be inserted, namely:

"Presumption as to electronic messages.

88A. The Court may presume that an electronic message forwarded by the originator through an electronic mail server to the addressee to whom the message purports to be addressed corresponds with the message as fed into his computer for transmission; but the Court shall not make any presumption as to the person by whom such message was sent.
Explanation. For the purposes of this section, the expressions "addressee" and "originator" shall have the same meanings respectively assigned to them in clauses (b) and (za) of sub-section (1) of section 2 of the Information Technology Act, 2000."

15. After section 90, the following section shall be inserted, namely:

"Presumption as to electronic records five years old.

90A. Where any electronic record, purporting or proved to be five years old, is produced from any custody which the Court in the particular case considers proper, the Court may presume that the digital signature which purports to be the digital signature of any particular person was so affixed by him or any person authorized by him in this behalf.
Explanation. Electronic records are said to be in proper custody if they are in the place in which, and under the care of the person with whom, they naturally be; but no custody is improper if it is proved to have had a legitimate origin, or the circumstances of the particular case are such as to render such an origin probable.

This Explanation applies also to section 81A.".

16. For section 131, the following section shall be substituted, namely:

"Production of documents or electronic records which another person, having possession, could refuse to produce.

131. No one shall be compelled to produce documents in his possession or electronic records under his control, which any other person would be entitled to refuse to produce if they were in his possession or control, unless such last-mentioned person consents to their production.".

The Third Schedule (See section 93) :

Amendments to the Bankers' Books Evidence Act 891 (18 of 1891)

1. In section 2

(a) for clause (3), the following clause shall be substituted, namely:

'(3) "bankers' books" include ledgers, day-books, cash-books, account-books and all other books used in the ordinary business of a bank whether kept in the written form or as printouts of data stored in a floppy, disc, tape or any other form of electro-magnetic data storage device.'

(b) for clause (8), the following clause shall be substituted, namely:

'(8) "certified copy" means when the books of a bank,

(a) are maintained in written form, a copy of any entry in such books together with a certificate written; the foot of such copy that it is a true copy of such entry, that such entry is contained in one of the ordinary books of the bank and was made in the usual and ordinary course of business and that such book is still in the custody of the bank, and where the copy was obtained by a mechanical or other process which in itself ensured the accuracy of the copy, a further certificate to that effect, but where the book from which such copy was prepared has been destroyed in the usual course of the bank's business after the date on which the copy had been so prepared, a further certificate to that effect, each such certificate being dated and subscribed by the principal accountant or manager of the bank with his name and official title; and

(b) consist of printouts of data stored in a floppy, disc, tape or any other electro-magnetic data storage device, a printout of such entry or a copy of such printout together with such statements certified in accordance with the provisions of section 2A.'.

After section 2, the following section shall be inserted, namely:

"Conditions in the printout.

2A. A printout of entry or a copy of printout referred to in sub-section (8) of section 2 shall be accompanied by the following, namely:

(a) a certificate to the effect that it is a printout of such entry or a copy of such printout by the principal accountant or branch manager; and

(b) a certificate by a person in-charge of computer system containing a brief description of the computer system and the particulars of

(A) the safeguards adopted by the system to ensure that data is entered or any other operation performed only by authorized persons;

(B) the safeguards adopted to prevent and detect unauthorized change of data;

(C) the safeguards available to retrieve data that is lost due to systemic failure or any other reasons;

(D) the manner in which data is transferred from the system to removable media like floppies, discs, tapes or other electro-magnetic data storage devices;

(E) the mode of verification in order to ensure that data has been accurately transferred to such removable media;

(F) the mode of identification of such data storage devices;

(G) the arrangements for the storage and custody of such storage devices;

(H) the safeguards to prevent and detect any tampering with the system; and

(I) any other factor which will vouch for the integrity and accuracy of the system.

(c) a further certificate from the person in-charge of the computer system to the effect that to the best of his knowledge and belief, such computer system operated properly at the material time, he was provided with all the relevant data and the printout in question represents correctly, or is appropriately derived from, the relevant data.".

The Fourth Schedule (See section 94) :

Amendment to the Reserve Bank of India Act, 1934 (2 of 1934)

In the Reserve Bank of India Act, 1934, in section 58, in sub-section (2), after clause (p), the following clause shall be inserted, namely:

(pp) the regulation of fund transfer through electronic means between the banks or between the banks and other financial institutions referred to in clause (c) of section 45-1, including the laying down of the conditions subject to which banks and other financial institutions shall participate in such fund transfers, the manner of such fund transfers and the rights and obligations of the participants in such fund transfers;".

Appendix–IV

Information Technology Policy of Andhra Pradesh

THE VISION

The Government of Andhra Pradesh has a clear vision for the all-round development of the State. This is reflected in the form of a well-conceptualized and cogent blueprint called Vision 2020. The Vision 2020 document sets the goals and milestones and suggests the strategies and plans necessary to realize the vision. The constantly inspiring and overarching goal is to build Swarna Andhra Pradesh—the ideal society of the future. The vision of the State for the IT sector is embodied in the following statement : " Andhra Pradesh will leverage Information Technology to attain a position of leadership and excellence in the information age and to transform itself into a knowledge society." — Vision 2020 (A collaborative effort of GOAP & Mckinsey & Co.).

The vision on the IT front is also nicely paraphrased in the following statement of Sri N. Chandrababu Naidu, Honorable Chief Minister of Andhra Pradesh. "My Vision is to make AP the foremost state in ten years time in terms of standard of living of my people through adoption of Information Technology in all aspects of development and governance." The IT policy for Andhra Pradesh is so formulated as to create the right environment for realizing the above vision.

Objectives of IT Policy

The policy objectives for the IT sector flow from the vision of the Government of Andhra Pradesh described in the foregoing section. The policy shall act as the beacon light for guiding the actions of all those interested in reaching the goal of the over all development of the

State using IT as the major vehicle. The set of such interested parties includes the State consisting of the legislative, executive and judicial arms, IT entrepreneurs, citizens, businessmen, academicians, students, intelligentsia, association of professionals etc. The policy contains guidance for each of these stakeholders. The objectives of the IT policy are enunciated below.

Economic Development

The first and foremost objective is to use IT as an instrument to foster the economic development of the State. This translates to specific action in the following areas:

- Growth of IT industry in the state
- Growth of software exports
- Creation of employment potential
- Attracting investments from outside the state
- Providing high quality services in all spheres
- Promoting knowledge as the key resource for economic progress of individuals and institutions.

One of the prime policy considerations of a democratic government is the need to ensure that the economic benefits that flow out of its initiatives spread evenly and reach the underprivileged population groups as well. While the benefits of citizen services projects reach the rich and the poor equally, IT projects aimed at improving the internal efficiencies benefit the poor indirectly through better planning and targeting of weaker section programmes and superior enforcement of law. Apart from this, the Government intends to make conscious efforts to see that IT percolates to the middle class and people below the poverty line. This translates to goals such as

- Taking Internet to the villages,
- Promoting IT-enabled education,
- Promoting Local Language interface, and
- Taking up socially relevant extension and outreach programmes.

Human Resource Development

Together with economic development, an improved quality of life to the citizens has to be assured. These include the following :

- Quality, standards and universalization of education
- Access to quality health care for all
- Availability of nutritious food for all
- Development of centres of excellence in knowledge

Good Governance

Good governance is a *sine qua non* for the orderly functioning of the society. IT can significantly impact on the quality of governance. The following facets of governance can be significantly improved with the use of IT:

- Government-Citizen Interface
- Government-Business interface
- Intra-Governmental processes

IT shall be used not merely to automate processes but as a strategic tool to simplify procedures and revamp processes. Electronic governance will bring in the following benefits :

- Anywhere, anytime services to citizens
- One-stop shop for all transactions in the G-C interface
- Better accountability, responsiveness and transparency of all systems
- Highly efficient government machinery and systems
- Reduced discretion and arbitrariness

This document on the IT Policy 2000 makes an endeavour to put in place the overall framework necessary for achieving the above objectives.

The IT Policy 2000 is not a static document. The nature and pace of development of Information Technology dictates that such a policy document has to be dynamic and evolutionary, to take into its fold emerging technologies and trends. It is, therefore, proposed to update the document as frequently as required.

IT STRATEGIES

The Harvard Business School defines entrepreneurship as 'the relentless pursuit of opportunity with no regard to the available resources'. This definition, however, is in the context of an individual entrepreneur. This definition has to be suitably tempered in the context of a State policy and a State initiative. In the context of the State, the policy objectives, however laudable, have to be assessed for their feasibility against the background of the socio-economic conditions prevalent in the State, the financial and human resources available with the Government, the conduciveness of the fiscal environment for growth of capital and entrepreneurship in the IT sector and, above all, the will of the people to support and encourage achievements in this sector. Given the fact that many of the above requisites are not available to the desirable degree in any State at any point, the Governments have to design and adopt a suitable set of strategies to derive optimum benefit from the available set of resources and mould the circumstances to advantage for achieving the policy objectives.

The set of strategies most appropriate for the overall development of the IT sector in the State are discussed below.

1. Putting the Enablers in Place

One strategy that is extremely relevant in the circumstances is to identify and put in place the enablers, which catalyze and foster a rapid growth of IT on all fronts. It is necessary for us to study the factors that were responsible for such rapid growth of IT sector in areas like the Silicon Valley, Route 128, Singapore, Taiwan and China. The following are believed to be the set of enablers that would be required in the Andhra Pradesh context.

Apex Policy-Making Bodies

The key to the design and development of a successful IT policy and monitoring its implementation is the existence of a high-powered policy making body that forms a think tank capable of drawing a large yet manageable canvas and that which can take quick decisions. This assumes special significance in the context of the IT sector, given the traditionally slow decision-making process associated with Governments and in contrast, the speedy decision making required to keep pace with the developments in this Internet age. In view of this, the Government of Andhra Pradesh has created a suitable institutional mechanism in the form of the following bodies.

AP FIRST : This is the apex body with the responsibility for the design of suitable IT policies, strategies and plans and reviewing their implementation. It is chaired by the Chief Minister and consists of Ministers for Finance and Revenue besides experts of the Indian IT industry. This IT Board meets on a fixed day of every alternate month.

ITPC (Information Technology Promotion Committee) : This Committee, headed by the Chief Secretary and consisting of Senior Secretaries of the Government, is responsible for evaluation of major IT projects besides implementing the IT policy and reviewing its progress.

C-IT (Departmental Committee on Information Technology) : These Department-level Committees headed by the respective ministers are responsible for drawing up suitable IT plan for the department and its implementation and review. The structure described above has been created through GOMs 4, Finance & Planning (Plg IT&C) Department dated 24-1-2000, a copy of which can be seen at Annexure I.

The Technology Think Tank : When the policy objective is to develop IT within the Government and outside in a ubiquitous way, it is necessary to be clear about the technology options available so that the state has the advantage of keeping itself on par with the best in the world. It is equally important to forge technical standards so that we do not create islands of excellence which cannot communicate with each other! These standards could cover simple things like the way we define data to complex things like communication and networking standards. For considering these matters, a Technical Advisory Board (TAB) is to be constituted.

The Right Regulatory Regime

Efforts shall be made to ensure that starting and running of businesses in the State in general and IT industries in particular, is fast and smooth and to see that the interface with Government is required to be minimal and positive. Efforts shall be made to put in place a regulatory regime that regulates the least ! The G2B interface shall be through electronic means within 3 years. The areas identified to be reformed in this regard are :

- Licensing and registration of a business
  - Declaratory and filing requirements under
  - Income Tax Act
  - Customs & Central Excise
  - Sales Tax
  - FERA
  - Compliance requirements under various Acts like
  - Water & Air Pollution Act
  - Factories Act
  - Employment Exchange (Notification of Vacancies) Act
  - Payment of Wages Act
  - Minimum Wages Act
  - Contract Labour (Regulation & Abolition) Act
  - Workmen Compensation Act
  - A P Shops & Establishments Act
  - Employees State Insurance Act
- Facilitating regulatory regime conducive to formation of capital, under the
  - SEBI Act
  - RBI Act

While some of the Acts are under the purview of the State Government, the items shown in italics are under the purview of the Central Government. In respect of a majority of the State laws requiring liberalization at the hands of the State Government, suitable orders have already been issued through GOMs 114 dated 25-5-1999 (Copy at Annexure II). It shall be the endeavour of the Government of Andhra Pradesh to use its good offices to bring about desired reforms in the legal, taxation and regulatory matters relating to the

Central Government also.

2. Building Infrastructure

One of the most important pre-requisites for fostering the growth of IT industry is the building up of the required infrastructure in the government sector to the extent necessary and in the private sector to the extent desirable. The infrastructure for IT is broadly in the form of the following.

Hi-tech Habitat

Ready availability of Hi-tech space with the required amenities like built-in electrical and communication ducts, data ports, central air-conditioning etc. will be a great incentive for IT companies to set up shop on a fast track. It is the endeavour of the Government to facilitate creation of large extents of hi-tech space not only in and around Hyderabad but in the important cities and towns in the state.

The first major effort at this is the Hi-tech City at Madhapur, 7 km from the heart of the city. It is a 1 million square-feet of world class IT space. The phase I of the Hi-tech city is fully booked already. It is noteworthy that the Hi-tech city has come up in a mere 11 months through a joint venture, L&T Infocity, between the AP Industrial Infrastructure Corporation and Larsen & Toubro Ltd. in keeping with the strategy of leveraging the best private sector strengths. This JV is actively engaged in developing phase II of the Project to create about 860,000 sq ft of high tech space in blocks of 250,000 sq ft. The first block will be operational by December 2000.

In addition to developing Phase II of the Hi-tech city, the Government has also enabled IT majors to develop space of their own by allotting plots of land adjacent to the Hi-tech city, at a confessional rate. Wipro, Baan, SoftSol, Infotech have already brought up their development centres in this area. An extent of about 100 acres of land is available in the vicinity of the Hi-tech city, for allotment to IT companies, as of January 2000.

Given the policy objective of developing all parts of the state using IT as the instrument, it is imperative that Hi-tech space is built in and around all the major cities and towns in the districts. Such space would be extremely useful to spawn the growth of IT-enabled services in a sector that has the promise of providing jobs to millions. It is the policy of the Government to encourage and promote the building of mini-Hi-tech cities in this hinterland at medium to low rates within the reach of start-up IT entrepreneurs. A suitable framework for promoting such efforts will soon be brought in place.

Cyber City

The march towards a knowledge society requires the establishment of intelligent cities which are planned and constructed with all features conducive to give a free play to the explosive development of IT. These features include a suitable city plan, energy-conserving and environment-friendly building architectures, in-built connectivity with bandwidth on futuristic scales, recreational facilities that induce innovative thoughts and entrepreneurship, excellent transportation facilities and logistics, education and healthcare of international standards with highly focused IT education and an ideal networking environment for entrepreneurs, investors and academics.

The services of an international consultant have to be hired for the preparation of a blueprint for the Cyber-city.

Bandwidth

Bandwidth is to IT what oxygen is to human existence. Bandwidth is an electronic highway, which is critical for the conduct of all human interactions in the new millennium. However, by international standards, the State is still way behind. Viewed in the above perspective, Andhra Pradesh must take the lead in creating this mission-critical infrastructure by designing an attractive model for acquiring bandwidth in an economically viable manner, quite like constructing other IT infrastructure.

Optical Fibre Connectivity

Government will facilitate and promote the establishment of broadband digital networks in the State. For example, the existing transmission and distribution network of the Electricity utilities and the highways could be used to establish a digital backbone network in association with the private sector.

Policy on Right of Way

The Government has announced its policy on right of way along all the highways of the state, for the telecommunications sector. The salient features of this policy are given below :

- The policy is modelled after that of the Ministry of Surface Transport, Government of India in respect of National Highways.
- Any entrepreneur holding the necessary licences from Department of Telecommunications, can apply for permission to lay optic fibre along the State Highways, forest roads, district roads, Municipal and Panchayati Raj roads, along with a set of plans.
- Permission will be accorded by the respective Engineer-in-Chief within 14 days.
- The applicant has to enter into a licence agreement with the concerned department agreeing to restore the road margin/road to its original standard after laying the cable.
- The right of way is given free of any charges or licence fee.

A copy of the GOMS 5 Fin. & Planning (IT&C) Department dated 11-2-2000 can be seen at Annexure III.

Satellite Communications

The Government will promote the use of satellite communication systems to provide connectivity, especially to the remote locations in the State. The Government has two proposals on hand in this area.

The Government will also promote the use of wireless communication technologies to provide better communication services especially in the last mile. The Government will ensure the efficient management of the radio frequency spectrum to maximize convenience to users. An integrated approach to wireless communications to meet governmental requirements will be developed.

The use of CORDECT technology is being experimented to connect the villages in Kuppam constituency, in Chittoor district. It is being implemented by the Telecom Department.

The other approaches for bandwidth creation being explored currently are :

- Getting permission for a landing point for fibre carriers on the East Coast.
- Promoting the building OF link with the US West Coast via Singapore and Japan.
- Broadband high speed links with the metropolitan centres of the country.
- Early implementation of Sankhya Vahini Project—a joint venture of IUnet, DoT and IIIT which envisages laying down optical fibre backbone touching all major cities in India. This project has received the approval of the Union Government in January 2000.

A Modern International Airport

International Airport is essential for speedy and convenient travel and cargo movement to international IT centres. It facilitates

- Travel of IT professionals to Silicon Valley and to other IT hubs of the world;
- Quick cargo movement of computer hardware produced by Hardware manufacturers to the International markets; and
- Importing IT equipment required for research and development.

The Government of Andhra Pradesh is promoting an international airport at Shamshabad, about 40 km from Hyderabad. A notification has been issued calling for expressions of interest (As of January 2000). Following are some of the salient features of this project :

- Suitable site admeasuring 2000 acres is being acquired.
- Tata Consultancy Services with Speedwing UK (British Airways) were appointed as consultants.
- Bids invited for expression of interest under Design, Finance, Build, Operate and Maintain basis.
- 50-year planning horizon.
- World class International Convention Centre Complex.
- Engineering & Maintenance Centre.
- Airport Management & Aviation Academy.
- World Class Export Promotion Zone Cargo Complex.
- Airport to be positioned as Regional Hub in the domestic and

International sectors.

International Convention Centre

Another piece of essential infrastructure is the establishment of an International Convention Centre with facilities to host International IT exhibitions, Seminars and Conferences. Hyderabad with its multifarious advantages like availability of quality manpower, central geographic location, competitive real estate prices, good social and civic infrastructure, decent quality of life and a facilitating proactive Government is perceived to be an ideal investment destination in India.

The State Government offers 5 hectares of picturesque land in the Central Business District, where other tourism and leisure development projects are envisaged, for establishment of the Convention Centre. The Government intends to establish it through a partnership between the AP Industrial Infrastructure Corporation and the private sector.

3. Creating the Right Social Environment

The development of IT industry in a region is an evolutionary process. It happens over a period of time in typically a decade or two. This continuous process of evolution needs a continuity also in the policy environment, which, in turn, depends on the socio-economic milieu. A climate conducive to the development of IT has, fortunately, emerged in India in general and in Andhra Pradesh in particular. It is the firm intention of the Government to exploit these climatic conditions fully on one hand and take steps that would ensure its consolidation on the other.

The creation of confidence in society in the capability of IT to manage its day to day affairs and the generation of the widespread belief that IT can be an effective instrument for the economic well being of a people are essential in this context. Fortunately for the State, such a confidence and belief have already begun to take root due to the successful and visible effects of some of the projects taken up or promoted by the State. Examples are the Hi-tech city, the IIIT, CARD and TWINS projects, which have fired the imagination of not only the citizens of the state but also of the other States and countries. This is an excellent and highly conducive situation.

Building Public Awareness

However, good the objectives of the IT policy may be, its successful implementation depends to a large extent on the extent to which the citizens in general and the benefit groups in particular appreciate its usefulness and derive the fruit it provides. Very well implemented IT projects could not achieve the desired objectives due to the disinterest — bordering on apathy — and ignorance of what benefit the project could offer to the citizen. A well designed campaign to continually enhance the public awareness of the benefits of the various programmes is quite relevant and essential in this context. This campaign could be in several forms like

- Advertisements through press and media
- Electronic Display Boards
- Project-specific seminars and workshops
- Press conferences
- Web-sites
- Mega IT Events
- Road shows
- Participation in exhibitions

The cost and effort required to create the right degree of awareness among the user groups — be it the citizens, the entrepreneurs, the employees — has to be built into the design of all IT projects.

4. Leverage Private Sector Initiative

One other strategy critical to derive massive investments into the IT sector that it rightly needs at this point, is to leverage the financial, managerial and technological strengths of the private sector. For such a strategy to take root and work, it is necessary for the Government to spell out the areas in which such investments are invited and to spell out the ground rules for private initiatives. Some of these areas are :

- Creation of IT infrastructure
- Implementation of e-Governance Projects on BOO and BOOT

basis
- Development of software for e-governance projects
- Facilities management
- Distance education and healthcare
- Community Internet Infrastructure
- E-commerce

While it is not possible in this document to detail the ground rules required for participation of the private sector, it is necessary to lay down the principles governing the same. The government intends to be guided by the following principles in this regard :

- Transparency of procedures adopted for selection of private parties.
- Designing a suitable scheme for creation of a stream of revenue linked to the transactions, in relation to implementation of e-governance projects on BOO, BOOT basis, before throwing a project to the process of open bidding.
- An institutional mechanism for empanelling players in the IT sector who intend to work on Government IT projects, and awarding projects based on pre-determined eligibility criteria on a fast-track basis. The range of IT players include system designers, developers, system integrators, facility managers, ISP's, IT training institutes, Internet companies, website developers and hosts etc.

The Government believes that the adoption of such a strategy would have three advantages. Firstly, it will pave the way for pumping in large amount of investments into the priority areas of IT, which Government cannot hope to do at the required pace. Secondly, it would give a fillip to the development of a variety of IT skills locally and create job opportunities. Thirdly, it will give the required experience to the local IT players and give them enough confidence and credentials to compete globally.

5. Strategic Alliances and Partnerships

One of the key objectives of the policy is to make the State globally competitive in the IT sector. This requires emulation of global best practices. Strategic alliances and partnerships with global leaders in specific thrust areas of IT, especially in IT infrastructure and IT education, is ideally suited to achieve this end. This strategy will have several distinct advantages. Firstly, the global player would bring to the table the state-of-the-art technology and skill set. The government need not invest its resources on a technology hunt. Secondly, the financial and managerial resources of the State are not put to undue strain. This strategy has already been successfully used in the development of Hi-tec city, IIIT and the international IT schools around IIIT and the Indian School of Business. The government intends to take up more such projects through the alliance/partnership route in diverse areas. While it is not possible to straight-jacket the policy or the norms for arriving at and concluding such alliances/partnerships, it is certainly possible to indicate the areas in which proposals are welcome. The following is the list of priority areas in which the government intends to follow the alliance/partnership route :

- IT-enabled education
- Data centres/server farms
- Digital libraries
- Smart cards
- Electronic payment systems

6. Collaboration

The Government intends to foster strategic collaborations with other countries to derive the synergies in bringing the best practices of the world into the State. An MOU has been signed with Singapore in 1997.

7. International Consultancies

It is crucial to design an overall architecture for the development of IT in the State and for assessing global trends and the competitive advantages of the State. Though such an architecture is likely to be dynamic due to the very nature and pace of advancement of information technology, it is felt desirable to have an initial blue print, which can be updated at yearly intervals. Putting such an architecture in view would benefit the State immensely by eliminating redundancies and enabling interoperable solutions to be developed in all sectors of governance. To this end, the government proposes to retain the services of an International consultancy firm in designing large systems.

8. Thrust Areas

It would be strategically important to identify and focus on the thrust areas in IT based on the strengths of Andhra Pradesh. This would give visible results in the medium and long run. The Government considers that the focus of Andhra Pradesh should be on IT-enabled education, e-governance and IT-enabled services.

E-GOVERNANCE

The Government of Andhra Pradesh firmly believes that e-governance is one of the pillars of the edifice of IT. The Government exists for the people. All the efforts and initiatives of the Government should, therefore, be directed to the goal of providing good governance. It is well recognized principle of public administration that a good government is that which governs the least ! Hence, fundamental to the concept of good governance is a process of administrative and legal reforms aimed at reducing State controls and regulations to the barest minimum and developing a system that can administer the minimum required controls in the most efficient manner. The Government cherishes the vision of establishing a Simple, moral, accountable, responsive and transparent government in SMART government.

governance is one of the vehicles that can be gainfully used in reaching the goal of SMART governance. The Government is aware of the fact that transition to e-governance is a difficult exercise, which can be costly, time-consuming and fraught with several organizational and behavioural impediments. In the face of these constraints, the Government desires to adopt a pragmatic and graded approach to the issue.

1. Ground Gained So Far

Andhra Pradesh has already gained the pride of place in the area of e-governance owing to the efforts made over the last five years. Several major projects are on ground and beginning to yield good results. A brief survey of these efforts is made below.

APSWAN : Connectivity is perceived to be the backbone of all efforts at e-governance. A 2Mbps optical fibre connectivity has, therefore, been established between Hyderabad and all the District Headquarters plus two other major towns (Vijayawada and Tirupati). The network has been operational from 1-11-99. It has been implemented under the BOO concept. The Government has the following policy perspective for the APSWAN

- putting an alternative backbone in position with higher capacities and better technologies.
- taking the connectivity to the next logical levels of the mandal and village levels in one and 2 years. The vision of the Government to take to its villages, the benefits of access to the Internet can thereby be achieved.
- the WAN infrastructure already created and planned in future is proposed to be optimally used by the government departments and agencies to translate the concept of e-Governance into a reality.

Video-Conferencing Facility : A video-conferencing facility between Hyderabad and the 25 cities/towns has been operational from 1-11-1999. It rides on the APSWAN. The facility has to be eventually extended to all major departments at Hyderabad and their officers at the district level. It should be used also as a tool for specialized professional education and extension activities.

CARD (Computer-aided Administration of Registration Department) : This is one of the major success stories of e-governance in India. 214 registration offices have been completely computerized from 4-11-1998. The process of registration of deeds is completed in one hour and several other miscellaneous services like issue of Encumbrance Certificates and valuation certificates are accomplished in 15 minutes. The Government is seriously contemplating provision of registration services on a remote access basis as it would promote public convenience tremendously. About 700,000 documents have been registered under CARD till end of February 2000.

COMPACT (Computer-aided Administration of Commercial Taxes) : 220 offices of Commercial Taxes Department, including 16 check posts have been computerized from 1-4-96. The database of the details of over 350,000 registered dealers has been built up. Over 1 million returns are fed annually into the computers at 182 CTO offices for processing and analysis. About 5,000,000 transactions are captured online in the computers at 16 check posts annually and the data is analysed and used for taking up investigations to detect evasion of sales tax.

TWINS (TWIN cities Network Services) : A pilot project to provide one-stop services to the citizens has been launched in December 1999. It provides an initial set of 18 services to the citizens of ward 8 of Hyderabad. These include payments of utility bills, issue of certificates, licences and provision of information useful to the citizens. The Government proposes to

- replicate the TWINS pilot to all parts of the twin cities initially and to all other areas of the State eventually.
- add more citizen services to the project.
- introduce electronic payment systems.
- provide some of the services on the Internet.

The extension of the concept to several other locations in the State is sought to be achieved adopting BOOT model, involving the private sector. This model is expected to provide cost-effective services to the citizens in a speedy way. It is planned to extend the project to entire twin cities by October 2000 and to all major cities and towns subsequently.

An experiment in providing such single-window services in the rural areas is being currently planned.

SKIMS (Secretariat Knowledge and Information Management System) : This project is designed to develop a generic product that efficiently manages the information and knowledge of a large organization like the secretariat. Secretariat being the seat of the Government, is a repository of a fund of information and knowledge. Public interest lies in efficiently managing this pool. The Government feels that IT holds the key to this delicate management exercise. The

Government intends to implement the SKIMS project in a phased manner over 12 months (FY 2000-01) to achieve the following goals

- increase employee productivity and satisfaction
- create a knowledge bank
- exploit the power of the network
- automate the work flows in the secretariat
- prioritize areas of work
- provide effective tools for performance evaluation.

The functional requirements have been arrived at and the RFP is likely to be released in March 2000 for outsourcing the mammoth work of developing application software for the Central Information System and for each of the 40 departments. The product to be developed can be customized to be deployed in any major government organization that deals with files, like the following :

- Other State Secretariats
- Central Secretariat
- Departments of Government of India
- Pubic Sector Undertakings

FAST (Fully Automated Services of Transport Department) : The Fully Automated Services of Transport project is another e-governance project that aims at providing all transport department services like issue of learners licences, driving licences and registration of vehicles through a comprehensive networked solution. A pilot project is ready to be launched at 3 sites in the State — Secunderabad, Vijayawada and Tirupati. It is being implemented on a BOO basis. The Government intends to implement it at 30 more sites across the State on a BOO basis with extensive participation of the private sector.

Computerization of Treasuries : This is one of the oldest e-governance projects taken up in the State. All the accounting needs of the Treasuries Department are taken care of under this project. 23 District Treasuries and 300 sub-treasuries have been computerized under this project. It is possible to know the receipts and expenditure of the government on a dynamic basis.

MPHS (Multi-Purpose Household Survey Project) : This is one of the largest IT projects undertaken by the Government. It aims to create the database of the socio-economic data of all the citizens of the state. The project is proposed to be implemented at all the 1122 mandals, which are the pivotal administrative units of the government at the cutting edge level. The package of applications implemented under this project include in creation and maintenance of a citizen database that can be used in a variety of ways like for the public distribution system, issue of individual identity cards, in ensuring better targeting in all the poverty alleviation programmes, land records, land acquisition and grievance redressal system. The MPHS project has been implemented so far in 320 mandals. The remaining mandals are likely to be covered by July 2000. The Government proposes to use the infrastructure created under this project for being used as the nucleus of all efforts aimed at taking the benefits of IT to the common man.

APDMS : The Andhra Pradesh Development Monitoring System is a GIS-based system that has been launched on 26-1-2000. It has created the base maps of all the 1122 mandals and the constituent revenue villages and habitations together with a suite of applications which superimpose the thematic data on the road network, the community infrastructure, basic demographic data, soil and geo-morphological data etc. This information is accessible on the web and provides a tremendous support to research, analysis, project design and monitoring in the area of development planning.

2. Approach to Computerization of All Departments

Given the resource constraint, it is not possible for the government to attempt computerization of all the departments and agencies at one time. A thin spread of the resources is likely to result in a large number of failures and non-starters. The government, therefore, considers it a better strategy to prioritize its departments and agencies on rational criteria and focus on the priority areas so as to computerize all of them over the next 3 years. The objective of an e-governance project could be any or all of the following :

- improve the quality of citizen services

- improve the internal efficiencies of the government department or agency
- better enforcement of law
- promotion and outreach activities
- education and information

It is necessary to identify and prioritize the IT projects in different departments along the above lines. An exercise has already been started in this direction.

The next step is to impart the necessary skills to the senior functionaries of the government like the secretaries and the Heads of the Departments and to draw up plans of action that identify the clear objectives of each IT project, the resources required, the HRD and change management required and the phasing.

Local Language Initiative

All the major IT projects have adopted English as the medium. However, for administration to be effective and for the benefits of computerization to reach the common man, it is desirable to adopt Telugu as the medium. The Government of AP has appointed a Committee headed by the Chairman of the Official Language Commission to design and develop standards for use of the Telugu Font on computers, development of Internet content in Telugu, translation of English content to Telugu and suggest the steps necessary to promote the use of Telugu in computers.

Security Policy

Security of the data is of paramount importance for a reliable and stable administration. The Government of AP intends to develop a security policy by engaging an international consultancy firm for the purpose and implement fire walls around all major databases.

Computerization of Collectorates

The Collectorates are still the pivotal units for maintaining and improving the standards of administration. The computerization of collectorates is one of the major components of e-governance as this is an institution that has a large citizen interface and the common man sees the collectorate as the enduring symbol of governance. The Government intends to computerize all the 23 collectorates by developing common software with the following objectives :

- provide a computerized interface to the citizen for all his needs
- workflow automation of all standard licensing and permit procedures
- dissemination of information useful to the citizens
- monitoring of all developmental activities.

A number of programmes have been developed in different Districts over a period of time. Some of them have registered stable and useful operations over the last 2 years. It is proposed to integrate all such packages into the proposed comprehensive system so as to save time and effort.

Mandal Level Horizontal Integration of Departments

There are 1122 mandals in the state. All the mandal offices are going to be provided with computers under the MPHS project. Computerized systems are available at 214 sub-registrar offices and 300 sub-treasuries also. It is envisaged that major IT projects would be taken up in at least 25 departments over the next 5 years, out of which around 10 will extend to mandal level administrative units as well. Examples are police, agriculture, education, health, panchayati raj, engineering, welfare, cooperation, veterinary and self-help groups etc. It is necessary to network these institutions horizontally so that we derive optimum synergy from the efforts of various departments. By integrating thus, we add to the citizen convenience as he need not go to several government institutions but can get things done at a single location. We also add to the efficiency and effectiveness of administration by eliminating duplication of work in several departments.

It is proposed to undertake a pilot project at one representative mandal initially to gauge the technicalities and complexities involved in this proposal. The pilot project, once perfected, can then be extended to all other mandals in a phased manner.

Internet and E-mail Policy

The entire secretariat workplace comprising of 2000 nodes has been brought on to a LAN with a bandwidth of 10 Mbps to 622 Mbps over optic fibre. Internet facility has been provided to all the users of the rank of Deputy Secretary and above. Simultaneously Internet facility through dial up is in the process of being extended to all the Heads of Department at Hyderabad. Similarly all the Dist. Collectors, Heads of different offices in district level will also have Internet facility through APSWAN. To provide quality Internet facility, it is proposed to provide 2 Mbps Internet leased circuit connecting APSCAN to VSNL. The feasibility of securing a 2 Mbps satellite connectivity through NIC is also under consideration.

E-Mail

E-mail has caught the imagination of one and all and going to be the most effective way of communication from end to end. Realizing the importance of e-mail communication, Government of Andhra Pradesh has extended this facility to all its employees in Secretariat and the facility is also being extended to HoDs through dial up to start with. This facility will also be available to all the Offices at District level very soon.

Data Warehouse

The Data Warehouse project jointly implemented by the Andhra Pradesh State Government and C-DAC, Pune has two core objects, i.e. (i) Person object and (ii) Land object. The main source of data for these core objects is MPHS data and Land Records data. The data will be cleansed and loaded into PARAM Super computer which is scheduled to be installed at Secretariat, Hyderabad in March 2000. The web-enabled data will be made available to all Government Agencies for planning and analysis. The person object has information like name, father's name, sex, religion, caste, occupation and land object contains name of the owner, extent of land, nature of land, nature of crops raised, type of irrigation source. Different types of analysis can be made on both the objects with different permutations and combinations. The pilot level implementation of project is planned to be achieved by

April, 2000.

Electronic Kiosks

To enable the citizens to have access to Government information and development activities and to bring transparency in the administration it is proposed to commission 10 electronic kiosks in the State on a pilot basis. The Government intends to encourage setting up the Internet kiosks on the lines of public telephone booths not only to serve the information needs of the citizens but also to provide employment to a large number of educated youth. For the kiosk to be viable, it has to handle several types of services.

CIOs

Can there be an institutionalized programme to produce champions who understand Government and Information Technology? A fund of officers who can make many e-governance projects bloom. That was the idea which inspired the Government of Andhra Pradesh, Indian Institute of Management, Ahmedabad and Satyam School of Applied Information Systems, IIIT-Hyderabad to conceptualize and design a unique Advanced Management Programme (AMP) in Information Systems and Electronic Governance. What makes the programme unique is not just its first-class pedigree but also the fact that it envisages a direct linkage with a live e-governance project implementation in the field in AP. Thus, the programme would juxtapose theory and practice, academic rigour and pragmatic realism so that one can have several more e-governance projects happen in myriad spheres of interface between government, business and citizens in AP. We believe that initially individuals produce institutions. Later Institutions produce individuals. This is the touchstone if any, to judge the Chief Information Officer Programme of Andhra Pradesh.

The first batch of 25 CIOs is proposed to be trained from April 2000. It is proposed to continue the efforts and train a total of 100 CIOs in the next 4 years.

Centre for Electronic Governance

It is proposed to start a Centre for E-Governance for showcasing all successful e-governance projects and conducting research and training on the methodologies and technologies appropriate for these projects. This project will be useful to all other governments also.

Financing E-Governance Projects

In a world of increasing fiscal deficits, it is inappropriate for governments to think of finding financial resources for implementation and maintenance of major IT projects in the area of e-governance.

Many good IT projects decline in performance for want of timely availability of funds for maintenance of systems, consumables and upgradation. These gaps are much more devastating as the technologies change by the month.

At the same time, the Government's firm intention is to use IT in all aspects of development and governance. In this context, it was felt essential to put in place a framework to create local equilibrium within each IT project that matches the need for funds with a source of revenue from the transactions.

The Government intends to create sources of income to each major IT projects in the area of e-governance within the framework of the functioning of the department. The policy of financing e-governance projects by collecting service charges from the users, has been 23 announced by the Government in March 2000. The policy allows the departments to fix service charges after ensuring that quality of service is defined precisely and that the solution offered is the most cost-effective one. A copy of this policy can be seen at Annexure IV.

Cyber Laws

Andhra Pradesh is committed to ensuring that the overall legal regime is in consonance with the requirements of transactions and interactions in the electronic medium. The State Government shall examine all the state level legislations and statutes so as to ensure the necessary harmonization, with the above objective in mind. The overall objective is to provide a transparent, simple and enforceable set of laws, which shall facilitate e-business and all other IT-enabled activities.

Reorganization and Strengthening of IT and C Department

The Information Technology and Communications department has functioned as a thin organization deriving strengths from sister organizations like the AP Industrial Infrastructure Corporation, APTS etc. However, sustained efforts are not possible unless the Department has adequate human resources to drive the ambitious initiatives. An organizational structure consisting of the following wings is proposed to be established for this purpose :

- Policy formulation and Planning
- Promotion of IT
- E-governance
- HRD in IT
- Infrastructure
- Administration

Private sector talent is proposed to be drawn in areas like promotion and infrastructure planning.

HUMAN RESOURCE DEVELOPMENT

The spectacular growth of software industry all-over the world has generated a huge demand for highly skilled Information Technology manpower resulting in projections of a long-term global demand-supply gap for such manpower. Unlike the traditional industries, human resource constitutes the single most important resource in the Information Technology industry and the finest companies in Information Technology funnel their growth into areas that have the richest availability of skilled IT manpower.

Tremendous potential exists in Andhra Pradesh for generating such skilled software professionals. Among the states of India, Andhra Pradesh contributes the highest percentage of IT professionals. The IT industry in Andhra Pradesh has been consistently registering a growth of more than 100% per year for the last several years, necessitating rapid increase in the number of highly skilled IT professionals to sustain such growth.

There has been a significant increase in the academic institutions, such as engineering, MCA and BCA colleges and polytechnics that offer IT education in the state. The state now has 102 engineering colleges with an annual intake of 24,135 students (out of which 4,750 students pursue computer science and 2,200 are in IT programmes). Colleges offering MCA number 118 and enroll 3730 students annually and there are 413 BCA colleges that enroll 16520 students annually. In addition, there are 103 Polytechnics with an annual intake of 17,100 out of which 3,500 students are enrolled in IT related courses. This educational infrastructure will generate a significant number of IT professionals to fuel the growth of IT industry in the state. In order to generate highly skilled IT professionals, the areas that need attention are:

- Addressing problems that colleges face in attracting and retaining high calibre faculty,
- Getting high bandwidth access to the Internet and thereby to resources available from other institutions, and
- Providing students and faculty members with state-of-the-art technologies on a continuing basis.

It is also relevant to note that generation of highly skilled IT professionals requires high initial as well as ongoing investment to provide access to state-of-the-art-technology. In view of the rapid developments in Information Technology, keeping pace with the requirements of the Industry calls for regular and frequent changes in curriculum, provision of access to new technologies, new hardware as well as software, along with highly qualified researchers and academicians. Competition in IT industry is not confined within traditional geographical boundaries. The compensation offered by the Industry for persons holding high qualifications and experience in Information Technology is very high as compared to what is offered by conventional academic institutions.

Certain strengths have been built in the recent past that can be tapped to address some of these issues.

Indian Institute of Information Technology

The Government of Andhra Pradesh has played a lead role in the establishment of Indian Institute of Information Technology (IIIT) at Hyderabad. The Institute is established with the active participation, support and contribution of the finest global and Indian IT companies. The aim is to pool the strengths and resources of the best companies with facilitation and support of the Government to create an institution designed to play the role that Stanford University has played for Silicon Valley. IIIT commenced its main academic programme in the year 1998 with a four-year Undergraduate Programme in Information Technology.

While the Government has provided land and initial infrastructure on a long-term lease, major global IT companies like IBM, Oracle, Microsoft, Metamor and Satyam are directly participating in the establishment of this Institution and have signed agreements with the Government of Andhra Pradesh to set-up Schools of Excellence within IIIT, which would focus on IT education and training in their respective areas of core competence. Three of the schools, viz. "IBM School of Enterprise Wide Computing", "Metamor School of Excellence in Software Development Methodologies" and "Oracle School of Advance Software Technology" have already commenced operations. The conceptual model of IIIT has emerged as an embodiment of industry-academia interaction across a spectrum of academic, research and training activities.

IIIT plans to conduct interdisciplinary research and development in IT. Research centres of international standards are planned that will focus on areas and problems of most significance to IT and the nation. The first research centre of IIIT, Language Technologies Research Centre (LTRC), has already become operational. Its research activity focuses on language translation especially among Indian languages and from English to Indian languages, search engines for Indian languages, information extraction from text, summarization, information retrieval, speech recognition/generation for Indian languages, and optical character recognition for Indian scripts.

Networked Universities and Colleges within the State

With the rich pool of technology, research and faculty resources at IIIT, the institute can spearhead the process of networking universities, colleges and research centres within the state and the country. It can also serve as a resource centre for upgradation of curriculum and training of teachers of various colleges and institutions across the state. IIIT is expected to be an active participant in the establishment of Sankhya Vahini, a high bandwidth optic fibre based national network that would connect research institutions, universities and educational institutions in all the major Indian cities with each other, thereby enabling sharing of resources among all of them. Through this network, excellent multimedia educational content created by IITs, IISc, IIIT as well as from foreign institutions like the Carnegie Mellon University is expected to become available to all the participating institutions all over the country. Coupling the AP State Wide Area Network that is now connecting 25 locations within AP with a 2 Mbps link, with the Sankhya Vahini, will provide a robust network that would bring rich academic content and resources into the entire technical education system.

Distance Education and Electronic Classrooms

High quality academic programmes can be conducted in electronic classrooms in several locations across the state to generate a high number of IT professionals. Such programmes can be tailored not only to the requirements of students of computer science or information technology but also for students in other engineering disciplines and in diverse academic streams like Medicine, Law, Economics, Commerce, Sciences, Mathematics, etc. Electronic classrooms equipped with suitable projection equipment would be set up for receiving and effectively using digital content. Existing computer labs would be strengthened and made available to students to browse content received in the form of CDs. Universities and major institutions would also be encouraged to create suitable infrastructure like classroom studio/video recording equipment etc.

Universities and their research centres and laboratories have strengths in certain areas. Each university and participating institution would be encouraged to identify areas in which it would be willing to digitize educational content to make it available for other participating institutions. Teachers and resource persons to be entrusted with the responsibility of creating content would also be identified by the respective Universities and participating institutions.

Each of the universities and institutions would be encouraged to create significant web presence. Existing websites would be strengthened and new websites would be created by the institutions. A central website of the A.P. State Council of Higher Education would be created to serve as a portal that would catalog the content and resources available on the websites of various universities and institutions and would provide links to all the relevant sites.

Private Computer Training Institutions

There has been a remarkable growth in the number of private training institutions offering computer-related courses. Such institutions are now available even in small towns across the state. Their offerings cover a wide spectrum of technologies and skills. There is a wide variation in the quality of infrastructure and facilities available with these institutions. The quality of instruction imparted by them ranges from very high to indifferent quality.

The Government will encourage collective efforts by the institutions engaged in computer training to define common standards and self-regulatory mechanisms, as well as the establishment of independent credible rating mechanisms for such training institutions. The Government will also support high quality institutions by involving them to meet the internal training requirements within the government.

Use of IT in Education

Information Technology will be used in the area of school education in two distinct segments, one comprising computer literacy and skills in information technology and the other related to its use to enhance the effectiveness of teaching in other subjects. Government of Andhra Pradesh is planning various initiatives in both these segments. These would take into account the requirements in these segments in primary, secondary, higher secondary and intermediate levels of education. As a part of these initiatives, mechanisms for imparting rudimentary computer literacy as well as skills in use of various software and hardware products would be created. The latest teaching and learning technologies would be applied to increase effectiveness of teaching in other subjects.

The Government has earlier implemented the CLASS project in various schools. This project is now being implemented with appropriate changes in curriculum, software and hardware.

The Smart Schools programme taken up by the Ministry of Human Resource Development, Government of India will also be implemented in the state.

The Government will focus on early implementation of computer literacy and training in IT skills in schools. Residential schools and junior colleges run by the AP Social Welfare Residential Educational Institutions Society would be accorded high priority while implementing such programmes.

In the recent months, some projects taken up elsewhere have been studied. The Tamil Nadu Schools Project has leveraged existing infrastructure of high schools and has involved companies engaged in computer training to conduct computer literacy and IT skills programmes for high school and intermediate students. Some innovative and cost effective technologies being used in various schools have also been studied.

Appropriate implementation models suitable for schools and institutions in Andhra Pradesh are being worked out, both for creation of multimedia content in various subjects and the establishment of cost effective delivery mechanisms. The Government will encourage the participation of multiple entities in the creation of multimedia educational content for various subjects. The Government will encourage development and deployment of cost effective technologies and delivery mechanisms that can bring about a quantum jump in the number of schools and students that have access to IT-enriched education.

National Institute for Smart Government

Based on a suggestion made by the Government of Andhra Pradesh, the National IT Task Force had recommended the establishment of a National Centre for SMART Government (NISG). Here SMART is an acronym for Simple, Moral, Accountable, Responsive and Transparent.

The Institute is expected to be an independent, autonomous, non-profit, viable and self-sustaining institution, which would focus on effectively harnessing Information Technology to bring about significant improvement in the citizen services, and would at the same time use IT to create opportunities for the people while protecting them from the risks involved in these processes. The proposed Institute would serve as a think tank and resource centre with expertise on all issues related to effective use of Information Technology in governance.

The Government proposes to play the role of a lead promoter of this institution. The services of the NISG would help the government in its endeavour to improve the efficiency of operations in its departments and improve the quality, convenience and range of services offered to the common man.

PROMOTION

IT Investment Promotion and Incentive Policy

India's software exports have been growing at a compounded annual growth rate (CAGR) of around 56% while only one state has been consistently notching up triple figures of almost 121% CAGR over the last four years. From a mere Rs. 0.2 crore in 1992 the state will be touching Rs.1000 crores at the end of this financial year. When Microsoft wanted to establish an Overseas Development Centre it chose Hyderabad, making it the second one anywhere outside the US. General Electric is setting up a 4000-person facility here. Hyderabad is also the home to Oracle, Metamor, HSBC, Ericsson, Tata Teleservices, Aristasoft, Motorola, Toshiba, Baan, TCS, Pentafour, Satyam, Wipro, to name just a few. From software development to IT enabled services to Internet startups, to e-business companies to small and medium IT companies to logistics companies—they are all here and thriving!

The state has, as part of a unique IT Incentives Policy, incentivised software employment by subsidizing land to the extent that one can even get it completely free! Further the state has reviewed all the major Acts and rules that regulate the IT industry and in most cases has either done away with the red tape completely or else has resorted to a self-certification process.

What is even more paramount is that AP is perhaps the only state in India, which has even begun to understand the first principles of doing business with business! Andhra Pradesh is one of the few examples of success wherein the public and private sectors have worked in mutual synergy so as to bring out the best of each. A harmonious construction of the State and Market is the ultimate mantra of economic development. Something AP has internalized in its day-to-day functioning.

The bigger underlying shift for the Government is the one from mistrust to trust. And the Government aggressively and probatively invites industry to be partner in its Development Dream.

E-Commerce

All belief is against it, all argument is for it ! — Samuel Johnson would probably forgive us for misquoting him if only he knew how e-commerce is dramatically rewriting every known relationship across the globe. E-business in India would be a market worth Rs. 400 million by 2003 say Pricewaterhouse Coopers (PWC) in the first ever Indian E-Commerce survey, while McKinsey pegs the figure at \$1.5 billion by 2004 and around \$10 billion by 2020, which would be approximately 1% of the world's e-commerce business. E-Commerce is something more than just buying and selling commodities across the globe. It is more about rewiring an entire set of relationships between consumers and producers, between corporations and within them, and between government, business and civil society. In fact the Internet is like a huge business super channel and anyone who does not tap it is actually losing revenue and losing opportunities, both at once.

Andhra Pradesh has clearly recognized this opportunity and is in the process of putting in place world-class infrastructure to enable this revolution to touch every aspect of human life in AP. For e-commerce to boom, one needs bandwidth, almost as much as people need oxygen. Recognizing this truth, the state endeavours to make available adequate bandwidth with international quality of service (QoS) at competitive prices to e-businesses and IT enabled services that wish to set-up shop in the state. Further with a slew of e-governance projects happening all over the state, it is virtually an open invitation to the private sector to be partner and participate in these exciting endeavours. VCs and Angels are all over the place trying to fund potential winners in the battle of ideas. Further AP is also catalyzing the development of various soft issues like lifestyle, entertainment and leisure, which are critical to the creation of the correct ambience for e-commerce and Net startups in the state. To summarize, just as E-Commerce is the future of IT; so is AP. Indeed, useless is each without the other.

Promotion of Venture Capital

Venture capital is an effective answer to meet the ambitious goals set by the Government of India for software exports (US$ 50 billion by 2008). A number of policy initiatives are required at the GOI level, mostly, if the ambition is to be realized. A SEBI committee headed by Sri KB Chandrasekharan, Chairman, Exodus, USA has made a few recommendations in this regard. It shall be the endeavour of the State to pursue with GOI in this regard. The initiatives required are mentioned below :

- IT start-ups look for capital typically based on the IP they hold rather than against any physical assets they can show as security. The investment climate has to change suitably to recognize the value of the IP and provide 'smart capital'.
- Implementation of the VC Committee of SEBI involving
  - Notification of SEBI as the single window for all requirements of VCs
  - Tax-pass through benefit to avoid double taxation, irrespective of the form of VC:
  - Creation of LLP's (Limited Liability Partnerships)
  - ESOP (Employee Stock Option)
  - Permitting the Banks to invest in VC's
  - Provide flexible options for entry and exit
- Simplify pricing norms of RBI
- Develop managers for the VC sector
- Conducting seminars on VC's to increase the awareness and tap the hidden potential of sources of capital for VC's
- Creation of incubators for start-up facilitation and providing mentoring and the benefits of networking with VC's
- Promote the concept of angel investors

A few of the items on the above agenda can be done at the State level itself. For instance, developing managers for the VC sector, organizing seminars and increasing awareness on VC's and angels, establishing incubators for the benefit of start-ups etc.

Several VC funds have been created in the recent past in India—

the 100 crore fund at the National level, a US$ 100 million fund at the international level besides the funds created by several State governments like Andhra Pradesh (Rs. 15 cr), Tamil Nadu and Gujarat. It is necessary to ensure that these funds are managed professionally with the least involvement of the government.

Annexure I

Government of Andhra Pradesh

Abstract

Government of Andhra Pradesh —Establishment of Apex bodies for promotion of Information Technology and e-governance —Orders —Issued.

Finance & Planning (Plg. I.T.&C) Department

G.O.Ms.No.4 Dated: 24-1-2000

Order

The vision of the Government is to substantially enhance the standard of life of the citizens of the State, among other initiatives, through the use of Information Technology in all aspects of development and governance. The Government has recognized that development of Information Technology is the key to all-round economic development and prosperity in the State. Government has also identified the uses of Information Technology within Government for better governance, particularly for providing improved citizens' services. It has also been recognized very clearly that this enormous task has to be undertaken in manageable steps and that both the IT&C department and individual departments and organizations in government have definite roles to play in achieving this goal. Government recognized very clearly the need to institutionalize a mechanism to help departments to evolve, pursue and reach clearly identified goals in IT usage. The Government has felt the need for establishing a suitable apex structure within Government to drive the whole process of architecturing, guiding and monitoring the overall development of Information Technology industry in the State and its deployment within the Government for achieving the desired goals of economic development and good governance. It is therefore decided that a two-tier structure would be created for this purpose with the role and constitution as suggested at paras 3.I and 3.II below. Information Technology and Communications wing would play the role of the Secretariat for these bodies.

2. It has also been decided that individual departments need to work out clear plans defining their information needs and the citizen services which are of priority for improvement. Constitution of departmental IT implementation committees is also felt necessary to drive these efforts. Indicative structure of the Departmental Information Technology Implementation Committees with their scope is given in para 3.III.

3. Government hereby constitute the following committees (I & II) and suggests the composition for the departmental committees for which separate orders will be issued by the respective departments involving all the concerned and following the procedure prescribed.

The composition and the terms of reference for each of the committees is as detailed hereunder :

I. AP FIRST: Composition : 1. Chief Minister, Chairman. 2. Minister for Finance, Member. 3. Minister for Revenue, Member. 4. Minister for Home, Member.5. Adviser to Government on IT, Member. 6. Chief Secretary, Member. 7. Sri F.C. Kohli, Vice Chairman, Tata Consultancy Services, Member. 8. Sri Azim Premji, Chairman, Wipro Infotec, Member. 9. Sri Narayana Murthy, Chairman, Infosys Technologies, Member. 10. Sri Ramalinga Raju, Chairman, Satyam Computers, Member. 11. Dr. Raj Reddy, Professor, Carnegie Mellon University, USA, Member. 12. Sri Dewang Mehta, Director, NASSCOM, Member. 13. Secretary, IT Member, Convenor. 14. Minister, Prl. Secretary/ Secretary/HOD(s) concerned will be invited as special invitees, when specific projects are discussed.

Terms of reference of AP FIRST

- Formulation of IT Policy for the State.
- Promotion of investment in IT industries in the State.
- Clearance of major IT projects to be set-up in the State.

- Clearance of IT plans of Government Departments.
- Promotion of Centres of Excellence in IT education.
- Promotion of citizen-centric projects of e-governance.
- Coordination with the Central Government agencies as required
- Review of the progress of major IT projects in the State.
- Any other issue(s) concerning IT as found necessary from time to time.

The committee will meet once in two months preferably on a fixed date of alternate months.

II. State Information Technology Promotion Committee (ITPC): Composition : 1. Chief Secretary, Chairman. 2. Chief Commissioner Land Administration, Member. 3. Spl. CS/Prl. Secretary, G.A. (AR&T) Dept., Member. 4. Director General, MCR HRD Institute, A.P., Member. 5. Prl. Secretary, Revenue, Member. 6. Prl. Secretary, Finance. Member. 7. Secretary, Law, Member. 8. Secretary, G.A. (Co-ordination) Dept., Member. 9. Secretary, Planning, member. 10.Secretary, I.T.& C. , Member/Convenor. 11. Prl.Secretary/ Secretary/HOD(s) concerned will be invited as special invitees when specific projects are discussed, Member.

Terms of reference of ITPC

- Evolve/Design IT architecture(s) for the State.
- Examination of proposals for major investment in IT industries in the State.
- Examination of IT plans of Government Department.
- Design of centres of excellence in IT education.
- Design of citizen-centric projects of e-governance.
- Promotion of development of IT infrastructure in the State.
- Review of the progress of major IT projects in the State.
- Approval of Technical Standards for implementation of IT applications.
- Evolve guidelines for cost-effective implementation of IT projects in government.
- Any other issue(s) concerning IT as found necessary from time to time.

The committee will meet once a month, preferably on a fixed date of a month.

III. Departmental Committees on IT (C-IT) : (To be constituted by the Departments separately according to their actual requirements).

Suggested Composition of C-IT: Minister, Chairman, Prl. Secretary/Secretary. Vice-Chairman & Convenor, Heads of Departments, *Members:* Nominee of IT Department, Chief Information Officers (CIOs), any other member as deemed fit by the constituting authority of the committee. (In cases where the CIOs are so far not appointed the departments will do so under intimation to IT&C).

Proposed terms of reference

- Design of IT plans for the Dept(s).
- Review of the progress of ongoing IT projects.
- HRD required for e-governance.
- Approval of major IT projects relating to the Dept(s).
- Implementation of IT projects with direct funding of the government or through involvement of private sector.
- Re-engineering the administrative processes to suit IT implementation.
- Change management within the department.
- Individual Departments depending on their specific requirements will be adding to the scope of the committees as and when required.

4. The Committees I & II will come into force with immediate effect.

(By Order and in the Name of the Governor of Andhra Pradesh)

V. Anandarau, Chief Secretary to Government

Annexure II

Government of Andhra Pradesh

Abstract

Information Technology (IT) Policy of the Government of Andhra

Pradesh — Incentives for promoting the IT Industry and IT Enabled Services in the State — Orders — Issued.

Finance and Planning (Plg.IT&C) Department.

G.O.Ms. No. 114. Dated 25-05-1999.

Read the following :

1. G.O.Ms.No.506, Revenue (CT.II) Department, dated 27-6-96.
2. G.O.Ms.No. 67, Energy (Power. II) Department, dated 21-07-98.
3. G.O.Ms.No.161, EFS&T (Environment) Dept. dated 15-10-98.
4. G.O.Rt.No. 58, Finance and Planning (Plg.IT&C) Dept. dated 1-2-99.
5. T.T.O(Commercial), No.173, Transmission Corprn. of A.P. Ltd dt. 10-5-99.

Order

Government of Andhra Pradesh has clearly recognized the strategic importance of information technology in creating a competitive economy equipped to face the challenges and exploit the opportunities of the future. Information Technology is increasingly permeating every facet of human endeavour and has radically transformed the way societies work, play, gather and access knowledge and govern themselves. Apart from the enormous benefits accruing from usage of information technology, it is also universally well recognized now that India enjoys a unique comparative advantage globally as a natural base for the information technology industry. The primary strength of the country in this sector is the vast, highly cost-effective, highly skilled and mostly English-knowing technical personnel available in the country.

2. Within the country, it is being increasingly recognized that Andhra Pradesh in general and Hyderabad in particular, is a favoured destination for the IT industry. Surveys reveal that Andhra Pradesh is the State from which the highest percentage (23%) of Indian IT professionals worldwide originate. The quality of urban infrastructure in Hyderabad, the low cost of living in relation to other destinations in the country for the industry, and the large number of technical personnel

graduating from the various institutions in the state are some of the other factors that have added to the comparative advantages of Hyderabad.

3. In order to build on these strong fundamentals, the state has embarked on certain key initiatives in order to foster the rapid growth of the industry. It has established a major state-of-the-art IT park, the Hyderabad Information Technology and Engineering Consultancy (HI-TECH) city at Madhapur, on the outskirts of the city through L&T Infocity, a joint venture between the State owned AP Industrial Infrastructure Corporation and M/s Larsen and Toubro, together with the Software Technology Park, Hyderabad, the HI-TECH City provides all requisite infrastructure for IT companies such as reliable telecommunication links, uninterrupted power, etc. along with speedy procedural clearances. The first phase of the project has already been inaugurated and a number of IT companies are now based there. Subsequent phases of the project are expected to ensure that the availability of infrastructure is always ahead of the demand in a sector that has been consistently growing at over 100% every year.

4. Recognizing that human resource development is the key to sustained growth in the sector, the Government embarked on another major initiative, the establishment of the Indian Institute of Information Technology (IIIT), Hyderabad. This Institute has been established as an autonomous industry—led and driven institution supported by the Government. Major IT companies including several Multi National Companies (MNCs) have participated in the establishment of the institution. As a result of this joint effort, the IIIT is endowed with state-of-the-art facilities and highly competent faculty. With its emphasis on IT enabled and distance education, the Institute is expected to make a major contribution both directly and indirectly (in conjunction with the technical institutions in the state) to the continuous generation of the increasing number of skilled personnel that the industry needs. A large number of training institutions that have sprung up in the state in general and Hyderabad in particular, have seen the emergence of Hyderabad as a major IT training Centre of the country.

5. Other initiatives taken by the State include the establishment of a venture capital fund, HITVEL (Hyderabad Information Technology Venture Enterprises Limited). A special package for start-up companies, which includes venture capital, leased space (including fully furnished space) is also being worked out by APIIC, HITVEL

and Software Technology Park of India (STPI), Hyderabad.

6. Another major initiative of the State Government that has implications for the growth of the IT industry in the State is the move towards ushering in an electronic Government in the State. The primary objective of this effort is to leverage the power of modern Information and Communication Technology to provide more convenient, accessible and transparent government services to citizens and at the same time, improve efficiency in government. As far as possible, the Government intends to utilize the capabilities and resources of the local IT software and services industry in its efforts towards ushering in an electronic government. This would also provide a strong domestic market for the IT industry, in addition to the offshore market. Some of the major computerization projects undertaken include Mandal computerization project, Treasuries, Commercial Taxes, Registration, Land Records, Employment Exchanges, Rural Development, Twin Cities Network Services project, etc. Major IT infrastructure projects, namely the State Wide Area Network, Secretariat Campus Network, Video conferencing project etc. are nearing completion and are expected to provide a sound basis for a modern Information and Communication Technology enabled governance system.

7. The above initiatives together with the efforts of the Software Technology Park Hyderabad have seen the industry reach an export turnover of nearly Rs. 600 crores in 1998-99 with nearly 200 registered companies. This turnover is expected to touch Rs.1200 crores in 1999-2000.

8. The State Government has been actively and constantly monitoring the incentives necessary to foster the rapid growth of the industry. A major growth area identified is IT Enabled Services (ITES) or 'Remote Services'. In 1998, this segment generated more than Rs. 980 crores in revenues in India. It is estimated that by the year 2008, the ITES industry in India would generate annual revenue of US $ 20 billion (Rs. 85,000 crores) leading to opportunities for more than 10,000 full-fledged units. The ITES sector, like the software industry, requires a conducive environment and access to large pools of skilled to semi-skilled professionals. ITES affords a unique opportunity for providing employment to large numbers of qualified unemployed youth in the state as well as business opportunities for budding knowledge entrepreneurs. Keeping in view the intensely cost-competitive nature of this sector globally, the need to have a

specific set of incentives tailored to the requirements of this sector has been considered by the Government in order to attract the maximum employment potential of the industry to the state. An employment-linked incentive has accordingly been worked out to link the incentives given by the State directly to the employment generated.

9. Feedback received during deliberations with the industry also indicated that there is a need to provide certain incentives to the IT/IT infrastructure industry to ensure conditions conducive to its establishment and sustained growth in the State. A number of suggestions were also received for simplification of procedures for compliance with various regulatory Acts and Rules. Following are some of the aspects on which the industry had proposed incentives/ procedural simplification:

(a) Exemption from environmental clearance;
(b) Exemption from zoning regulations for purposes of location;
(c) Fiscal incentives;
(d) Power tariff at rates applicable to industry;
(e) Exemption from sales tax;
(f) Self-certification for purposes of compliance of the following Acts:
(i) Water and Air Pollution Act; (ii) Factories Act; (iii) Employment Exchange (Notification of Vacancies Act); (iv) Payment of Wages Act; (v) Minimum Wages Act; (vi) Contract Labour (Regulation and Abolition) Act; (vii) Workmen Compensation Act; (viii) Andhra Pradesh Shops and Establishments Act; and (ix) Employees State Insurance Act.
(g) General permission to run a three-shift operation;
(h) Rebate in land cost keeping in view the high employment potential;
(i) Relaxation of FAR for IT parks;
(j) Exemption from stamp duty, transfer of property and registration charges for all IT parks' etc.

10. Against the background narrated above, the Government of Andhra Pradesh decided to frame an appropriate package of incentives for the IT and IT Infrastructure industry. The purpose of the package is to enable the State to leverage its resources and facilitate their optimal utilization to the best advantage of the State; provide a

relative competitive edge over other competing markets; tap the massive employment potential of the global IT market in IT (software and hardware) and IT enabled Services. Accordingly, a proposal was prepared and discussed with all the departments concerned either individually or in the SIPC/SIPB. The Cabinet Sub-Committee constituted in the orders 4th read above also considered the proposed incentives.

11. After careful consideration of all relevant aspects of the issue, Government approve the following package of incentives for the IT industry and for IT Infrastructure:

Note: 1. IT includes IT and Telecommunications , 2.IT Industry includes IT hardware and software industries; IT software industry includes IT software, IT services and IT enabled services, 3.IT Infrastructure means the physical Infrastructure built by a firm or a builder and sold to an IT Industry for its own use or the Infrastructure built by an IT Industry for its own use, 4.In case of any ambiguity in implementing/interpreting this policy, clarifications issued from time to time by IT & C Department shall prevail :

(a) IT Software industry is exempted from the purview of the AP Pollution Control Act, except in respect of power generation sets (orders issued by Environment, Forest, Science and Technology Department *vide* reference 3rd cited);

(b) IT industry is exempted from the purview of statutory power cuts (orders issued by Energy department *vide* reference 2nd & 5th cited);

(c) Industrial power tariff and all other admissible incentives and concessions applicable to industries in respect of power shall be applicable to the IT Industry including those in the urban areas (orders issued by Energy Department *vide* reference 2nd & 5th cited); 25% confessional power tariff shall be allowed to the new IT Industrial units for a period of 3 years from the date of release of power or of going into actual commercial production whichever is earlier.

Note:Concessions provided by the A.P. TRANSCO, to the IT industry are elaborated in the reference 5th cited.

(d) The Government *vide* reference 1st cited have totally exempted, computer software from the payment of Sales Tax payable under the provisions of A.P. General Sales Tax Act, 1957.

(e) IT Software Industry is exempted from zoning regulations for purposes of location.

(f) Government agree in principle to self-certification/exemption as far as possible for the IT Software Industry from the provisions of the following Acts/Regulations (subject to issue of specific orders by the departments concerned in consultation with the IT & C Department); i. Factories Act; ii. Employment Exchange (Notification of Vacancies) Act; iii. Payment of Wages Act; iv. Minimum Wages Act; v. Contract Labour (Regulation and Abolition) Act; vi. Workmen Compensation Act; vii. Andhra Pradesh Shops and Establishments Act; and viii. Employees State Insurance Act.

(g) General permission is accorded to run a three-shift operation to the IT Software industry (subject to issue of specific detailed order separately by the department concerned).

(h) Rebate in the cost of land allotted to an IT industry at Rs.20,000 (Twenty thousand only) per job created subject to the following conditions:

(i) The rebate shall be applicable only in respect of lands allotted by Government/APIIC with prospective effect; (ii) The rebate shall be restricted to Rs. 20,000 per job created or the cost of the bare land (excluding development charges/cost) whichever is less subject to a ceiling computed at the rate 0.30 acres for every 100 jobs created [e.g. If 3250 jobs are created the limit for allotment of land at concessional price would be 9.75 acres]. (iii) The minimum number of employees to be hired by a company in order to avail of the concession on land cost shall be 100 (corresponding to a ceiling of 0.30 acres of land). (iv) On areas allotted in excess of the limit, i.e. the ceiling of 0.30 acres for every 100 jobs created, no concessions would be applicable; (v) The minimum gross salary/wage for an employment to be considered to have been created would be Rs. 5000 per month; (vi) The period for which such employment would have to be sustained to be eligible to be reckoned for this incentive shall be two years; (vii) The number of employees to be considered for the purpose of this provision shall not exceed the number arrived at by the formula [No. of computer work stations at a location × (1.33) X number of shifts (of 8 hours each) operated by the company at the location]; (viii) APIIC shall specify suitable guidelines to ensure that the benefit of this provision reaches a company only after it meets the stipulated conditions regarding job creation and that the employment figures reported are corroborated by other supporting data such as investment, turnover, returns filed with RBI, returns filed with STPI, Hyderabad, etc.; (ix) Cost of these incentives to APIIC shall be offset against cost of government lands alienated to APIIC; (x) The concessions linked to employment generation will be limited to the extent of the number of persons of Andhra Pradesh origin employed by the company. A company will be free to employ persons as per their own policies subject to conformity with local regulations as applicable. However, the concessions available under this incentive will be restricted to the number of persons of AP origin employed by the company. For the purposes of this provision, a person of AP origin is defined as a person who, at the time of employment by the company has been:

- A resident of the State of AP;
- Domiciled in the State of AP;
- Born in the State of AP;
- Studied in a school/college/university in the State of AP;
- A person either of whose parents was born or attended school/ college/University in AP or was domiciled in AP.

(i) For IT infrastructure companies establishing facilities on private/APIIC/government lands, concessions will be in the form of rebate on registration and transfer of property charges and exemption from stamp duty on a tapering scale for sale/ lease of built-up space to the IT Industry.

For facilities established and sold/leased before 1-4-2000, 90% rebate; (ii) For facilities established and sold/leased on or after 1-4-2000 but before 1-4-2001, 70% rebate; and (iii) For facilities established and sold/leased on or after 1-4-2001 and up to 31-3-2002, 50% rebate. (iv)This concession would be available only to IT parks notified by the Department of Information Technology and Communications and which provide certain minimum facilities like uninterrupted/ backup power, reliable telecom links, etc. (v) The rebate would be applicable on the combined levy of registration fee, stamp duty and transfer of property duty and no total exemption of stamp duty would be extended. (vi) This concession would be available only for the first transaction, when the first sale by the infrastructure company is made to an IT industry. (vii) The above concession would also be available on the purchase of land by an IT Industry establishing an IT park for its own use provided it does not avail of the concession in para (h) above, i.e. rebate on cost of land linked to employment. IT & C Department would stipulate such conditions as may be necessary in this regard while notifying such IT parks.

(j) For IT Industry/IT infrastructure companies establishing facilities on private lands outside the limits of the Municipal Corporations and the nine surrounding municipalities of Hyderabad and Gaddiannaram village, relaxation of FAR to the extent of 50% of the prevailing norm will be available. For example, if the normal FAR is 1.5, the FAR allowed in such cases would be 2.25.
   - This concession would be available only to IT parks notified by the Department of Information Technology and Communications and which provide certain minimum facilities like uninterrupted/backup power, reliable telecom links, etc.
   - This incentive would not be available in respect of Government/APIIC lands allotted at a concessional price.

(k) District headquarters and other major economic nodes in the State like Vijayawada and Tirupathi offer highly competitive locations for siting IT parks for IT Enabled Services as skilled and semi-skilled manpower is readily available at these locations and the cost of living is very low. Government will consider providing required telecommunication linkage through the A.P. State Wide Area Network (APSWAN) to such IT parks coming up at these locations. This will also enable APSWAN to meet one of its targeted objectives of serving as a highway for jobs in ITES to flow down to the hinterland.

(l) Investment subsidy for new IT (hardware and software) industries: Investment subsidy: 20% of the fixed capital investment but not exceeding Rs.20.00 lakhs; however in respect of entrepreneurs belonging to Scheduled Caste and Scheduled Tribe categories the investment shall be 25% of Fixed Capital Cost, not exceeding Rs.50.00 lakhs. This subsidy shall not be available to IT Industries availing of the rebate on land cost as provided in para (h) above. (i) Fixed capital investment, wherever referred to in this order shall always mean the original fixed capital invested in the project before depreciation. (ii) The IT & C Department shall prescribe a procedure for scrutiny and sanction of the claim of units involving eligible capital investment as specified from time to time. The Commissioner of Industries shall pay the sanctioned amounts to the units from the same provision and head of account from which investment subsidy is paid to industries. (iii) The decisions of the Information Technology and Communications Department shall be final in scrutinising and deciding the eligible investment and sanctioning the incentives for eligible industries.

(m) Special Incentives for Mega Projects/Pioneering Projects: For Mega Projects, with investment exceeding Rs. 100 crores, Government may consider Special Package of Incentives, on a case to case basis, based on the gestation period of projects, pioneer nature of projects, locational aspects, state of the art technology, profitability, scope for further related investments, etc.

(n) The above incentives will be inclusive of any similar incentives of State Government/Central Government institutions/ Agencies already availed/Central incentives which may be announced from time to time by the Government of India and other such incentives extended by any other government agency.

(o) The package of concessions will initially be valid for a period of three years and subject to review thereafter.

12. This order issues with the concurrence of the Finance wing of this department *vide* U.O. No.1961/P.F.S./99 dated 22-05-1999.

(By Order and in the Name of the Governor of Andhra Pradesh)

S/d. R. Chandrashekhar, Secretary to Government

Appendix–V

Information Technology Policy of the Government of Kerala

Executive Summary

1. Information Technology (IT) is the world's fastest growing economic activity. The IT industry has been found to be ideal for Kerala in terms of its potential to generate opportunities and employment with little pressure on land, environment and other resources. This is one of the most people-friendly and environment-friendly industries of modern times.

2. The Government understands the enormous potential of Information Technology not only as a tool for improving governance and creating more jobs, but more significantly, as a means to greatly enhance the standard of living of the people. Use of IT in enhancing the delivery of government services leads to a very responsive and transparent administration facilitating the empowerment of the people and satisfying their right of information.

3. The Policy Statement addresses the following components:

- Increased application of Information Technology in all walks of life.
- Enhancing the IT industry base so as to make Kerala a very fertile location for ventures in Information Technology.
- Creating a robust State Information Infrastructure.
- Human Resource Development for Information Technology.

4. To promote the use of Information Technology, the following mission targets have been spelt out.

- PC penetration of 10 per 1000 of the population by the year 2001,
- All colleges to be hooked to Internet by the year 2000 and all the schools by 2002,
- Internet kiosks in every Panchayat ward, and
- Modernization and integration of government functions using Information Technology.

A High Power Committee has been proposed, chaired by the Chief Minister, to co-ordinate and direct strategies to achieve rapid penetration and use of IT in all sectors.

5. Kerala is a fertile ground for the growth of the IT industry. Government realizes the significance and potential of this sector in the economic development of the State and will facilitate the creation of a sound IT production base through conscious efforts and policy initiatives which will combine the following:

- Creation of IT-specific infrastructure in different parts of the State.
- Removal of hassles in the regulatory environment, making it pro-active and sensitive to the needs of the industry.
- Incentives and concessions for IT ventures.
- Special package for financing IT ventures.
- Promoting Kerala as a location for IT investments.

Specific proposals include strengthening of Techno park and setting up of Software Technology Parks and Software Complexes in major cities in the State. A venture capital fund is also proposed to cater to the financing requirements of the IT industry.

6. The establishment of a sound State Information Infrastructure with a communication backbone, switches, nodes, access networks and data warehouses has been identified a high priority area. The existing infrastructure will be harnessed, developed and integrated to create an Information Infrastructure that can effectively handle the traffic for several years to come. The mission targets for SII have been spelt out as follows:

- Connectivity at 2 MBPS to any user in the three major cities of the State and at multiples of 64 KBPS in other parts of the State by the year 2000.

- All District Head Quarters be provided with the connectivity of 622 MB capacity by 1999, all Taluk Head Quarters by 2000 and all Village Offices by 2002. Concurrently, one Sil node in each Block by 2000 and in each Panchayat by 2002.
- Strengthening data warehousing for promoting trade, tourism and for enhancing delivery of government transparency and empowerment of the people.

7. Human Resource Development is a very critical aspect in the development of Information Technology. The Government is seized of the urgency for consolidating and strengthening the core competence of the state on the human resources front to propel the development of IT industry. The proposals in this regard include establishment of an Institute of Information Technology, introducing Information Technology as a specialized branch of study, development of Centres of Excellence in Information Technology, creating a fund for up-gradation of training/educational infrastructure and introduction of a system for accreditation.

1. Preamble

1.1 Information Technology (IT) is the world's fastest growing economic activity. It is transforming resource-based economies to knowledge-based economies. Information services, products and production processes are evolving rapidly. Knowledge engineering is replacing pure data and information oriented engineering. The application and impact of Information Technology is so pervasive that it is effecting issues as diverse as balance of payment, skill development, design competence, mass media reach, industrial competitiveness, publication, communication, transportation, health, financial infrastructure, industrial productivity and managerial efficiency.

1.2 Information Technology is a tool of productivity and efficiency and will lead to better transparency in the functioning of the administration. With its appropriate use the governance of the State can be made highly effective and citizen-friendly, contributing to the standard of living of the people. Internet is becoming wide-spread and popular and electronic commerce is going to be the way the world will do business in future. Entirely new ways will evolve by which future governments will function.

1.3 "Leadership in the world's largest industry" is a dream which any economy would work towards. More so, if such industry contributes to redistribution of wealth through the creation of large scale employment. And further so, if the pressures on land and environment are less and the demands for capital and energy are modest. This is precisely what Information Technology promises. Very truly the most people-friendly and environment-friendly industry of modern times—one of the greenest industries of all times.

1.4 Kerala is a highly advanced society. The wide-mass base which the media enjoys in the State and the penetration that communication technologies have been able to make, will see Kerala emerging soon as a 100% internetised State—very truly, an Information Society.

1.5 The Government of Kerala feel the silent revolution that is taking shape and realize the need for an appropriate policy and strategy for Information Technology in the State. This IT Policy document has been the result of elaborate discussions that have taken place at various levels, involving manufacturers, users, service providers, R&D organizations, educational institutions and various other interest groups.

2. Policy Mission

2.1 Up-gradation of the standard of living of the people of the State through use of Information Technology in all sectors as a tool to enhance productivity, efficiency and optimum utilization of resources, and through full exploitation of the employment potential of the IT sector.

2.2 Establishment of a State Information Infrastructure (SII) comprising of high speed broad band communication backbone, nodes, access network, distributed data warehouses and service locations to cater to the needs of trade, commerce, industry and tourism and also to enhance the delivery of Government Services to the people.

2.3 Establishment of the State as a fertile location for the growth of Information Technology Industry, facilitating flow of investments from within the country and abroad, achieving in the process, rapid growth in domestic and export earnings.

2.4 Development of human resources for IT through increased use of IT in educational institutions and through academic and training programmes that improve the employability of educated youth in the IT sector.

2.5 Facilitation of decentralized administration and empowerment of people through the application of Information Technology.

3. Components of the IT Policy

The following components have been identified for the speedy and effective realization of the policy mission :

- Diffusion and Dissemination of Information Technology.
- Enhancement of Information Technology industry base.
- Creating a robust State Information Infrastructure.
- Human resources development for Information Technology.

4. Diffusion and Dissemination of IT

The State of Kerala offers tremendous potential for application of IT due to reasons which include :

- High literacy and phenomenal growth in education, health and other services.
- Ease of geographical access in extent and stretch both longitudinal and lateral.
- Large migrant population with extensive demands for connectivity.
- Extensive telecom network reaching all towns and villages Availability of educated youth.
- Exportbased trade and commerce potential for tourism industry.

The mission targets for promoting the use of Information Technology in various fields is spelt out as follows:

1. PC penetration of 10 per 1000 of the population by year 2001.
2. All colleges to be hooked on Internet by 2000, and all schools by 2002.
3. Internet Kiosks in every Panchayat ward, accessible to any member of the public.

4. Modernization and integration of government functioning using IT :
   (a) IT will be used to deliver government services in a manner that is affordable, reliable, accessible and delivered to the citizens in a short span of time. All government departments will have facility to place as much information as possible on their respective websites for the benefit of the public.
   (b) Services will be provided in an integrated manner to the public from single point of access. A common screen based proforma will be made available to all Internet users who want to interact with the government.
   (c) IT will be used at every government-business interface to provide better services and to enhance speedy execution of government policies.
   (d) Computer proficiency of a specified level will be stipulated as essential qualification for all appointments in government and as a desirable qualification for being considered for promotions/increments. A state level examination is envisaged similar to KGTE to test computer proficiency and to provide necessary certification.

4.0 Policy Initiatives

4.1 A high power committee will be constituted to co-ordinate and direct strategies to achieve rapid penetration and effective use of IT in all sectors. The high power committee is proposed to be chaired by the Chief Minister. Minister for Industries will be the Vice-Chairman and other members will include representatives from industry and professional groups. The committee will promote the use of IT in government to achieve a more efficient and responsive administration, and will spell out broad guidelines for this purpose.

4.2. The following action will be initiated for facilitating decentralized administration

- Building up resource-based data repositories and citizen databases for decentralized planning.
- Implementing computerized services at the Panchayat level in issue of certificates, licences, etc. and in tax-collection which can result in perceptible improvement of services available to the common

man.

- Providing Internet/Intranet services at the Panchayat level with the specific objective of fulfilling the right of information of the community at large.

4.3 Enhancement of the IT-base in educational institutions will be taken up on priority :

- Internet connectivity will be provided to schools, colleges and other Institutions. The connectivity also envisages linkages to Research Libraries and other knowledge repositories including the archives of various educational and research institutions. Interconnectivity between institutions and exchange of knowledge will be actively encouraged.
- A network will be developed for linking high schools in the state and to facilitate distance learning. A programme to strengthen the application of Educational Technology at the school level will be taken up.

4.4 Pilot projects of high visibility for strengthening and fostering IT applications in government will be initiated, to effectively understand and demonstrate the benefits and effects of using IT in various walks of life.

5. Enhancement of IT Industry Base

Kerala is a fertile ground for the growth of the Information Technology industry. The Government realises the significance and potential of this sector in the economic development of the State and will facilitate the creation of a sound IT production base through conscious efforts and policy initiatives which will combine the following:

- Creation of IT-specific infrastructure in different parts of the State.
- Removal of hassles in the regulatory environment, making it pro-active and sensitive to the needs of the industry.
- Incentives and concessions for IT ventures.
- Special package for financing IT ventures.
- Promoting Kerala as a location for IT investments.

Policy Initiatives to Create Infrastructure

5.1 Technopark: The Government of Kerala has set up Technopark as a location of international standards for Electronics and IT companies. Today, the campus is the most advanced IT location in the country and has been a model for many other states to emulate. The Government will further strengthen the campus and will continue to build infrastructure to meet the needs of the new enterprises being set up.

5.2 Software Technology Parks/Software Complexes will be set up in major cities like Kannur, Kozhikkode, Kochi, Palakkad, Thrissur, Kottayam and Kollam.

5.3 Specific areas will be ear-marked for Information Technology in all industrial areas developed by Kerala State Industrial Infrastructure Development Corporation (KINFRA). KINFRA will construct and make available built up space in these industrial areas for IT units.

5.4 Participation of the private sector will be encouraged in the expansion of Technopark and in the setting up of Software Technology Parks in the State.

5.5 Private sector will be encouraged to set up Software Complexes on the lines of the STPs.

5.6 In STPs and Software Complexes set up by Government or in joint-sector, there will be an executive authority, who function as a single point contact for all statutory clearances required for units within them. No clearance will be required from local development authorities, local bodies, local government etc.

Policy Initiatives at Pro-active Government Support

5.7 The Government is of the opinion that Information Technology is a tool of productivity and efficiency to be promoted in all walks of life. It is proposed to do away with all restrictions, clearances and permissions required to set up software units in the State. Any software unit or software centre may be set up without obtaining prior clearance from State, District or Local Government Agencies. A statement may be filed with the District Industries Centre, if necessary, based on which the District Industries Centre will allot a registration number which can be used for all other Government related purposes.

Incentives and Concessions Envisaged

For Information Technology industries :

(a) IT industries will continue to be exempted from the purview of Pollution Control Act.
(b) Priority for IT industries in sanctioning and servicing of power.
(c) Exemption from Sales Tax to IT industries for 7 years.
(d) For captive power generation sets installed by IT industries.
 (i) Exemption from payment of electricity tax/duty.
 (ii) 50% subsidy for installation of captive generation sets.
(e) All IT Units to be eligible for subsidy of 20% of capital investment subject to a maximum of Rs.25 lakhs.

For Technopark, Software Technology parks and other Software complexes :

- Technopark, STPs and Software Complexes will be eligible for all the concessions, benefits and exemptions available to the companies in these Parks/Complexes.
- Executive authority of Technopark, STPs and Software Complexes in the public/joint sector will be empowered to give all clearances required by units within them.
- Exemption from stamp duty/registration charge for purchase and sale of land/built-up space by Technopark, STPs and Software Complexes.

Policy Initiates: Special Package of Financing

5.9 Venture capital financing is an alternative financing source, particularly when an industry is technology-based, entrepreneur inexperienced and investment carries high risk. The wider definition of venture capital envisages it as long-term growth capital invested in start-ups, expansion, management buy-outs of industrial units using higher level technology.

A corpus will be set aside for creating a venture capital fund.

This fund will be separately created by KSIDC and not as part of the on-going programmes.

Policy Initiates: Promotion of the State as an IT Investment Location.

5.10 Promotion and publicity is crucial for the success of any initiative. The Government attaches primacy to the promotion of Kerala as an IT-oriented investment location.

5.11 Senior people in the IT Sector from different parts of the world will be invited to the state to get their advice and to enlist their participation in these efforts.

5.12 Promotional campaigns and visits targeting investments into the IT industry from countries like Singapore, Germany, USA, Japan, UK, Sweden, Switzerland etc. will be undertaken with support from embassies, Government and International industry/trade development organizations in these countries.

6. State Information Infrastructure

The first World Telecom Development Conference held at Buenos Aires in 1994 gave a call to all nations of the world for establishment of "Global Information Infrastructure (GII)". The Global Information Infrastructure shall enable people to securely use a set of communication services supporting an open multitude of applications and embracing all modes of information, any time and anywhere, at acceptable cost and acceptable quality. It is expected that from GII, we will derive robust and sustainable economic progress, strong democracies, better solutions to global and local environmental challenges, improved health care and ultimately a greater sense of shared stewardship of our planet.

If GII has to become a reality it is evident that several National Information Infrastructure (NII) units will have to be built and interconnected. The Department of Electronics of the Government of India has formulated a systematic strategy for building up NII in the country.

A state level Information Infrastructure to meet the IT goals in the State has to be conceived, designed and executed in a phased manner to act as the backbone of the IT Policy implementation. The State Information Infrastructure (SII) will be a major factor for the economic prosperity and competitiveness of the State. In Kerala, with its high literacy levels, high information awareness, and the sizable population of educated youth who can be rapidly trained, the information infrastructure will turn out to be the ideal mechanism for reducing the information gap in the society, promoting transparency, facilitating an efficient and responsive administration and ensuring rapid and sustained industrial and commercial growth. The mission targets for SII have been spelt out as follows :

- Connectivity at 2 MBPS to any user in the three major cities of the State and at multiples of 64 KBPS in other parts of the State by the year 2000.
- All District Head Quarters be provided with the connectivity of 622 MB capacity by 1999, all Taluk Head Quarters by 2000 and all Village Offices by 2002. Concurrently, one SII node in each Block by 2000 and in each Panchayat by 2002.
- Strengthening data warehousing for promoting trade, commerce and tourism and for enhancing delivery of Government services, its transparency and empowerment of the people.

The State Information Infrastructure would essentially comprise the following elements :

- *Communication Infrastructure:* Communication infrastructure covering High Speed broad band and Digital Telecom infrastructure for transfer of information in all forms reliably and interactively throughout the State and to the NII. A three-tier paradigm of connectivity comprising, backbone transmission fabric, switches/nodes and lastmile segments/access network will form the infrastructure.
- *Computing Platforms and Data warehouses:* A range of computing hardware covering Servers, Workstations etc. to act as the Public Database and provide storage, processing and information services across the network.
- *Networks:* State level networks (LANS and WANS) with specific focus on State level, District level and Village level information processing and dissemination needs.

Policy Initiatives

6.1 The Department of Telecommunications, Government of India has fibre optic backbone reaching the entire State and is planning additional microwave capacity of 6 GHz by the year 2000. In addition, high capacity backbone running all along the State with ready microwave connectivity to several towns can be easily put in place using the infrastructure created/being created by mobile communication companies. MAR radio access can be had from anywhere in these towns. The infrastructure created by cable TV companies can also be harnessed to set up the access network. The availability of these infrastructural resources is an important factor in the establishment of SII.

The State Government will take initiative to establish the State Information Infrastructure with one or more international gateways by harnessing, developing and integrating these infrastructural resources. The State Government will form a task force with appropriate representation from the industry, users and service providers to prepare a proper scheme and to work towards the realisation of the State Information Infrastructure.

6.2 The Government will endeavour to ensure that internet access is available to PSTN analog dial up subscribers in all districts by 1999. The access shall be provided at various Points of Presence (POP) in the state and the internet traffic aggregated and linked through the gateways to the internet.

6.3 The Government will take the initiative to strengthen the links to Districts and Taluks in the State with support from DoT, VSNL and other operators. Pressure will be put on Government of India to include all districts in Kerala in the NII and for strengthening the DoT network in the State.

6.4 Non-stop high-reliable scaleable servers will be established to serve as information repositories. A single host shall be developed in each district to focus on network information content relevant to the development sector, government databases, support services etc.

6.5 Malayalam user interface and web browser tools will be promoted to exploit the capabilities of SII for applications like access to Government databases in Malayalam.

6.6 The establishment of State Information Infrastructure will be carried out with the active participation of private sector.

6.7 Concurrent with the above efforts, the Government will encourage initiatives to normalise and standardise the backbone to make it a universal plug and play fabric that is conducive to all users and service providers across a wide range of bandwidth requirements. This is necessary to mitigate the possible fractious and unbridled proliferation of connectivity crisscrossing the state.

7. Human Resource Development for IT

One of the critical factors that determine the growth and development of the IT industry is the availability of trained manpower. It is noteworthy that human resources have played an important role in the development of electronics and computer software industry in Kerala. The Government is seized of the urgency for consolidating and strengthening the core competence of the state on the human resources front to propel the development of IT industry.

Policy Initiatives

7.1. Detailed Study of the Needs of the IT Sector

A detailed study will be undertaken to assess the quantum and caliber of manpower required for the IT industry in Kerala as also to ascertain the industry expectations about the scope and nature of educational training to be imparted by the institutions. An organized census of the educational and training institutions in Kerala offering courses on Software Development/IT will be an integral part of this study and the census will focus on critical aspects such as training infrastructure, course coverage/curriculum, quality of trainers, affiliations/acceptance of the courses offered, placement of the students etc. A database of computer professionals in Kerala — covering both urban as well as rural areas — will also be developed.

The comprehensive database that emerges from the detailed study mentioned above would provide as the basic document for proper management of HRD in the IT-sector in Kerala. This document shall be continually updated.

7.2 Establishment of Institute of Information Technology in Kerala

The Government will encourage the industry to set up an institute of excellence in Information Technology. The educational/training programmes to be undertaken at the institute is expected to be highly specialized in nature, targeting higher-end requirements of the industry and R & D institutions within and outside the country. The institute should also rovide infrastructure/facilities and expert assistance for result oriented R & D projects initiated by other institutions and industrial concerns.

7.3 Introducing Information Technology as a Specialized Branch of Study

Information Technology will be popularised as specialized branch of study. Well-defined graduate and post graduate courses in Information Technology will be introduced in select engineering colleges in Kerala. Affiliations with national/international institutions in faculty support as well as sharing of infrastructure will be encouraged to maintain the quality of output at the desired levels. Also, diploma level programmes in IT will be introduced in identified polytechnics in the State to enhance the resource base for highly trained supervisory personnel to cater to the ever increasing demand from the industry. The courses to be offered by the engineering colleges as well as the polytechnics will be designed and closely monitored through proper linkages with the industry. Necessary action on this aspect will be initiated by the Directorate of Technical Education, in consultation with the industry.

7.4 Development of Centres of Excellence in Information Technology

The Government will pursue a policy of providing freedom of operation to the institutes offering courses in Information Technology subject to their satisfying norms relating to the adequacy of infrastructure and other facilities. The objective will be to develop centres of excellence in Information Technology. In respect of the engineering colleges where Information Technology will be introduced as a branch of study, the department managing such courses will be given sufficient freedom of operation. Necessary action in this regard will be initiated by the Directorate of Technical Education.

7.5 Fund for Up-gradation of Training/ Educational Infrastructure

Focus will be laid on strengthening/up-grading the educational and training infrastructure in the existing institutions offering programmes on IT as well as institutions that may be selected for introducing specialized courses in IT. A corpus fund will be formed with the participation of the government, institutions and the private sector for this purpose. The fund will be made available on soft terms to deserving institutions, particularly for investing in technologies, up-gradation of laboratories/R&D facilities, purchase of new software etc.

7.6 Introduction of a System for Accreditation

A body of experts of international caliber and senior representatives from leading corporate groups from the IT sector within India and abroad will be constituted for ranking and providing accreditation to the IT courses offered by various institutions.

7.7 Financing HRD in IT

Private investments for human resource development in the IT sector will be encouraged. New institutes for education and training in the IT sector will be promoted in the private/joint sectors at appropriate locations in the State. Educational, Training and R & D institutions will be treated on par with industries for assistance from financial institutions. Necessary directions in this regard will be given to the State level financial institutions.

7.8 Improving Computer/IT Literacy

Kerala has the credit of having achieved a notable level of computer literacy. While computer systems have been set up in the work place in large numbers of offices — in both private and public sectors — the percentage of users of computers needs be enhanced. This requires well-conceived training programmes targeting employed personnel.

Further, adequate training programmes in computer-based communication, use of Internet etc. needs be introduced. Such (in-house) training programmes will be organized. Internet booths will be established at appropriate centres aiming at the popularization of the use of Internet. Specific emphasis would be given and appropriate programmes evolved to impart training to the rural population who otherwise do not have access to computers. It is expected that the computer literacy in Kerala can be greatly enhanced through such initiatives.

7.9 Ensuring Linkages Between Industry and Institutions

Thrust will be laid on facilitating linkages between industry and institutions to eliminate mismatch between the output from institutions and industry expectations. It would be made mandatory for institutions to ensure guest faculty support from the industry in key areas. Project work/assignments to be undertaken at the industrial units — at different stages — by the student of IT courses will be an integral part of curriculum.

Institutions will be encouraged to take up research projects addressing specific problems encountered by the industry. Expert assistance and infrastructure support will be made available for such projects, by the proposed Institute of Information Technology.

Specific programmes/activities aimed at fostering closer linkages between institutions and industry will be formulated and implemented on a regular basis.

8. Support Institutions and Resource Centres

Centre for Development of Imaging Technology (C-DIT) : A leading Research and Development Institution in the State actively involved in Science and Technology, Development Communication and the application of IT in the decentralized planning and medicine. C-DIT has the capability and expertise to emerge as a resource centre for dissemination of Information Technology in the State and also in the setting up of State Information Infrastructure.

Directorate of Industries and Commerce : The Directorate of Industries and Commerce co-ordinates industrial development activity in various sectors — tiny, small, medium and large — throughout the State helping entrepreneurs to acquire the required infrastructure and providing financial incentives and concessions on industrial investments.

Kerala State Industrial Development Corporation (KSIDC) : The primary industrial development arm of the State providing a range of services including finance to prospective investors and supporting them from conception to commissioning and beyond. KSIDC focuses mainly on the medium and large sectors.

Kerala Financial Corporation (KFC) : The primary industrial financial institution focusing on offering term-loan assistance to entrepreneurs.

Kerala Industrial Infrastructure Development Corporation (KINFRA) : A statutory corporation set up by an Act of the Kerala Assembly in 1993 for creating infrastructure for industrial development. KINFRA has several industrial infrastructure projects in different parts of the State.

Kerala State Electronics Development Corporation (KELTRON) : The first State Electronics Development Corporation in India, actively involved in manufacture and marketing of a wide spectrum of electronic products. Keltron is a leader in communication products and has the capability of being a partner in popularizing the use of Information Technology in Government and also in the creation of the State Information Infrastructure.

Technopark : India's first and most advanced Technology Park for Information Technology. Technopark provides the ideal infrastructure and environment for setting up ventures in Information Technology and is already home to a large number of successful software and IT companies.

Appendix–VI

Information Technology Policy of West Bengal 2000

1. Preamble

The Task Force on Information Technology set up by the State Government has submitted its recommendations on a policy for IT and on an Action Plan. The State Government will in partnership with industry and educational institutions, promote the growth of the IT industry in the State. This will offer benefits of Information Technology applications for all types of industry, enterprises, private and public organizations and institutions. Increasing information appliance access to the people of the State will be a major goal. The Government will also seek to orchestrate a conducive policy environment that can provide efficient growth in all important sectors including software development for the domestic and international market, help in creation of a durable multimedia, as also Web-enabled technologies and promote setting up of venture capital companies.

2. This policy is expected to help in providing better and more efficient services to citizens, promote social and economic development through broad-based computer access and contribute towards the development of e-commerce and efficient connectivity.

2.1 The State Government sees a substantial potential of employment in the IT sector, particularly in the area of IT enabled services and back office processing in the next five years. The high level of education among the youth and the general aptitude for creative thinking, should afford an appropriate environment lead to high level growth in this sector.

2.2 The State's IT goals are to :

2.2.1 Realize 20% of the National Software Export Target by the year 2005.

2.2.2 Build on the State's creative intellectual wealth including the abundance of skilled and educated manpower and focus on one or two areas of excellence for rapid growth, e.g., multimedia, Web enabled technologies etc.

2.2.3 Stimulate the growth of IT enabled services and back office support services.

2.2.4 Transit from an IT aware Government to an IT enabled Government by adopting e-governance appropriately.

2.2.5 Provide easily affordable infrastructure and incentives for progress in the IT sector.

2.2.6 Set up an integrated State-wide delivery backbone for a WAN (Wide Area Network) which can facilitate OFC backed data, voice and video communications which can support e-governance, e-commerce, distant education and provide efficient government-citizen interface.

2.2.7 Address IT education and education in related spheres to :

2.2.7.1 Produce adequate numbers of industry ready IT professionals in the State through public and private institutions.

2.2.7.2 Develop IT culture in the State through IT literacy programmes.

2.2.7.3 Promote setting up of IT Venture Fund companies.

3. The IT Policy covers the following broad heads for the present :

- IT in Communication.
- Strategic areas of E-Governance and Citizen-Government interface.
- IT education and Human Resource Development, research.
- IT in Industry and the Service Sector.
- Role of Webel (West Bengal Electronics Industry Development Corporation Limited).
- E-Commerce.
- Special incentives for the IT Sector.

3.1 IT in Communication

Government-wide Electronic Information Infrastructure will be appropriately created to simplify service delivery, reduce duplication and improve the level and speed of service to the public. Telecommunication linkages through optical fibre cable and VSAT systems will be installed to form a communication backbone [The Department of Telecommunication are engaged in laying of such cables and the WBSEB is in the process of setting a State-wide VSAT system.]

3.1.1 In order to provide high speed connectivity to a wide range of end-users, the State Government will help to set up an extensive network with appropriate bandwidth. The latest communication strategies using fibre optics will be used appropriately to connect institutions of higher learning, research centres, health, commercial, manufacturing and financial sectors. Initially some fibre optic cable network will be provided by the Department of Telecommunication and VSAT linkages by the West Bengal State Electricity Board. The West Bengal Telecom Department has provided 2.81 lakh additional lines during 1998-99. Internet modes have been commissioned at Durgapur, Siliguri, Kharagpur and Haldia. It is expected that all district headquarters will be connected to Internet by January 2000. The optical fibre cable link between Calcutta and Kharagpur is expected to be in place soon. A state-wide fibre optic cable based backbone project is being planned. This will comprise of a 1600 km. Long backbone network over the WBSEB Transmission network, connecting all the 17 district headquarters, an additional 10 centres with population over one lakh, 10 Engineering Colleges, 6 Medical Colleges, 9 Universities, 13 Industrial Growth Centres, the Falta Export Processing Zone and the border posts of Petrapole and Hilly. Rural locations have been identified where 100/50 KVA power sub-stations are required to be located to facilitate reliable telecommunication services. The gap in requirements of the communication network will be met through separate projects of fibre optic cable, VSAT/VSNL systems and later networks on a variety of platforms like VSAL satellite and Microweb LAN / WAN to be financed by the State Government with the help of financial institutions/International Agencies.

3.1.2 Government will issue necessary directives to concerned government agencies to facilitate laying of a fibre optic network for the purpose of internet connectivity and other requirements.

3.2 E-Governance

The State Government recognizes the importance and scope of e-governance and will promote use of necessary technologies for efficiency and transparency in its functions. The Government is identifying areas which require introduction of IT in the overall functional framework of the Government. Towards this end IT literacy and training will be encouraged within the Government along with the suitable infrastructure. Attention will be paid to models, network design and overall systems management. As a beginning, for a better citizen interface the following will be emphasized for computerization, viz., vehicle registration, land records, birth and death registrations, employment exchanges, payment of excise duty, sales tax and local tax, electronic bill payment of water and electricity, computerization of health records, relevant education through internet, work of police and police stations, criminal justice etc. Government departments and organizations will have E-mail communication. All important government policies, Acts, Rules, Regulations, Notifications which have a direct bearing on the members of the public would be made available through internet or other suitable networks.

3.2.1 A Department of Information Technology will be set up by the State Government to co-ordinate and assist in adoption of various Information Technology techniques in the Government according to a structured plan. The IT Department will provide appropriate technological inputs to be gleaned from the open market and from interaction with other States and IT bodies. The IT Department will obtain assistance from Webel and other organizations dealing in different areas of IT, to ensure adoption of common standards in hardware and software applications. The IT Department would also help different Government departments in examining/evaluating proposals for introduction of IT in their functioning and for administrative approval to such projects within budgetary provisions. In the case of a plan schemes, the IT Department will have necessary interaction with the State Planning Board. The State Government will :

3.2.1.1 Accord priority to the development, adoption and use of IT in PRIs/field offices having a direct interface with the public.

3.2.1.2 Develop computerized information bases in a phased manner, to include programmes and projects at all levels under implementation with budgetary support of the Government, taking advantage of commonality in applications.

3.2.2 Progressively network the information bases of all departments and field offices into an appropriate Management Information System for the government. Each department will have a CITO (Chief Information Technology Officer) for monitoring and assisting in implementation of IT applications.

The following measures will also be taken :

3.2.2.1 Use of appropriate IT at the field level; the Zilla Parishads will gradually adopt GIS based planning to establish a District-wide network with Blocks/Municipalities for speedy transmission of relevant date and information. This network will be suitably coupled with the State-wide network in due course.

3.2.2.2 Formulate strategies for training, hardware acquisition, designing network and software development for : Phase-wise implementation at the headquarters of districts and blocks including local Government Institutions and other notified authorities, development agencies, Panchayati Raj institutions and other field offices. Emerging global technologies will be identified and appropriately adopted in different functional units of the government.

3.2.3 Indian language based systems are crucial for impact of IT at the grassroots level. Government will actively promote broad based use of software tools in Bengali, Nepali/Gorkhali and other local languages etc.

3.2.4 The right of citizens to have access to information through electronic media will be progressively ensured. Access will be given to the various acts, rules, application forms, services, existing Government processes and procedures, etc. by the concerned government departments and public bodies. Web-sites will be progressively set up for Government Departments, PRIs, Public sector organizations etc. with a mother Web-site for the entire State Government.

3.2.4.1 Initiate actions for setting up an independent Wireless Satellite based communication system which will not only provide connectivity to remote locations day and night but will also remain operational even during emergency situations unaffected by man-made or natural calamities. This system will provide exclusive connectivity for the State Police with a main control centre in Calcutta, each of 17 District Headquarters and all police stations and a few more remote rural locations. Each centre or location will provide with a Telephone set, Fax machine and a PC for data communication using state-of-the-art technology. The same system will be extended later to other additional village centres, as required.

3.2.5 Service Delivery Points (SDPs) will be set up progressively at convenient locations for citizens to access services. These can be established by the private sector and may include the following in the long run —

- Information kiosks having intelligent public interface with touch screen monitors, or cord operated phones in public places such as shopping centres.
- post offices, railway stations and libraries, private centres etc.
- PCOs (upgraded to manned public access terminals). All STD/ ISD booths can be converted into IT booths through necessary steps with the co-operation of the Department of Telecommunications, Government of India. They can operate as Public Telephone Information Centres (PTICs).
- Front office terminals of Government offices.
- Home PC through the Internet and/or through private cable operators.

3.2.6 SDPs services will be available in the local language in due course.

3.2.7 Services will be delivered to citizens in rural areas in the following sectors on a priority basis :

- Agricultural Sector :
    - Weather forecasting at the district level in the short term and the medium term.
    - Price of commodities in all major centres of the State and other States.
    - Crop Disease Management.
    - Crop loans.
- Extension Programmes and supply of inputs according to schedule.
- Educational Opportunities.

- Employment Exchange Registration.
- Employment opportunities etc.
- Mail.
- Trade & Business.
- Health & Medicine.
- Land Records.
- Public Grievances Registration.
- Police Stations, Crime and Crime Records.
- Natural Calamities and Emergencies.
- Income or Caste certificates.

3.2.8 Utilities billing/payment is a major problem area for citizens in urban areas. Projects will be taken up for computerized billing and electronic payment of the following utilities :

- Electricity bills
- Telephone Bills
- Gas Bills
- Water Bills
- Property tax payment/records
- Road Tax
- Fines
- Sales Tax
- Other taxes and charges

3.2.9 Smart cards, stored value cards, credit/debit cards will be integrated into the Electronic System for payment of bills to utilities. A business model will be evolved for joint partnership of government and the private sector to electronically deliver services on a sustained basis so as to ensure that government does not incur much expenditure while the private sector invests initially and recovers money on a transaction fee basis.

3.2.10 A system of Career Guidance for youth will be set up with the following components:

3.2.10.1 Electronic Employment to enable youth to register themselves for jobs based on their qualifications, capabilities and interests.

3.2.10.2 Career options available in different areas including options for higher studies in any professional area. Links will be provided to the Web Sites of different institutes/organizations dealing with the subject.

3.2.10.3 Career guidance for school, college and university pass-outs will be separately dealt with. Information on universities, professional institutions and vocational institutions will be available. All private institutions would be required to pay a normal fee for registering their names at this site.

3.2.10.4 Career options in sports will be specially addressed on the Web to enable the detection and nurturing of talents.

3.2.10.5 Information will also be made available on job opportunities abroad.

3.2.10.6 Results/enrolment and other such services.

3.2.10.7 DOE accredited organizations in the government sector also will be relied upon for easy access to the mechanisms/ systems already developed in different States and at the National level.

3.2.10.8 E-governance should eventually provide integrated government services through a single window by re-engineering of government processes.

3.3 IT Education and Human Resource Development

3.3.1 Government will address the question of quality of IT education and also accreditation with a well defined target of increase of output of accredited IT professionals every year.

3.3.2 Existing Engineering Degree Colleges, Polytechnics and other specialized institutions will be encouraged to expand their intake in Information Technology courses. [Action in this direction has commenced as computer science and technology, electronics and communication engineering degree courses have been introduced in Kalyani Engineering College, Haldia Institute of Technology (Govt. aided) and Institute of Engineering and Management (private). Five new Engineering Colleges (private) have been established at Asansol, Berhampore, Kolaghat, Bankura, Garia where along with other disciplines Computer Engineering, Electronics and Communication Engineering and Information Technology degree courses have been introduced. Five more institutions have been started in 1999. At present the total student intake is 1910 per annum. Post-Graduate courses are also being conducted in some institutions. In addition proposals have been sent to the AICTE for introduction of courses on Information Technology in eleven institutions.]

3.3.3 Government will promote the setting up of an Indian Institute of Information Technology at Calcutta (IIT-C) as an Apex Institute with the active participation of industry, within the year 2000. A unique model is being developed independently which wiil be a centre of excellence in IT. District branches will be set up in North and South Bengal.

3.3.4 State Government will promote a new Technology University by the year 2001.

3.3.5 Government will aim to progressively promote IT literacy at senior secondary level. [The Department of Youth Services, Government of West Bengal have set up computer training centres in the districts for imparting basic computer skills of youth. More centres will be set up in the next year increasing the total capacity to around 30,000 trainees. This training programme was launched in the year 1996 and has generated a lot of interest at the district level and below.]

3.3.6 IT literacy will be gradually made an essential requirement for some categories in Government and Public Sector employment.

3.3.7 Courses on IT enabled Services will be introduced as vocational courses.

3.3.8 A high level Information Technology Development Board (ITDB) will be set up to focus on Research & Development efforts of the State. Awards will be given to Institutes for achieving excellence in R & D in IT related subjects. The board will encourage meaningful linkage between academic, R & D Organizations and IT Industries. Research positions in selected Institutions will be provided together with award of Fellowships.

3.3.9 The rich cultural heritage of the state will be preserved and propagated through judicious use of IT. Efforts will be made to channelise manpower possessing special skills into multimedia and web content creation. Training programmes for professionals in multimedia would be initiated in Engineering Colleges, Polytechnics and other commercial institutions.

3.3.10 The Government will encourage the world-wide trend of employment of women in the IT sector. The following promotional measures will be taken.

3.3.10.1 Telecommuting will be encouraged for allowing

professionally qualified women in IT to facilitate their continued association with their work place in case they are not in a position to attend their offices on a regular basis due to family constraints. They may be offered special loans/financial grants by their employers to set up infrastructure at their homes to be able to telecommute.

3.3.10.2 Virtual institutes to evolve special HRD programmes to help educate women to enter the field of IT enabled services and back office processing.

3.3.10.3 Banks and FI's will be encouraged to offer special financial packages on a proactive basis to support enterprising and professionally qualified women to set up home based IT services in various areas of IT led economic activities.

3.3.11 Students and teachers in institutions would have ready access through electronic connectivity to a wide source of data, information and research material. Specialised teaching methods would also be designed and adapted through this system to the level of skills of teachers.

3.3.12 Assistance of ISRO would be sought wherever required for dissemination of information, training and education in rural and tribal areas.

3.3.13 A public awareness programme will be designed and implemented.

3.3.14 The MOU between WEBEL and WorldTel will be examined in the light of requirement of information kiosks and IT powered services.

3.4 IT in Industry

3.4.1 An Industry Consortium will be formed with active collaboration of the State Government, NRIs, leading industrial houses, software companies and venture capital companies to address the huge opportunity offered by IT enabled services and back office services.

3.4.2 Government will promote the creation of venture capital funds towards funding start-ups and entrepreneurial efforts for also catering to the IT Enabled Service Market.

3.4.3 Courses on IT Enabled Services will be introduced as vocational courses.

3.4.4 Government will review and suitably amend laws where necessary to enable re-location and reorganization in the IT industry including special incentives.

3.4.5 In order to encourage IT entrepreneurship, incubation facilities will be encouraged at Calcutta as well as other important towns in the districts.

3.4.6 Adequate quality office space with State of the Art telecom connectivity for the IT industry will be promoted from 2000.

3.4.7 Government will promote the setting up of at least two world class software technology parks by 2004.

3.4.8 Software units and software technology parks will be given fast track clearance while focusing on —

- Expeditious clearance to building plans.
- WBSEB/CESC will give such units the status of continuous process industry and give priority for providing dedicated lines. Exemption from statutory power cuts and supply of power at the proper frequency.
- For approved software technology parks, sale and purchase of spaces may be made freely transferable and may be considered for exemption of payment of some percentage of stamp duty.
- Self-certification/exemption from provisions of some statutes/ regulations is being examined.
- Permission to run three-shift operations.
- Relaxation of FAR norms.
- Use of excess and/or vacant land of sick/closed industries.

3.5 Role of Webel

Webel (West Bengal Electronics Industry Development Corpn. Ltd.), the Government IT Company, will be a facilitator for development of information technology in the State with in-house or contracted expertise from the open market.

Webel will —

- Assist in e-governance.
- Provide a common platform for meeting of representatives of premier institutes like IIM Calcutta, IIT Kharagpur, BE College, leading Universities, other Educational Institutions, majors in IT industries and in IT education so that up-gradation of curriculum

through modernization may take place regularly.

- Identify projects in collaboration with the private sector for facilitating ready use of the Internet by the common man and initiate steps for setting up of research and development projects.
- Set up a single window computerized clearance mechanism for processing IT applications to assist the government in according fast track clearances.
- Co-ordinate engineering of software for Bengali and English voice recognition and dictation to facilitate dispensing of keyboards in due course.
- Standardize a Bengali keyboard and appropriate user-friendly software for interface with the public.
- Provide a forum for interaction between academia, IT industry, government and the public at regular intervals to enable constant improvement of e-governance.
- Set up training centres in the districts by introducing distance learning through duly accredited centres in collaboration with the private sector.
- Progressively take up the manufacture of high speciality software/ hardware for the niche market.
- Promote initiatives between the Government and industry, IT firms in software and IT education so that the Government can play a proactive role in not only promoting growth of the IT sector in all aspects but can also afford and obtain advice in some aspects of e-governance.
- Upgrade Webel's in-house capabilities for facilitating promotion of IT in e-governance and the IT Sector.

3.5.1 Webel will be placed under the administrative control of the newly formed Information Technology Department to provide for more effective coordination.

3.6 E-Commerce

3.6.1 E-commerce is another rapidly emerging area which will facilitate international as well as domestic and regional trade and commerce and will require IT-enabled activity at varied levels. A major focus area for the government will therefore be to spearhead the structure and networking that will enable the e-commerce users in all categories.

3.6.2 Legislation will have to be enacted primarily by the Government of India to provide legal sanctions for presentations and transactions through electronic data interchange and other electronic systems. Amendments to existing laws like the IPC and the Indian Evidence Act are required to be carried out. Consequent to this suitable amendments would then have to be brought in to provide for Cyber codes in existing State Acts.

3.7 Venture Funds

The State Government recognizes the importance of venture capital financing for promotion of the IT industry, IT in education, IT enabled services market and in providing last mile connectivity in the districts and urban agglomerations. The State Government would promote the setting up of specialised financing bodies in the joint sector along with Financial Institutions and other interested parties like the Chambers of Commerce, IT industry majors etc.

3.8 Incentives Under Consideration for the IT Sector

3.8.1 Exemption/permission to sell excess vacant land held by a sick/closed industry unit is being considered if it sets up a non-polluting IT/software/electronic/IT education/training sector. However, the process of such sale as well as utilization of the sale proceeds will be overseen by a Committee to be set up by the Government. Various Corporations and other Municipal Authorities will examine the modalities for according necessary sanction speedily for setting up for such non-polluting IT related industries.

3.8.2 The Government is examining the possibility of allowing building activity in a certain percentage of the cases on vacant land held by sick/closed industry units provided a bulk of the excess land is utilized for setting up of an industry in the IT/software/electronic/IT education/training sector. Such permission would be granted on a case by case basis only, according to individual merit. A committee will be set up to decide and monitor these cases.

3.8.3 For promoting the construction of buildings directly relating to IT in the State, some concessions are being examined. This would, however, be subject to certification of the usage of the building for IT.

3.8.4 Areas having cluster of IT industries are being considered for exemption from the purview of statutory power cuts and for ensuring supply of power at the proper frequency.

3.8.5 IT software industries will be considered for installation in residential areas with the approval of the concerned urban authority/ district industries centre etc. and on proper certification on a case by case basis.

3.8.6 New IT industries may be provided special escort services and concessions on a case by case basis if the units are located outside metropolitan city limits.

3.8.7 Government and District Authorities will pay special attention to telecommunication linkages for IT parks.

3.8.8 For establishments of IT companies outside limits of urban local bodies, question of relaxation of FAR norms is being examined by the MA Department and will be done on a case by case basis.

3.8.9 Venture Capital activity would be encouraged by offering concessions to Venture Capital Companies.

3.9 State Level Monitoring

3.9.1 For monitoring and implementing the policies outlined, at the apex level, a high Level Committee on Information Technology will be set up to be chaired by the Chief Minister. Consultative Committees will be formed under the High Level Committee to focus on different areas of specialization.

Appendix–VII

Karnataka : The Millennium IT Policy: Information Technology for the Common Man

Introduction

1.0 Karnataka is in the forefront of Information Technology and is called the Silicon State of India. In addition, the state capital Bangalore has shown tremendous growth in the IT Sector and is the IT Capital of India.

1.1 Karnataka is the first state to announce IT Policy in the year 1997. This Policy has acted as an important catalyst for the growth of IT Industry in the State. The industry however is growing in leaps and bounds. The type and nature of business are rapidly expanding. Karnataka is becoming the centre for more and more companies in sophisticated IT products and services. The value addition from IT professionals of Bangalore is getting at the higher end of the spectrum. Thanks to Moore's Law, the cost of technology is dropping and technology is advancing exponentially. Thus, the prices of the new products are dropping rapidly and the same products are becoming more intelligent. The IT usage is becoming more widespread and relevant. It is necessary to re-focus on the IT Policy and define it in a way that is most suited for the present.

1.2 Hence, the Government of Karnataka is pleased to announce Mahithi, the Millennium IT Policy.

Objectives

2.0 Objectives of the Millennium IT Policy are:

- to utilize the power of Information Technology in the overall goal of the Government of Karnataka in eradicating poverty and empowering women,

- to effectively reduce unemployment by absorbing the major share of educated youth into the IT Industry,
- to promote the usage of Kannada in Information Technology,
- to use e-governance as a tool and deliver a government that is more proactive and responsive to its citizens,
- to unleash the Karnataka Incubation engine,
- to encourage business with non-English speaking countries, and
- to maintain the pre-eminent position of both Bangalore and Karnataka in the field of Information Technology.

Eradicate Poverty and Empower Women

3.0 One of the primary goals of the Government of Karnataka is to eradicate poverty and empower women. The eradication of poverty was attempted via several poverty alleviation schemes. These schemes generally targeted the poorest beneficiaries and provided credit for them.

3.1 The latest technology in eradicating poverty is via self-help groups for women. These women groups are encouraged to save money. The Government steps in with revolving fund as well as bank credit. This method is found to be the most effective in delivering rural credit as well as eradicating poverty.

3.2 One of the critical components of this scheme however involves tracking these beneficiaries that save money as well as receive funding from the government and credit from the banks. The Government of Karnataka proposes to use Information Technology to track all these beneficiaries. The Information Technology is proposed to be used as a tool to eradicate poverty and empower women.

3.3 It is proposed to document every self-help group in Karnataka. This documentation will include the name of the beneficiary, the family particulars, her contribution to the corpus of the group fund or borrowings from the group fund, revolving fund received from the Government of Karnataka, credit received from the concerned bank, the interest due and paid etc. These particulars will be computerized and stored in the respective bank branches where groups would be investing their savings.

3.4 The programme will include complete training of the

organizer, the concerned official and non-officials involved in the implementation of the programme and includes intensive review and monitoring.

3.5 In addition, the IT Department would be involved enthusiastically in several rural development projects. These include providing drinking water via follow-on project of the World Bank, computerizing Village Panchayats, building MIS system for the Zilla Panchayats, etc. Karnataka has a very effective decentralized democratic system of Government. All the Zilla Panchayats in the state spend more than Rs. 4,000 crores a year. This amount is spent on several social sector schemes. The Zilla Panchayats' money is kept in treasury as well as commercial and regional rural bank accounts. Several thousand drawing and disbursing officers spend money. It is proposed to build 'Panchayat' an exhaustive Management Information System for Zilla Panchayats. This system will include both routine accounting reports for the review at various levels, as well as decision support systems for critical management decisions. The same system will have an effective interface with the Khajane the Treasury, Computerisation System.

Employment

4.0 The IT Sector provides vast employment opportunities. Presently, 280,000 IT Professionals are employed all over India. In Karnataka alone the estimated number of professionals is about 75,000. It is estimated that in the year 2010, the potential for employment in Karnataka in the IT Sector alone will reach 10 lakhs. The employment is likely to be generated in sectors of Information Technology that include the hardware development, software services, network services as well as several sectors in the IT Enabled Services. The examples of the IT enabled services are customer interaction, financial and accounting services, call centres, medical transcription, engineering and design data management, remote education, net work consulting, web-site services as well as market research. It is proposed to meet the demand for professionals by organizing Human Resource Development schemes. These schemes will be implemented to train people at different levels like unemployed graduates, engineering college students, college students, polytechnics, ITI as well as schools.

Incentives for Companies

4.1 This policy offers several incentives for companies that create employment in Information Technology. These incentives could be in the areas of cost of land, registration charges, FAR, zonal regulations, etc. The new companies that provide employment of more than 250 in Bangalore and 100 in other areas will be eligible for these concessions.

Training Centres

4.2 This policy seeks to establish 225 training centres all over the state, primarily for the purpose of training the unemployed educated youth in various IT skills. The Government will encourage private sector initiatives in setting up such centres. These centres would receive appropriate concessions from the Government.

College Students

4.3 The Government would like to develop the IT skills amongst college students. This programme will initially cover all the engineering colleges, about 100 polytechnics, 150 ITIs, and 300 colleges. The programme will encourage private sector to set up research centres, training centres, upgrade the laboratories, etc. The scheme will allow the usage of such centres for partial commercialization.

IT in 1000 Schools

4.4 The Government plans to take Information Technology to school children in all parts of the state. This involves setting up of training centres and encouraging private companies to set up training centres in schools. The centres will impart computer education as well as regular education in multimedia format for the students during the school hours. These centres will also provide resources for the students for their class projects. The private companies will also be allowed to use the same centres for commercial use before and after the school hours.

Liberalize Higher Education

4.5 Even though Karnataka's population is only 5% of Indian population, its share in higher education is close to 15%. The state is committed to maintaining this advantage. The government would like to thank the private managements who are running several institutions of higher learning. They will be invited to open more colleges. New institutions that concentrate primarily on IT will be encouraged. Old institutions desiring to convert their seats from other streams into IT will be allowed to do so. Technical standards and quality will be kept up.

Indian Institute of Information Technology

4.6 The Government of Karnataka has established this autonomus Institution which has world class infrastructure and state of the art facilities. The Institute has laboratories sponsored by Sun Microsystems, IBM, Microsoft, Informix, Oracle, Apple & Abode, Novell, Compaq, PTC, CISCO, Ramco, SAP, Computer Associates. The Institute offers advanced courses in post-graduation and doctoral programmes. The Institution is playing a pivotal role in the human resources development in producing high quality professionals as well as training consultants.

Promoting Kannada in IT

5.0 The Government of Karnataka is totally committed to usage of Kannada in the State. While Kannada is being used in all the Government offices it is important to promote Kannada usage via Information Technology. The Government of Karnataka has already taken steps in this direction. Presently, Kannada usage is primarily through software developed by private companies. Each of these companies uses its own proprietary internal code. The result is that the files saved in one software cannot be read or edited using another software. The primary reason for this is that the software developers are not using a common code. In addition, private companies are using different keyboard layouts.

5.1 The Government of Karnataka with the active co-operation of the Kannada Abhivruddhi Pradhikara, Kannada Ganaka Parishad,

Kannada and Culture Department as well as several Kannada researchers has already evolved a common keyboard. The Government is committed to complete the process of standardization and prescribe standard formats and codes for all the software companies.

5.2 The Government is pleased to constitute a committee under the Chairmanship of Secretary to Government, Kannada and Culture Department to standardize the formats and codes so that the development of Kannada software can take place rapidly. The Government will provide incentives for the development of Kannada software.

E-Governance

6.0 The Government of Karnataka believes that effective implementation of e-governance will take IT to the common man. The Government would like to be proactive and responsive to all its citizens particularly the poor. Presently, computers are used in several departments and such decisions are taken in a decentralized manner. While the Apex Committee headed by the Additional Chief Secretary lays down the general guidelines, the committees under the Secretaries to Government are empowered to take all decisions and implement computerization in their respective departments. The departments are supported by Karnataka Government Computer Centre as well as the National Informatics Centre. In fact, the Government of Karnataka is a pioneering state that established Karnataka Government Computer Centre as early as 1971.

Centre for E-Governance

6.1 While statistical progress has been achieved in several departments in a decentralized manner, the Government now proposes to establish a Centre for e-governance under the Department of Information Technology. This Centre will facilitate the use of Information Technology for the common man rapidly and effectively. It will provide technical support to all the Government departments in their IT Projects. It will play a vital role in coordinating with the Government departments as well as undertake a few critical projects that are likely to be used in more than one department.

6.2 A few important initiatives in the e-governance are:

Mukhya Vahini

6.3 Karnataka State has a decentralized set-up in which people do not have to come to Bangalore for their day-to-day routine business. Most decisions are taken at the village and district levels. It is however felt that an exhaustive database needs to be developed at a single point and be made available to all the decision makers in Karnataka. A comprehensive database will be developed and portions of the database will be made available to respective decision makers. It is also planned to analyse the data in an intelligent manner and provide a sophisticated decision support system for the use of the Chief Minister. The Government has already commenced a systems requirement study on the project.

Education Department

6.4 The Government of Karnataka's commitment to education shows up in the projects implemented here. The department already has a computerised payroll accounting system of all 2.4 lakh teachers in the state. The details of over 18 lakh students that take SSLC, PUC and university examinations have already been computerised and the results of SSLC are made available on the website. The department has used IT in Common Entrance Test for professional courses in an astounding manner. The Common Entrance Test is conducted by the Government of Karnataka for admitting students to professional courses in engineering, medicine, dental courses. Over 55,000 students appear for these examinations every year seeking admission to more than 128 colleges covering 27 courses. More than 20,000 students from outside Karnataka State also participate in the process. The examination is conducted in a most transparent manner. The students are admitted by computerised counselling process, the best ever designed in any education system in India.

Bhoomi

6.5 The record of rights (RTC) play a vital role in the life of farmers. The records are required for establishing ownership of land, for recording the succession of ownership, for recording the agricultural crop details and for obtaining loans from banks. The land records of all the villages in Karnataka have already been computerised. Immediate steps will be taken to make these computerised land records available to the villagers.

Nondani

6.6 This project is aimed at making land registration simple and easy for the citizens. People go to the sub-registrar offices for registering sale deed, mortgage deed, etc., as well as for an encumbrance certificate. This process requires a lot of manual operation and is extremely cumbersome. To simplify the procedures for citizens, the government has already initiated computerisation of the department. The sub-registrar offices in Shivaji Nagar, Kengeri and Bangalore South have facilities to scan the registration deeds and return the registered documents. So far, over 100,000 documents have been registered in a computerised environment. For giving the encumbrance certificate the 13 year data need to be incorporated into the computer. This process has already been taken up and is expected to be finished early. This will give relief to Bangalore citizens. Later, the project will be extended to entire Karnataka.

Khajane

6.7 This involves intensive computerization of the treasuries all over Karnataka. The treasury payment system handles over Rs.20,000 crores annually through 225 treasuries. This system serves 4.7 lakh pensioners of Government service, art and culture, sportsmen, journalists, freedom fighters, etc. In addition, the system serves 13.15 lakh old age pensioners, the physically handicapped and destitute widows. The treasuries act as bankers to 4,500 zilla panchayats, taluk panchayats, grama panchayats, municipal corporations and other funds. A comprehensive computerization is planned using the V-sat terminals. There will be a main database centre at Bangalore and a disaster recovery centre at Dharwad.

Therige

6.8 The Commercial Taxes Department has already computerised several facets of its operations. The details of about one lakh dealers are computerised by the department. In addition, important check posts are being computerised where the invoices will be scanned and the details of the transactions will be made available to the assessing officers to check evasion of taxes on certain commodities.

Karnataka Government Insurance Department (KGID)

6.9 Karnataka has the oldest insurance department started in the year 1891. It undertakes life insurance as well as vehicle insurance for its employees. The department offers life insurance policies for the employees as well as third party and comprehensive insurance for the vehicles. The motor branch of the department that offers insurance for vehicles is completely computerised. The computerisation of life insurance business is under progress.

Reshme

6.10 Karnataka has introduced online transactions in the silk market. The cocoons are brought to the market, displayed and the trades are recorded online. This system has brought lot of transparency in market operations.

Agricultural Price Information

6.11 The Government of Karnataka has already got a system of recording and displaying the spot prices of agricultural commodities at APMC, Bangalore. It is proposed to expand the system to other APMCs so that the prices of commodities are easily available for the farmers all over the state.

Employment Department

6.12 Karnataka has computerised data on registration of candidates for employment, employment market information as well as the all India trade tests for the employment training wing.

Police IT 2000

6.13 Karnataka boasts of a peaceful law and order situation in the country. The Government is committed to maintaining the law and order for the benefit of its own citizens as well as citizens from outside and foreign nationals. The Police Department is already computeriseed to a large extent and has an ambitious project which will improve the state crime record bureau, connect the police stations located in Bangalore, enhance the capabilities of the intelligence wing, etc.

Environment

6.14 The Government believes in the protection of the state's natural environment and has used IT as a tool to do that. The Forest Department has already implemented computerised systems to track poaching and other forest offences, track the land use data, improve the wild life management system as well as manage rare species under the Western Ghats programme.

Saarige

6.15 Under this project, the Government has plans to computerize all the RTO offices in Bangalore. Once implemented, the citizens will be able to get the driving licences faster. Vehicle registration process will also be simplified. This project is already under implementation and is expected to be launched in the next few months.

Municipal Corporation

6.16 The Government has initiated action to computerise the Bangalore, Mangalore, Mysore, Belgaum, Hubli-Dharwad and Gulbarga Corporations. The project involves simplification of the payment of property tax, early issue of birth and death certificates and grievance redressal.

Small Scale Industries

6.17 The State has computerized the permanent registration of over 2.5 lakh Small Scale Industries. All the districts as well as 26 taluk industries centres have been completely computerised.

Common Systems

6.18 The centre for e-governance plans to develop certain common systems in the areas of payroll processing (Vethana), personnel information system (Sibbandhi) as well as GIS. Already many government departments have their own systems in place. The centre for e-governance seeks to standardize them to enhance the scope and implement the systems uniformly and more effectively across the departments. The Sibbandhi system includes operation of a Sibbandhi Card that gives important details of employees. The Secretariat employees will have the benefit of receiving this card, very soon.

6.19 In addition, the centre for e-governance is expected to complete Sachivalaya Vahini, the Secretariat LAN System for intelligent sharing of information between the departments.

6.20 The centre also plans to start an information network to connect all the district and taluk headquarters. Presently, all the districts as well as 140 taluks out of 175 taluks have already been connected via Fibre Optic Network. Video conferencing facility is in place in most of the district headquarters facilitating direct interaction between the district level officers and the higher authorities at the State level.

Unleash Karnataka Incubation Engine

7.0 Karnataka is already in the forefront of Information Technology and a number of new ventures come up in Bangalore regularly. The companies in Bangalore are in the forefront of Information Technology and several core technology areas such as Voice over IP, MPEG, Products on Blue Tooth, WAP, GPRS, Home RF, etc., are increasingly becoming focus areas. Many multi-national companies have applied for international patents. For instance, the Texas Instruments, the first MNC in Bangalore has already applied for 115 patents. Bangalore boasts of over 55,000 very high quality professionals in the areas of integrated chip design communication software, application software as well as other services.

7.1 The Government of Karnataka is committed to keep up the pace of such venture creation in Karnataka and unleash the Karnataka Incubation Engine. The state has the right environment for this to happen. The Mckinsey NASSCOM Report indicates the critical ingredients, viz., idea generation, anchor companies, research centres and universities. The following table provides a comparison between the Silicon Valley (California) and the Silicon State (Karnataka).

7.2 The Government plans to encourage the Incubation Centres primarily with private initiative. The Government will also set up a few Incubation Centres that provide complete start up facilities with the computer systems and telecommunication link for a limited period of time. The entrepreneurs are expected to pay a reasonable rent for the premises and move out in a short period to commercial space.

	Silicon Valley (California)	Silicon State (Karnataka)
Anchor Companies	HP, Fair Child, Sun Micro System	WIPRO, Infosys, Microland, i-Flex, TCS, Motorola, Texas Instruments
Research Centres	XEROX, Palo Alto Research Centre	ISRO, NAL, LRDE, GTRE, CSIR, CAIR
University	Standford	Indian Institute of Science, Indian Institute of Management, Indian Institute of Information Technology
Venture Financing	Draper, Walden NICCO, Kleiner Perkins	Draper, KITVEN, ICICI Ventures, IL&FS Ventures, Indus Ventures, CAN Bank, ICF Ventures

To encourage Business with non-English speaking Countries

8.0 Currently the Karnataka companies have substantial interaction with English speaking countries. While this will be intensified, the Government believes that the companies can add tremendous value for the non-English speaking countries in Europe, Asia as well as South America. Presently, Karnataka has ties with many countries and Bangalore has representative councils/representative offices, trade offices from China, Denmark, France, Germany, Italy, Israel, Japan, Netherlands, Singapore, etc. The Government will welcome and encourage initiatives from all these countries and will promote cross-interaction initiatives as well as cross-cultural activities. They will also be encouraged to set up their country specific IT Parks.

Where IT Really Happens

9.0 Karnataka has a pre-eminent position in the IT Industry not only in India, but also in the World Map. In fact, Bangalore was rated as one of the "top 10 Hot Spots" by the *News Week magazine*. It was also considered as one of the "top 10 Tech Cities" in a survey conducted by *Business Week*. The German publication *Diezeit* called Bangalore as "City of Future".

9.1 Karnataka boasts of a stable democratic Government, peaceful law and order, welcoming locals, a vast pool of IT Professionals, a large array of higher educational institutions, diversity of culture, pleasant climate, excellent labour relations and premier research institutions.

9.2 Almost 100 multi-national companies from almost all parts of the world — USA, UK, Japan, Germany, France, Singapore, Malasya, China, Korea, Belgium, Ireland, etc., are located here. Bangalore has been home for Indian multi-national companies like Infosys Technologies, Wipro, Microland, etc.

9.3 Karnataka has the thriving presence of 9 of the 19 CMUSEI Level 5 companies. Several companies located in Karnataka are conducting high technology research and are registering patents all over the world.

9.4 The Government of Karnataka is committed to maintaining its pre-eminent position in the field of Information Technology.

9.5 An IT company could be any company in the sectors of computing devices, network controller cards memories, the storage units, printers and output devices, networking products, software, power supplies to computer systems, networking/cabling and related accessories, consumables, electronic components, telecommunication equipments, etc.

9.6 The major initiatives of the Government are described below.

The Lowest Ever Taxation in India

9.7 The Government of Karnataka has specified the lowest ever taxation of only 0.25% on computers and computer peripherals effective from 2nd March 1999. In addition, 4% work contract tax on the annual maintenance contract on hardware has been totally waived effective from 2nd March, 1999. In addition, the following Fiscal Incentives are offered:

Fiscal Incentives

9.8 Information Technology Industries will be exempt from payment of entry tax and purchase tax on computer hardware, computer peripherals and other capital goods including captive power generation sets, during the implementation stage which can be extended up to five years from the date of commencement of implementation.

9.9 Information Technology Industries irrespective of level of investment and location of the unit will be offered sales tax exemption for a period of 10 (ten) years or deferment for a period of 12 (twelve) years, subject to a ceiling of 200% (two hundred per cent) of the value of fixed assets. Such exemption/deferment will also cover turnover tax payable by the unit.

9.10 Captive power generation sets installed by the Information Technology Industry will be eligible for the following incentives :

(a) total exemption from payment of electricity tax without any time limit;
(b) total exemption from payment of sales tax on fuel used for captive power generation without any time limit.

Mega Projects

9.11 The concessions detailed above are primarily meant for IT companies where initial investment in a new company, or in expansion, modernization is less than Rs. 100 crores. If the investment is more than Rs. 100 crores, the Government considers that project as a Mega project and a special set of initiatives and concessions will be worked out with reference to the needs of the company. Also, a project that employs more than 1000 employees will also be considered as a Mega project and these concessions are applicable for both the new units as well as for existing units that create an additional employment by incremental investment.

Pollution Control

9.12 The Karnataka State Pollution Control Board has simplified the procedure for seeking clearances under the Air Act and the Water Act for the software companies that use captive DG Sets.

Power

9.13 Software companies will be treated as industrial (and not commercial) and electricity tariff applicable to the industrial consumers will be levied on such companies.

9.14 Continuous uninterrupted and quality power supply being one of the prime requirements for sustenance and growth of Information Technology Industries, these industries would be given priority in sanction and servicing of power and would also be exempt from power-cuts without any time limit.

Zonal Regulations

9.15 The IT companies that use power up to 5 KVA will be permitted to be established without any locational restrictions. The companies can be established in residential, industrial or commercial areas.

Urban development

9.16 The Government is pleased to relax FAR for all IT projects set up outside the limits of the municipal corporations in the state. This concession would be available to the projects notified by the department of IT that sets up excellent infrastructure, water, uninterrupted power, dedicated connectivity etc. A maximum relaxation up to 50% of the existing FAR would be available.

Venture Capital

9.17 Karnataka offers the widest array of venture capital for any start-ups. Apart from the state promoted venture capital fund KITVEN, special packages are available for financial assistance from both Karnataka State Industrial Investment and Developmental Corporation Ltd., as well as Karnataka State Finance Corporation. The state has several major players such as Draper International, Indus Ventures, ICICI Ventures, IL&FS Ventures, CAN Bank, ICF Ventures, Gujarath Ventures, etc.

Registration Charges

9.18 The tiny and Small Scale Industries taking up expansion, diversification and modernization get concession on registration charges. These companies pay nominal stamp duty on lease-cum-sale deeds executed with the State Government agencies like Karnataka State Small Scale Industries Development Corporation, Karnataka Industrial Areas Development Board, KEONICS etc. Even when the absolute sale deeds are executed the stamp duty also depends on consideration amount agreed at the time of lease date. These concessions are also applicable for companies in the IT sector.

Concessions for Creating Employment

9.19 Karnataka recognizes the potential of IT companies to create new employment opportunities. All new IT companies which create employment of more than 250 in Bangalore and 100 in other areas during the first year are eligible for rebate on the stamp duty and rebate on the cost of the land. A rebate of 15% on cost of land will be applicable to those companies that get land from the state agencies like Karnataka State Small Industries Development Corporation, Karnataka Industrial Areas Development Board, KEONICS etc. For other companies rebate of 15% on stamp duty is applicable. This rebate on stamp duty is also applicable to the existing IT companies expanding or modernizing as well as creating additional employment.

Labour Laws Simplified

9.20 The IT sector is subject to several labour legislations, like

State Enactments

1. Karnataka Industrial Establishments (National and Festival Holidays) Act, 1963.
2. Karnataka Shops and Commercial Establishments Act, 1951.

Central Enactments

1. Contract Labour (Regulation and Abolition) Act, 1970
2. Employees' State Insurance Act, 1948
3. Employment Exchanges (Compulsory Notification of Vacancies) Act,1959
4. Employee Provident Fund & Miscellaneous Provisions Act, 1952
5. Industrial Employment (Standing Orders) Act, 1946
6. Maternity Benefit Act, 1961
7. Minimum Wages Act, 1948
8. Payment of Wages Act, 1936

9.21 The State is committed to simplify all the enactments for the IT sector. The State proposes to exempt the IT companies from furnishing returns and maintain certain registers. A specific notification will be issued by the Labour Department. The Labour Department has issued an administrative circular that streamlines several procedures pertaining to labour enactments. The Labour Department has also initiated procedures to exempt the IT companies from the preview of Industrial Employment (Standing Orders) Act, 1946.

9.22 The department is also aware of industry's concerns—declaring EOU units as public utilities, allowing flexi timing in IT industries, submitting returns through electronic media etc. Specific notification will be issued shortly.

Infrastructure

9.23 The Government recognizes that the provision of infrastructure has to keep pace with the development and needs of the IT sector. The various initiatives taken by the government have been described below.

IT Parks

9.24 Karnataka is a pioneering state where several International Standard IT Parks have already been established. For instance, International Technology Park was established in the year 1997. This Park was established through a joint venture of Government of Karnataka, the TATA group and the Singapore Consortium. This park is the largest in the country with 12 lakh sq. ft. space, has world class infrastructure facilities/telecom connectivity, power security, housing etc. The ITPL is expanding rapidly and the second phase will be started very soon. The park will have a capacity of 1.8 million square feet and 1.45 million square feet residential area. There are several other IT Parks in Bangalore and in other parts of Karnataka. The Parks have been built by reputed real estate builders. The Government is pleased to offer the following special incentives and concessions for IT Parks.

9.25 Exemption from payment of entry tax on machines, equipment, capital goods and construction material procured for implementation of infrastructure projects, for a period of three years or till the date of completion of the project, whichever is earlier, subject to the condition that each invoice should be for not less than Rs.25 lakhs (Rs.1 lakh for construction materials).

9.26 Exemption from sales tax/works contract tax arising in the construction of the infrastructure facility for a period of three years or till the date of completion of the project, whichever is earlier.

9.27. 50% exemption from payment of stamp duty and registration charges on the first sales of land in the case of IT Parks.

9.28 These concessions will be available for IT Parks certified by the IT Department. The Parks shall have a minimum built up area of 1 lakh sq. ft. They shall provide world class facilities in water, power, security, telecommunications, etc.

Single Window Agency

9.29 All these incentives and concessions will be administered through a single window agency headed by the Principal Secretary of Department of Commerce and Industries. This agency will be supported by Udyog Mitra in scrutinizing these proposals. In addition, Karnataka Information Technology Services will be set-up to support these IT projects to get quick clearances.

IT Corridor

9.30 The Government of Karnataka announces a special IT corridor that will be planned in and around Bangalore. This corridor will be planned with active assistance and consultation with reputed international agencies that have complete experience in IT Parks. The corridor will provide for the best quality Parks. Exclusive parks for international companies/countries will be encouraged with schools of international standards, housing, water, electricity as well as facilities for amusement and leisure activities. The corridor will be self-content with the state of the art facilities.

Electronic City

9.31 Karnataka established an Electronic City way back in 1985. This city provides IT entrepreneurs with land, water, incubation centre and excellent communication facilities. It is a matter of pride for Karnataka that the headquarters of Infosys is located in the Electronic City. The government has already planned Electronic City phase II which involves developing over 303 acres of land for IT entrepreneurs.

Export Promotion Industrial Park

9.32 This is a 288 acres exclusive park for export oriented industries. The park is situated near ITPL and has excellent facilities — water, electricity and communication. The General Electric Company has chosen to locate its India Technology Centre here. The Centre is expected to employ over 700 top class scientists in Biotechnology. The project may fuel reverse brain drain from foreign countries to Bangalore.

Software Technology Park of India

9.33 This institute has played a pivotal role in the development of IT industry in Karnataka. STPI began with only 13 companies in 1992 and as of now services 396 world class companies that are involved in integrated circuit design/communication software etc. STPI has already established earth stations in Manipal and Mysore. It will soon be establishing an earth station in Hubli. In addition to this, STPI is planning an earth station in Mangalore where several IT companies lead by Infosys have established Software Development Centres. STPI is also planning to establish more earth stations in Karnataka.

Incubation Centre

9.34 Karnataka already has Incubation Centres in the private sector. The Government of Karnataka and STPI are planning Incubation Centres at Bangalore and Hubli. These centres will be set up in active consultation with the private sector so that the centres function effectively.

IT Backbone

9.35 All district head quarters in the state of Karnataka and also 140 out of 175 taluks have already been connected with a fibre optic network. The video conferencing facility of the Government of Karnataka is already functioning on this network. The State has received a lot of requests from the private sector to set up high bandwidth networks. The State is committed to make high bandwidth available to all its citizens. The Government of Karnataka is committed to complete liberalisation and simplification of the right of way procedures.

International Gateway in Mangalore

9.36 The Government is committed to the establishment of another international gateway at Mangalore immediately. Right now private fibre carrier already has submarine cables running just 6 kms away from Mangalore. The Government is pursuing with the Department of Telecommunication for making a high bandwidth connection available at Mangalore.

Bangalore Agenda Task Force

9.37 The Government has constituted the Bangalore Agenda Task Force which is headed by Mr. Nandan Nilekani, Managing Director, Infosys Technologies Ltd. This is one of the efforts of Government to actively involve private sector in planning for and providing infrastructure for citizens. The Bangalore Agenda Task Force has already suggested several plans for the implementation of critical infrastructure for Bangalore citizens to be implemented both in short term and medium term. The Government is committed to honour and involve private initiatives to improve infrastructure and standard of living of its citizens.

Bangalore International Airport

9.38 The State has already made available over 2000 acres of government land for the location of International Airport near Bangalore. The State has appointed a special officer for this project. 7 bidders of international standing have shown interest and the State will be finalising the bidder very soon. The project will be implemented by Government of Karnataka in a joint venture with the Airport Authority of India and the private sector bidders. In addition to the airport, a 6-lane highway has also been planned.

Outer Ring Road for Bangalore

9.39 Around 12000 trucks and heavy vehicles from Pune-Bombay pass through Bangalore city to go to Chennai. The outer ring road which will divert these directly to Chennai/Hosur will be completed by June 2000. Once completed, the city road will be freed up and city driving will be more enjoyable.

World Bank-HUDCO Assistance

9.40 The State with the assistance of World Bank and HUDCO has plans to spend over Rs.12,000 crores in several infrastructure projects. For instance, Road Development Corporation is expected to spend Rs.650 crores and improve Karnataka roads. The power sector initiative includes unbundling of the entities, rationalisation of tariffs, privatisation of distribution and new generation projects. The government plans to spend Rs.3000 crores in power sector and Rs.950 crores in improving urban infrastructure. In addition, many other infrastructure projects, viz. Bangalore mass rapid transit system/ Bangalore-Mysore Express Highway/Mangalore-Bangalore Petro Product Pipeline etc., are also planned.

Carnegie Centre for Software Engineering

9.41 The Carnegie Mellon University's Software Engineering Institute has developed the Capability Maturity Model (CMM). This institution assesses the capability of the software companies and classifies them into various levels (CMM/SEI/Level-1 to 5). Level-5 indicates the most sophisticated Software Company that has excellent human resources management as well as abilities in delivering quality Software Services. Karnataka is proud that its homegrown company, WIPRO is the 1st recipient of the Level-5 certification. All over the world there are 19 Level 5 companies. 12 of those are located in India and 8 of those in Bangalore.

9.42 The Government of Karnataka in a Joint Venture with the Carnegie Global Technologies Inc., Indian Institute of Science and LG Soft India Pvt. Ltd., has established the Carnegie Centre for Software Engineering at Bangalore. This Centre is expected to offer services in consultancy, training, education etc. in the whole of Asia-Pacific region.

Anti Piracy

9.43 The Government of Karnataka believes in the intellectual property rights of the IT Companies. The Government would like to encourage more and more patents and take steps against piracy of patented products. The Government will constitute a high level committee that will review serious piracy cases and initiate appropriate action.

Dot-Com Companies

9.44 The DOT COM Companies and the Internet have been making B2B & B2C transactions more efficient. This has resulted in cheaper products for the poor and middle class people. It has been estimated that DOT COM Companies / e-business has resulted in reducing the inflation in the United States of America. The Government is also committed to encouragement of e-business in the State. While encouraging the private sector initiatives in B2B & B2C, the Government will open offer several services of the government like water bill payments, electricity bill payments, property tax collections etc., to e-business companies.

Mahiti Bonds

9.45 The Government of Karnataka's commitment to IT is

unflinching. The Government proposes to announce that Rs.300 crores will be raised by floating Mahithi Bonds. The proceeds of the bonds will be utilised for human resource development; training in schools, ITIs, Polytechnics, Colleges, Pharmacy and Engineering Colleges; training centres for uneducated youth; Incubation Centres, earth stations, IT Parks and Communication Infrastructure, etc. The money will be used based on the action plan suggested by the high powered IT task force. We expect enthusiastic response for the Karnataka Mahiti bonds from IT companies, IT professionals, Trade and Industry as well as people of Karnataka.

Appendix–VIII

Information Technology Policy of Delhi

A. Vision

1. The rapid advancements in the field of Information, Communication and Entertainment Technologies and the resultant explosive growth of the information intensive services sector have radically changed the world economic landscape. These changes have given rise to a new society based on knowledge. This has further resulted in the new avenues of development, employment, productivity, efficiency, and enhanced factors of economic growth.

2. Government of Delhi recognizes the enormous potential of the IT and has decided to embark upon an ambitious journey to herald the benefits of IT to the people of the state.

3. It envisions that by the year 2003, Delhi shall have realized this huge potential and, as a result, would emerge as a premier Cyber state in the country with its citizens qualifying to be e-citizens.

B. Aspirations

1. The aspirations of the IT policy in the State of Delhi are governed by the following 6 E's, i.e. Electronic Governance, Equality, Education, Employment, Entrepreneurship and Economy. The objectives of the policy are as follows :

- ***E-Governance*** : To use e-governance as a tool and deliver a government that is more pro-active and responsive to its citizens.
- ***Equality*** : To use the power of the IT to achieve the objectives of eradicating poverty, improving healthcare, empowering women and economically weaker sections of the society. The Right to Information Act that the Government of Delhi proposes to enact

will empower the people and ultimately help to bring about social and economic justice.

- ***Education*** : To encourage the use of IT in schools, colleges and educational institutions in the state of Delhi so as to enable the students to improve their skills, knowledge and job prospects and enable them to obtain employment in this sunrise industry.
- ***Employment*** : To use IT for generating additional employment for the new digital economy. To facilitate localization of software, so that benefits of IT could percolate not only in English language, but also in Hindi, Urdu, and Punjabi.
- ***Entrepreneurship*** : To unleash the Delhi incubation engine, promote entrepreneurship, earn foreign exchange, and increase IT's contribution to the economic growth of the state.
- ***Economy*** : To encourage and accelerate investments and growth in IT hardware, software, Internet, training, IT enabled services, telecom, e-commerce and related sectors in the state. To use IT effectively in industries to make them competitive and web-enabled. To provide adequate infrastructure in the state so that IT sector can flourish. To use IT for ushering world-class e-tourism in the state.

C. Enablers

1. While it is essential to announce an IT policy for the State of Delhi, it is equally important to put together an enabling process for its implementation. For this, we propose to put two processes in place. A high-powered committee under the Chairpersonship of the Chief Minister and formation of core-groups for implementing the policies of the government in respect of E-Commerce, IT enabled services, E-governance and E-Education.

Advisory Council : The government shall set up high-powered Information Technology Advisory Council under the Chairpersonship of Chief Minister of Delhi. This advisory Council would have representatives from the industry, government and academia. This Council will review the implementation of the IT policy and also advise the state on further improvements as may be required from time to time so that Delhi continues to keep pace with the global IT scenario.

Core Groups : To oversee the implementation of the policy in key areas of Information Technology such as E-Commerce, IT enabled services, E-Governance and E-Education, as also to assist the Advisory Council, the government shall set up Core Groups for each of these key areas, which shall have representatives from the industry, government and academia.

Strengthening of the Department of Information Technology: The Department of Information Technology will be suitably strengthened to enable it to discharge its role of acting as a single window agency for an all-round implementation and monitoring of the state's IT policy.

Milestones on the Road Map to Cyber City : While Government of Delhi is committed to achieve its objective of transforming Delhi into a premier Cyber city by the year 2003, the government realizes that it is equally essential to set up important milestones on this journey. These milestones will allow the government to take stock of what has been achieved, what hurdles need to be removed, and whether any mid-course correction is required to reach the destination. These milestones are December 2000, June 2001 and December 2001. At appropriate places this policy document will enumerate the objectives, which the departments are expected to achieve by these dates.

D. Strategy

The private sector has been in the forefront of developments of IT sector. As the government seeks to translate its vision into reality, it expects the private sector to continue to play its pivotal role. However, the vision will not be realized early without the government playing an active role in the following three areas :

- Promoting IT for masses.
- Ushering E-Governance.
- Creating an atmosphere conducive for the growth of IT Industry and IT Infrastructure.

Promoting IT for Masses : IT to Improve the Quality of Life

Strategies : The two strategies — promoting the IT sector and infrastructure and promoting e-governance — will bring enormous benefits of IT to the citizens of Delhi. While the government will take a number of pro-active steps to promote the growth of IT industry and e-governance, it is equally conscious that these developments do not create new division in society — referred to as digital divide by some people — divide between those who have access to IT based industry and those who do not. Government is therefore determined to see that the benefits of Information Technology do not remain confined to higher classes of society. In fact government intends to use IT as a major instrument to provide new opportunities to those segments of society who do not see opportunities to improve their quality of life and tend to reconcile to their fate.

Bridging Gap Between Haves and Have-nots : It is the firm view of the government that if any technology can create new opportunities to bridge the gap between the haves and the have-nots in society in the present times, it is IT.

Enabling Process : To give a concrete shape to this thinking, the government shall take the following catalytic, pro-active and enabling steps :

- Enabling Literacy and Education for the masses
- Fulfilling local information needs of the people
- Educating citizens about their duties
- Enabling e-tourism
- Enabling women

Enabling Literacy and Education for the Masses

Information Technology with convergence of various technologies related to communication and delivery of information such as video, audio, telephone, television, newspapers, computers etc. into one unified network, provides for the first time a unique opportunity to spread literacy and education on a mass scale at affordable costs. The convergence enables ease of providing educational material, which is one of the pre-requisites to spread literacy and education. The government proposes to spread literacy and computer education by initiating action under the following broad policy framework.

"Teach the Teachers" Programme : The government shall

start a "Teach the Teachers" programme for upgrading the IT knowledge and skills of teachers on a regular basis. A Special Cell will be set up in State Council for Education, Research and Training to work out details of this programme. The government intends to take up training of at least 10% of teachers in Higher Secondary Schools during 2000-01. There shall be an incentive scheme to attract teachers to this programme and to encourage them to complete it successfully.

Computer Labs : The government will establish computer laboratories in all government schools by the year 2003 in collaboration with private sector. About 115 schools will be covered in the first year, i.e. 2000-2001. The Government will also encourage aided schools to set up computer labs in collaboration with private sector.

Computer Literacy Campaign in Slums : The government will launch a literacy campaign in slum areas using ICT. It proposes to start a pilot project in a slum colony under which 30 computer kiosks will be set up with Internet connectivity to enable the children to learn computing skills on their own without any adult intervention.

Upgrading ITIs : The government shall upgrade Industrial Training Institutes for providing training of skills for data entry, marketing, transcription, call centres, content creation and data processing. This will give necessary boost to the IT enabled services in the state.

Training Centre for Unemployed : The government will encourage private sector initiatives in setting up Training Centres for the Unemployed Educated Youths. The government aims to start at least 10 Centres in the year 2000-01.

IT Open University : The government will take steps to establish an IT Open University. It will also encourage technical courses in its university, schools and ITI's. The government hopes to take education and literacy to a much larger section of population in the next three years.

Setting up an IIIT : The government will also set up a premier Indian Institute of Information Technology to impart high quality IT education and training to the people.

Digital Library : It will also set up a Digital Media Library that would be a central storehouse of digitalized data containing government records, industry information and information on education, tourism and archaeology.

Fulfilling Local Information Needs of the People : Citizen Service Points

The government has also proposed to set up Suwidha Points at each of its major offices. These Suwidha Points will be single user-friendly window for deadline-based handling of applications. At this point a citizen will also be given an acknowledgment with a probable date of response to his application.

Suwidha Points : The government has already proposed setting up of Citizen Service Points all over the state, which could be used by the citizens to access any information about government services from any location within the state and outside. These CSPs will be electronically linked to government departments through their web sites. These will be set up by the private sector that will be allowed to recover the costs by charging the user an affordable transaction fee.

Cyber Cafes and Information Kiosks : In addition the government will encourage the private individuals to set up information kiosks all over the city. The kiosks shall provide free access to a wide range of citizen-oriented information. In particular, all the e-governance related information should be available through these kiosks. They need not have Internet connections. They could simply have data stored for access to the citizens. These kiosks will be encouraged to use touch-screens requiring no use of either the keyboard or the mouse. The government will assist the entrepreneurs in getting space where demand for kiosks could be foreseen. Some examples of such places are bus stops, markets, colleges, community centres, resident association offices, clubs, tourist places, airports, railway stations and schools. In addition the government will encourage the owners of STD/ISD booths to convert them to Cyber cafes all over Delhi.

Educating Citizens about Their Duties : Internet based information delivery systems in combination with conventional broadcast media, TV and Radio, could act as a major vehicle to educate citizens regarding their duties to the nation and the state. This will immensely help in people's participation in programme like family welfare, conservation of environment, and preservation of ethical, moral and cultural values. The people could also be informed about the rich heritage of the capital and the need to preserve the ancient monuments which dot the city landscape and the dangers of vandalizing them. The nuisance created by littering public places, parks, roads and places of religious and tourist interests will be highlighted using IT technology.

Enabling E-Tourism : Tourism is one industry that can effectively use IT to promote itself. The use of Internet for promoting tourism is only one example. Innovative solutions using IT can help Delhi to attract more visitors and tourists by providing them with information about the many places of historical interest in the city. To take advantage of IT in the tourism sector the government would encourage and initiate the following:

E-Tourism Portal : There are currently many web sites providing information about the tourism sector of the state. However, there is a need for setting up comprehensive tourism portal for the state of Delhi. This portal could have comprehensive information on the tourism industry, hotels, places of religious and historical interest etc. The idea is to not only provide basic information but also cybercasting, video clips, and graphics etc. The portal will have cybercasting of major events in the State of Delhi. The portal will also encourage e-commerce by selling local handicrafts, agriculture and industry products through the web site. The portal will also have a revenue model of earning through on-line bookings, advertisements and brokerage from e-commerce transactions.

Tourism Marketing : An aggressive marketing plan would be designed to market the state of Delhi through the net.

Enabling Women

Empowerment of women is an integral part of the process of development of any economy. The transition to a knowledge-based economy includes the participation of all sectors of the society. The government of Delhi considers the role of women to be very important in the economic and social development. With the increased emphasis in IT by the government, there is a need to introduce special scheme for providing the benefits of IT to the women in the state. The IT can play a catalytic role in the process of empowering women. Government will take the following initiatives in this regard.

Literacy Campaign for Women : An IT literacy programme specially directed towards spreading literacy among women would be launched by the year 2001.

Setting up Web Sites : Government will encourage NGOs to set up B2C (business to consumer) and B2B (business to business) web sites to promote interest of women doing business in the state.

Re-inventing Government Processes : Ushering E-governance

Citizen Interface : Government of Delhi will use IT not merely to automate its existing procedures but also to reinvent government processes and to redefine the role of bureaucracy. This would enable the government to make its functioning citizen-centric, transparent and efficient.

Nine Departments to go "On-line" : The government has identified nine major public dealing departments that will go 'on-line' by the year 2002. These departments are revenue, transport, sales tax, excise, education, social welfare, co-operatives, health and labour. Of these sales tax, excise and transport will go on-line by June 2001. The government will provide assistance for computerization of Local and Autonomous Bodies such as MCD, NDMC, DVB, DJB etc. working under it.

Government Transaction Through Internet : In order to do this, the government will set up the legal machinery to implement Cyber law provisions regarding recognition of digital signature and electronic records and their use in government. By December 2003, it shall enable the citizens to conduct most of their transactions with the government through the Internet. Some examples of these transactions are: obtaining driving licences, registration of vehicles, registration with employment exchanges, registration of births and deaths, obtaining ration cards, payment of various bills, lodging of various complaints and their redressal, delivery of pensions, tendering, filing of tax returns and applying for admissions. To ensure that this process is monitored periodically some important milestones have been fixed.

Heads of Departments and the OSDs : The heads of departments shall be responsible for the preparation and implementation of their respective departmental action plans. An Officer on Special Duty will assist each head of department in this task. He will also act as the nodal officer in the department for implementing IT policy. The heads of departments shall allocate 3% of their departments' budget for implementation of this policy.

Employee Support : In addition, a detailed plan for employee training shall be implemented. The Civil Service Training Institute shall design new modules for IT courses for imparting computer training and education to produce knowledge workers in the government. The annual confidential reports of the employees shall reflect the employee performance in implementation of this policy. The possibility of relaxing the scheme for loan to employees for purchase of computers and peripherals shall be explored. For all new employees appropriate level of computer literacy shall be made an essential requirement in the recruitment rules.

Information Through Internet

Milestone One: December 2000 : By the end of December 2000, the citizens will be able to access information relating to transactions with the government through the Internet. Some examples of such information are: downloading of non-priced forms, information about eligibility, rules, documents required to be submitted along with various application forms, formats of affidavits, and information relating to tenders. The filing of complaints of suggestions through the Internet will also be made possible.

Simultaneously, the government will also put on the Internet information that ought to be in public domain. This will enable the citizens to play the role of a watchdog and to ensure transparency. Some examples of this type of information are: land owned by the government and the gaon sabha, details relating to the civil works and payments made for them, mandi market prices, availability of hospital beds, citizens' charters, cause list of various revenue courts, names of licensees under different provisions of law and the terms and conditions thereof.

Right to Information Act : Later this information set will be further expanded and their placement in public domain will be made legally enforceable through the Right to Information Act.

Citizen Service Points

Milestone Two: June 2001 : By this date some transactions with the government will be carried using telephones, stored-value credit or debit cards. This will be achieved through the intermediation of the banks. Paying bills for government services is one example. IT will make travel to the government offices unnecessary. The citizen will be able to transact business with a few major public-dealing departments from one place. These points — Citizen Service Points (CSPs) — will be electronically linked to these departments. These points will be set up in private sector that will recover its initial cost of setting up these points by charging the citizens a transaction fee.

Suwidha Points : Besides these CSPs, the government will set up Suwidha Points in each department to enable the citizens to interact at only a single point called the Suwidha or single user-friendly window for handling applications which have to be submitted by a certain date. At these Suwidha Points the applications will be accepted and acknowledged and the citizens will be given a date by which they may expect a response from the department. The government proposes to allot these Suwidha Points to senior citizens who will be allowed to charge handling costs.

Self-Certification Exemption for IT Industry : By this date the department will explore the possibility of introducing self-certification/exemption for IT software industry under various Acts/Regulations mentioned in para D (a) (viii) above.

Use of Smart E-Cards

Milestone Three : December 2001: The third milestone will be reached when citizens will be able to use electronic cards for accessing services offered by different departments. The government will consider issuing multi-purpose cards to citizens that would serve the purpose of being a ration card, an identity card, a driving licence etc. The citizens will be required to register their personal details only once. To begin with, ration cards and a single electronic card in selected areas on an experimental basis will replace driving licences by June 2001.

Race to the Finishing Line

Similar milestones will be identified between December 2001 and March 2003 in detailed departmental plans in such a manner that the goal of transacting business over the Internet is achieved.

Improving Internal Efficiency

A More Efficient Government : IT will also be deployed to improve government's internal efficiency. This will be done in two main areas: in internal communication and in data handling.

Use of E-mail, Bulletin Boards and Video Conferencing : Internal communication will be improved by increasing use of e-mail, bulletin boards and video conferencing in the government. Routine circulars, meeting notices, and minutes will be communicated through e-mail. Video-conferencing will be used to decide urgent matters in consultation with senior officers without calling them over from their offices. This will make them accessible to the people even while being in a position to confer with other officers in matters which are urgent and cannot wait for a formal meeting to be convened.

Data Handling

Data handling comprises data capture, data sharing, data storage, and data retrieval, data processing and data presentation. Some examples of the projects which lend themselves to data handling are Executive Information Systems for the departmental heads, computerization of land records and hospital OPDs, ICT based delivery of education in formal, informal and non-formal sectors of education, data capture on violation of laws/rules using remote cameras or other recorders with online data updating and generation of reports in such areas as traffic violation and pollution monitoring. These projects with their target dates of completion shall be detailed in departmental plans of action. The expected progress at the milestones identified earlier, i.e. December 2000, June 2001 and December 2001 are stated below :

Routine Communications : Milestone One: December 2000: By December 2000, all routine communication between CM's Office and departments and among departments themselves shall be done through e-mail and bulletin boards. A beginning in the use of video conferencing will be made by that date.

Networking Departments : Milestone Two: June 2001: The next milestone will be reached in June 2001 By this date all the departments shall be internally networked and projects of all departments will be under implementation.

Land Records Computerization : Milestone Three: December

2001: By December 2001 some important projects would have been completed. These include networking of different departments, the departmental Executive Information Systems and the Land Record Computerization.

Task Force

Implementation enabling mechanism: A mechanism to ensure that these milestones are reached is necessary. This is specially so because at the time of implementation many complex technical, legal, financial and institutional problems will arise. Some of these will be related to the need for process change and culture change. The government will, therefore, constitute a Task Force headed by the Chief Secretary to implement this policy. It will lay down uniform guidelines for the departments to follow so that common issues are not handled differently by different departments. A technical committee comprising representatives from IT industry and academia will assist the task force. The Task Force's first main responsibility will be to ensure that all the major public departments prepare their respective plans to implement this policy.

Incubation Centre

Creating an atmosphere conducive for the growth of IT Industry and IT Infrastructure : The State Government will set up an "Incubation Centre" that will guide entrepreneurs to make business plans, advise on mergers and acquisitions and network with venture capital companies including the Venture Capital Fund Company to be created by the Government of Delhi. The Centre will undertake financing of small IT companies.

Zero Sales Tax on IT Software and Hardware

The Government is in favour of zero sales tax on the transactions of the following IT related hardware and software :

- Sale and leasing of computers and its accessories.
- Inter-state sales of computers, parts, accessories and computer consumables.

- CD-ROMS, optical disc media or magnetic media containing text, data, or multimedia.

However in keeping with the ruling of a uniform sales tax in all states, the government shall fix the sales tax on hardware and software not above the agreed Uniform Floor Rate (UFR). The State Government would however lobby for zero sales tax on all IT products along with other states and Central Government.

IT Industries in Residential Localities : The State Government shall strongly recommend to the Government of India to permit software and service units to function in residential areas subject to such reasonable restrictions as may be imposed by the government in public interest.

IT Software & Service Industry Entitle to Industry Status: All IT software and service industries including Services and Training Institutions in IT will be entitled to "Industry" status. Such units shall be eligible for all concessions and incentives applicable to Industries. For the purpose of this clause, accredited Training Institutions will also be eligible to claim industry status subject to certain norms which will enable them to obtain Term Loans and Bank Finance at industry rates.

Exemption from Routine Inspection for IT Industry and Facility for Self-Certification : IT Software and IT services companies, being constituents of the knowledge industry, shall be exempted from routine inspection by inspectors like those for Factory, Boiler, Labour, Pollution, Environment, Industry in line with the approved policy of Government of India. Moreover, the State Government agrees in principle to self-certification/exemption as far as possible for the IT software Industry from the provisions of the following Acts/Regulations—

Factories Act; Employment Exchange (Compulsory Notification of Vacancies) Act; Payment of Wages Act; Minimum Wages Act; Contract Labour (Regulation and Abolition) Act; Workmen Compensation Act; Shops and Establishments Act; and Employees State Insurance Act.

Permission for Three-Shift Operation : General permission is accorded, subject to such orders issued by the Police Commissioner of Delhi as may be necessary from time to time in public interest, to run a three-shift operation to the IT software and Services industry.

ROW Clearance : The government shall assist in getting speedy clearance for Right of Way and use of infrastructure of utilities like DVB.

Protection of IPR : The government shall set up a regulatory framework to implement Cyber laws. The intellectual property rights of creator of content and software shall be protected through vigorous enforcement of relevant copyright laws.

IT Parks : The government will establish modern IT parks in collaboration with private sector. The park will have high speed telecom facility and plug and play built up modules for minimizing gestation period of new projects. The first such park will be established by the year 2002.

International Gateway : The government will encourage private companies to set up international gateway for providing high-speed Internet connectivity.

Campaign for E-Commerce : A massive campaign will be launched to encourage e-commerce and computerization in the local industries. It shall attempt to increase e-commerce activities by at least three times in the next two years. A suitable framework to encourage and support electronic money transfer, electronic benefited transfers (EBT cards) and electronic tagging like bar coding will be established.

IT for Industries : The government will initiate an "IT for industries" project. Under this project, advice will be given to the local industries to adopt use of IT or to diversify into IT activities.

IT Enabled Services : IT enabled services like Medical Transcription, Call Centres, Data Processing, Back-Office Operations, GIS, Revenue Accounting etc. are considered as niche areas for the state. A special scheme will be announced to help local industries to diversify into IT enabled services. The benefits of the scheme would also be applicable for companies setting up IT enabled services in the State.

Seminars and Workshops : The government will encourage conduct of seminars/workshops to disseminate information of IT to local industries and thus work towards increase in usage of IT in local industries.

Establishment of Regional Hub : With an extremely widespread telecommunication system, the state of Delhi can take lead in establishing and serving a regional hub for Internet,

E-commerce and digital services traffic.

State Level Awards : State level awards will be given to IT companies with outstanding performance in exports and in domestic segments.

Appendix–IX

Information Technology Policy of Uttar Pradesh,1999

Vision

To use IT as a vehicle for economic development and to create a high-tech society with a high quality of life in Uttar Pradesh.

Background

Information Technology is going to be the vehicle of technological revolution in administration, education, industries and services in the 21st Century. Realizing this, the Government of India has resolved to make India a global superpower in this field and has sought cooperation of all the states in doing so. Uttar Pradesh which saw rapid growth of the Electronic Industry in the 80s and occupied the top position in the country till 1991 is eminently suited for the development of this Sector.

The world market for IT products in hardware and software is expected to jump from the level of US $ 1081bn in 1996 to US $ 1814bn in 2000 AD. The present annual growth rate in most of the developed countries is 10 to 15%. However, India with its strength software is witnessing a growth rate of 50% annually. By the year 2000 India is likely to reach the 4bn dollar mark, according to the IT vision of Government of India the expected level of this by the year 2007-2008 is expected to reach US $ 50bn. UP cannot ignore the voluminous growth in a sector in which it has great strength and therefore the need for a focused policy in IT is self-evident.

IT Industry is basically knowledge based and the location in UP of IIT, Kanpur, a world renowned institute in this field, is a major pillar of strength. UP has other great engineering institutions like BHU, in the fields of metallurgy and electrical engineering, Roorkee in the field of civil engineering, HBTI in the field of chemical engineering colleges and research laboratories which are capable of providing trained manpower of high quality in various fields of application in IT. Therefore, the IT Policy attempts to give a thrust to incorporation of IT education in the existing educational framework.

Objectives

To harness the advantages offered by the State of Uttar Pradesh and to place it on the global map of IT as the new Silicon Valley of India, a proactive, responsive and action oriented IT Policy is being formulated. The objectives of the Policy are as follows:

1. Accelerated development of Information Technology Industry in the State and increase in both domestic and export earning in the software and hardware sector in IT. 2. To create a SMART Government, Smart Government means, use of IT for speedy, transparent accountable and efficient conduct of the Government systems and services. 3. To encourage and accelerate the use of Information Technology in schools, colleges and educational institutions in the State, to enable the youth of the State to acquire necessary skills and knowledge of IT, thereby making them highly employable. The IT Sector will be developed in order to provide increased employment opportunities. 4. To bring IT within the easy reach of the common man and make it useful to his daily need.

Definition

Broadly the definition of IT will be as per the Government of India guidelines. This may be suitably altered to suit the needs of the State from time to time by a high level Authorized Committee constituted under this policy.

Infrastructure

The State shall make efforts to upgrade the existing infrastructure for the rapid growth of the IT Sector in UP. Efforts will be made to facilitate provision of cheap communication infrastructure for ensuring better efficiency and productivity. The State Government endeavours to provide a well developed infrastructure in the form of: Internet Connectivity.

Measure would be taken to provide strong basic Internet infrastructural support to increase Internet penetration in the State of UP. The Governmental will, in coordination with the Central Government and private vendors, expand the international network to all the districts, towns and villages of the State. Microwave link and VSAT facilities of telecom licensees/cellular service operators will effectively employed in partnership with them for this purpose. Right way on UPSEB network to private Internet Service Providers will be considered on mutually negotiated terms.

High Speed Telecom Links

The State will endeavour to create a high speed Telecom Backbone to match the National Telecom Backbone. For this the already existing facilities of Railways, Power Department and other National entitles will be optimally employed. Impetus will be provided for creation of a reliable and cheap communication link between the State headquarters and district headquarters, sub-divisions and blocks.

Earth Stations : Earth Stations at NOIDA/Dehradun/Lucknow/ Allahabad/Varanasi and Agra.

Gateways : The State will arrange for provision of easy international connectivity through the VSNL international Gateway at Kanpur and Lucknow for achieving the overall high economic growth rate. This will also include the facility for electronic commerce and electronic data interchange.

Rural Telephony : Appropriate telecom infrastructure will be created in the private/joint sector to provide connectivity to all the 1.12 lakh villages of the State.

Multi-purpose Info Centres : The State will also promote provision of infrastructure for establishment of tele-kiosks, Internet booths and DTP booths for delivery of information to common man. This will also ensure employment to large number of educated youth in the State.

IT Cities : Electronic cities at Noida and Agra and a Cyber city at Kanpur by Noida/UPSIDC.

IT Parks : Software Technology Parks at Noida, Dehradun Moradabad, Agra, Lucknow, Kanpur, Alahabad and Varanasi in joint sector.

WAN for Connecting Various Organizations : Development of WAN for the State to connect all district HQ with State HQ. and so provide Internet connectivity, e-mail facility and other value added services in this area in every part of the State. This would also include inter-connecting universities, colleges and schools for providing a reliable and cheap distant education facility for human resource development.

NIC Infrastructure : The already existing IT infrastructure of the NIC will be optimally utilized. NIC will be pursued to provide high bandwidth based VSAT links so that most of the government businesses can be transacted online.

IT in Industry

The State Government recognizes the need to develop a strong bond of partnership between Government and private sector the proper and rapid development of IT in the State. Adequate representation would be provided to the representatives of IT industry in policy formulation and designing of incentives. For creating an investor friendly environment in the State, the Government will ensure

- Preferential allotment of land for IT industry by Noida/Greater Noida/UPSIDC/Development Authorities in the State.
- Continuous and uninterrupted power supply for IT industries. Exemption from power cuts without limit.
- Encouragement to captive power generation in IT locations.
- Creation of Venture Capital Fund with State Government/PICUP/ UPSIDC/UPFC/Private Enterprises/SIDBI and others for IT Industry.
- Special financing packages will be developed by the State Financial Agencies to fulfil the unique needs of the IT sector. PICUP has already formulated a special package for the purpose.
- Key person insurance/sweat equity concept as developed by Government of India/RBI/All India Financial Institutions/Banks shall be recognized by the State level institutions as well.
- Special efforts will be made to develop high quality social infrastructure like schools, housing, health and entertainment/leisure facilities in IT locations.

- To create a pool of highly qualified professional for use of IT Industry State help will be provided to software companies to set up a shop in Uttar Pradesh.
- Facilitate setting up of quality certification centres with the help of industry and academia for getting ISO 9000 and software engineering certification.
- Escort services will be provided for obtaining easy clearances and approvals from various government departments.
- ER&DC Noida will be developed to provide R&D back up to IT industry.

Fiscal and Other Incentives

- No trade tax on computer software.
- Two per cent trade tax on computer hardware including all surcharges.
- No Trade Tax on raw material used for exports.
- Software lease/work contract or licences to use in any form will be exempted from trade tax.
- IT products produced in the State will be provided quantity and price preference.
- IT industries, which fulfil the definition under the policy, irrespective of level of investment and location of the unit shall be offered trade tax exemption for a period of 12 years and deferment for a period of 15 years.
- IT unit in Information Technology Parks and STPs will be charged the same power tariff as the SSI.
- Units with 5KVA power requirement can be set up anywhere irrespective of master plan or land use classifications.
- 'Green Card' for priority treatment to IT Industry in all government offices and industrial/urban authorities.
- Trade tax Form-31 will be given through Industry Associations or through authorities managing industrial parks or STPs.
- Complete exemption to software industry from the provisions of Pollution Control Act both for air and water pollution.
- IT software and IT services companies, being constituents of the knowledge industry shall be exempted from inspections by inspectors like those for Factory/Boiler/Labour/Pollution/ Environment etc.

- 50% more FAR to be allowed for IT units in earmarked areas/ Information IT Parks and STPs.
- Units situated in private sector STPs will be provided the same concessions and the government STPs.
- Special package of incentives will be formulated for IT industries involving an investment of Rs.50 crore or more.
- Escort services to be provided by Department of IT, Udyog Bandhu and PICUP for obtaining easy clearances and approvals.
- All clearances and approvals required by units within a STP will be provided by a single executive authority acting on the concept of Single Table Under One Roof. The entrepreneur himself will not be required to go to any other organization for this.

IT in Government

The focus will be on making UP as a Smart State in 10 Years as Far as Application in Government is concerned. This will be achieved by:

- Training of all Government employees in use of IT and its products over a period of 5 years. UPDESCO will undertake this job with the help of other public sector/private sector bodies.
- Linking of all government offices up to district level by the year 2000, up to tehsil level by 2001 and Block level by 2004 with the help of suitable funding mechanism to be finalized with national/ international funding agencies.
- District offices-State HQ to be linked through high speed data communication facilities to provide Internet access, e-mail, video conferencing etc. by the year 2000.
- Developing NOIDA/Greater NOIDA and Ghaziabad and Lucknow as Smart Cities by the year 2000, Gorakhpur, Kanpur, Aligarh, Bareilly and Agra by the year 2002. Allahabad, Moradabad and Varanasi will be developed into smart cities by the year 2003, rest of the Divisional headquarters by 2005 and the remaining State by the year 2008.
- World class GIS solutions wherever available in the fields of land record management, watershed management, master plan preparation, revenue collection, registration of documents, tourism facility management, agricultural input management, hospital and health management, State plan preparation, law and order

administration etc. Will be procured and applied in the State Government departments.

- Active help of UPDESCO and other suitable agencies like NIC and other public sector corporations will be taken for increasing the use of computers in Government Departments.
- Promotions and crossing of efficiency bars of Government officials will be linked to computer literacy.
- All tax collection activities will be computerized in two years.
- The State Government will earmark one per cent of the departmental budgets for computerization and training of personnel.
- To begin with the following departments will be taken up for computerization up to the field level:

    - Revenue
    - Social Welfare and Women's Welfare
    - Rural Development
    - PWD
    - Energy
    - Jal Nigam/Jal Sansthan
    - Education
    - Food and Civil Supplies
    - Medical and Health
    - Policy
    - Local Bodies and Urban Authorities

IT in Education

A four-tier education system will have to evolve for IT in education sector:

- Training in high tech software to take up design and development of software
- Software programme for code writing
- IT application for office application/data entry and processing
- IT literacy in rural areas by opening at least one learning centre in each development block over 5 years.

To achieve a 5% computer literacy level in 10 years (1 crore computer literate) and to have a 20% computer literacy level in 20 years the following will be the essential features of this policy in education sector.

- Helping all educational institutions in the urban centres to put up computer education facilities in the next 3 years.
- Opening at least one Computer Education Centre in an intermediate/ degree college in each block. An additional Computer Education Centre in another intermediate college in a second Nyaya Panchayat of the same block, for increasing IT penetration in rural areas in the next 5 years.
- Covering all students from class VI level to degree level in the State of over the next 10 years.
- Opening state and divisional level training institutions for training the teachers in computer education. Computer education will be introduced in all DIETS at the district level for training of teachers.
- Developing appropriate course material in Hindi as per requirement of different classes.
- Establishment of IIITs at Kanpur and Allahabad.
- To involve premiere institutes such as IIT Kanpur, IIM Lucknow etc. to act as nodal agencies for development of IT course material/ teachers training etc. for the universities of the State for their B.A./B.Sc./B.Com. level courses.
- Use of network of NIC/private VSAT networks/cable TV networks/wireless network/Internet/INET/SAT to link all schools/ colleges/universities/engineering colleges/research organizations.
- Encouraging private sector investment in IT education and training and ensuring quality through a Board of Computer Education.
- Encouraging setting up of virtual campuses of reputed overseas universities for IT education and establishing suitable linkages in IT between state universities.

Enabling Administrative System

State of UP shall make all efforts to put itself as the ideal destination for IT industries. For this the following institutional arrangement will be set up :

- A full-fledged Department of Information Technology and Electronics at the Government level to act as the nodal agency for the sector.

- State level steering committee headed by the Chief Secretary and consisting of all Secretary/Principal Secretary to Government will be formed to accelerate IT application in all departments.
- A vision group with Secretary, Information Technology as Chairman. This group will also have representatives of industry associations, users and academia.
- A Bureau of IT shall be formed (utilizing the existing resources of USDESCO, initially) which shall act as the agency for implementation and development of IT in the State.
- A district/divisional steering committee will be set up under the chairmanship of DM/Commissioner/CEOs for implementation of computerization programme. The steering committee will also include academicians and professionals.
- Escort services to be provided by the Department of IT PICUP and Udyog Bandhu.
- A MOU will be signed with specialized agencies to take advantage of facilities like ASCET, Software Engineering Centre, Prototype and Tool Department Centre, Technical Incubation and Development Centres etc. for the benefit of IT industries in the State.
- Organizing annual IT events with the help of industry associations.

Appendix–X

State Policy and Initiatives on Information Technology MP : The Next Destination for IT

1. Introduction

1.1 Individuals and communities are at the centre of all developmental enterprises and policy priorities in Madhya Pradesh. The State acknowledges that it has the obligation to provide simple, moral, accountable, responsive, transparent governance to its citizens. The State's policy environment is built around a staunch commitment to decentralization of administration and encouragement to community participation in decision making through Panchayat Raj Institutions and Urban Local bodies. The State believes that every citizen has a right (a) to information pertaining to his own welfare needs and opportunities for individual and social development; (b) to understand the processes of governance; (c) to know the rationale for decision making affecting citizen welfare and welfare of communities; and (d) to quick and effective delivery of citizen services. The State also believes that the use of technologies would enable information to bring about human development.

1.2 The strength of the State lies in the strong telecom infrastructure available through both public and private basic service providers and the strategic location at the heart of India. Madhya Pradesh has some of the finest institutions in telecommunications, electronics and management, which not only have current and prospective utility, but also have a cadre of alumni many of whom are

Non-Resident and Resident entrepreneurs and IT professionals. The number of private institutions in the training sector as well as public institutions offer Madhya Pradesh as a source for low cost competent human resources. Political stability, high quality social infrastructure and quality of life, tranquil public order, and a progressive and forward looking policy environment are strengths that few States in India can match. These strengths would be converted and exploited as opportunities.

1.3 A State Task Force on Information Technology was constituted by the State Government under Prof. Yash Pal, in addition to giving a number of recommendations, about setting up infrastructure, encouraging industry and private initiative; the Task Force has also indicated measures to promote IT in Government and social sectors as well as measures for human resource development to utilize employment opportunities in the IT sector within and outside the state. The recommendations of the Task Force have been approved by the Government of Madhya Pradesh, as its State policy on Information Technology.

2. Vision — Seamless Society with Global Opportunities

2.1 The vision statement for the State's IT Policy is the creation of a "Seamless Society with Global Opportunities". The Statement implies that there should be no islands of elitism or conclaves of wisdom in the information society of the future — where access to information and knowledge would be symmetric among all seekers and users. Every citizen must feel comfortable in accessing information through the facility of Technology — whether directly or where essential through public or private intermediaries. It is to create such a confident society of the future that human resources should be developed in the State.

2.2 The State would aim for contributing 5% to 10% of the IT output of the country by the year 2008. This would translate into employment opportunities for between Four hundred thousand to One million persons in IT related activities.

2.3 To make Madhya Pradesh a lead IT State in India by the year 2003, the State aims to provide cost effective infrastructure, and transparent and responsive governance based on a high level of stability in policies in the medium and long term.

2.4 The State has set a target of providing information access to all citizens at an affordable cost and for achieving IT literacy in all the High Schools and Colleges by the year 2003 and aims to do so in all the schools by the year 2008. IT penetration would be achieved through aiming for an optimistic average of one internet connection per 100 population and coverage of every habitat by 2003.

2.5 Computerization in Government departments and agencies must be the engine of growth of IT in Madhya Pradesh, in the initial period. An optimistic goal for computer penetration in the Government, its organizations including the Panchayat Raj Institutions and other local self-government institutions has been kept at one per ten employees by the year 2003, raised to one per five employees by the year 2005 and finally to one per two employees by the year 2008.

2.6 A targeted share of 10% of the national IT output by the time frame indicated earlier, i.e. the year 2008 would be in the region of appx. Rs. 42000 crores and would require a direct private sector investment of the order of Rs. 4500 crores appx. Such a scale of economic activity is possible if the intermediate mile stones are in the region of appx. Rs. 200 crores or so in year 2001 and a four fold growth in investments by the year 2003, leading to output of approximately Rs. 1700 crores by 2001 and appx. Rs. 6500 crores by year 2003.

2.7 The targeted share in national IT output would also be reflected in the aim for a share in the software exports in the region of Rs. 300 crores in year 2001 and Rs. 2900 crores or more by year 2003 and Rs. 28000 crores by year 2008.

2.8 The State Domestic Product (SDP) is currently growing at the rate of 5.50% annually; and the share of IT in the Madhya Pradesh SDP is appx. 0.2% or appx. Rs. 100 crores. Assuming pessimistically that the SDP in all other sectors would grow at the current rate, a goal of achieving a 10% share in the national output would translate to roughly one-third of the SDP being contributed by IT.

2.9 The State aims to provide employment opportunities in the range of four hundred thousand to one million by the year 2008 engaged in the IT related activities. An estimated sixty % of the jobs could come from services, of which some 20% would be low-skilled data entry jobs and the balance from the growth of Internet related services such as information kiosks in urban and rural areas. Software development could give employment to another 20%, trade and commerce could contribute 10%, and the rest of the employment opportunities could be contributed by training related jobs and jobs relating to communications and hardware maintenance.

3. Policy Initiatives

Creating an Enabling Environment and Niche Marketing

3.1 The nodal point and the prime mover for propelling IT growth and implementation of plan of action would be a registered society promoted by the Government — "Madhya Pradesh Agency for Promotion of Information Technology" ("MAP-IT"). The Agency's high powered governing body would be headed by the Chief Minister and would include the Ministers of Industry, Higher Education, School Education, Chief Secretary of the State Government, distinguished representatives from the IT industry, NIC, Science and Technology institutions, social sectors. The Chief Executive Officer of MAP-IT world be an IT professional of repute and would hold the rank of ex-officio Secretary to the State Government.

The objectives of MAP-IT would be the following :

- To propel the growth of Information Technology (IT) in Madhya Pradesh and implementation of the State IT Action Plan for socio-economic development of the state.
- To coordinate with all the Government Departments/agencies for sectoral and cross-sectoral promotion and use of IT in Government and prescribe guidelines to enable smooth and widespread induction of IT.
- Coordinate and Network with investors and industry, trade organizations and financial institutions in public and private sector to promote growth in IT sector.
- To generate awareness amongst citizens and demystification of IT so as to promote its use as a comprehensive and cost effective means of disseminating information.
- Coordinate manpower needs and human resource development efforts for the above objectives.
- Coordinate and pursue development of all support infrastructure including telecom infrastructure in the State with the State

Government and the Government of India and their agencies.
- Marketing the State as an attractive IT destination for investment.
- Identifying and developing opportunities for furthering innovative research of world standard on its own or in collaboration with one or more institutions and/or industry.

3.2 Hindi is the medium of communication among governments and the population over the largest landmass of India. All the web pages of Government departments would also be in Hindi to increase their reach. The use of Hindi would also be promoted in all IT based databases and applications. Further, necessary action would be taken towards the following:

- To make Hindi E-mail as an important medium of communication between departments and field level offices.
- To ensure that in all public purchases of hardware/software, the systems being procured would have bilingual capabilities, e.g. all keyboards would be bilingual facilitating.
- Partnering the Hindi language newspapers and other media organizations based in the state for popularization, dissemination as well as access to Hindi formats.
- Collaboration with the other Hindi speaking states such as UP, Bihar, Rajasthan, Delhi and HP for a joint programme of promoting Hindi's presence on the Internet by uploading and enhancing Hindi resources. Easy availability of standardized fonts would be part of this exercise.
- Collaboration with C-DAC for the setting up of an institute and research centre of world standing for addressing problems relating to use of IT in Hindi computing in these languages, promotion of software applications in the vernacular, etc.

3.3 IT cannot grow in isolation to the general pace and status of economic development of the State and so the IT policy will be dovetailed, giving it the pride of place in the Industrial Policy of the State. Commercial tax administration would provide opportunities for such incentives by accepting computerized tax returns, encouragement to computerized billing, bar coding of inventory etc.

Promotion of Infrastructure, Industry and Investments

3.4 The State Government would move the Government of India to permit International Private Operators to create an international gateway hub each at Bhopal and Indore.

3.5 Sub-block level connectivity to the villages/village Panchayats is a must for the introduction of IT for the social sectors including rural development. The Government would enter into MOU's with private entrepreneurs to establish Information kiosks and Community Facilitation centres in the rural areas.

3.6 The State Electricity Board (MPEB) would actively examine whether it can leverage the right of way its vast supply network by partnering with suitable private national or international communications companies with capital and technology in return for such right of way for connectivity.

3.7 Indore, Raipur, Gwalior and Bhopal would be developed as IT 'cities'. The required land will be identified and the norms for the allotment of the land so identified would be made to attract investments in the IT industry.

3.8 Content industry and remote services will be pro-actively and vigorously promoted in the State to position MP as a lead State, in the country, in this area as well as, generate large employment opportunities in IT and IT enabled services sector.

3.9 Venture Capital availability would be given special focus by inviting FIs to be an integral part of State's IT vision. The MP Industrial Development Corporation or the MPFC would work out a detailed proposal for dedicated venture capital fund for IT.

3.10 MPSIDC and MPFC would formulate a special package for providing financial assistance to the IT industry.

3.11 Hardware technology parks for manufacturing units in computers, telecommunication equipment, entertainment electronics and related ancillaries would be promoted and established at Pithampur, Mandideep and Malanpur and other industrial growth centres.

3.12 The existing schemes of self-employment generation such as the IRDP, TRYSEM, PMRY etc. would be utilized to provide assistance to youth for setting up of Information Kiosks or 'soochana gumtis' to provide e-mail, internet and other value added services. The State has over 28000 STD/PCOs at present. A phased strategy to upgrade these into information kiosks would be worked out in consultation with basic service providers, banks and industry department.

3.13 State Government would facilitate a single window clearance system and a universal overriding permission that gives the right to enterprises to carry on with activities without barriers of any kind. Residential premises would be allowed to setup IT units, particularly related to content industry and remote services.

3.14 IT industries requiring electrical power upto 15 KVA could be established without any locational restrictions. Necessary amendment would also be made in Pollution Control Act and the rules therein.

3.15 Procedures in respect of some of the existing regulatory legislation relating to labour, factories, shops and establishments for the IT related units would be rationalized.

3.16 Leasing would be incorporated as a preferred option in out-sourcing policies for items of high obsolescence. Amendments to Store Purchase Rules would be worked out.

Promotion of IT in Government

3.17 IT Sub-plans: The annual plan of each department/sector in Government would have a detailed sub-plan for IT. Every department would be required to establish IT working group consisting of senior officers and representative of employees, a representative from MAP-IT, and also co-opting IT professionals on voluntary or contractual basis from other departments or agencies. There would be a nodal officer or executive for IT related matters in every department.

3.18 Budgetary outlay: A distinct budgetary head of account for IT related activities would be introduced in the annual budget from this fiscal year.

3.19 The State Government would impress upon the XI Central Finance Commission of the need to modernize administration at the level of State Government as well as at the level of the PRIs. Additionally, modernization and computerization of systems in the Panchayats, would be included in the list of priorities for grants given as per the recommendations of the State Finance Commission.

3.20 The financial resources for computer penetration for Gram Panchayats presently numbering 31,126 would be met out of the grants-in-aid for basic services, and/or by financing one educated unemployed Youth/Panchayat Karmi at each Gram Panchayat HQ to own/operate a computer unit for various value added services including information retailing through kiosks.

3.21 An action plan would be prepared to ensure that all offices of the district Government including those at the sub-district levels are computerized and networked by the year 2003. In particular, the tehsil offices dealing with land records, revenue legislation, land acquisition information, collection and allocation of land revenue and cess to Panchayats, payments of compensation, planning an execution and expenditure on relief operations, information on listing of revenue court cases, monitoring of progress in disposal of revenue case work etc. would be taken up for computerization by year 2003. Offices such as those of the district governments and the PRIs should be in a position to enable single window facilitation after computerization.

3.22 E-mail facility would be extended to all employees to encourage greater use of e-mail facility for communication.

3.23 The 'mantra' for introduction of IT in Government departments would be Zero additional personnel costs, except costs on training and re-tooling of the serving employees. The present pace of training would be stepped up to match computer penetration goals.

3.24 A special scheme of incentives would be introduced to motivate all Government employees to become computer literate. To do so in the shortest possible time frame, there would be a strategy of contracting with public and private sector training institutes for specially designed short-term courses for different groups of users.

3.25 All hardware supplies would be contracted with a compulsory clause on familiarization of employees in the operations. All bulk procurement of generic software as well as contracts on specialized application software development would be out-sourced on similar conditionalities for training.

3.26 Proposal to tie up with banks for hire purchase schemes for the employees and provide interest-subsidy for purchase of computers for personal use by employees would be worked out.

3.27 All departments will move towards electronic communication within the department. Necessary changes in the office manuals would be worked out for this purpose.

3.28 Networks : Every department would establish a LAN by the year 2003. The District Government offices, the Collectorate and the Zila Panchayats as well as all other large offices would also establish respective intra-office networks.

3.29 The state unit of NIC provides a wide range of IT services in Madhya Pradesh. The NICNET facility has enabled networking with the districts and creation of many information systems and databases in various departments/sectors. These systems/databases would be upscaled and/or augmented and made on-line seamlessly. Detailed plans would be prepared especially in respect of the following:

- The Agriculture Market Information System on commodity arrivals and price movements in the major mandies.
- The Treasury Accounting Information System.
- The Commercial Taxes Information System.
- The databases under the DISNIC-PLAN, Village Information System and Gram Sampark Abhiyan.
- The Transport Management System.

The schedule for implementation of IT based systems in Government departments would be in phases.

Promoting IT in the Social Sector

3.30 Role of NGOs: NGOs and non-government organizations would be encouraged to establish Janpad (block) level centres — 'samadhan kendras' for providing Hardware/Software or other support services. NGOs volunteering to establish such centres would be encouraged to tie up with the mini ITIs, rural polytechnics and ITIs for man power and skill development under TRYSEM and other schemes.

3.31 Awareness campaign : Using both formal and non-formal channels, the State would disseminate information about the applications, advantages to communities of the use of IT.

3.32 For the widest possible involvement of people and communities in IT, benefits of computers and communication resources to be provided at the village Panchayat and sub-block or cluster levels must be utilised for rural development activities, agricultural and horticultural extension for farmers, career guidance for youth, technology guidance for rural enterprises, micro level planning etc. Communities and user groups or beneficiaries would be actively encouraged to participate, in all such activities, including in designing reporting formats and in deciding on control systems or entering data as it is an important way of demystifying the use of IT by and through communities.

3.33 All existing web sites relating to both government and non-government agencies of Madhya Pradesh would be linked on a reciprocal basis.

3.34 The present public grievances redressal system of the State Government would be upgraded to facilitate access to citizens through any of the kiosks, Samadhan Kendras, public facilitation centres or Government offices. It would be made e-mail based and strengthened to facilitate monitoring and on-line responses.

3.35 The wired village's concept would be replicated with a pilot in each district.

3.36 The State Government would stake its share of the claim in the various schemes, which form part of the recommendations of the National Task Force. Preparations for drawing up suitable proposals in order to leverage assistance as soon as GOI formally announces or launches these would be started straightaway by the corresponding departments of the State Government.

3.37 The District Sainik Welfare Boards would list ex-service personnel with background in communications and computers. The services of IT hardware specialists from the Defence Forces can be beneficially exploited by local hardware/ancillary industry. Financial arrangements and schemes would be proposed in collaboration with the Defence Ministry, Banks/FIs for retired Defence personnel for setting up IT training/services enterprises and IT kiosks. The services of retired IT qualified Defence personnel would be utilized at school level for creating IT awareness in the villages/districts.

3.38 Creation of Intranet: Creation of Intranet among institutions in each social sub-sector would qualitatively improve the services/training being provided by institutions with resource and faculty constraints. To begin with, all medical colleges in the State would be linked for leveraging each other's faculty strengths. Similarly, Tele or remote referral consultancy through linkages with medical colleges would be used to virtually upgrade the referral facilities at sub-district and district hospitals. The medical colleges would in turn tap institutions of excellence outside the state for consultations.

3.39 UGC is sponsoring the INFLIBNET which seeks to network all 176 Universities in the country. This would spur the use of Internet and Intranet resources by not only the campuses but even those local area networks that the University is able to create. Madhya Pradesh would take advantage of the INFLIBNET by promoting and developing LANs for every University in the State by working out a detailed strategy. Creation of virtual libraries in colleges would also be a priority.

3.40 Creation of a Citizen Database: A unique social security ID number would be introduced for those availing various benefits such as social assistance, social security pension etc. The BPL household survey, survey conducted for electoral photo identity cards, etc. would form the database for such an exercise to improve delivery of services and eliminate leakage.

Manpower Development for IT

3.41 Training for Government Employees: Training efforts, which are at present confined to largely the NIC initiative, would be multiplied. The existing Training institutions for the training of employees of the various departments as well as the State Academy of Administration would be upgraded to meet the requirements. Training tie up with private institutes using a common modular training package would also be used for re-tooling of employees.

3.42 Employees engaged in course studies in IT through distance education or other certification programmes would be allowed to use office computers after work hours. Recognition of computer time thus spent would be given due credit by the institutions awarding certificates.

3.43 Computer penetration in all the high schools in the next three years would be an effective way of spreading IT usage. All PRIs and urban local bodies would get at least one teacher or shiksha karmi in each high school, under their control, trained in IT usage or familiarity.

3.44 The National Task Force has recommended suitable floor space in Government buildings, which are not utilised during non-office hours, could be given to private educational institutions for IT training purpose in return for a proportionate number of free nominations of Government employees for IT training. This concept would be extended to permit commercial utilisation of schools/colleges/ educational institutions after academic hours in return for free training of teachers, staff and students. Transparent norms to facilitate this arrangement would be evolved.

3.45 Familiarization of PRI functionaries with benefits of IT uses would expedite introduction of IT based practices in these institutions. To begin with, Zila Panchayats and Janpad Panchayats would be introduced to IT during the training programmes to be conducted for the newly elected members in September 1999.

3.46 To meet the manpower needs of the State in IT, private sector training institutions, and distance education format would also be encouraged along with other Government supported institutions.

3.47 The courses of study in the ITIs and polytechnics would be upgraded and the training of teachers of these institutions would be taken up simultaneously where required.

3.48 Action would be initiated for capacity enhancement of institutions imparting IT education in the State.

3.49 The State would gear for leveraging its share of benefits from the GOI's decision to make computers and internet access available to schools, polytechnics and colleges by the year 2003. Proposals would be prepared for accepting these benefits in a phased manner each year.

3.50 The National Task Force has suggested setting up of IIITs. The State would propose to the Government of India setting up of at least one of the proposed IIITs in Madhya Pradesh fully funded by the Centre and in addition, promote private investment for setting up institutions of excellence in IT at par with IIITs by land grants.

3.51 The Universities in the State would look at how IT course modules can be introduced in the existing degree programmes so that every student is exposed to concepts and rudiments of applications in his or her own area of study.

3.52 The State would set-up a Virtual University as an enhancement of Open University model and also a Virtual School as an another dimension to the M.P. Open School.

3.53 For Demystification of IT and computers, the State Council of Education Research and Training would develop and include course material of an elementary nature to arouse curiosity and satisfy young minds at the primary school level.

3.54 Madhya Pradesh would aim at creating computer awareness among its masses of a magnitude far higher and not yet achieved or aimed by any other State. It would be universal in

character. Only then can people benefit from the IT policy and drive up demand for IT in the State as also throw up the trained manpower. In the ultimate analysis people must feel comfortable in using technology

Appendix–XI

Information Technology Policy of Tamil Nadu

Introduction

The Information Technology Industry in India is a fast growing segment of the Indian economy, with growth rates exceeding 50% per annum. In 1995-96, the Indian Information Technology Industry comprising hardware, software, peripherals and training had a turn over of Rs. 9037.85 crore. The Hardware Industry in India has mainly catered to the needs of domestic consumers, with only marginal exports. On the other hand, 60% of Software revenues are from exports, and the main growth is in this sector.

Tamil Nadu's contribution to the IT industry has been significant. The key elements which have made Tamil Nadu an important player in this area are availability of skilled and educated manpower, comparatively higher standard of educational institutions, reasonably good infrastructure, and lower costs of operation. Apart from these, the presence of an International Airport and a major Seaport in Chennai have also helped the growth of IT industry in Tamil Nadu. After the liberalization process in 1991, and especially after reduction of import duties on hardware in July 1996, Multinational Companies were able to export large volumes to India, thereby boosting the domestic market for both hardware and software. Despite all these advantages, Tamil Nadu accounts for only 7% of the total revenue from hardware and software in the country. The turnover of the industry in Tamil Nadu in 1995-96 was Rs. 289 crore of which Rs. 139 crore was in hardware and Rs. 150 crore in software. The potential for growth of Information Technology in Tamil Nadu is enormous with IT penetrating all spheres, including government departments, educational institutions, banking, shopping, entertainment and a whole gamut of other consumer applications. The Industry while drawing up the programme for the IX Five Year Plan has projected that by the year 2001-2002, I.T. revenue in Tamil Nadu will be of the order of Rs. 13,000 crore (Rs. 5000 crore in Hardware and Rs. 8000 crore in Software). The industry has predicted that this level of achievement can be obtained provided the State Government announces and implements an industry-friendly IT policy. With the aim of achieving the goals spelt out in the IX Plan and to focus attention on the IT Industry as an engine of growth in the State, it has been decided to formulate an industry-specific policy for the IT Industry.

Objectives of the IT Policy

The main objectives of the policy are :

- To encourage and accelerate the growth of hardware and software industries and associated services in the State and to remove the bottlenecks for starting and running of such Units in Tamil Nadu.
- To increase both domestic and export earnings of software and hardware sectors in the State.
- To upgrade and develop manpower skills required for the IT industry by facilitating training, to accelerate the use of IT in schools, colleges and educational institutions with a view of providing skills and knowledge to the youth to make them fit for employment in this sector.
- To upgrade the quality of life the citizens of the State by facilitating access to consumer application of Information Technology.
- As part of the above objectives, the Government will also encourage use of IT in Government institutions and Departments with a view to improving productivity and efficiency of Government services, revenues and tax collections, and assist in the process of decision-making by Government, and monitoring of Government programmes. A high Power Committee headed by the State Finance Secretary has been constituted to draw up a plan for phased use of IT in Government Departments. A separate policy paper will be prepared on this for speedy implementation.

Existing Incentives Available to the Industry

- There is no system of Entry Tax or Purchase Tax in Tamil Nadu. IT Industry will continue to enjoy facilities of unrestricted movement of capital equipment including hardware, peripherals, captive power gen. sets, UPS sets and Telephone Exchanges, subject only to Sales Tax payments as per orders in force.
- Due to self-sufficiency in power, Tamil Nadu does not have power cuts for industry. The facility of uninterrupted power will continue to be offered to IT industry.
- Tamil Nadu has already announced fiscal and tax concessions for investments of various slabs starting from an investment of Rs. 50.00 crore (mega projects) up to investments exceeding Rs.1500.00 crore (super mega projects). The orders issued in G.O.Ms.No.43, Industries, dated 13-12-1992 (for 'mega' and in G.O.Ms.No.1, projects) industries dated 2-1-1996 (for 'super mega' projects) will be applicable for IT industries also in addition to other incentives.
- Capital subsidy as applicable to electronics industries @ 20% of fixed assets subject to a maximum of Rs. 20.00 lakhs will be available for all IT industries, irrespective of their location in the State. Where the unit is also eligible for capital subsidy for backward / most backward areas, this special subsidy will become part of such subsidy. The existing incentives available for industries employing at least 30% of women workers will also be available to IT industries.

New Initiatives

- The State Government will set up Information Technology Parks (ITPs) at Chennai, Coimbatore, Tiruchirappalli and Madurai in a phased manner through ELCOT during the IX Plan period in association with the private sector. The ITPs will have full-fledged facilities with adequate modules for software development as well as sites for non-polluting hardware units, commercial and residential areas, schools, Convention and Business Centres as well as the connectivity required for communication and information exchange globally.
- Apart from ITPs in the Government and joint sectors, Government

will facilitate setting up of ITPs by the private sector in potential locations for the development of IT industries. Private ITP developers will be given assistance in land acquisition and re-zoning, wherever required, by State Government. State Government will also facilitate provision of water, power connection and roads. State Government will also help the ITP promoters in obtaining necessary cable and satellite links through VSNL/DOT for the necessary connectivity. An ITP will be treated as an "industry" and be eligible for backward area capital subsidy and ST benefits.

- The Government will provide assistance to VSNL and Department of Telecommunications to expand communication links in the State and also provide the land and power wherever required by such agencies. State Government will liaise with Government of India to ensure dedicated VSNL connectivity/Earth Stations as well as Electronic Telecom facility for each ITP.
- All ITPs set up by private promoters will have the same status as ITPs promoted by Government agencies for the purpose of eligibility for the concessions/incentives granted by Government from time to time to SIPCOT, ELCOT, TIDCO and TACID industrial estates, subject to conformity to certain quality standards, and subject to location (whether backward/most backward area). Units in private ITPs will be entitled for exemption from stamp duty and registration charges at the time of allotment of sites/ built up space as in the case of units in ELCOT/SIPCOT industrial estates. Private ITP promoters will be granted exemption of tax for works contracts within the complex as in the case of SIPCOT/ ELCOT, etc. Software/hardware units set up in private ITPs established in accordance with the standards prescribed by the Government will enjoy the same facilities and incentives on par with units in Government industrial estates.
- In all the Technology Parks set up by Government and Joint Ventures, there will be an Executive Authority of the Park which will function as the Single Window for all statutory clearances required for the units, within the Parks. In the case of private sector Technology Parks, ELCOT will assist in getting all clearances fast.
- Apart from development of software and hardware Industry through ITPs/STPs the Government will also encourage software development outside the Parks by giving such stand-alone units the same incentives as the Units in the ITPs/STPs. There will be

no locational restrictions for setting up units exclusively engaged in software development/training.

- All software industries including Services and Training Institutions in IT will be entitled to "Industry" status. Such units shall be eligible for all concessions and incentives applicable to Industries. For the purpose of this clause, accredited Training Institutions will also be eligible to claim industry status, subject to certain norms which will enable them to obtain Term Loans and Bank Finance at industry rates.
- Government will provide continuous power supply in industry rates to all IT units, whether set up in ITPs, or in stand-alone locations, and also ensure quality of power as required by the industry. Software Training units will also be eligible for these facilities.
- For the purpose of power tariff, maintenance and servicing units and hardware units will be treated as Industrial and not Commercial consumers and electricity staff as applicable to Industry consumers will be charged.
- All software industries will be exempted from the purview of Tamil Nadu Pollution Control Act. Hardware units will require clearance from Pollution Control Board as applicable to other industries.
- Government of Tamil Nadu will also facilitate setting up of a T-Net with an "Information Back bone" connecting all District Head Quarters, using the Cable TV network all over the State whose penetrating at present is 4 times that of Telephone lines.
- Government of Tamil Nadu will encourage setting up of Venture Capital Fund for development of IT Industry through TIDCO in association with private sector partners.

Human Resource Development

A sub-group set up to discuss the prospects of the Information Technology Industries in the IX Plan period has assessed the man-power requirements for the industry. The sub-group has estimated the Tamil Nadu manpower in the Information Technology Industry by the end of the Plan period. The following are the policy initiatives planned for Human Resources Development in Information Technology.

Government of Tamil Nadu will set up an Information

Technology Institute of Tamil Nadu (TANITEC) to take care of the training and technology upgradation aspects of IT in the State. The Institute will also co-ordinate in preparation of syllabus for IT courses in Colleges and Technical Institutions, create Centres of Excellence in Universities, and also support funded research programme and specific technology applications.

Training Institutes for hardware, software, servicing and maintenance will be deemed to be "Industries" and will be eligible for all facilities offered to Industries including Bank Finance and SSI or IEM registration. Certification for Software training will be governed by existing standards prescribed by the Department of Electronics, Government of India. For quality certification of training in hardware, servicing and maintenance ELCOT will be the Nodal Agency to prescribe minimum standards for eligibility.

Basic training in computers will be introduced in all schools from the high school level. The endeavour will be to cover all schools within a 5-year period. Training of teachers will also be done in a phased manner over the 5-year period. In addition to Government sponsored training programmes, State Government will facilitate and co-ordinate with other sponsors like INTEL, IBM, APPLE, etc., for training of teachers.

Government of Tamil Nadu will encourage IT industries to obtain ISO 9000 process certification. Small Scale Industries (SSIs) will be eligible to claim the incentives offered by TIIC for obtaining such certification.

Special Assistance for Information Technology Industries

Government of Tamil Nadu will offer relaxation of FSI (Floor Space Index) in metropolitan areas to the extent of 50% for IT Parks.

Government of Tamil Nadu will co-ordinate with Government of India facilitate setting up of 'Internal Container Depot' to take care of exports of specified industrial products through Chennai Port, including products of electronic and hardware units.

Government of Tamil Nadu will facilitate setting up an Air Freight City near Chennai Airport, for improving the cargo movement for imports and exports from Chennai Airport. The Air Freight Centre will have sufficient space for handling equipment and necessary facilities for customs clearances, with staff posted round the clock.

Such a centre will be formed as a Joint Venture between TIDCO, TACID, and FIEO. With these facilities, Government of Tamil Nadu will facilitate a 72-hour cycle for import of components and export of finished products by the hardware units.

Concessions/Incentives Available for Industries

Special Subsidy for Mega Projects

An industry set up anywhere in Tamil Nadu having an investment of Rs.50 crores and above and below Rs. 100 crores is eligible for a Capital subsidy of Rs. 25 lakhs.

An industry set up anywhere in Tamil Nadu with an investment of Rs. 100 crores and above and below Rs. 200 crores is eligible for a subsidy of Rs. 50 lakhs.

An industry set up anywhere in Tamil Nadu having an investment of Rs. 200 crores and above is eligible for a subsidy of Rs. 100 lakhs.

They will be eligible for Sales Tax deferral/waiver for 14 years. The company can exercise its option either to avail deferral/waiver.

The limit of only one revision of the Eligibility Certificate as stipulated in Government Letter Ms. No. 1414, Industries (MIG-2) Department dated 14-12-1990, will not be applicable to Super Mega Projects. They are permitted a maximum of five number of revisions of the Eligibility Certificate. The Eligibility Certificate indicates the investment made in fixed assets upto the date of its issue and represents the Eligibility Limit for availing Sales Tax Deferral/Waiver at any point of time. Once the "Investment Limit" and "Time Limit" for making the investment as specified for 'Super Mega Project' are reached, the company will be eligible for the concessions indicated in succeeding paras below.

These companies can continue to avail sales tax deferral / waiver upto the specified period of 14 years, even if the quantum of Sales Tax Deferral/Waiver availed reaches the limit of 100% of the value of installments in fixed assets the Super Mega Project before 14 years.

If the quantum of Sales Tax Deferral/Waiver availed by these companies does not reach the limit of 100% of the investment in fixed assets for the Super Mega Projects by the end of the 14th year, they can continue to avail Sales Tax Deferral/Waiver for a further period not exceeding 7 years or till the limit of 100% of the value of the investment in fixed assets for the Super Mega Project is reached, whichever is earlier.

The deferred sales tax will be repayable in 5 equal annual installments as follows :

Sales Tax deferred in Year 1 will be repayable in 5 equal annual installments from Year 15 to Year 19 ; Sales Tax deferred in Year 2 will be repayable in 5 equal annual installments from Year 16 to Year 20 and so on. The deferred amount repayable in any particular year will be paid in 4 equal quarterly installments before the last day of each quarter.

Existing Industries taking up expansion /diversification, at their existing plant location/sites or at new sites, for which investment in fixed assets exceeds Rs.1500 crore (excluding the investment already made) within a time frame of 5 years (relaxable up to 7 years in special cases), will also be eligible for the concessions referred to as in above foregoing paras, provided they satisfy the additional turnover norms for expansion/diversification.

Additional Subsidy for Employing Women Workers

New industrial units (small, medium or major) where more than 30% of the total workers employed are women shall be eligible for an additional Capital Subsidy of 5% of investment in fixed assets subject to a ceiling of Rs. 5 lakhs.

Special Subsidy for Electronics Industry

Electronics—20% of fixed assets subject to maximum of Rs. 20 lakhs.

INDEX